THE

WILLARD J. GRAHAM SERIES

IN ACCOUNTING

THE IRWIN SERIES IN MANAGEMENT

CONSULTING EDITOR   JOHN F. MEE   *Indiana University*

Management
Accounting
Principles

Management Accounting Principles

ROBERT N. ANTHONY, D.C.S.
Ross Graham Walker Professor of Management Control
Graduate School of Business Administration
Harvard University

1970 · Revised Edition
RICHARD D. IRWIN, INC., Homewood, Illinois   60430
Irwin-Dorsey International, London, England   WC2H 9NJ
Irwin-Dorsey Limited, Georgetown, Ontario   L7G 4B3

Revised Edition

First Printing, February, 1970
Second Printing, May, 1970
Third Printing, August, 1970
Fourth Printing, January, 1971
Fifth Printing, August, 1971
Sixth Printing, September, 1971
Seventh Printing, December, 1972
Eighth Printing, June, 1973

Library of Congress Catalog Card No. 79–98243
Printed in the United States of America

LEARNING SYSTEMS COMPANY—

a division of Richard D. Irwin, Inc. has developed a PROGRAMMED LEARNING AID to accompany texts in this subject area. Copies can be purchased through your bookstore or by writing PLAIDS, 1818 Ridge Road, Homewood, Illinois 60430

To my daughter,
Vicky

PREFACE

THERE ARE two general approaches to a study of accounting. One takes the viewpoint of the *accountant*, the person who is responsible for collecting and reporting accounting information. A generation ago, nearly all books on accounting took this approach, and many of them still do. The other type of book approaches the subject from the viewpoint of the *user* of accounting information. The latter is the approach I have taken in this book. More specifically, my objective is to show how accounting information can be used by members of management, at all levels, and by their staff assistants.

The user should be familiar with the underlying structure of accounting; otherwise, he will misunderstand the real meaning of accounting information. Part I of the book describes this structure. It shows how accounting rules and procedures can be logically related to a few underlying concepts, which in turn have been developed to meet the criteria of relevance, objectivity and feasibility. Without an appreciation of the significance of these concepts, one might think, for example, that depreciation attempts to measure the decline in value of an asset, or that the balance sheet indicates approximately what a company is worth, or that an increase in net income is closely related to a build-up of cash. These are all misconceptions. In order to make intelligent use of accounting information, one needs to know not only that they are misconceptions, but also what depreciation, the balance sheet, and net income really mean.

Although in Part I, I have attempted to discuss all the main aspects of the accounting structure, the treatment is briefer than that in most books that take the accountant's viewpoint. This is because I can safely omit or condense many of the detailed rules of recordkeeping and much of the minutia that are of interest to the accountant.

The balance of the book is organized according to the main purposes for which accounting information is used. Part II discusses its use in an analysis of the business as a whole, which is of interest both to investors and other outside parties and to the management. Parts III and IV focus on the use of accounting inside the enterprise, that is, in the management control process, and in the decision-making process.

In Part III, I have tried to merge techniques such as cost accounting, the analysis of costs, and budgeting, with concepts drawn from social psychology. I think it unrealistic to discuss the quantitative techniques without bringing in the human equation which is so important in real-life control situations. Part IV discusses the use of accounting and other information in the analysis of alternative choice problems, such as make-or-buy problems, pricing problems, and problems involving the acquisition of plant and equipment. There is a chapter on automated data processing and its effect on management accounting.

This book consists essentially of the text of the Fourth Edition of my *Management Accounting: Text and Cases*, with the addition of some illustrative material.

ROBERT N. ANTHONY

Boston, Massachusetts
January 1970

TABLE OF CONTENTS

Financial Accounting and Management Accounting. Plan of the Book: *The Structure of Accounting. Uses of Accounting. Analyzing Financial Statements. Management Control. Decision Making.* Some General Considerations: *Figures for a Purpose. Different Figures for Different Purposes. Accounting Figures Are Approximations. Working with Incomplete Data. Figure Evidence Is Only Partial Evidence. People, Not Figures, Get Things Done.* Summary.

PART I. The Accounting Structure

Accounting as a Language. Nature and Source of Principles: *Criteria. Sources of Principles.* Basic Concepts: *1. The Money Measurement Concept. 2. The Business Entity Concept. 3. The Going-Concern Concept. 4. The Cost Concept. 5. The Dual-Aspect Concept. 6. Conservatism.* The Balance Sheet: *Account Categories. Assets. Current Assets. Fixed Assets. Other Assets. Liabilities. Current Liabilities. Other Liabilities. Owners' Equity.* Balance Sheet Changes. An Overall View of the Balance Sheet. Summary of Basic Concepts.

The Accounting Period. The Accrual Concept. Measurement of Expenses: *Expenses and Expenditures. Expenditures That Are Also Expenses. Assets That Become Expenses. Expenditures That Are Not Yet Expenses. Expenses Not Yet Paid. Asset or Expense?* Measurement of Revenue. The Realization Concept: *Matching.* The Consistency Concept. The Materiality Concept. Other Changes in Owners' Equity: *Extraordinary Items.* Tax Accounting versus Business Accounting. The Income Statement: *Revenues. Cost of Goods Sold. Gross Profit. Expenses. Retained Earnings.*

xi

graph. Interpretation of the Profitgraph. Improving Profit Performance. Limitations on Profitgraph Analysis. Marginal Income Analysis Statement. Learning Curves. Controllable Costs: *Degree of Influence. Converting Noncontrollable Costs to Controllable Costs. Recording Noncontrollable Costs.* Engineered, Discretionary, and Committed Costs: *Engineered Costs. Discretionary Costs. Committed Costs. Spurious Relationships.* Summary. Appendix: *Fitting a Straight Line by Least Squares.*

Types of Budgets. The Operating Budget: *Relationships among the Budgets. The Budget Process. Choice of Time Periods. Organization for Preparation of Budgets. The Budget Timetable. Setting Guidelines. The Sales Estimate. Initial Budget Preparation. Negotiation. Coordination and Review. Final Approval. Variations in Practice. Revisions. Uses of the Budget.* The Cash Budget. The Capital Budget. Summary.

Structure of Analysis: *Inputs and Outputs. The Search for a Standard.* Difficulties in Performance Measurement: *Difficulty in Measuring Outputs. Long-Run versus Current Performance. The Special Problem of Investment Centers.* Performance Reports: *The Time Interval of Control. Content of Reports. Management by Exception. Feedback.* Formal Analytical Techniques: *Validity of the Standard.* Structure of Analysis: *Noncomparable Data. Price and Quantity of Inputs. Mix of Inputs. Quality of Output. Output Price and Volume. Volume and Overhead Costs. Measuring Stick Variance.* An Illustrative Analysis: *Marketing Variance. Manufacturing Variances.* Attacking an Appraisal Problem. Summary.

PART IV. Accounting in Business Decisions

Approach to Alternative Choice Problems: *Criteria. Outline of Approach. Definition of the Problem and of Alternative Solutions. Weighing and Measuring the Quantitative Factors. Evaluating and Weighing the Unmeasured Factors. Reaching a Decision.* Problems Involving Costs: *Future Costs. Differential Costs. Mechanics of the Calculation. The Margin of Error. Example: Operating an Automobile. Example: Economic Lot Size.* Pricing: *Theoretical Considerations. Full-Cost Pricing. Contribution Pricing.* Advanced Techniques: *Probability Theory. Mathematical Models. Linear Programming.* Nonprofit Organizations: *Cost-Benefit Analysis.* Some Practical Pointers. Summary.

APPENDIX TABLES

CHAPTER 1

INTRODUCTION

Accounting is a system for collecting, summarizing, analyzing, and reporting, in monetary terms, information about an organization. The reader has already been exposed to a great deal of accounting information. The cash register receipt at the stores where he trades, the checks that he writes or (hopefully) that he receives, his bank statement, the bills which he is expected to pay, all these are parts of accounting systems. He reads in his newspaper about the profit of a company or of an industry, about dividends, about money being spent to build new buildings, and this information comes from accounting systems. Even before he begins a formal study of the subject, therefore, the reader has accumulated a number of ideas about accounting.

The trouble is that some of these ideas are likely to be incorrect. For example, it seems intuitively sensible that accounting should report what a business is "worth," but accounting does not in fact do this, or even attempt to do it. As another example, there is a general notion that the word "asset" refers to valuable things, good things to have; but the skill and ability of the chief executive of a company is not an asset in the accounting sense, even though it may be a principal determinant of the company's success.

Thus, as is the case with many other subjects, the student of accounting must be wary of his preconceptions. He will discover that accounting "like it really is" may be different in important respects from what he surmises it to be, or from what common sense tells him it should be. He will find that there are sound reasons for these differences, and it is important that he understand these reasons.

FINANCIAL ACCOUNTING AND MANAGEMENT ACCOUNTING

This book deals primarily with accounting in business organizations, although essentially similar concepts are used in government and other

1

nonbusiness organizations, and even in national income accounting, which provides information about an entire nation. In studying a business accounting system, it is useful to consider it as consisting of two parts, labeled, respectively, financial accounting and management accounting. These two parts are not in fact neatly separable in practice, but the concepts and purpose related to each part are sufficiently different so that it is well to consider them separately.

Financial accounting has the primary objective of providing information to parties outside the business, that is, to shareholders, bankers and other creditors, government agencies, and the general public. Only in rare instances can these outside parties insist that a business furnish information that is tailor-made to their specifications. In most cases they must accept the information that the business chooses to supply. They could not conceivably understand this information without knowing the ground rules that governed its preparation. Since the typical outsider uses accounting information from many different businesses, there is a clear need for having the basic ground rules apply to all businesses, both so that the information from one business can be compared with that of another and also to obviate the necessity of learning a separate set of ground rules for each business. These ground rules are the subject matter of financial accounting.

When an outside party reads information that has been prepared in accordance with these ground rules, it is meaningful to him, provided, of course, that he understands what the ground rules are. Without such rules, clear communication between a business and the outside world would be practically impossible.

> EXAMPLE: When a person familiar with accounting sees on an accounting report the item "Inventory at Fifo Cost or Market, $1,435,655," he understands that this refers to a certain category of property, and that the amount of this property has been measured according to certain prescribed rules; and he can rely on this understanding even though he has had no personal contact with the accountant who reported this information.

The ground rules of financial accounting therefore facilitate communication between a business and outside parties who need information about that business.

The persons responsible for operating a business—that is, the management—also need monetary information to aid them in doing their jobs effectively. Although much of this information is the same as that contained in reports prepared for outsiders, management also needs a considerable amount of additional information. *Management Accounting*[1] is concerned with accounting information that is useful to management.

---

[1] Some persons prefer the phrase "managerial accounting." The choice turns on a fine point of grammar and is of no practical consequence.

The management of a business can establish whatever ground rules it wishes for the accounting information collected for internal use. Thus, although the rules of financial accounting are applicable to all businesses, the rules of management accounting are tailor-made to meet the needs of the management of a specific business.

There is nevertheless a similarity in the management accounting of most businesses, for two reasons. First, there are obvious economies in using financial accounting information wherever possible for management accounting purposes, rather than devising two completely different systems for the two purposes; thus the rules of financial accounting have a great influence on management accounting. Second, there are principles of management accounting that have wide applicability, and these tend to shape the management accounting practices of a great many companies.

This book is focused on management accounting. Because of the close relationship between financial accounting and management accounting, however, it starts with a description of financial accounting.

The terms "financial accounting" and "management accounting" are not precise descriptions of the activities they comprise. All accounting is *financial* in the sense that all accounting systems are in monetary terms, and *management* is responsible for the content of financial accounting reports. (This is the first of many problems in terminology that will be noted throughout this book. The reader is cautioned against drawing inferences from the labels alone; he must learn the concepts that the labels represent.)

PLAN OF THE BOOK

The Structure of Accounting

The structure of financial accounting underlies all accounting. This structure consists of a few basic principles and concepts, a set of relationships among the elements comprising the accounting system, a terminology, and a number of rules and guides for the application of the principles and concepts to specific situations. This underlying structure will be described in Part I.

The end product of financial accounting, the objective toward which the financial accounting system is directed, is a set of financial statements called the balance sheet and the income statement. We shall therefore emphasize the principles underlying the construction of these statements. Our objective, however, is not to discuss financial accounting per se; rather, it is to develop the concepts and terminology that underlie all accounting.

Furthermore, we do not describe in detail the techniques used to collect and summarize accounting information. Our point of view is that of the *user* of accounting information. The user needs to know something about these techniques in order to understand the nature and limitations of the information that they produce, but he does not need the detailed knowledge that the accountant must have.

The approach to accounting taken in Part I is something like that used by an airplane pilot in learning to use his instruments. The pilot needs to know the meaning of the message conveyed by each of his instruments; that is, he needs to know such things as the fact that a clockwise movement of a certain arrow probably means one thing and that a counterclockwise movement probably means another thing, that the flashing of a red light probably means that a certain component is not functioning, that a certain sound in his earphones probably means that he is on course, and so on. The word "probably" is used because, for one reason or another, an instrument may not always give the reading that it is supposed to give; the pilot must realize this, and he must also understand something of the likelihood of, and the reasons for, these abnormalities. On the other hand, the pilot does not need to know how to design airplane instruments, how to construct them, how to check them for accuracy, how to maintain them, or how to repair them. Specialists are available for these important functions.

Similarly a person who is to make intelligent use of accounting information must understand what a given accounting figure probably means, what its limitations are, and under what circumstances it may mean something different from the apparent "signal" that it gives. He does not, however, need to know how to design, construct, operate, or check on the accuracy of an accounting system. He can rely on accountants for these important functions. The discussion of accounting in Part I is limited, then, to matters which the *user* of accounting information needs to know about.

Uses of Accounting

Knowledge of the meaning of an instrument reading is by no means all, or even a very important part, of what the pilot needs to know in order to fly his plane. In addition, he must know how to use this knowledge to solve the problems that arise during flight, and he must know a great deal about the "art" of flying, which includes many matters that have little or nothing to do with the instruments. Parts II, III, and IV of this book deal with the use of accounting information. Just as there is much more to the art of piloting an airplane than the ability to read instruments, so there is much more to the art of management than the ability to use accounting information; this book is in no sense a book on the whole art of management.

Analyzing Financial Statements

Since the material in Part I focuses on the principles underlying the construction of financial statements, a good place to begin our examination of the use of accounting information is the use made of these statements. This is the subject matter of Part II.

The two principal financial statements are the balance sheet, which reports the financial position of a business at one moment in time, and the income statement, which summarizes its financial performance over a period of time. We shall discuss how the businessman can obtain from these statements useful information both about his own business and about other businesses in which he may be interested. We shall at the same time point out the inherent limitations of financial statement information, limitations which prevent these statements from providing the answers to all, or even the most important, questions that are raised about a business.

Management Control

An important process in which accounting information is used within a business is called *management control.* This is the process of assuring that resources are obtained and used effectively and efficiently in the accomplishment of the organization's objectives. In Part III, we discuss the role of accounting information in this process.

Management control has to do with the ongoing operation of the business. It consists of a more or less regularly recurring sequence of interrelated activities. For convenience in exposition, these activities may be classified as either control activities or planning activities. Nevertheless, the whole process is a single, indivisible one, in which the two types of activities interact and merge into one another; the same people are involved in both. Although pedagogical considerations make it desirable to discuss these activities separately, we shall emphasize throughout this text the relationship between them.

CONTROL. Control is the process by which management assures itself, insofar as is feasible, that actions taken by the members of an organization conform to management's plans and policies. Accounting information is useful in control as a means of communication, of motivation, and of appraisal.

As a means of *communication,* accounting reports can assist in informing the organization about management's plans and policies and, in general, the types of action that management wishes the organization to take.

Unless the business is a one-man enterprise, it is not management's job to do the work; that is, management does not personally manufacture and sell the product. Rather, it is the responsibility of management to see to it that the work gets done by others. This requires, first, that personnel be hired and formed into an organization and, second, that this organization be motivated in such a way that it will do what management wants it to do. Accounting information can help (and also, unless properly used, can hinder) this *motivation* process.

Periodically, management needs to evaluate how well the employees are doing their jobs. Such an *appraisal* of performance may result in a salary increase, promotion, reassignment, corrective action of various kinds, or, in extreme cases, dismissal. Accounting information can assist in this appraisal process, although an adequate basis for judging a man's performance cannot be obtained solely from information revealed by accounting records.

PLANNING.   Planning is the process of deciding what action should be taken in the future. The area covered by one plan may be a tiny segment of the enterprise, or it may be the whole enterprise. Thus, a decision as to whether the price of one product should be increased 10 cents is a plan, and so is a decision to merge or not to merge the company with another company.

The essential characteristic of a plan is that it involves a decision about action to be taken in the future. Planning is therefore to be distinguished from *forecasting*. A forecast is an estimate of what will happen in the future, but the forecaster makes no attempt to influence the future by his own decisions or action. People *forecast* the weather, but they do not— except in the few areas where cloud-seeding operations are carried on— attempt to *plan* the weather.

Some businesses have planning staffs whose full-time job is to assist in making plans. The planning function, however, is much broader than the work done by these staffs; it is performed at all levels in the organization and in all organizations, whether or not they have separate planning staffs. The foreman who decides to route a certain job through Machine A rather than through Machine B is planning in the same sense as, but on a smaller scale than, the president who decides how much the company will spend on research.

A systematic form of planning, called *budgeting*, occurs as part of the management control process. Budgeting is the process of planning the overall activity of the enterprise for a specified period of time, usually a year. An important objective of this process is to fit together the separate plans made for various segments of the enterprise so as to assure that these plans harmonize with one another and that the aggregate effect of all of them on the whole enterprise is satisfactory. For example, the budgeting process might reveal that the sales organization has planned a considerable increase in the sales of one product line but that the production organization has not planned for the additional facilities and manpower necessary to turn out the increased volume; or an expansion of facilities might be planned without adequate consideration of where the funds required to build these facilities are to be obtained. In a very small business, top management may have a sufficient personal awareness of overall plans so that formal, written budgets are unnecessary, but a business of any considerable size is likely to be so complex that some systematic process of formulating and balancing the plans for the separate parts of the enterprise is essential.

Decision Making

Part IV describes how accounting information is used as an aid in making business decisions. Although in one sense all business activities involve decision making, our focus in Part IV is on the type of decision that relates to some specific segment of the business, rather than to operations as a whole. This might be a decision to buy a new machine, to enter a new market, to use a new type of raw material or a new method of manufacturing, to borrow money from a bank, or any of a host of other decisions.

All these decisions are arrived at by, essentially, recognizing that a problem exists, identifying the alternative ways of solving the problem, analyzing the consequences of each alternative, and comparing these consequences so as to decide which is best. Accounting information is useful especially in the analysis step.

SOME GENERAL CONSIDERATIONS

Before we plunge into detail, it may be well to consider briefly a few general matters that apply to all sorts of problems and to all types of figures, both accounting and nonaccounting. Although they are introduced here, it is not expected that these points will become entirely meaningful or concrete until the reader has had an opportunity to examine them and to think about their relevance in specific situations. It may therefore be desirable to refer back to these points from time to time.

Figures for a Purpose

Unlike mathematics, accounting is not an end in itself. As is indicated in the preceding section, accounting is done for some purpose—to convey information about what has happened in a business, to provide data that are of assistance in solving a business problem, to express future plans, and so on. The work of accountants is justified only insofar as it contributes to some activity that is external to accounting. Both the beginning student and also the person who has been long immersed in accounting have a tendency to think of accounting as being conducted for its own sake. This is regrettable, and we shall here try to avoid the creation of such an attitude by frequent references to the purposes for which accounting data are intended to be used.

Different Figures for Different Purposes

In mathematics, and in most of the physical sciences, there are definitions that are valid under a wide variety of circumstances. Such is not the case with most accounting definitions. Each of the purposes described in the preceding section requires a different kind of accounting figure. Since these different figures may superficially resemble one another and since they may even be called by the same name, a person who is not familiar with them may easily become confused or frustrated. The most common source of confusion is the word "cost." As will be seen in later chapters, there are historical costs, standard costs, original costs, net costs, residual costs, variable costs, differential costs, incremental costs, marginal costs, opportunity costs, direct costs, estimated costs, full costs and other kinds of costs. Some of these terms are synonymous; others are almost but not quite synonymous; still others, although not synonymous at all, are used by some as if they were.

Accounting figures should always be discussed in terms of the particular problem that they are intended to help solve, rather than in any abstract sense. A statement that "the cost of such-and-such is $100" literally has no meaning unless those who hear this statement understand clearly which of the several possible concepts of cost was intended. A useful procedure to follow in approaching a specific problem is to define, as carefully as possible, the purpose for which figures are to be used in that problem and then to consider how the figures should be assembled and used for that specific purpose.

Accounting Figures Are Approximations

Accounting is a system for recording and summarizing measurements of business facts, and, as is the case with any measurement, an accounting figure is an approximation rather than a precisely accurate statement. Most of the data used in the physical sciences are also measurements, and like scientists and engineers, the user of accounting information must acquire an understanding of the degree of approximation that is present in the data.

Consider, for example, the concept of temperature. With the proper instruments, the temperature of the human body is easily measured to a tenth of a degree and that of a room to a degree or so, but the temperature of the sun is measurable only with an accuracy of a hundred degrees or so. Although these measurements differ widely in their degree of accuracy, each is useful for a particular purpose. Similarly, some accounting figures, such as the amount of cash on hand, may be accurate within very narrow limits, while others are only rough approximations.

There are many reasons for the roughness of accounting figures. A few are mentioned here, and others will become apparent in later chapters. One of them is simply that a business is a complicated organism which includes vastly dissimilar elements—money, buildings, morale, machines, incentives, materials, policies, and so on. There can be no precise way of adding all these diverse elements together so as to form a completely accurate picture of the whole enterprise.

The problem of obtaining reasonably accurate measurements is further complicated by management's desire to obtain information quickly. A rough approximation that is available today is often more useful to management than a more accurate figure published a year from now. For instance, consider the cost of owning and operating an automobile. This cost includes the purchase price of the automobile, plus the cost of gasoline, repairs, and other operating items, less anything that is received when the automobile is sold or traded. The total cost cannot be known exactly until after the automobile has been sold or traded. Businessmen are unwilling to wait this long for information about what an automobile costs, however; they want information every year, every month, or even oftener. In order to provide this information, the accountant must work with estimates of how many years or months the automobile will be used in the future and how much will be received when it is eventually sold or traded. The accuracy of any interim figure on the cost of the automobile depends on the validity of these estimates.

For the same reason that automobile costs cannot be precisely determined until the automobile is sold, the profit of a whole company cannot be precisely determined accurately until the company goes out of business. Also, for reasons to be discussed subsequently, the profit of a division, a product, or other segment of a company usually cannot be measured with close accuracy. Nevertheless, management needs information on costs and profits for short periods of time, such as a month, and for individual divisions, products, or other segments of a business. Accounting will furnish such information, and it can be most helpful to management. (After all, one needs only a rough approximation of the outside temperature in order to decide whether to wear an overcoat.) Management must clearly understand, however, the approximations that are inherent in most accounting figures.

The degree of approximation is especially high in the case of the figures used for planning purposes. Such figures are always estimates of what will happen in the future. But businessmen are not clairvoyant; they do not *know* what will happen in the future, and the figures used for planning purposes can be no better than their estimates of what the future holds.

Working with Incomplete Data

No one could ask a person to solve a problem in mathematics without furnishing him all the information he needs. In a business problem, on the other hand, one almost never has exactly the information he would like to have. In nearly every practical situation, the person who is struggling with the problem can think of additional information that would be helpful if it were available. On the other hand, there are many business situations in which page after page of figures are available, but only a small fraction of them are at all relevant to the problem at hand, and perhaps none of them is quite what one needs to solve the problem.

It is a fact of life, however, that problems must be solved, business decisions must be made, and often the decision cannot be delayed until all the pertinent information is available. One does the best he can with what he has, and then moves on to the next problem. John W. Gardner writes:

> Anyone who accomplishes anything of significance has more confidence than the facts would justify. It is something that outstanding executives have in common with gifted military commanders, brilliant political leaders, and great artists. It is true of societies as well as of individuals. Every great civilization has been characterized by confidence in itself.[2]

On the other hand, a decision should not be made if a vital, obtainable piece of evidence is missing. Deciding whether or not to act on the available evidence is one of the most difficult parts of the whole decision process. As the late Dean Wallace B. Donham has put it: "The art of business is the art of making irrevocable decisions on the basis of inadequate information."

Figure Evidence Is Only Partial Evidence

Few, if any, business problems can be solved solely by the collection and analysis of figures. Usually, there are important factors that cannot be, or have not been, reduced to numbers. For example, think of how you would judge the performance of a baseball player. Every time a baseball player comes to bat, and almost every time he handles the ball in the field, a statistic is generated. Detailed records are published on his times at bat, walks, hits, slugging, singles, two-base hits, three-base hits, home runs, strikeouts, putouts, sacrifices, fielding chances, assists, errors, earned run

---

[2] *Annual Report 1965,* Carnegie Corporation.

average, and so on. Nevertheless, when the manager of the team must decide whether A is a better ball player than B, he knows better than to rely completely on the numerical information. Such factors as how well a man gets along with his colleagues, his ability to hit in the pinches, and other unmeasurable characteristics must also be taken into account. If the question of a ball player's ability could be answered solely by an analysis of statistics, there would be no reason for the millions of man-hours of discussion by the "hot-stove league" during the winter months.

Most business organizations are much more complicated than baseball teams; the "game" of business goes on all day, every day, rather than 156 discrete times a year, and business results are not expressed by the number of games won and lost. Business measurements are therefore much more difficult and less precise than baseball measurements.

Some people act as if problems could be completely solved by numerical analysis. They have the erroneous idea that solely from a knowledge of loads, stresses, and material strengths the engineer can figure just how a bridge should look, disregarding the element of judgment completely. At the other extreme, there are those who believe that intuition is the sure guide to a sound decision, and who therefore pay no attention to the figures. Although the correct attitude is clearly somewhere between these extremes, there is no way of describing precisely where it is. The reader must reach his own conclusion on the relative importance of figure and nonfigure data in the solution of management problems.

People, Not Figures, Get Things Done

An obvious fact about business organizations is that they consist of human beings. Anything that the business accomplishes is the result of the actions of these people. Figures can assist the people in the organization in various ways, but the figures themselves are nothing more than marks on pieces of paper; by themselves they accomplish nothing. But figures don't talk back; they give the appearance of being definite and precise, and it is a comforting illusion to imagine that the construction of a set of figures is synonymous with acting on a real problem.

An accounting system may be beautifully designed and carefully operated, but the system is of no use to management unless it results in action by human beings. For instance, three companies may use exactly the same system—the same chart of accounts, the same set of records and reports, the same procedure for collecting and disseminating information—with entirely different results. In one company, the system may be *useless* because management never acts on the information collected, and the organization has become aware of this fact. In the second company, the system may be *helpful* because management uses the information as a general guide for planning and control and has educated the organization to use it in the same spirit. In the third company, the system may be *worse than useless* because management overemphasizes the importance of the figures and therefore takes unwise actions.

SUMMARY

In this book we shall discuss some powerful tools that can assist management in the tasks of operating a business. The invention and refinement of these tools have, in a significant way, made possible the creation and efficient operation of large enterprises, and it is scarcely conceivable that any business, except the smallest ones, could operate without them. At the same time we shall explore the limitations on the use of these tools. We shall see that in the real world, formulas or mechanical techniques rarely provide the complete solution to a problem. The essential reason for these limitations has been well summed up by G. K. Chesterton:

The real trouble with this world of ours is not that it is an unreasonable world, nor even that it is a reasonable one. The commonest kind of trouble is that it is nearly reasonable, but not quite. Life is not an illogicality; yet it is a trap for logicians. It looks just a little more mathematical and regular than it is; its exactitude is obvious, but its inexactitude is hidden; its wildness lies in wait.[3]

---

[3] *Orthodoxy* (London: Bodley Head, 1949 reprint), p. 131.

PART I

The Accounting Structure

CHAPTER 2

BASIC ACCOUNTING CONCEPTS: THE BALANCE SHEET

Suppose you were asked to keep track of what was going on in a business so as to provide useful information for management. One way of carrying out such an assignment would be to write down a narrative of important events in a diary or in a log similar to that kept by the captain of a ship. After some experience with your log or diary, you would gradually develop a set of rules to guide your efforts. For example, since it would be impossible to write down every action of every person in the business, you would frame rules to guide you in choosing between those events that were important enough to record and those that should be omitted. Thus, if your business was a retail automobile dealership, you certainly would want a record of each car sold, but you might well decide not to make a record of every person who came into the showroom.

You would also find that your diary would be more valuable if you standardized certain terminology. People who studied it would then have a clearer understanding of what you meant. Furthermore, if you standardized terms and definitions of these terms, you could turn the job of keeping the diary over to someone else and have some assurance that his report of events would convey the same information that you would have conveyed had you been keeping the diary personally.

In devising these rules of keeping a diary, you would necessarily be somewhat arbitrary. There might be several ways of describing a certain event, all equally good; but in order to have a common basis of understanding, you would select just one of these for use in your record-keeping system. Thus, since the products handled by your automobile dealership could be called "vehicles," "autos," "cars," or "trucks," some of

15

which are synonyms and others not, it would clearly be desirable to agree on a standard nomenclature.

All the foregoing considerations were actually involved in the development of the accounting process. Accounting has evolved over a period of several hundred years, and during this time certain rules and conventions have come to be accepted as useful. If you are to understand accounting reports—the end products of an accounting system—you must be familiar with the rules and conventions lying behind these reports. The purpose of this and the next eight chapters is to describe the more common of these rules and conventions.

Accounting as a Language

Accounting is often called "the language of business." In an important sense, this is an apt phrase, since accounting provides the principal formal means by which information about a business is communicated (although of course there are many other types of business communication). In any event, the task of learning accounting is essentially the same as the task of learning a new language.

This task is complicated by the fact that many of the words used in accounting mean almost, but not quite, the same thing as the identical words mean in everyday, nonaccounting usage. If you are an American learning French, you realize from the beginning that the words and the grammar in French are completely new to you and must therefore be learned carefully. The problem of learning accounting, however, is more like that of an American learning to speak English as it is spoken in Great Britain. Unless he is careful, the American will fail to recognize that words are used in Great Britain in a different sense from that used in America.

> EXAMPLE: The grain that Americans call "wheat" is called "corn" by the British, and the British use the word "maize" for the grain that Americans call "corn." To complicate the matter further, a grain grown in certain parts of America is called "maize," and it is almost, but not quite, like American corn. Unless they understand these differences in terminology, Americans and Englishmen will not communicate what they intend when talking with each other.

Perhaps the greatest difficulty that a beginning student of accounting encounters is that of distinguishing between the accounting meaning of certain terms and the meaning that he has attached to these terms in their nonaccounting, everyday usage.

> EXAMPLE: An amount labeled "net worth" appears on many accounting reports. The commonsense interpretation is that this amount refers to what something is "worth"—what its value is—but such an interpretation is incorrect. For the correct meaning, see p. 37.

As is the case with language, accounting has many dialects. There are differences in terminology and practice among industries and among companies within industries. In this introductory treatment, we shall not attempt even to list all these differences, although the principal ones will be mentioned.

Accounting also resembles a language in that some of its rules are definite, whereas others are not; and there are differences of opinion among accountants as to how a given event should be recorded, just as there are differences of opinion among grammarians as to many matters of sentence structure, punctuation, and choice of words. Nevertheless, there are many practices that are clearly "poor English," and there are also many practices that are definitely "poor accounting." In these chapters, therefore, an attempt is made to describe the elements of "good accounting" and to indicate areas in which there are differences of opinion as to what constitutes good practice.

Finally, languages evolve and change in response to the changing needs of society, and so does accounting. The rules described here are currently in use, but some of them will probably be modified to meet the changing needs of business.

NATURE AND SOURCE OF PRINCIPLES

The rules and conventions of accounting are commonly referred to as "principles." The word "principle" is here used to mean "a general law or rule adopted or professed as a guide to action; a settled ground or basis of conduct or practice."[1] Note that this definition describes a principle as a *general* law or rule, that is, to be used as a *guide* to action. This means that accounting principles do not prescribe exactly how each detailed event occurring in a business should be recorded. Consequently, there are a great many matters in accounting practice that differ from one company to another. In part, these differences are inevitable, because a single detailed set of rules could not conceivably apply to every company. In part, the differences reflect the fact that the accountant has considerable latitude within the "generally accepted accounting principles" in which to express his own idea as to the best way of recording and reporting a specific event.

The reader should realize, therefore, that he cannot know the precise meaning of many of the items on an accounting report unless he knows which of several equally acceptable possibilities has been selected by the person who prepared the report. For example, as mentioned in Chapter 1, the simple word "cost" has many different meanings, and there is agreement on the definition of this word only in the broadest sense. The

---

[1] AICPA, *Accounting Terminology Bulletin No. 1*, p. 9.

meaning intended in a specific situation requires knowledge of the context.

Criteria

Accounting principles are man-made. Unlike the principles of physics, chemistry, and the other natural sciences, accounting principles were not deduced from basic axioms, nor is their validity verifiable by observation and experiment. Instead, they have evolved, and the process of evolution is essentially as follows: a problem is recognized; someone works out what he thinks is a good solution to this problem; if other people agree that this is a good solution, its use gradually becomes widespread, and then it becomes an accounting principle. Moreover, some hitherto accepted principles fall from favor with the passage of time. This evolutionary process is going on constantly; accounting principles are not "eternal verities."

The general acceptance of an accounting principle or practice usually depends on how well it meets three criteria: relevance, objectivity, and feasibility. A principle is *relevant* to the extent that it results in information that is meaningful and useful to those who need to know something about a certain business. A principle is *objective* to the extent that the information is not influenced by the personal bias or judgment of those who furnish it. Objectivity connotes reliability, trustworthiness. It also connotes verifiability, which means that there is some way of ascertaining the correctness of the information reported. A principle is *feasible* to the extent that it can be implemented without undue complexity or cost.

We shall illustrate and expand on the significance of these criteria in connection with the discussion of the principles themselves. At this point it is sufficient to point out that these criteria often conflict with one another. The most relevant solution is likely to be the least objective and the least feasible.

> EXAMPLE: The development of a new product may have a significant effect on a company's real value—Xerography and Polaroid cameras being spectacular recent examples. Such information is most useful to the investor. It is indeed relevant. But the best estimate of the value of a new product is likely to be that made by management, and this is a highly subjective estimate; that is, some persons would make extremely optimistic estimates, whereas others would be equally extreme on the conservative side. Furthermore, many managements have a natural tendency to make the figures look as good as possible. Accounting therefore does not attempt to record such values. It sacrifices relevance in the interests of objectivity.
>
> The measure of the value of the owners' interest in the Xerox Corporation obtained from the stock market quotations (i.e., multiplying the price per share of stock times the number of shares outstanding) is a much more accurate reflection of the true value than the amount at

which this item appears in the corporation's accounting records. As of December 31, 1967, the marketplace gave this value as $6,657 million; the accounting records, $406 million. The difference does not indicate that there is an error in the accounting records. It merely underlines the fact that accounting does not, and does not attempt to, report market values.

In developing new principles, the essential problem is to strike the right balance between relevance on the one hand and objectivity and feasibility on the other. Failure to appreciate this problem often leads to unwarranted criticism of accounting principles. It is easy to criticize accounting on the grounds that accounting information is not as relevant as it might be; but the critic often overlooks the fact that proposals to increase relevance almost always involve a sacrifice of objectivity and feasibility. On balance, such a sacrifice may not be worthwhile.

Sources of Principles

Accounting principles are not codified in a single source that resembles, either in the amount of detail or in its authority, the codification of legal principles on which lawyers rely so heavily. Of the various sources, by far the most authoritative is the set of *Opinions of the Accounting Principles Board* of the American Institute of Certified Public Accountants (AICPA). As of 1968, there were a dozen of these opinions, each consisting of a paragraph, or a few paragraphs, describing the principle, together with several pages of explanatory material. In addition, the Accounting Principles Board has adopted certain of the opinions issued by its predecessor organization, the Committee on Accounting Procedures of the AICPA. These are published in Paul Grady's *Inventory of Generally Accepted Accounting Principles.*[2]

These statements are known as "generally accepted accounting principles." The AICPA emphasizes, however, that "generally accepted accounting principles" are those principles which have substantial authoritative support, and that although opinions of the Accounting Principles Board constitute "substantial authoritative support," "substantial authoritative support" can also exist for accounting principles that differ from opinions of the Accounting Principles Board.

The accounting reports of most companies of any substantial size are examined by certified public accountants, who are members of the AICPA. A company is not required to adhere to the set of principles stated by the Accounting Principles Board, but if the certified public accountant finds that the company has used a different principle, he

---

[2] Published by American Institute of Certified Public Accountants as its *Accounting Research Study No. 7, 1965.* References to these opinions will be cited herein as "Grady."

must call attention to this fact. The alternative principle is acceptable if the company can demonstrate that it has "substantial support." Such a demonstration can be made by showing that several reputable companies use the alternative principle.

As we shall see, the principles so far enunciated by the Accounting Principles Board do not encompass the whole of accounting, and in many cases they specifically permit alternative methods of treatment.

Another authoritative source of principles is publications of the U.S. Securities and Exchange Commission, particularly its *Regulation S–X* and its *Accounting Series Releases*. In general, these are consistent with the *Opinions of the Accounting Principles Board*. They amplify these opinions and describe their application to specific situations.

The American Accounting Association also publishes a statement of accounting principles, but these are to be regarded as normative rather than descriptive; that is, they state what accounting principles *should be*, rather than what they *are*. Thus, they are not necessarily a guide to current practice.

Various regulatory bodies also prescribe accounting rules for the companies they regulate. Among those subjected to such rules are banks and other financial institutions, insurance companies, railroads, airlines, pipelines, radio and television companies, and electric and gas companies. These rules are not necessarily consistent with those of the Accounting Principles Board.

> EXAMPLE: The Union Pacific Railroad company reported that in 1967 its net income, measured in accordance with generally accepted accounting principles, was $80.7 million. Measured in accordance with rules prescribed by the Interstate Commerce Commission, its net income was $102.1 million, or 26 percent greater.

The authority of these agencies exists, of course, only in the United States of America. Accounting principles in other countries differ in some respects from these, but there is a basic similarity throughout the world, including the USSR, but with the notable exception of the Chinese Peoples Republic, whose principles differ from these in some significant respects.

BASIC CONCEPTS

The principles of accounting are built on a foundation of a few basic concepts. They are so basic that most accountants do not consciously refer to them. Some of these concepts are currently undergoing a critical reexamination by the profession, but in this initial contact with them, the reader is asked to understand and accept them rather than to criticize them. As is the case with a language, one can criticize the way certain words are spelled (e.g., "bough," "cough," "doff"), but the fact remains that the words *are* spelled in a certain way. If a person is to use the language effectively, he must understand what the rules actually are.

Accountants differ as to how many basic concepts there are, and as to how they should be labeled and defined. Nevertheless, there probably is fairly general support for the following list:

1. Money measurement	2. Business entity
3. Going concern	4. Cost
5. Dual-aspect	6. Conservatism
7. Accrual	8. Realization
9. Consistency	10. Materiality

The first six of these are discussed below, and the remainder are discussed in Chapter 3.

1. The Money Measurement Concept

In accounting, a record is made only of those facts that can be expressed in monetary terms. The advantage of expressing facts in monetary terms is that money provides a common denominator by means of which heterogeneous facts about a business can be expressed in terms of numbers that can be added and subtracted.

> EXAMPLE: Although it may be a fact that a business owns $10,000 of cash, 6,000 pounds of raw material, six trucks, 10,000 square feet of building space, and so on, these amounts cannot be added together to produce a meaningful total of what the business owns. Expressing these items in monetary terms—$10,000 of cash, $5,000 of raw material, $20,000 of trucks, and $100,000 of buildings—makes such an addition possible.

This concept imposes a severe limitation on the scope of an accounting report. Accounting does not record the state of the president's health; it does not record the fact that the sales manager is not on speaking terms with the production manager; it does not report that a strike is beginning; and it does not reveal that a competitor has placed a better product on the market. Accounting therefore does not give a complete account of the happenings in a business or an accurate picture of the condition of the business. It follows, then, that the reader of an accounting report should not expect to find therein all, or perhaps even the most important, facts about a business.

Money is expressed in terms of its value at the time an event is recorded in the accounts. Subsequent changes in the purchasing power of money do not affect this amount. Thus material purchased in 1969 at $10,000 and land purchased in 1939 at $10,000 are each listed in the 1969 accounting records at $10,000, although the purchasing power of the dollar in 1969 was only 40 percent of what it was 30 years previously.

2. The Business Entity Concept

Accounts are kept for *business entities,* as distinguished from the *persons* who are associated with these entities. In recording facts in the accounts, the important question is, How do they affect the business? not, How do they affect the persons who own, operate, or otherwise are associated with the business? When the owner takes cash out of his business, for example, the accounting records show that the *business* has less cash than previously, even though the real effect of this event on the *owner* himself may have been negligible; he has taken cash from his business "pocket" and put it into his personal "pocket," but it remains his cash.

It is sometimes difficult to define the business entity for which a set of accounts is kept. Consider the case of a man and his wife who run a small unincorporated retail store. In *law* there is no distinction between the financial affairs of the store and those of the people who own it; a creditor of the store can sue and, if successful, collect from the owners' personal resources as well as from the resources of the business. In *accounting,* by contrast, a set of accounts is kept for the store as a separate business entity, and the events reflected in these accounts must be those of the store; the nonbusiness events that affect the couple must not be included in them. Clearly, this means that the family's expenses for food, clothing, shelter, and the like should be separated from the expenses of running the store. But suppose that the couple lives on the business premises. How much of the rent, the electric light bill, and the property taxes of these premises are properly part of the business and how much are personal expenses of the family? Because of questions like these, the distinction between the business entity and outside interests is a difficult one to make in practice.

In the case of a corporation, the distinction is often quite easily made. A corporation is a legal entity separate from the persons who own it, and the accounts of many corporations correspond exactly to the scope of the legal entity. There may be complications, however. In the case of a group of legally separate corporations that are related to one another by stock-holdings, the whole group may be treated as a single business entity for certain purposes, giving rise to what are called "consolidated" accounting statements. Conversely, within a single corporation, a separate set of accounts may be maintained for each of the principal divisions of the corporation, especially when they are physically separated from the home office.

There follows from the distinction between the business entity and the outside world the idea that an important purpose of financial accounting is to provide the basis for reporting on *stewardship*. The managers of a business are entrusted with funds supplied by owners, banks, and others. Management is responsible for the wise use of these funds, and financial accounting reports are in part designed to show how well this responsibility, or stewardship, has been discharged.

3. The Going-Concern Concept

Unless there is good evidence to the contrary, accounting assumes that the business will continue to operate for an indefinitely long period in the future. The significance of this assumption can be indicated by contrasting it with a possible alternative, namely, that the business is about to be liquidated or sold. Under the latter assumption, accounting would attempt to measure at all times what the business *is currently worth* to a buyer; but under the going-concern assumption there is no need to do this, and it is in fact not done. Instead, a business is viewed as a mechanism for adding value to the resources it uses, and its success is measured by the difference between the value of its output (sales of goods and services) and the cost of the resources used in creating that output. Resources which have been acquired but not yet used in creating output are shown on the accounting records, not at their current value to an outside buyer, but rather at their cost. Their current resale value is irrelevant, since it is assumed that they will not be sold as such, but rather that they will be used in the creation of future output values.

4. The Cost Concept

Resources (i.e., rights in tangible and intangible property) owned by a business are called, in accounting language, *assets*. A fundamental concept of accounting, closely related to the going-concern concept described above, is that an asset is ordinarily entered on the accounting records at the price paid to acquire it—that is, at its cost—and that this cost is the basis for all subsequent accounting for the asset.

Since, for a variety of reasons, the real worth of an item may change with the passage of time, the accounting measurement of assets does not necessarily—indeed, does not ordinarily—reflect what assets are worth, except at the moment they are acquired. There is therefore a considerable difference between the accounting concept of cost and the everyday, nonaccounting concept of value, since in its ordinary usage "value" means what something is currently worth.

EXAMPLE: If a business buys a plot of land, paying $5,000 for it, this asset would be recorded in the accounts of the business at the amount of $5,000. Subsequent changes in the market value of this land would ordinarily not be reflected by changes in the accounts. If a year later the land could be sold for $10,000, or if it could be sold for only $2,000, no change would ordinarily be made in the accounting records to reflect this fact. (The word "ordinarily" is used since there are a few situations in which accounting records are changed to reflect changes in market value; these will be described subsequently.)

Thus, the amounts at which assets are listed in the accounts of a company do *not* indicate what the assets could be sold for. One of the most common mistakes made by uninformed persons reading accounting reports is that of believing that there is a close correspondence between the figure at which an asset appears on these reports and the actual value of the asset. Of course, there may well be a correspondence between accounting measurements and real market values in the case of certain assets. The asset "cash" is the best example. Readily marketable securities and inventories held by the company for only a short period of time may appear on the books at figures that are close to their actual worth. In general, it is safe to say that the longer an asset has been owned by a company, the less likely it is that the amount at which it appears on the accounting records corresponds to its current market value.

The cost concept does not mean that all assets remain on the accounting records at their original purchase price for as long as the company owns them. The figure for an asset that has a long, but nevertheless limited, life is systematically reduced over that life by the process called *depreciation*, as discussed in more detail in Chapter 6. The purpose of the depreciation process is systematically to remove the *cost* of the asset from the accounts and to show it as a cost of operations; depreciation has no necessary relationship to changes in market value or in the real worth of the asset to the company.

It follows from the cost concept that if the company pays *nothing* for an item it acquires, this item will usually *not* appear on the accounting records as an asset. Thus, the knowledge and skill that is built up as the business operates, the teamwork that grows up within the organization, a favorable location that becomes of increasing importance as time goes on, a good reputation with its customers—none of these appears as an asset in the accounts of the company.

On some accounting reports the term "goodwill" appears. Reasoning from everyday definition of this word, you may conclude that it represents the accountant's appraisal of what the company's name and reputation are worth. This is not so. Goodwill appears in the accounts of the company only when the company has *purchased* some intangible and valuable property right. A common case is when one company buys another company and pays more than the fair value of its tangible assets. The amount by which the purchase price exceeds the value of the tangible assets may be called goodwill, representing the value of the name, the reputation, the location, or other intangible possessions of the purchased company. Unless the business has actually purchased such intangibles, however, no item for "goodwill" is shown in the accounts. If the item does appear, it is shown initially at the purchase price, even though the management may believe that its real value is considerably higher.

It also follows from the cost concept that an event may affect the true value of a business without having any effect on the accounting records. To take an extreme case, suppose that several key executives are killed in a plane accident. To the extent that "an organization is but the lengthened shadow of a man," the real value of the company will change immediately, and this will be reflected in the market price of the company's stock, which reflects investors' appraisal of value. The accounting records, however, will not be affected by this event.

The cost concept provides an excellent illustration of the problem of applying the three basic criteria discussed in the preceding section: relevance, objectivity, and feasibility. If the *only* criterion were relevance, then the cost concept would not be defensible. Clearly, investors and others are more interested in what the business is actually worth today rather than what the assets cost originally.

But who knows what a business is worth today? The fact is that any estimate of current value is just that—an estimate—and informed people will disagree on what is the right estimate. (For illustrations, see the judgments about companies that are reported in the financial press. On the same day, some people will say that the stock of a given company is "overpriced" and others will say that it is "underpriced.") Furthermore, accounting reports are prepared by the management of a business, and if they contained estimates of what the business is actually worth, these would be management's estimates. It is quite possible that such estimates would be biased.

The cost concept, by contrast, provides a relatively objective foundation for accounting. It is not *purely* objective, for, as we shall see, judgments are necessary in applying it. It is much more objective, however, than the alternative of attempting to estimate current values. Essentially, the reader of an accounting report must recognize that it is based on the cost concept, and he must arrive at his own estimate of current value, partly by analyzing the information in the report and partly by using nonaccounting information.

Furthermore, a "market value" or "current worth" concept would be difficult to apply, because it would require that the accountant attempt to keep track of the ups and downs of market prices. The cost concept leads to a system that is much more feasible.

In summary, adherence to the cost concept indicates a willingness on the part of those who developed accounting principles to sacrifice some degree of relevance in exchange for greater objectivity and greater feasibility.

To emphasize the distinction between the accounting concept and the ordinary meaning of worth, the term "book value" is used for the amounts as shown in the accounting records and the term "market value" for the actual value of the asset as reflected in the marketplace.

5. The Dual-Aspect Concept

As stated above, the resources owned by a business are called "assets." The claims of various parties against these assets are called "equities." There are two types of equities: (1) *liabilities,* which are the claims of creditors, i.e., everyone other than the owners of the business; and (2) *owners' equity* (or "capital," or "proprietorship"), which is the claim of the owners of the business.[3] Since all of the assets of a business are claimed by someone (either by the owners or by some outside party) and since the total of these claims cannot exceed the amount of assets to be claimed, it follows that—

$$\text{Assets} = \text{Equities} .$$

Accounting systems are set up in such a way that a record is made of *two aspects* of each event that affects these records, and in essence these aspects are changes in assets and changes in equities.

Suppose that a man starts a business and that his first act is to open a bank account in which he deposits $10,000 of his own money. The dual aspect of this action is that the business now has an asset, cash, of $10,000, and the owner has a claim against this asset, also of $10,000, or—

$$\text{Assets (Cash)}, \$10,000 = \text{Equities (Owner's)}, \$10,000 .$$

If the business then borrowed $5,000 from a bank, the accounting records would show an increase in cash, making the amount $15,000, and a new claim against this cash by the bank in the amount of $5,000. At this point the accounting records of the business would show the following:

Cash.	$15,000	Owed to bank.	$ 5,000
		Owner's equity.	10,000
Total Assets.	$15,000	Total Equities. . . .	$15,000

Every event that is recorded in the accounts affects at least two items; there is no conceivable way of making only a single change in the accounts. Accounting is therefore properly called a "double-entry" system.

An accounting system conceivably could be set up with some concept other than the one stated here. As a matter of fact, there is a system called "single-entry" accounting that records only one aspect of a transaction, very much like the record maintained in a ship's log or a diary. However,

---

[3] Some accountants use the word "liabilities" to include both the claims of creditors and the claims of owners; when so used it is synonymous with the word "equities" as used here. The narrower definition is used here for the sake of clarity.

as will become apparent in later chapters, there are many advantages, both mechanical and conceptual, in the dual-aspect concept, and this is so universally accepted that no further mention will be made of any other possibility.

6. Conservatism

The conservatism concept means that when the accountant has a reasonable choice, he ordinarily will show the lower of two asset amounts for a given item, or will record an event in such a way that owners' equity is lower than it otherwise would be. This concept is often stated as follows: "Anticipate no profit, and provide for all possible losses." It is especially important as a modifier of the cost concept. To illustrate, inventories (material held for sale, supplies, etc.) are ordinarily reported, not at their cost, which is what one would expect in accordance with the cost concept, but rather at the *lower* of their cost or their current replacement value.

The conservatism concept affects principally the category of assets called "current assets" (see page 32). It is ordinarily not applied to noncurrent assets.

The conservatism concept is applied much less strongly now than was the case a few decades ago when it was a common practice to report some assets at far less than either their cost or their current market value. Nevertheless, the concept still has an important influence on accounting. Many informed persons would say that this concept is illogical and that the accountant should attempt to report the figures either consistently on the basis of cost or consistently on the basis of market value rather than choosing the more conservative of these two possible approaches. Nevertheless, few would question the fact that the concept does exist and that it is important.

THE BALANCE SHEET

The balance sheet is the fundamental accounting report in the sense that every accounting transaction can be recorded in terms of its effect on the balance sheet. It shows the financial status of the business as of a given moment of time.[4]

A balance sheet for a hypothetical corporation is shown in Illustration 2–1. Let us examine this statement in terms of the basic concepts listed

---

[4] A balance sheet dated "December 31" is implicitly understood to mean "at the close of business on December 31." Sometimes the identical balance sheet may be dated "January 1," meaning "at the beginning of business on January 1," which is the same moment of time. Ordinarily, the "close of business" connotation is the correct one.

Illustration 2-1

GARSDEN CORPORATION

Balance Sheet as of December 31, 1968

ASSETS

Current Assets:

Cash.	$ 3,448,891	
Marketable securities (market value, $248,420).	246,221	
Accounts receivable.	5,943,588	
Inventories.	12,623,412	
Prepaid expenses and deferred charges	388,960	
Total Current Assets.		$22,651,072

Fixed Assets:

Land, buildings, and equipment. . .	$26,945,848	
Less: Accumulated depreciation. . .	13,534,069	13,411,779

Other Assets:

Investments	$ 110,000	
Goodwill.	63,214	173,214
Total Assets.		$36,236,065

EQUITIES

Current Liabilities:

Accounts payable.	$ 6,601,442	
Estimated tax liability	1,672,000	
Accrued expenses payable.	640,407	
Deferred income	205,240	
Total Current Liabilities		$ 9,119,089

Other Liabilities:

Mortgage bonds payable.		3,000,000

Stockholders' Equity:

Common stock.	$15,000,000	
Retained earnings	9,116,976	24,116,976
Total Equities.		$36,236,065

above. The figures are *expressed in money* and reflect only those matters that can be measured in money amounts. The *business entity* involved is the Garsden Corporation, and the balance sheet pertains to that entity rather than to any of the individuals associated with the company. The statement assumes that the Garsden Corporation is a *going concern*. The asset amounts stated are governed by the *cost concept*. The *dual-aspect* concept is evident from the fact that the assets listed on one side of this balance sheet are equal in total to the equities, or claims against the assets, listed on the other side.

Incidentally, the practice of listing assets on the left-hand side and equities on the right-hand side of the balance sheet is common in the United States. An alternative practice of listing assets at the top of the page with equities underneath them is also common. The former format is called the *account* form, and the latter is called the *report* form of balance sheet. In certain other countries, assets are listed on the right-hand side and equities on the left-hand side. None of these differences have any real significance.[5]

It should be emphasized that the fact that the two sides add up to the same total necessarily follows from the dual-aspect concept; it does not tell anything about the company's financial condition. This equality of the two sides of the balance sheet is always found unless a clerical error has been made.

Since the term *balance* sheet may give the erroneous impression that there is something good or something significant about this balance or equality of the totals, the Accounting Principles Board recommends that this term be replaced by "statement of financial position" or "position statement." Many companies comply with this recommendation in their published reports, but the term "balance sheet" is still so widely used in ordinary business conversation that it is retained here.

Note also that the amounts are rounded to dollars. Pennies are eliminated in many published statements. In reports prepared for internal purposes, the amounts may be rounded even further, to thousands of dollars, or in large corporations to millions of dollars, so as to highlight the important figures.

Account Categories

Although each individual asset or equity—each building, each piece of equipment, each bank loan, etc.—could theoretically be listed separately

---

[5] Most of the balance sheets in this book are given in the report form for the simple reason that this fits better on a printed page. Most balance sheets typed on regular 8½ × 11 paper are in the report form for the same reason. In published annual reports, the balance sheet is often in the account form, since this makes an attractive two-page spread.

on the balance sheet, it is more practicable and more informative to summarize and group related items into categories or *account classifications*. There is no fixed pattern as to the number of such categories or the amount of detail reported; rather, the format is governed by the accountant's opinion as to the most informative way of presenting significant facts about the status of the business.

As in any classification scheme, the categories are defined in such a way that (1) the individual items included in a category resemble one another in some essential and significant respect, and (2) the items in one category are essentially different from those in all other categories. Although the items included in a category are similar to one another, they are not identical.

EXAMPLE: The category labeled "Cash" usually includes money on deposit at savings banks as well as money on deposit in commercial banks. These two types of money are *similar* in that they both are in highly liquid form, but they are *not identical* because certain restrictions may apply to withdrawals from savings banks that do not apply to withdrawals from commercial banks. If an accountant thought this difference was important enough to report, he would set up two separate categories. This would, however, increase the amount of detail shown on the balance sheet.

The balance sheet in Illustration 2–1 gives a minimum amount of detail. The terms used on this balance sheet are common ones, and they are described briefly below.

Assets

We shall now supersede the short definition of "asset" given in the preceding section by the following more exact statement: *Assets are valuable resources owned by a business which were acquired at a measurable money cost.* The three key points in this definition are the following: (1) the resource must be valuable; (2) the resource must be owned; and (3) the resource must be acquired at a measurable money cost.

A resource is *valuable* either if it is cash or an item that probably will be converted into cash, or if it is expected to benefit the future operation of the business. In some cases the presumed benefit for the future is rather nebulous and debatable; for example, some accountants regard the cost of organizing a corporation as an asset on the grounds that the corporate form of organization is valuable to the business, but others do not.

EXAMPLE: Amounts due from customers are assets, to the extent that customers are likely to pay their bills. The protection promised by an insurance policy is an asset, since the insurance provides a valuable protection against losses from future misfortunes. Merchandise that, because of damage or obsolescence, cannot be sold is not an asset, even though it is owned by the business.

Ownership is a legal concept which is to be distinguished from possession or control. The accounting concept is close to, but not exactly the same as, the legal concept. Thus, when a business buys an automobile on the installment plan, the business may not own the car, in the legal sense, until the last installment has been paid; nevertheless, the automobile is regarded as substantially owned by the business and is shown as an asset. But possession or control, without substantial ownership, is not enough to qualify the item as an asset.

EXAMPLE: A leased piece of equipment is not an asset of the lessee even though it is in his possession and he has complete control over its use. Goods on consignment are assets of the consignor who owns them, not of the consignee who has possession of them.

The *acquisition at a measurable money cost* test is usually clear-cut, but in some instances is difficult to apply. If the resource was purchased for cash or for the promise to pay cash, it is an asset. If the resource was manufactured by the business, then money was paid for the costs of manufacture, and it is an asset. If the resource was acquired by trading in some other asset or by issuing stock, then the item is an asset, although there may be problems in measuring its amount because of the difficulty in valuing the traded-in item or the stock. Ordinarily, the solution to this problem is to determine what the asset would have cost had cash been paid for it; but when no objective evidence of this amount can be found, the best possible estimate is made from whatever information is available. On the other hand, as already pointed out (p. 24), a valuable reputation or an efficient organization is not an asset if it arose gradually over a period of time, rather than being acquired at a specifically measurable cost.

EXAMPLE: Both "Seagrams" and "Schenley" are valuable trade names. Nevertheless, the December 31, 1967, balance sheet for Joseph C. Seagrams and Sons shows a zero amount for this item, whereas the December 31, 1967, balance sheet for Schenley Industries shows $18,595,000 for "Brands, Trademarks, and Goodwill."

Assets are recorded at their total cost, not the company's "equity" in them.

EXAMPLE: If a business buys land for $100,000, pays $30,000 cash, and gives a $70,000 mortgage, the asset is recorded at $100,000, not $30,000.

On most business balance sheets, assets are listed in order of their liquidity; that is, in order of the promptness with which they are expected to be converted into cash. On some balance sheets, notably those of public utilities, the order is reversed, and the least liquid assets are listed first.

Assets are customarily grouped into categories. Current assets are almost always reported in a separate category. All noncurrent assets may be grouped together, or various groupings may be used, such as "Fixed Assets" and "Other Assets" as shown on the Garsden Corporation balance sheet.

Current Assets

"The term *current assets* is used to designate cash and other assets or resources commonly identified as those which are reasonably expected to be realized in cash or sold or consumed during the normal operating cycle of the business."[6]

The distinction between current assets and noncurrent assets is important since much attention is given by lenders and others to the total of current assets. The essence of the distinction is *time*. Current assets are those that will be owned only for a short period of time, usually not more than a year from the balance sheet date, whereas noncurrent assets are those that are expected to be owned for a longer period of time.

Although the usual time limit is one year, exceptions occur in companies whose normal operating cycle is longer than one year. Tobacco companies and distilleries, for example, include their inventories as current assets even though tobacco and liquor remain in inventory for an aging process that lasts two years or more.

Cash consists of funds that are immediately available for disbursement without restriction. Usually, most of these funds are on deposit in checking accounts in banks, and the remainder are in cash registers or other temporary storage facilities on the company's premises.

Marketable securities are investments which are both readily marketable and which are expected to be converted into cash within a year. They are investments made so as to earn some return on cash that otherwise would be temporarily idle. According to generally accepted accounting principles, marketable securities are reported on the balance sheet at their cost or their current market value, whichever is lower, unless the decline in market value is believed to be only temporary. When reported at cost, a parenthetical note of the current market value is customarily given. Many insurance companies, banks, investment companies, and other financial institutions report marketable securities at market value.

Accounts receivable are amounts owed to the company, usually by its customers. Sometimes this item is broken down into *trade* accounts receivable and *other* accounts receivable; the former refers to amounts owed by customers, and the latter refers to amounts owed by employees and others.

---

[6] *Accounting Research Bulletin No. 43*, in Grady, *op. cit.*, p. 234.

Accounts receivable are reported on the balance sheet at the amount owed less an allowance for that portion which probably will not be collected. Methods of estimating this "allowance for doubtful accounts" are described on page 96.

If the amount owed is evidenced by a note or some other written acknowledgment of the obligation, it would ordinarily appear under the heading *notes receivable* rather than accounts receivable.

As defined by the Accounting Principles Board, the term *inventory* means "the aggregate of those items of tangible personal property which (1) are held for sale in the ordinary course of business, (2) are in process of production for such sales, or (3) are to be currently consumed in the production of goods or services to be available for sale."[7] Inventory is reported at the lower of its cost or its current market value.

The item *prepaid expenses and deferred charges* represents certain assets, usually of an intangible nature, whose usefulness will expire in the near future. An example is an insurance policy. A business pays for insurance protection in advance, often for a three-year or a five-year period. Its right to this protection is an asset—a valuable, owned resource —but this right will expire within a fairly short period of time.

Prepaid expenses and deferred charges are reported at the cost of the unexpired service. Thus, if a business has purchased insurance protection for a three-year period, paying $1,200, and one year has expired as of the balance sheet date, the asset is reported at two thirds of its cost, or $800, representing the cost of the protection for the next two years.

The distinction between "prepaid expenses" and "deferred charges" is not important. In some businesses, prepaid expenses and deferred charges are shown, not as current assets, but rather as "other assets" near the bottom of the balance sheet.

Fixed Assets

Fixed assets are tangible, relatively long-lived resources. The business has acquired these assets, ordinarily, in order to use them in the production of other goods and services. If the assets are held for resale they are classified as inventory, even though they are long-lived assets. In the balance sheet shown in Illustration 2–1 fixed assets are lumped together into the single item "land, buildings, and equipment," but in the balance sheets of many companies the figures for land, for buildings, and for various kinds of machinery and equipment are shown separately. In accordance with the cost concept, the figure $26,945,848 on the Garsden Corporation balance sheet represents the cost of these assets to the company at the time they were purchased. The next item, "accumulated

---

[7] *Ibid.*, p. 244.

depreciation," means that a portion of the original cost amounting to $13,534,069 has been already allocated as a cost of doing business, as will be described in Chapter 6.

Other Assets

Investments are securities of one company owned by another for reasons other than the temporary use of excess cash. They are therefore to be distinguished from "marketable securities," which is an item in the current asset section of the balance sheet. A company acquires such securities either to control another company or in the anticipation of earning a return from them. Investments are ordinarily reported at cost.

Intangible assets include goodwill (which was described briefly earlier in this chapter), patents, copyrights, leases, licenses, franchises, and similar valuable but nonphysical things owned by the business. They are distinguished from prepaid expenses, which are intangible current assets, in that they have a longer life-span than prepaid expenses.

Liabilities

Liabilities are the claims of outsiders against the business, or, to put it another way, the amounts that the business owes to persons other than the owners. Unless otherwise noted, all the liabilities shown on the balance sheet are claims against all the assets; ordinarily they are not claims against any *specific* asset or group of assets. Thus, although accounts payable typically arise through the purchase of material for inventory, accounts payable are claims against all the assets, not merely against inventories.

Even if a liability is a claim against a specific asset, it is shown separately on the right-hand side of the balance sheet, rather than as a deduction from the asset amount to which it relates.

EXAMPLE: If land is purchased for $100,000, and a $70,000 mortgage is given, secured by the land, the balance sheet reports land at $100,000 on the asset side, and the mortgage payable of $70,000 on the equities side, *not—*

<pre>
Land........................$100,000
Less: Mortgage.............. 70,000
    Net Amount..............$ 30,000
</pre>

Liabilities are reported at the amount owed as of the balance sheet date, including interest accumulated to that date. Interest that will be owed subsequent to the balance sheet date is excluded. Note that it is the amount *owed* that governs, not the amount *payable* as of the balance sheet date. A loan is a liability even though it is not required to be repaid for another 10 years.

Current Liabilities

In brief, current liabilities are obligations which become due in the near future, usually within the next year, except for those obligations which are expected to be met by the incurrence of a noncurrent liability (as in the case of a maturing bond issue which is to be refunded). The Accounting Principles Board gives a more detailed definition, as follows:

The term *current liabilities* is used principally to designate obligations whose liquidation is reasonably expected to require the use of existing resources properly classifiable as current assets, or the creation of other current liabilities. As a balance-sheet category, the classification is intended to include obligations for items which have entered into the operating cycle, such as payables incurred in the acquisition of materials and supplies to be used in the production of goods or in providing services to be offered for sale; collections received in advance of the delivery of goods or performance of services; and debts which arise from operations directly related to the operating cycle, such as accruals for wages, salaries, commissions, rentals, royalties, and income and other taxes. Other liabilities whose regular and ordinary liquidation is expected to occur within a relatively short period of time, usually 12 months, are also intended for inclusion, such as short-term debts arising from the acquisition of capital assets, serial maturities of long-term obligations, amounts required to be expended within one year under sinking fund provisions, and agency obligations arising from the collection or acceptance of cash or other assets for the account of third persons.[8]

Accounts payable represent the claims of vendors and others. Usually these claims are unsecured. If the claim was evidenced by a note or some other written acknowledgment of debt, the item would be called *notes payable, bank drafts payable,* or some other term that describes the nature of the obligation.

Estimated tax liability is the amount owed the government for taxes. It is shown separately from other obligations both because of its size and because the amount owed is not precisely known as of the date of the balance sheet. Often, the liability for federal and state income taxes is shown separately from other tax liabilities.

Accrued expenses are the converse of prepaid expenses. They represent certain obligations which are indeed valid claims against the assets but which are "intangible" in the sense that they are not evidenced by an invoice or other document submitted by the person to whom the money is owed. An example is the wages and salaries owed to employees for work they have performed but for which they have not been reimbursed.

Deferred income represents the liability that arises because the com-

---
[8] *Ibid.*, p. 277.

pany has received advance payment for a service it has agreed to render in the future. An example is precollected rent, which represents rental payments received in advance for which the company agrees to permit the tenant to use a specified building (or other property) during some future period.

Other Liabilities

Other liabilities are claims of outsiders that do not fall due within one year. Evidently the mortgage bonds of the Garsden Corporation do not mature within the next year, nor do any fraction of them; otherwise all or part of this liability would appear as a current liability (unless, as stated above, it is planned to refund them).

Owners' Equity

The *owners' equity* section of the balance sheet shows the claims of the owners, in this case the shareholders. The terminology used in this section of the balance sheet varies with different forms of organization.

In a corporation, the claims of the owners are evidenced by documents called *stock certificates.* The first item in the shareholders' equity section of the Garsden Corporation balance sheet is the "stated value" of this stock. This may be the par value of the stock, or the price at which it was sold, or some other figure fixed by the board of directors. In the interest of consistency, once the basis of stating each share of stock has been determined, it is rarely changed.

The owners' equity increases through *earnings* (i.e., the results of profitable operations) and decreases when earnings are paid out in the form of dividends. The difference between the total earnings to date and the total amount of dividends to date is *retained earnings;* that is, that part of the total earnings which have been retained for use in the business.[9] If the difference is negative, the item is labeled *deficit.*

The term "surplus" was formerly used instead of "retained earnings," and is still used by some companies. The word "surplus" is apt to be misleading, since to the uninitiated "surplus" represents something tangible, something "left over." There is, in fact, nothing tangible about retained earnings. All the tangible things owned by the business appear on the assets side of the balance sheet. It is because of this misleading connotation that use of this word is no longer recommended. The word "surplus" is sometimes used with appropriate modifiers (capital surplus,

---

[9] Shareholders' equity is also affected by events other than the accumulation of earnings and the withdrawal of these earnings. Examples are the sale of stock at a premium or a discount, the revaluation of stock, and the creation of special reserves. Some of these events will be discussed in Chapter 8.

paid-in surplus, etc.) for certain special items that will be described in Chapter 8.

The term "net worth" is another obsolete term that should be noted. It was formerly used as a synonym for owners' equity, but is being abandoned because of the connotation that the amount states what the owners' interest is "worth," in the ordinary sense of this word. Such a connotation is completely erroneous.

In unincorporated businesses, different terminology is used in the owners' equity section. In a *proprietorship*, which is a business owned by one person, it is customary to show the owner's equity as a single figure, with a title such as "John Jones, capital," rather than making a distinction between the owner's initial investment and the accumulated earnings retained in the business.

In a *partnership*, which is an unincorporated business owned jointly by several persons, there is a capital account for each partner, thus:

```
James Smith, capital. . . . . . . . $15,432
John Smith, capital . . . . . . . .  15,432
     Total Partners' Equity. . . . . $30,864
```

In addition to these basic owners' equity items, a proprietorship or a partnership may, for convenience, use a temporary item called a *drawing account* in which amounts withdrawn from the business by the owner(s) are recorded. Periodically, the total accumulated in the drawing account is subtracted from the capital item, leaving the net equity of the owner(s). For example, a balance sheet might show the following:

```
John Jones, capital . . . . .  $25,000
     Less: Drawings. . . . . .   2,400
     Net Proprietorship Equity        $22,600
```

After the two items have been combined, the balance sheet would read simply:

```
John Jones, capital . . . . . $22,600
```

The reader may have heard of the terms "partnership accounting" and "corporation accounting," and from these he may have formed the impression that different accounting systems are used for different forms of business organization. As a matter of fact, the treatment of assets and liabilities is generally the same in all forms of organization; differences occur principally in the owners' equity section as noted above.

BALANCE SHEET CHANGES

At the moment a business starts, its financial status can be recorded on a balance sheet. From that time on, events occur that change the figures on this first balance sheet, and the accountant records these changes in accordance with the concepts given above. Full-fledged accounting systems provide a means of accumulating and summarizing these changes and of preparing new balance sheets at prescribed intervals.

In learning the accounting process, however, it is useful to consider the changes one by one. This makes it possible to study the effect of individual events without getting entangled with the mechanisms used in practice to record these events. The technical name given to an event that affects an accounting figure is *transaction*. An example of the effect of a few transactions on the balance sheet will now be given. For simplicity, they are assumed to occur on successive days.

Jan. 1. John Smith starts a business, called Glendale Market, by depositing $10,000 of his own funds in a bank account which he has opened in the name of the store. The balance sheet of Glendale Market will then be as follows:

GLENDALE MARKET

Balance Sheet as of January 1

ASSETS	EQUITIES
Cash. $10,000	John Smith, capital. . . .$10,000

Jan. 2. The business borrows $5,000 from a bank giving a note therefor. This transaction increases the asset "cash," and the business incurs a liability to the bank. The balance sheet after this transaction will appear as follows:

GLENDALE MARKET

Balance Sheet as of January 2

ASSETS		EQUITIES	
Cash.	$15,000	Notes payable, bank. . . .$ 5,000	
		John Smith, capital. . . . 10,000	
Total	$15,000	Total. $15,000	

Jan. 3. The business buys inventory in the amount of $2,000, paying cash. The balance sheet is as follows:

GLENDALE MARKET

Balance Sheet as of January 3

ASSETS		EQUITIES	
Cash.	$13,000	Notes payable, bank. . . .$ 5,000	
Inventory	2,000	John Smith, capital. . . . 10,000	
Total	$15,000	Total. $15,000	

Jan. 4. The store sells, for $300 cash, merchandise that cost $200. The effect of this transaction is that inventory has been decreased by $200, cash has been increased by $300, and John Smith's own equity has been increased by the difference, or $100. The $100 is the profit on this sale. The balance sheet will then look like this:

GLENDALE MARKET

Balance Sheet as of January 4

ASSETS		EQUITIES	
Cash.	$13,300	Notes payable, bank.	$ 5,000
Inventory	1,800	John Smith, capital.	10,100
Total	$15,100	Total.	$15,100

These illustrations could be extended indefinitely. As we delve more deeply into the mechanics of accounting, it is worth remembering that every accounting transaction can be recorded in terms of its effect on the balance sheet.

AN OVERALL VIEW OF THE BALANCE SHEET

We have described the balance sheet as a list of assets and of claims against those assets. This is one useful way of thinking about it, especially when trying to decide how to record the effect of a specific transaction. In trying to understand the picture of a business that the balance sheet conveys, it is often useful to use a different, but equally correct, description, as given in the following paragraphs.

The right-hand side of the balance sheet may be viewed as a description of the sources from which the business has obtained the capital with which it currently operates, and the left-hand side as a description of the form in which that capital is invested on a specified date. On the right-hand side of the balance sheet, the several liability items describe how much capital was obtained from trade creditors (accounts payable), from banks (notes payable), from bondholders (bonds payable), and other outside parties. The owners' equity section shows the capital supplied by the shareholders. If the business is a corporation, the shareholders' contribution consists of two principal parts: capital directly supplied (capital stock) and capital which the shareholders provided by permitting earnings to remain in the business (retained earnings).

Capital obtained from various sources has been invested according to the management's best judgment of the optimum mix, or combination, of assets for the business. A certain fraction is invested in buildings, another fraction in inventory, another fraction is retained as cash for current needs of the business, and so on. The asset side of the balance sheet therefore shows the result of these management judgments as of the date of the balance sheet.

When the balance sheet is viewed in this way, some of the apparent inconsistencies in accounting principles and definitions described above may be resolved. Considering assets as items in which capital has been invested makes it reasonable to record assets at their cost rather than at market value, for the cost basis shows the amount of capital tied up in each asset category. Furthermore, a description of retained earnings as one source of capital—the accumulated earnings of past periods not paid out as dividends—is probably easier to understand than a description of retained earnings as someone's "claim" against the business; it is difficult to see how earnings can be a "claim" against anything.

In any event, either one of these approaches to the balance sheet is at best only a brief introduction to the balance sheet idea. Real comprehension comes through constructing and using balance sheets in practical business situations.

SUMMARY OF BASIC CONCEPTS

The basic concepts discussed in this chapter may be briefly summarized as follows:

1. Money Measurement. Accounting records only facts that can be expressed in monetary terms.

2. Business Entity. Accounts are kept for business entities as distinguished from the person(s) associated with those entities.

3. Going Concern. Accounting assumes that a business will continue indefinitely and that it is not about to be sold.

4. Cost. Assets are ordinarily entered on the accounting records at the price paid to acquire them, and this cost, rather than market value, is the basis for subsequent accounting for the asset.

5. Dual Aspect. The amount of assets equals the amount of equities.

6. Conservatism. An asset is recorded at the lower of two reasonably possible values, or an event is recorded in such a way that the owners' equity is lower than it otherwise would be.

SUGGESTIONS FOR FURTHER READING ON ACCOUNTING PRINCIPLES

(For Chapters 2–10)

There are several excellent textbooks, any of which may be useful either for additional information or to obtain a different viewpoint on topics discussed here.

Eric L. Kohler. *A Dictionary for Accountants.* 3d ed.; Englewood Cliffs, N.J.: Prentice-Hall, Inc., 1963. Much more than a dictionary, it contains a good discussion of many terms and concepts, and because of its dictionary format provides a quick way of locating desired information.

RUFUS WIXON (ed.). *Accountants' Handbook.* 4th ed.; New York: Ronald Press Co., 1966. A standard source for detailed information.

NORMAN J. LENHART and PHILIP L. DEFLIESE. *Montgomery's Auditing.* 8th ed.; New York: Ronald Press Co., 1957. Contains accounting principles arranged so they are easy to find.

Publications of the AICPA, AMERICAN ACCOUNTING ASSOCIATION, and U.S. SECURITIES AND EXCHANGE COMMISSION, referred to in the text, are important sources of the latest information on what constitutes "generally accepted accounting principles." *APB Accounting Principles,* published by Commerce Clearing House, Inc., contains all pronouncements of the Accounting Principles Board of the AICPA. In Volume 1, these are classified by topics, and in Volume 2 they are reproduced chronologically. *A Statement of Basic Accounting Theory,* American Accounting Association, 1966, gives the standards proposed by that organization. *Accounting Trends and Techniques,* published annually by the American Institute of Certified Public Accountants, gives detailed information on the accounting practices of 600 leading corporations as revealed in their annual reports.

CHAPTER 3

BASIC ACCOUNTING CONCEPTS: THE INCOME STATEMENT

Owners invest money in a business in the expectation of earning a return on that money. In the terminology of the preceding chapter, they expect that owners' equity will increase. The increase in owners' equity resulting from operation of the business over a specified period of time is called *income* or *profit*. Owners, and indeed all parties interested in the business, have a keen interest in how much profit has been earned and in an explanation of how it was earned. The accounting statement that conveys this information is called the *income statement*. The income statement and the concepts governing its preparation are discussed in this chapter.

In the course of this discussion, the last four of the ten basic concepts listed in Chapter 2 are explained, namely:

7. The accrual concept	8. The realization concept
9. The consistency concept	10. The materiality concept

THE ACCOUNTING PERIOD

It is relatively easy to measure income for the whole life of a business. This is simply the difference between the money that comes in and the money that goes out (excluding, of course, money invested by the owners or paid to the owners).

EXAMPLE: John Wainwright operated a boys' camp for one summer, renting all the necessary facilities and equipment. Before the camp opened, he invested $1,000 of his own money for food, the initial rental payment, and certain other costs. At the end of the summer, after all affairs were wound up, he had his $1,000 back and $2,179 additional. This $2,179 was the income of the camp business. It was the difference

42

between the fees he received from parents and the money he paid out for food, wages, and other costs. The income statement for the business would look like this:

Campers' fees.............................		$21,400
Less costs:		
Food...............................	$6,252	
Wages.............................	8,645	
Rental.............................	2,500	
Other costs.........................	824	
Total costs.............................		18,221
Income.............................		$ 2,179

Over the whole life of any business, income is as simple to determine as it was for the summer camp; that is, it is the difference between the money the owners get out of the business and the money they put into it.

Relatively few business ventures have a life of only a few months, as was the case with John Wainwright's summer camp. Most of them operate for many years. For these businesses, management and other interested parties are unwilling to wait until the business has terminated before obtaining information on how much income has been earned. They need to know at frequent intervals "how things are going." Therefore, accountants choose some convenient segment of time and they measure the income for that period of time. The time interval chosen is called the *accounting period*.

For the purpose of reporting to outsiders, the year is the usual accounting period. Pacioli, the first author of an accounting text, wrote in 1494: "Books should be closed each year, especially in a partnership, because frequent accounting makes for long friendship."[1] Most corporate bylaws require an annual report to the shareholders, and income tax reporting is also on an annual basis.

Formerly, the accounting year, or *fiscal* year, corresponded to the calendar year, but an increasing number of businesses are finding that there are advantages in using the *natural business year* instead of the calendar year. For example, nearly all department stores end their fiscal year on January 31, after the Christmas rush and its repercussions in the form of returns and clearance sales.

Management invariably needs information oftener than once a year, and reports for management are therefore prepared more frequently. The most common period is a month, but the period may be as short as a week or even a day. These reports are called *interim* reports to distinguish them from the annual reports.

Businesses are living, continuing organisms. The act of chopping the stream of business events into time periods is therefore somewhat arbi-

---

[1] Lucas Pacioli, *Summa de Arithmetica Geometria Proportioni et Proportionalita,* from the translation by John B. Geijsbeck.

trary since business activities do not stop or change measurably as one accounting period ends and another begins. It is this fact that makes the problem of measuring income in an accounting period the most difficult problem in accounting.

> EXAMPLE: If, instead of a summer camp, John Wainwright operated a year-round hotel, his income for a year could not be measured as simply the difference between the money taken in and the money paid out. As of the end of the year, some of his guests would not have paid their bills, but these unpaid bills are an asset, accounts receivable, which surely increase the "well-offness" of the business, even though the cash has not yet been remitted. Conversely, some of the cash paid out may have been for the purchase of an asset, such as the hotel itself, and this asset still has value at the end of the accounting period; it would be incorrect to conclude that his income has been decreased by the amount of such payments.

In sorting out the transactions occurring during an accounting period so as to measure the income of that period, the basic guides are the accrual concept and the realization concept.

THE ACCRUAL CONCEPT

The essence of the accrual concept is that income is measured by operating transactions that affect owners' equity, and only by such transactions.

Let us refer back to the January 4 transaction of Glendale Market (p. 39). On that day, merchandise costing $200 was sold for $300 cash. Looking first at the effect of this transaction on assets, we note that although inventory decreased by $200, cash increased by $300, so that the total assets increased by the difference, $100. From the dual-aspect concept, which states that the total of the assets must always equal the total of the equities, we know that the equities side of the balance sheet must also have increased by $100. Since no liabilities were affected, the increase must have occurred in the owner's equity item. In summary, because assets were sold for more than was paid for them, the owner's equity increased. Such increases in owner's equity are called income. In understanding how this income came about, it is useful to consider two aspects of this event separately: the $300 received from the sale, and the $200 decrease in inventory. If we look only at the $300, we see that it is an increase in cash, and a corresponding *increase* in the owner's equity. The $200, taken by itself, is a decrease in the asset, inventory, and a corresponding *decrease* in the owner's equity. These two aspects illustrate the only two ways in which business operations can affect owner's equity: they can increase it, or they can decrease it.

Any increase in owners' equity resulting from the operation of the business is called a *revenue*. Any decrease is called an *expense*. Income is therefore the excess of revenues over expenses. (If expenses exceed revenue, the difference is called a *loss*.) Restating the transactions described above in these terms, there was revenue of $300, expense of $200, and income of $100.

As an aside, it should be noted that the word *income* is often, but erroneously, used where *revenue* is intended. This is because the approved definitions are of relatively recent vintage and some companies have not kept up with the latest developments. For example, Western Electric Company, Incorporated, reported "gross income" in 1967 of $3,733,906,000; the term should have been "revenue." In this situation, the intended meaning was obvious, since no company has income of $3 billion; but in other situations, the misuse of the term "income" causes confusion. For example, if someone says Company X had an income of a million dollars, he gives a completely false impression of the size of the company if he actually meant that Company X had *revenues* of a million dollars.[2]

It is extremely important to recognize that income is associated with changes in owners' equity, and that it has no necessary relation to changes in cash. Income connotes "well-offness." Roughly speaking the bigger the income, the better off are the owners. An increase in cash, however, does not necessarily mean that the owners are any better off—that their equity has increased. The increase in cash may merely be offset by a decrease in some other asset or an increase in a liability, with no effect on owners' equity at all.

Again, reference to the transactions of Glendale Market may help clarify this point. When Glendale Market borrowed $5,000 from the bank on January 2 (p. 38), its cash was increased, but this was exactly matched by an increase in the liability to the bank. There was no change in owner's equity since Mr. Smith, the owner, had no greater claim on the assets. No income resulted from this transaction; the $5,000 was not revenue. Similarly, the purchase of inventory for $2,000 cash on January 3 (p. 38) resulted in a decrease in cash, but there was an exactly corresponding increase in another asset, inventory, and therefore owner's equity was not changed.

As we have already seen, the sale for $300 of inventory costing $200 did result in income, but it should be noted that the income was $100, whereas cash increased by $300, so even here the income is different from the amount by which the cash changed. In short, although the typical person measures his personal income by the amount of money he receives,

[2] The income tax Form 1040 still contains the phrases "dividend income," "interest income," and "pension and annuity income" for items that actually are *revenues*. The government is not always quick to change its ways.

he must be careful *not* to use a similar line of reasoning when thinking about the income of a business.

MEASUREMENT OF EXPENSES

The diagram in Illustration 3–1 shows a portion of the life of a business that has been divided into annual accounting periods. For each of these accounting periods an income statement is prepared, and for each point between periods (i.e., the close of business December 31) there is a balance sheet. In this section, the measurement of expenses in "this year" will be discussed.

Expenses are the costs incurred in connection with the earning of revenue. The term "expense" connotes "sacrifices made," "the cost of services or benefits received," or "resources consumed" during an accounting period. The term "cost" is not synonymous with "expense." As just explained, *expense* means a decrease in owners' equity that arises from

Illustration 3–1

the operation of a business during a specified accounting period, whereas *cost* means any monetary sacrifice, whether or not the sacrifice affects owners' equity during a given accounting period.

The American Accounting Association Committee gives the following definition:

> Expense is the expired cost, directly or indirectly related to a given fiscal period, of the flow of goods or services into the market and of related operations. . . . Recognition of cost expiration is based either on a complete or partial decline in the usefulness of assets, or on the appearance of a liability without a corresponding increase in assets.[3]

Expenses and Expenditures

An *expenditure* takes place when an asset or service is acquired. The expenditure may be made by cash, by the exchange of another asset, or by

[3] "Accounting and Reporting Standards for Corporate Financial Statements," 1957 Revision, *Accounting Review*, October 1957, p. 541.

incurring a liability. Over the entire life of a business most expenditures made by a business become expenses, and there are no expenses that are not represented by an expenditure. In any time segment *shorter* than the life of a business, however, there is no necessary correspondence between expense and expenditure.

EXAMPLE: In 1968, $1,000 of fuel oil was purchased for cash. This was an *expenditure* of $1,000, the exchange of one asset for another. If none of this fuel oil was consumed in 1968, there was no *expense* in 1968. If the fuel oil was consumed in 1969, there was an *expense* of $1,000 in 1969.

The American Accounting Association Committee describes the recognition of expenses as follows:

Expense is given recognition in the period in which there is (*a*) a direct identification or association with the revenue of the period, as in the case of merchandise delivered to customers; (*b*) an indirect association with the revenue of the period, as in the case of office salaries or rent; or (*c*) a measurable expiration of asset costs even though not associated with the production of revenue for the current period, as in the case of losses from flood or fire.[4]

The expenses of "this year" therefore include the cost of the products *sold* during the year, even though these products were purchased or manufactured in a prior year; the wages and salaries *earned* by employees who sold these products, whether or not they were paid during the year; and the supplies, telephone, electricity, and other assets or services *consumed* or *used* during the year in connection with the production of this revenue, whether or not the bills for these items were paid.

Four types of events need to be considered in distinguishing between amounts that are properly considered as expenses of a given accounting period, and the expenditures or cash payments made in connection with these items. Focusing on "this year" in the diagram in Illustration 3–1, these are as follows:

1. Expenditures this year that are also expenses of this year.
2. Expenditures made prior to this year that become expenses during this year. These appeared as assets on the balance sheet at the beginning of this year.
3. Expenditures made this year that will become expenses in future years. These will appear as assets on the balance sheet at the end of this year.
4. Expenses of this year that will be paid for in a future year. On the balance sheet at the end of this year, these will appear as liabilities.

---

[4] *Ibid.,* p. 541.

Expenditures That Are Also Expenses

This is the simplest type of event, and the least troublesome to account for. If an item is acquired during the year, it is an expenditure; if it is consumed during the same year, it is also an expense of the year.

Assets That Become Expenses

On January 1, the balance sheet shows certain assets. During "this year" some of these assets are used up and hence are transformed into expenses. The three principal types of such assets are described below.

First, there are *inventories* of products; these become expenses when the products are sold.

Second, there are *prepaid expenses* and *deferred charges*. These represent services or other assets purchased prior to "this year" but not yet used up when the year begins. They become expenses in the year in which the services are used or the assets are consumed. *Insurance protection* is one such item; the premium on most types of insurance policies is paid in advance, and the insurance protection bought with this premium is an asset until the accounting period in which the insurance protection is received, at which time it becomes an expense. Prepaid rent follows the same pattern, with the expense being associated with the year in which the company receives the benefit of occupying the rented premises.

> EXAMPLE: A company purchased three-year insurance protection on December 31, 1967. The $900 appears as an asset on the balance sheet of December 31, 1967. In 1968, $300 becomes an expense and $600 remains as an asset on the balance sheet of December 31, 1968. In 1969, $300 more becomes an expense, and so on.

> EXAMPLE: A company paid $10,000 to its landlord on July 1, 1968, representing an advance payment of one year's rent. Of this amount $5,000 is rent expense of 1968. On the balance sheet of December 31, 1968, $5,000 appears as an asset, and this amount becomes an expense in 1969.

Another, and somewhat different, type of prepaid expense is *prepaid taxes*. Certain taxes are paid for in advance of the accounting period to which they apply, and although it is farfetched to say that this accounting period "benefits" from the taxes, it is reasonable to charge these taxes as an expense in the accounting period, or periods, for which the tax is levied.

The third category of assets that will become expenses is *long-lived* assets. Most fixed assets (with the exception of land) have a limited useful life; that is, they do not last forever. They are purchased with the expectation that they will be used in the operation of the business in future periods, and they will become expenses in these future periods.

The principle is exactly the same as that of the insurance policy previously mentioned, which also was purchased for the benefit of future periods. An important practical difference between a fixed asset, such as a building, and an insurance policy, however, is that the life of a building is usually difficult to estimate, whereas the life of an insurance policy is known precisely. It follows that estimating the portion of a building's cost that is an expense in a given accounting period is a more difficult task than that of determining the insurance expense of a period. The mechanism used to convert the cost of fixed assets to expense is called "depreciation" and is described in Chapter 6.

Expenditures That Are Not Yet Expenses

As the preceding examples show, some expenditures made to acquire assets "this year" are not expenses of "this year" because the assets have not yet been used up. These include not only the purchase of assets as such, but also expenditures incurred in connection with the *manufacture* of products that are to be sold in some future year. Thus, wages and salaries earned by production personnel and all other costs associated with manufacturing become part of the cost of the product manufactured and remain as part of the cost of an asset, inventory, until the product is sold. The distinction between manufacturing costs, which initially are added to inventory amounts, and other costs, which are expenses of the current period, will be discussed in more detail in Chapter 7.

Expenses Not Yet Paid

Some expenses which were incurred "this year" are not paid for by the end of the year. The parties who furnished these goods or services have a claim against the business for the amounts owed them, and these amounts are therefore liabilities of the company as of December 31. The liability for wages earned but not paid for is an example that has already been mentioned. Several other types of obligations have the same characteristic; namely, that although services were rendered in an accounting period prior to that for which the balance sheet is prepared, these services have not yet been paid for. The *incurrence* of these expenses reduces owners' equity; the subsequent *payment* of the obligation does not affect owners' equity.

For all obligations of this type, the transaction involved is essentially the same: the expense is shown in the period in which the services were used, and the obligation that results from these services is shown on the liability section of the balance sheet as of the end of the period.

    Example: In 1968 an employee earned $50 that was not paid him. This is an expense of $50 in 1968, and there is a corresponding liability of $50 (called accrued wages) on the balance sheet as of December 31, 1968. In 1969, when the employee is paid, the liability disappears, and there is a corresponding reduction in cash.

Note that in these examples, the basic equality, Assets = Equities, is always maintained. The earning of wages resulted in an expense of $50, which was a decrease in owners' equity, and there was an equal increase in the liability, accrued wages, so the total of the equities was unchanged. The payment of the $50 resulted in a decrease in cash and a decrease in the liability, accured wages; that is, both assets and equities were reduced by $50.

Another common item of this type is *interest*. Interest is the cost of borrowing money, and it is an expense of the period during which the money was borrowed. Interest rates are usually stated on an annual basis. The treatment is different depending on whether the interest is paid when the loan *matures* (i.e., falls due) or whether it is paid in advance. The latter practice is called *discounting* and is customary for short-term bank loans. An example of each will be given.

EXAMPLE: On December 1, 1968, the company borrowed $1,000 for four months at 6 percent interest, the interest and principal to be paid on March 31, 1969. The loan itself results in an increase of cash, $1,000, and creates a liability, loans payable, of $1,000. The total interest cost is $1,000 × 4/12 × 0.06 = $20. One fourth of this interest, $5, is an expense of 1968. Since it has not been paid, $5 also appears as a liability item, interest payable, on the December 31, 1968, balance sheet. The remaining $15 interest is an expense of 1969. When the loan is repaid on March 31, cash is reduced by $1,020, and this is balanced by the decrease in loans payable of $1,000, the decrease in interest payable of $5, and the interest expense for 1969 of $15.

EXAMPLE: On December 1, 1968, the company borrowed $1,000 for four months at 6 percent discounted. The company receives $980. Interest expense for 1968 is $5, as in the preceding example, but now there is an asset, prepaid interest, of $15 on the December 31, 1968, balance sheet, representing the interest cost that will not become an expense until 1969. Thus, the following items are affected by this transaction in 1968: cash has increased by $980; there is an asset, prepaid interest, of $15; owners' equity has decreased by the applicable $5 of interest expense; and there is a liability, notes payable, of $1,000. Note that, as always, the change in assets ($980 + $15) equals the change in equities ($1,000 − $5).

Asset or Expense?

When one part of a transaction results in a decrease in cash or an increase in a liability the accountant must often answer the question: Is the other part of the transaction an increase in an asset, or is it an expense?

If it is the former, income is unaffected; if the latter, income is decreased.

One useful way of approaching this problem is to consider whether, at the end of the accounting period, the business will own something that qualifies as an asset, as this word is defined in accounting. If not, the item must be "written off," as an expense.

There are many situations in which the answer is not clear-cut, and some of these can have a substantial effect on the income reported for a period.

> EXAMPLE: Consider expenditures for research and development. It can be argued, on the one hand, that such expenditures lead to new products or processes that will add to income in future periods and therefore that such expenditures, or at least part of them, create assets. It can also be argued, on the other hand, that the connection between an expenditure for research and development and the income from the new products or processes is so tenuous that no measurable asset value has been created. Often, there is no clear-cut right or wrong answer to such problems.

MEASUREMENT OF REVENUE

Revenues are also measured in accordance with the accrual concept; that is, revenues accrue in the accounting period in which they are earned, which is not necessarily the same as the period in which the cash is received.

As was the case with expenses and expenditures, a careful distinction must be made between revenues and cash receipts. Referring back to our diagram in Illustration 3–1, the balance sheet at the end of "last year" may show, as liabilities, some items that become revenues in "this year." On that balance sheet these are called *deferred revenues* or *precollected revenues*. They represent an advance payment which creates a liability to render a service in some future period. The building owner who receives rent in advance, the insurance company which receives insurance premiums in advance, and the magazine publisher who receives subscription revenue in advance will have such liabilities on their books.

Conversely, revenue may be earned "this year" even though payment is not received until "next year." In this case, the balance sheet as of the end of "this year" will show the asset *accounts receivable* representing amounts owed to the business on account of sales made "this year" for which payment has not yet been received. The year-end balance sheet may also show the asset, *accrued revenue* (or a more descriptive term such as accrued *interest* revenue), representing amounts due the business for services rendered during the accounting period that have not been actually invoiced to the recipient. For example, interest on funds loaned by the business is revenue for the period during which the loan is outstanding, and recognition of this revenue results in corresponding recognition of the amount of interest receivable from the borrower; the latter amount is an asset.

The difference between revenue and receipts is illustrated in the following tabulation that shows various types of sales transactions and classifies the effect of each on cash receipts and sales revenue for "this year":

		This Year	
	Amount	*Cash Receipts*	*Sales Revenue*
1. Cash sales made this year..............	$200	$200	$200
2. Credit sales made last year;.............			
cash received this year.................	300	300	0
3. Credit sales made this year;.............			
cash received this year.................	400	400	400
4. Credit sales made this year;.............			
cash received next year.................	100	0	100
Total.........................		$900	$700

Note that in the above illustration the total cash receipts do not equal the total sales revenue for the period. The totals would be equal in a given accounting period only (1) if the company made all its sales for cash, or (2) if the amount of cash collected from credit customers in an accounting period happened to equal the amount of credit sales made during that period.

THE REALIZATION CONCEPT

We have referred to the "earning" of revenues. A basic accounting concept is that revenue is considered as being earned on the date at which it is *realized;* that is, on the date when goods or services are furnished to the customer in exchange for cash or some other valuable consideration. For services, revenue is recognized in the period in which the service is rendered. For tangible products, revenue is recognized not when a sales order is received, not when a contract is signed, not when the goods are manufactured, but rather when the product is shipped or delivered to the customer.

There are many fine points concerning the exact date on which legal title passes from one party to the other. In general, the accountant uses the date the product was shipped or the date shown on the invoice to the customer, whichever is later.

There is a difference here between accounting and economics. In economics (and in fact), the manufacturing process is regarded as creating value, and this value includes an allowance for profit, but in financial accounting only the *costs* of manufacture are recognized as adding to the value of the product during the manufacturing cycle; all the profit (i.e., the increase in owners' equity) is recorded at the time of sale.

This difference between accounting and economics is explained by the importance of the criterion of objectivity in accounting. There is no objective way of measuring how much profit is created during the manufacturing process. The outcome of the whole process is known with reasonable certainty only when the buyer and seller have agreed on a price and the goods have been delivered. Also, at this time there is usually an invoice, a cash register record, or some other tangible evidence as to the revenue arising from the transaction—evidence that permits the facts to be verified by some outside party. This "test of the marketplace," or "arm's-length agreement," as it is called, provides an objective measure of the revenue, and this is the essential reason for the realization concept.

In cases where revenue can be objectively measured earlier than the date of exchange between buyer and seller, it is often recognized on this earlier date. In gold mining, for example, revenue is recognized in the accounting period in which the gold is mined, rather than the period in which it is sold, because gold always has a specified value, and a market exchange is not necessary to establish this value.

Conversely, revenue may not be recognized in the period in which the goods are delivered if there is considerable doubt as to the amount of cash that is actually going to be received from the customer. In certain types of installment selling, for example, a sizable fraction of the customers default on their contracts; and in view of the uncertainty of realizing the full amount of the sale, the seller may decide to recognize revenue only as the installment payments are received.

The general rule that realization occurs on the date when goods are shipped or services rendered implies a reasonable certainty, but not an absolute certainty, that revenue has been earned on that date. The customer may not pay his bill, or he may return the goods, or he may, perhaps several months later, ask to have repairs made under the terms of a warranty agreement. These subsequent events, which make the actual income turn out less than it was originally thought to be, are recognized in the accounts if reasonable estimates can be made of their impact. The method of doing this is described in Chapter 5.

EXAMPLE: A company manufactures a machine in March, ships and bills it to a customer in April, and receives payment in May. The machine carries a guarantee which provides for free repairs over the next five years. The revenue from this transaction is realized not in March, the month of manufacture, nor in May, the month in which cash is received, but in April, the month in which the exchange takes place. The fact that there may be future costs associated with this transaction is recognized by setting up, also in April, a provision for the estimated future repair cost. This is an expense item in April.

Matching

The accrual concept is often described as the "matching" concept. It is important that the expenses recognized in an accounting period be *matched* with (i.e., be measured in a manner consistent with) the revenues recognized in that period. This means that under the usual practice of recognizing revenue at the time of shipment, the total cost of the products shipped is an expense of this same period. In other words, the "cost of products sold" item and the "sales" item on an income statement should refer to the same physical products.

Expenses incurred in producing revenue are also matched against the revenue produced. For example, if "this year" a salesman received an advance commission for selling a product that is to be shipped and recognized as revenue "next year," the commission is an expense of "next year" rather than of "this year." This distinction is not always easily made in practice.

Note that expenses are matched to revenues, not the other way around; that is, the first step is to determine what revenues are to be recognized in a given accounting period, and the second step is to determine the expenses that are associated with these revenues.

> EXAMPLE: If a company decides that revenues on installment sales are to be recognized in the year in which the sale is made, then the cost of the products sold and any other costs associated with the sale are expenses of that year. If, on the other hand, revenues are recognized in the year in which the installment payments are received, then the costs are expenses in that same year.

If expenses cannot be traced to specific items of revenue, they are charged to the year in which they are incurred. Salary earned by a salesman whether or not he makes sales, as contrasted with a commission paid on a specific sale, is an example. Such salary is an expense of the period in which the salesman earned it.

THE CONSISTENCY CONCEPT

The eight concepts that have been described in this and the preceding chapters are so broad that there are in practice several different ways in which a given event may be recorded in the accounts. For example, when a company takes a cash discount in paying bills to its vendors, this discount may be treated as being revenue; it may be treated as a reduction in the purchase price of the goods purchased; or the cash discounts *not* taken may be treated as an expense. The consistency concept requires that once a company has decided on one of these methods, it will treat all subsequent events of the same character in the same fashion. If a company made frequent changes in the manner of handling a given class of events in the accounting records, comparison of its accounting figures for one period with those of another period would be difficult.

Because of this concept, changes in the method of keeping accounts are not made lightly. A company's auditors invariably include in their opinion (i.e., a letter summarizing the results of their annual examination of accounting records) the statement that the figures were prepared "in conformity with generally accepted accounting principles *applied on a basis consistent with that of the preceding year*"; or if there were changes in practice, these are spelled out in the opinion.

Note that consistency as used here has a narrow meaning. It refers only to consistency over time, not to *logical* consistency at a given moment of time. Some people argue that it is inconsistent to measure inventory at cost or market, whichever is lower, and to measure fixed assets at cost. Whatever the merits of this argument may be, it does not involve the accounting concept of consistency. This concept does not mean that the treatment of different categories of transactions must be consistent with one another, but only that transactions in a given category must be treated consistently from one accounting period to the next.

THE MATERIALITY CONCEPT

In law, there is a doctrine called *de minimis non curat lex,* which means that the court will not consider trivial matters. Similarly, the accountant does not attempt to record a great many events which are so insignificant that the work of recording them is not justified by the usefulness of the results. An example of these trivialities is the accounting treatment of pencils. A brand new pencil is an asset of the company. Every time someone writes with the pencil, part of this asset is used up, and the owners' equity decreases correspondingly. Theoretically, it would be possible to ascertain daily the number of partly used pencils that are owned by the company and to correct the records so as to show that fractional amount of the asset amount that remains, but the cost of such an effort would obviously be gigantic, and no accountant would attempt to do this. He would take the simpler, even though less exact, course of action and consider that the asset was used up at the time the pencils were purchased or at the time they were issued from inventory to the user.

There is no agreement as to the exact line separating material events from immaterial events. The decision depends on judgment and common sense. It is natural for the beginning student, who does not have an appreciation of the cost of collecting accounting information, to be more meticulous in recording events in the accounts than would the practicing accountant.

The *materiality* concept is important in the process of determining the expenses and revenue for a given accounting period. Many of the expense items that are recorded for a given accounting period are necessarily estimates, and in some cases they are not very close estimates. There is a point beyond which it is not worthwhile to attempt to refine these estimates. Telephone expense is a familiar example. Telephone bills, although rendered monthly, often do not coincide with a calendar month. It would be possible to analyze each bill and classify all the toll calls according to the month in which they were made. This would be following the accrual concept precisely. Few companies bother to do this, however. They simply consider the telephone bill as an expense of the month in which the bill is received, on the grounds that a system that would ascertain the real expense would not be justified by the accuracy gained. Since in many businesses the amount of the bill is likely to be relatively stable from one month to another, no significant error may be involved in this practice. Similarly, very few businesses attempt to match the expenses of making telephone calls to the specific revenues that might have been produced by those calls.

OTHER CHANGES IN OWNERS' EQUITY

If the logic of the accrual concept were considered narrowly, only those expenses that relate to operations of the current period would be shown on the income statement for that period. There are a number of events, however, that although not strictly conforming to this concept are nevertheless reported as expenses of the period in which they are recognized.

An example that happens frequently is the transaction required to correct an error made in a *prior* accounting period. Suppose that in 1969 a company receives a bill for services performed for it by a lawyer in 1968, but the cost of these services had been overlooked when the 1968 financial statements were prepared. This cost is not properly an expense of 1969, and the logical procedure, therefore, would be to make the deduction in owners' equity directly rather than to report it on the income statement for 1969 as an expense of that year. Until recently, such a procedure was followed by many companies, but the Accounting Principles Board has now adopted the doctrine of the *all-inclusive income statement*, which is that almost all changes in owners' equity, other than dividend payments and changes in capital structure, should be reported on the current year's income statement. Adjustments for prior periods are limited to those which:

1. Can be specifically identified with and directly related to the business activities of prior periods.

2. Are not attributable to economic events occurring subsequent to the date of the financial statements for the prior period.
3. Depend primarily on determinations by persons other than management.
4. Were not susceptible of reasonable estimation prior to such determination.[5]

Adjustments that meet these criteria are relatively rare.

Extraordinary Items

Transactions which affect owners' equity but which do not arise in the normal course of business operations appear on the income statement as a separate item. The Accounting Principles Board describes these extraordinary items as follows:

The segregation in the income statement of the effects of events and transactions which have occurred during the current period, which are of an extraordinary nature and whose effects are material requires the exercise of judgment. . . . Such events and transactions are identified primarily by the nature of the underlying occurrence. They will be of a character significantly different from the typical or customary business activities of the entity. Accordingly, they will be events and transactions of material effect which would not be expected to recur frequently and which would not be considered as recurring factors in any evaluation of the ordinary operating processes of the business. Examples of extraordinary items, assuming that each case qualifies under the criteria outlined above, include material gains or losses (or provisions for losses) from (a) the sale or abandonment of a plant or a significant segment of the business, (b) the sale of an investment not acquired for resale, (c) the write-off of goodwill due to unusual events or developments within the period, (d) the condemnation or expropriation of properties, and (e) a major devaluation of a foreign currency. . . .

Certain gains or losses (or provisions for losses), regardless of size, do not constitute extraordinary items (or prior period adjustments) because they are of a character typical of the customary business activities of the entity. Examples include (a) write-downs of receivables, inventories and research and development costs, (b) adjustments of accrued contract prices, and (c) gains or losses from fluctuations of foreign exchange. The effects of items of this nature should be reflected in the determination of income before extraordinary items.[6]

TAX ACCOUNTING VERSUS BUSINESS ACCOUNTING

In figuring its income tax, a business must determine its net taxable income. The amounts of revenue and expense used to determine federal taxable income are usually similar to, but not identical with, amounts measured in accordance with the principles of financial accounting. The

---

[5] AICPA *Opinions of the Accounting Principles Board No. 9*, Par. 23.

[6] *Ibid.*, pars. 21 and 22.

differences are such that it is unwise to rely on income tax regulations as a basis for solving business accounting problems.

Unless tax rates applicable to the business are expected to increase in the future, a business usually reports the minimum possible amount of taxable income in the current year, thus postponing tax payments as much as possible to future years. It does this generally by recognizing expenses as soon as legally possible, but postponing recognition of revenue for as long as possible. Note that this is a process of shifting revenue and expense from one period to another; over the long run in most businesses, there is little difference between the total expenses and revenues computed for tax purposes and the total expenses and revenues computed for financial accounting. The objective of minimizing current taxes is, as the Supreme Court has pointed out, a perfectly legal and ethical one, provided it is done in accordance with the tax regulations. It is also legal and proper under most circumstances to figure income one way for tax purposes and another way for accounting purposes.

The objective of minimizing current taxes is not by any means the same as the objective of financial accounting, which is to inform management and others as to the income earned. Therefore, the two measurements of income may well be different. For example, in order to encourage research, the tax regulations permit most research costs to be counted as expenses in the year in which the research is done; whereas if the research results in products that will produce revenue in future years, these costs can be spread over the years in which the revenue from the new products is earned.

As a practical matter, many businesses choose to pattern their accounting practices after the tax regulations. This policy is convenient in that it reduces somewhat the number of separate records that must be maintained. However, if it is carried to the point of complete subservience to the tax regulations, serious distortions in accounting reports can result. In constructing a business income statement, the accountant should not use the authority of a tax regulation as a substitute for careful thinking about the best way of measuring income in accordance with accounting principles.

Although tax regulations are not described in detail in this book, references are made to accounting practices which are or are not consistent with them. The businessman learns early the importance of becoming thoroughly familiar with the principal tax rules that affect his operations and also the importance of consulting an expert when unusual situations arise.

THE INCOME STATEMENT

The accounting report that summarizes the revenue items, the expense items, and the difference between them (net income) for an accounting period is called the *income statement* (or the "profit and loss statement," "statement of earnings," or "statement of operations"). In a technical sense the income statement is subordinate to the balance sheet in that it shows in some detail the items that together account for the change during an accounting period in one balance sheet category, owners' equity, and more specifically in one item in that category, retained earnings. Nevertheless, the information on the income statement is usually much more important than information on the balance sheet, since the income statement reports the results of operations and indicates reasons for the business's profitability or lack thereof. The importance of the income statement is illustrated by the fact that in situations where accountants in recording an event must choose between a procedure which distorts the balance sheet or one which distorts the income statement (a choice which is unfortunately necessary on occasions), they usually choose the former.

There is in practice considerable variation among companies in the format used for the income statement. The Accounting Principles Board has suggested a format along the lines shown in Illustration 3–2, but makes it clear that this is not mandatory.

The income statement in Illustration 3–2 gives information for the prior year, as well as for the current year, to provide a basis for compari-

Illustration 3–2

STATEMENT OF INCOME AND RETAINED EARNINGS

Years Ended December 31, 1967, and December 31, 1966

	1967	*1966*
Net sales	$84,580,000	$75,650,000
Other revenue	80,000	100,000
	$84,660,000	$75,750,000
Cost and expenses:		
Cost of goods sold	$60,000,000	$55,600,000
Selling, general, and administrative expenses	5,000,000	4,600,000
Interest expense	100,000	100,000
Other deductions	80,000	90,000
Income tax	9,350,000	7,370,000
	$74,530,000	$67,760,000
Income before extraordinary items	$10,130,000	$ 7,990,000
Extraordinary items	(2,040,000)	(1,280,000)
Net Income	$ 8,090,000	$ 6,710,000
Retained earnings at beginning, plus Net Income	$33,770,000	$30,060,000
Cash dividends on common stock—$0.75 per share	4,380,000	4,380,000
Retained Earnings at End of Year	$29,390,000	$25,680,000
Per share of common stock:		
Income before extraordinary items	$1.73	$1.37
Extraordinary items	(0.34)	(0.22)
Net Income	$1.39	$1.15

SOURCE: Slightly modified from Exhibit A of *Opinions of the Accounting Principles Board No. 9.*

son. The Accounting Principles Board recommends such a practice, both for the income statement and for the balance sheet.

Comments about the items listed on this income statement and variations often found in practice are given in the following paragraphs.

Revenues

An income statement often shows several separate items in the revenue section, the net of which is the *net sales* figure. For example:

Gross sales..............................		$15,400
Less: Returns and allowances............$450		
Sales discounts................... 350		800
Net sales...............................		$14,600

Gross sales is the total invoice price of the goods shipped (or services rendered) plus the cash sales made during the period. It does not ordinarily include *sales taxes* or *excise taxes* that may be charged the customer. Such taxes are not revenues, but rather represent collections which the business makes on behalf of the government. They are a liability to the government until paid. Similarly, postage, freight, or other items billed to the customer at cost are not revenues; they appear not in the sales figure but as an offset to the costs the company incurs for these items. Exceptions are made to these rules when it is not feasible to disentangle the revenue and nonrevenue portions of the transaction.

Sales returns and allowances represent the sales value of goods that were returned by the customer or on which he was given a credit because they were not as specified or for some other reason. The amount could have been subtracted from the sales figure directly, without showing it as a separate item on the income statement, but it is often considered as being important enough information to management to warrant reporting.

Sales discounts are the amount of *cash* discounts taken by customers for prompt payment. For example, if the business sells merchandise for $1,000 on terms 2/10, n/30 (2 percent off if payment is made in 10 days, and the net, or total, amount due in 30 days), and the customer takes advantage of the discount by paying within 10 days, the business receives only $980 cash and records the other $20 as a sales discount. On some income statements, sales discounts are listed as an operating expense rather than as a deducation from sales; but showing them as an adjustment to the billed price, as above, is probably more common and is more indicative of their character. *Trade discounts,* which are formulas used in figuring the actual selling price from published catalogues or price lists (e.g., "list less 40 percent"), do not appear in the accounting records at all.

Cost of Goods Sold

At the identical moment that income is increased by the sales value of a product sold, it is also decreased by the cost of that product. Indeed, were it not for the fact that the separate figures for sales revenue and the cost of products sold are useful to management, a record could be made only of the net increase in owners' equity that results from a sale.

Some businesses, especially those that sell high unit value merchandise in small quantities (such as automobile dealers), keep a record of the cost of each individual item sold. In these businesses, the total cost of the goods sold in an accounting period can be determined simply by adding up the costs recorded for the individual transactions. This same cost is also subtracted from the asset, inventory, so that at all times the asset item shows the cost of merchandise still on hand. This method is referred to as the *perpetual inventory* method.

If the business does not have such a direct method for ascertaining the cost of the products sold during an accounting period, it must deduce the cost by indirect means. The procedure for doing this is described in Chapter 5. The measurement of cost of sales in a manufacturing business involves special problems that are discussed in Chapter 7.

Gross Profit

The difference between sales revenue and cost of goods sold is the *gross profit* or *gross margin*. On many income statements this amount appears as a separate item.

Conversely, some companies do not show cost of goods sold on their income statement, but instead list expenses by *object*, such as salaries and wages, purchases of goods and services, interest. In such an income statement it is impossible to calculate the gross profit.

Expenses

The classifications given on Illustration 3–2 are a minimum. In many income statements, especially those prepared for internal use, the "selling, general, and administrative expense" category is broken down so as to show separately the principal items of which it is comprised.

In Illustration 3–2, income tax is listed with the other expenses. In many income statements, the item "income before income tax" is given and income tax expense is then subtracted.

Retained Earnings

Strictly speaking, the income statement ends with the item "Net Income." Illustration 3–2 goes beyond this to show the other changes, other

Illustration 3-3

A "PACKAGE" OF ACCOUNTING REPORTS

Balance Sheet
As of December 31, 1967

ASSETS

Current assets.	$23,839,904
Fixed assets.	14,255,720
Other assets.	180,535
Total Assets. . . .	$38,276,159

EQUITIES

Current liabilities . . .	$12,891,570
Other liabilities	3,000,000
Common stock.	15,000,000
Retained earnings	7,384,589
Total Equities. . . .	$38,276,159

Income Statement
For the Year 1968

Net sales.	$75,478,221
Less: Cost of sales. . . .	52,227,004
Gross profit	$23,251,217
Less: Expenses	10,784,830
Income before taxes. . . .	$12,466,387
Provision for income taxes	6,344,000
Net income	$ 6,122,387
Retained earnings,	
beginning.	7,384,589
	$13,506,976
Less: Dividends.	4,390,000
Retained Earnings, Ending	$ 9,116,976

Balance Sheet
As of December 31, 1968

ASSETS

Current assets.	$22,651,072
Fixed assets.	13,411,779
Other assets.	173,214
Total Assets. . . .	$36,236,065

EQUITIES

Current liabilities . . .	$ 9,119,089
Other liabilities	3,000,000
Common stock.	15,000,000
Retained earnings	9,116,976
Total Equities. . . .	$36,236,065

than net income, that have occurred during the period. This final section links the income statement to the retained earnings item on the balance sheet.

The Report Package

A moment's reflection will show that the two types of accounting reports, the balance sheet and the income statement, can be combined into a package that discloses important information about the events of an accounting period. Such a package would consist of (1) a balance sheet as of the beginning of the period, (2) an income statement for the period, and (3) a balance sheet as of the end of the period. A much condensed version of such a package, presented so as to show the relationships among the various components, is shown in Illustration 3–3. (The same December 31, 1968, balance sheet is shown in more detail in Illustration 2–1.)

A Reminder: The Dual-Aspect Concept

Each of the statements and examples given in the foregoing discussion is consistent with the dual-aspect concept. Going back to the fuel oil example on page 47, the purchase of fuel oil for cash is reflected on the balance sheet by a decrease in the asset, cash, and a corresponding increase in the asset, fuel oil inventory; the consumption of fuel oil is represented by a decrease in the asset, fuel oil inventory, and an equal decrease in owners' equity. The recognition of revenue, which increases owners' equity, is accompanied by an equal increase in cash or some other asset. Every other event described in this chapter can be analyzed in terms of its dual effect on balance sheet items, so that at all times the basic equation, Assets = Equities, is preserved. Expense and revenue items represent no more than decreases and increases in owners' equity during an accounting period. For purposes of management analysis, it is important to collect and report these items in some detail, but insofar as their effect on the balance sheet goes, they can all be expressed directly in terms of their effect on owners' equity.

SUMMARY

Management is especially interested in how the operations of the business change the owners' equity, that is, in revenues and expenses and the difference between them, net income. In measuring net income, the continuing life stream of the business is divided into accounting periods, and an income statement is prepared for each period. The basic concepts governing this measurement are those already discussed in Chapter 2, plus the following:

7. *The Accrual Concept.* Income is measured as the difference between revenues and expenses rather than as the difference between cash receipts and disbursements.

8. The Realization Concept. Revenue is recognized at the time it is realized.

9. The Consistency Concept. Events of the same character are treated in the same fashion from one period to another.

10. The Materiality Concept. Events that do not have a significant effect on the accounts are not recorded.

CHAPTER 4

ACCOUNTING RECORDS
AND SYSTEMS

Up to this point, the effect on the financial statements of each individual transaction has been described separately. Thus, starting with a balance sheet that contained the item "Cash, $10,000," a transaction involving an increase in cash of $5,000 would be recorded by, in effect, erasing the $10,000 and putting in the new figure, $15,000. This procedure was appropriate as an explanatory device in view of the small number of transactions with which we have been dealing. Clearly, however, such a technique is not a practical way of handling the large volume of transactions that occur in actual business operations. This chapter describes some of the bookkeeping procedures that are used in practice. It should be emphasized that *no new accounting concepts are introduced;* the devices described here are no more than the mechanical means of increasing the facility with which transactions can be recorded and summarized.

Some of the considerations that are important in designing and operating accounting systems are also described.

BOOKKEEPING

We are not concerned with bookkeeping procedures per se, that is, for the purpose of training bookkeepers. Some knowledge of accounting mechanics is useful, however, for at least two reasons. First, as is the case with many subjects, accounting is something that is best learned by doing —by the actual solution of problems—and although any accounting problem can theoretically be solved without the aid of the tools discussed in this chapter, their use will often speed up considerably the problem-solving process. Secondly, the debit-and-credit mechanism, which is the principal technique discussed here, provides a framework for analysis that has much the same purpose, and the same advantages, as the symbols and equations that are studied in elementary algebra. This mechanism can often be used to reduce an apparently complex, perhaps almost incomprehensible, statement of facts to a simple, specific set of relationships. Thus, the debit-and-credit mechanism provides a useful way of thinking about many types of business problems—not only strictly accounting problems but also problems of other types.

The Account

Consider again a balance sheet on which the item "Cash, $10,000" appears. Subsequent cash transactions can affect this amount in only one of two ways: they can increase it, or they can decrease it. Instead of increasing or decreasing the item by erasing the old amount and entering the new amount for each transaction, considerable effort could be saved by collecting all the increases together and all the decreases together and then periodically figuring, in a single arithmetic operation, the net change resulting from all of them. This could be done by adding the sum of the increases to the amount of cash shown at the beginning and then subtracting the sum of the decreases. The difference would be the new cash *balance*, reflecting the net effect of all the separate increases and decreases.

In accounting, the device called an *account* is used for just this purpose. The simplest form of account, called a *T account*, looks like this:

Cash

(Increases)		(Decreases)
Beginning balance	10,000	2,000
	5,000	600
	4,000	400
	100	1,000
	2,700	
	800	
	22,600	4,000
New balance	18,600	

All increases are listed on one side, and all decreases are listed on the other. The saving in effort can be seen even from this brief illustration. If the balance were changed for each of the nine transactions listed, five additions and four subtractions would be required. By using the account device, the new balance is obtained by only two additions (to find the 22,600 and 4,000) and one subtraction (22,600 − 4,000).

Note that the dollar sign ($) is omitted; this is the usual practice in most accounting procedures.

In actual accounting systems, the account form is set up so that other useful information, in addition to the amount of each increase or decrease, can be recorded. A common arrangement of the columns is the following:

CASH

Date	Explanation	(R)	Amount	Date	Explanation	(R)	Amount

The above headings are self-explanatory except that of *"R"* (standing for "reference") under which is entered a simple code showing the source of the information recorded. This is useful if it is necessary to check back to the source of the entry at some future time.

Debit and Credit

The left-hand side of any account is arbitrarily called the *debit* side, and the right-hand side is called the *credit* side. Amounts entered on the left-hand side are called debits, and amounts on the right-hand side, credits. The verb "to debit" means "to make an entry in the left-hand side of an account,"[1] and the verb "to credit" means "to make an entry in the right-hand side of an account." *The words debit and credit have no other meaning in accounting.* The preceding sentence is emphasized because in ordinary usage these words do have other meanings. Credit has a favorable connotation (such as, "he is a credit to his country") and debit has an unfavorable connotation (such as "Chalk up a debit against him."). In accounting, these words do not imply any sort of value judgment; they mean simply "left" and "right." Debit and credit are usually abbreviated to Dr. and Cr.

If an account were considered by itself, without regard to its relationship with other accounts, it would make no difference whether increases were recorded on the debit side or on the credit side. In the 15th century a Franciscan monk, Lucas Pacioli, described a method of arranging accounts in such a way that the dual aspect that is present in every accounting transaction would be expressed by a debit amount and an equal and offsetting credit amount. This made possible the rule, *to which there is absolutely no exception,* that for each transaction the debit amount (or the sum of all the debit amounts, if there are more than one) must equal the credit amount (or the sum of all the credit amounts). This is

---

[1] The verb "to charge" is often used as a synonym for "to debit."

why accounting is called *double-entry* accounting. It follows that the recording of a transaction in which debits do not equal credits is incorrect. It also follows that, for all the accounts combined, the sum of the debit balances must equal the sum of the credit balances; otherwise, something has been done incorrectly. Thus the debit and credit arrangement used in accounting provides a useful means of checking the accuracy with which the work has been done.

The reader could reason out such an arrangement for himself from the simple equation: Assets = Liabilities + Owners' Equity, taking into account also the fact that expenses and revenue accounts are subdivisions of owners' equity, since the rules of debit and credit are merely an expansion of the algebraic relationships that follow from this equation. He may find it easier, however, to memorize the following five rules:

1. Increases in *assets* are debits; decreases are credits.
2. Increases in *liabilities* are credits; decreases are debits.
3. Increases in *owners' equity* are credits; decreases are debits.
4. Increases in *expense* are debits; decreases are credits.
5. Increases in *revenue* are credits; decreases are debits.

Rule No. 4 follows from the fact that expense items represent decreases in owners' equity, and Rule No. 5 follows from the fact that revenue items represent increases in owners' equity.

Note that assets, which are "good" things, and expenses, which are "bad" things, both increase on the debit side, and that liability and revenue accounts both increase on the credit side. This is another illustration of the fact that "debit" and "credit" are neutral terms; they do not connote value judgments.

These rules are illustrated in the diagram shown in Illustration 4–1.

Debits and credits to certain special accounts are not covered by these rules, but they can be deduced from them. As an example, consider the account, Sales Discount, which is a deduction from sales revenue. We know that Sales is a revenue account and that increases are therefore recorded on the credit side. Since Sales Discount is a deduction from Sales, it must be treated in the opposite way from Sales. Sales Discount, therefore, increases on the debit side.

The Ledger

A ledger is a group of accounts. The reader has probably seen a bound book with the word "ledger" printed on the cover. All the accounts of a small business could be maintained in such a book. Or, the business might have an "Accounts Receivable Ledger," an "Accounts Payable Ledger," and a "General Ledger," each containing the group of accounts suggested by the title. The ledger is not necessarily a bound book; it may consist of

Illustration 4–1

RULES OF DEBIT AND CREDIT

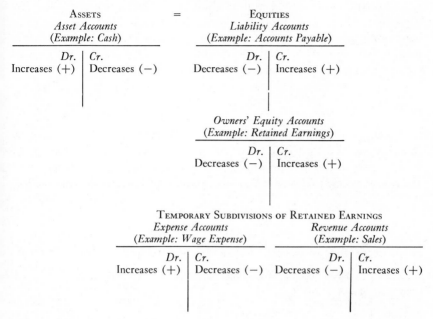

ASSETS = EQUITIES

Asset Accounts
(Example: Cash)

Dr.	Cr.
Increases (+)	Decreases (−)

Liability Accounts
(Example: Accounts Payable)

Dr.	Cr.
Decreases (−)	Increases (+)

Owners' Equity Accounts
(Example: Retained Earnings)

Dr.	Cr.
Decreases (−)	Increases (+)

TEMPORARY SUBDIVISIONS OF RETAINED EARNINGS

Expense Accounts
(Example: Wage Expense)

Dr.	Cr.
Increases (+)	Decreases (−)

Revenue Accounts
(Example: Sales)

Dr.	Cr.
Decreases (−)	Increases (+)

a set of loose-leaf pages, a set of punched cards, or, with the advent of electronic computers, a set of impulses on a reel of magnetic tape. No matter what its form may be, the essential character of the account and the rules for making entries to it remain exactly as stated above.

The ledger will contain at least as many separate accounts as there are items on the balance sheet and income statement. Usually there are many more accounts than this minimum number so that detailed information useful to management can be collected. The number of accounts is governed by management's need for information. For example, although the single item "accounts receivable" ordinarily appears on the balance sheet, a separate account for each customer is often maintained in a ledger so as to show how much is owed by each.

There is no limit, other than the cost of record keeping, to the proliferation of accounts that may be found in practice. Take, for example, transactions concerned with the inflow and outflow of merchandise in a store. In the simplest set of books, all such transactions could be recorded as debits or credits to a Merchandise Inventory account. Or, additional information could be obtained by setting up a Purchases account, in which all purchases of merchandise during the accounting period are recorded, or there could be several Purchases accounts, one for each type of merchandise. Carrying the detail further, the Purchases account (or accounts) could be further subdivided so as to record in separate accounts (1) the invoice cost of merchandise purchased, (2) inward freight, (3) discounts allowed on purchases, and (4) merchandise returned to vendors (i.e., purchase returns). The inward freight item could be subdivided according to the several means of transportation used, or into an account for the freight bills themselves and another account for transportation taxes, and so on.

The Journal

A journal is a chronological record of accounting transactions showing the names of accounts that are to be debited or credited, the amounts of the debits and credits, and any useful supplementary information about the transaction. A simple form of the journal is shown in Illustration 4–2.

Illustration 4–2

JOURNAL

1969		Transactions	LF	Debit	Credit
Jan.	2	Cash.	*1*	120.50	
		Sales	*41*		120.50
	2	Accounts Receivable	*2*	676.32	
		Sales	*41*		650.00
		Sales Tax Liability	*15*		19.50
		Postage	*32*		6.82
	2	Cash.	*1*	196.00	
		Sales Discount.	*43*	4.00	
		Accounts Receivable	*2*		200.00
	3	Sales Returns and Allowances.		47.00	
		Accounts Receivable			47.00

The entries shown relate to the sales transactions described on page 60. It helps in understanding these transactions if the reader reasons for himself the events that gave rise to each of them.

With respect to format, note that the debit entry is listed first, that the debit amounts appear in the first of the two money columns, that the account to be credited appears below the debit entry and is indented, and that credit amounts appear in the second money column. "LF" is an abbreviation for "ledger folio," that is, the page reference to the ledger account where the entry is to be made; these references are inserted at the time the entry is recorded in the account, and their presence indicates that the entry has been recorded. (In the illustration, the first nine items have been recorded in the accounts, and the remaining two have not yet been recorded.) In some businesses, a brief explanation of each entry is written beneath it.

The journal contains explicit instructions as to the changes that are to be made to the balances in the accounts. The process of making these changes is called *posting*. No account balance is ever changed except on the basis of a journal entry. (The balance in the account is periodically computed and recorded, as explained on page 66, but this process does not in any way *change* the balance in the account.)

Thus, the ledger is a device for *reclassifying* and *summarizing*, by accounts, information originally listed in chronological order in the journal.

THE ADJUSTING AND CLOSING PROCESS

Adjusting Entries

Most of the entries that are to be made in accounts come to the accountant's attention easily and obviously. When checks are drawn against the company's bank account, it is obvious that an entry must be made crediting cash and debiting some other account. When invoices are sent out, a credit to Sales and a debit to Accounts Receivable is obviously generated. Entries of this type are called *original entries* or *spot entries*. They constitute the bulk of the entries made in the typical business.

Some events that affect the accounts are not evidenced by such obvious documents. The effects of these events are recorded at the end of the accounting period by means of what are called *adjusting entries*. The purpose of the adjusting entries is to modify account balances so that they will reflect fairly the situation as of the end of the period.

CONTINUOUS TRANSACTIONS. Most adjusting entries are made in connection with events that are, in effect, continuous transactions. Consider a tank of fuel oil purchased for $1,000. On the day of delivery, the $1,000 of fuel oil was an asset, but each day thereafter some fuel oil was consumed in the furnace, whereupon part of the $1,000 became an expense. Rather than record this consumption daily, a single adjusting entry is made at the end of the accounting period to show how much of the fuel oil is still an asset at that time and how much has become expense during the period. There are two ways of handling these events, both of which come out to the same result. Under one method, the fuel oil is originally recorded as an asset, and at the end of the accounting period the asset account is adjusted by subtracting the cost of fuel oil consumed, thus:

```
*dr. Fuel Expense. . . . . . . . . . . . . . . . . . . . . 600
    cr.   Fuel Oil Inventory. . . . . . . . . . . . . . . .       600
```

*As a reminder to the reader, the notations *dr.* and *cr.* are used in Chapters 4 and 5 to designate the debit and credit portions of each journal entry. These notations are not used in practice since the accountant understands from the order and indentation of the accounts what is meant.

Under the other method, the $1,000 expenditure for fuel oil is originally recorded in an expense account, and the fuel oil remaining at the end of the period is subtracted and shown as an asset, thus:

```
dr.  Fuel Oil Inventory. . . . . . . . . . . . . . . . . 400
    cr.   Fuel Expense. . . . . . . . . . . . . . . . . . . .       400
```

Although neither method reflects the correct facts *within* the period (with the trivial exception that the first method does reflect the facts on the first day), both reflect a correct statement of the facts as of the *end* of the accounting period, namely, that the fuel oil inventory is $400 and that fuel oil expense for the period was $600. Since accounting focuses on deriving the proper amounts for the statements that are prepared at the end of the accounting period, and since both methods result in the correct final amounts, the choice between these methods depends solely on which is more convenient.

Several other types of events that require adjusting entries were described in the sections of Chapter 3 that dealt with the distinction between expense and expenditure (pp. 46–51) and between revenue and receipts (pp. 51–53). The following list gives the form of the adjusting entries for such transactions:

1. For insurance protection, originally recorded as Prepaid Insurance (an asset), $300 of which becomes an expense in the current period:

```
dr.  Insurance Expense . . . . . . . . . . . . . . . . . 300
    cr.   Prepaid Insurance . . . . . . . . . . . . . . . .       300
```

2. For a rent paid in advance and originally recorded as an expense, $5,000 of which is an asset at the end of the period since it covers rental for the next period:

```
dr.  Prepaid Rent. . . . . . . . . . . . . . . . . . . . 5,000
    cr.   Rent Expense. . . . . . . . . . . . . . . . . . .     5,000
```

3. For $200 of supplies consumed in the period:

```
dr. Supplies Expense. . . . . . . . . . . . . . . . . . 200
    cr.   Supplies Inventory. . . . . . . . . . . . . . . .       200
```

4. For $50 of wages earned by an employee during the period but not yet paid to him:

```
dr. Wages Expense . . . . . . . . . . . . . . . .      50
    cr.  Accrued Wages Payable . . . . . . . . . . . .      50
```

5. For interest expense of $5 which has not yet been paid:

```
dr. Interest Expense. . . . . . . . . . . . . . .       5
    cr.  Accrued Interest Payable. . . . . . . . . . .       5
```

6. For interest (i.e., discount) deducted from a loan in advance and originally recorded as Prepaid Interest (an asset), $5 of which becomes an expense of the current period:

```
dr. Interest Expense. . . . . . . . . . . . . . .       5
    cr.  Prepaid Interest. . . . . . . . . . . . . . .       5
```

7. For $20 of interest earned by the business during the period, but not yet received:

```
dr. Accrued Interest Receivable . . . . . . . . . . .      20
    cr.  Interest Revenue. . . . . . . . . . . . . . .      20
```

DEPRECIATION. Most fixed assets are continuously being converted to an expense, just like fuel oil, prepaid insurance, and supplies. This expense is called depreciation. Instead of subtracting the amount of expense for the period directly from the asset amount, however, a separate account, *Accumulated Depreciation*, is used. This account shows the total of such subtractions to date and is subtracted from the cost of fixed assets on the balance sheet, thus:

```
Equipment (at cost). . . . . . . . . . . . $1,000
    Less: Accumulated depreciation . . . . .    400
    Net Book Value . . . . . . . . . . .        $600
```

The adjusting entry to record the depreciation expense for a period is therefore of the following form:

```
dr. Depreciation Expense. . . . . . . . . . . . . .     200
    cr.  Accumulated Depreciation. . . . . . . . . . .     200
```

This process is described in more detail in Chapter 6.

OTHER ADJUSTMENTS. The accountant may make a variety of other adjusting entries in his attempt to make the accounts reflect fairly the results of operations and the status of the business. An example, discussed in more detail in Chapter 5, is that for *bad debt expense*, an adjustment made in order to recognize the likelihood that not all credit customers will pay their bills and that therefore the Accounts Receivable account may overstate the collectible amount of the company's claims against its customers. An adjusting entry that records the estimated amount of bad debts is as follows:

```
dr.  Bad Debt Expense. . . . . . . . . . . . . . . . . 300
   cr.   Allowance for Doubtful Accounts . . . . . . . . .         300
```

On the balance sheet, Allowance for Doubtful Accounts is subtracted from Accounts Receivable, thus:

```
Accounts receivable (gross). . . . . . . . . . . . $1,000
   Less: Allowance for doubtful accounts. . . . . .      50
      Net Accounts Receivable. . . . . . . . . . .         $950
```

Closing Entries

Revenue accounts and expense accounts are called *temporary* (or "nominal") accounts, as distinguished from asset, liability, and owners' equity accounts, which are called *permanent* (or "real") accounts. The temporary accounts are actually subdivisions of owners' equity. They are a means of classifying the various revenue and expense transactions that occur during an accounting period so as to provide the information needed to prepare the income statement for the period. The temporary accounts are periodically *closed* to owners' equity in order to determine the net effect (i.e., the profit or the loss) of all the revenue and expense transactions.

Closing procedures differ from company to company. Under all closing methods, however, revenue and expense accounts are ultimately closed to an account called *Profit and Loss* or *Loss and Gain* or *Expense and Revenue Summary*, which reflects the net income or loss for a given accounting period. Loss and Gain is a temporary account which in turn is closed to some owners' equity account, such as Retained Earnings, to complete the closing process. In many businesses, the revenue and expense accounts are not closed directly to Loss and Gain. Instead, one or more additional temporary or *clearing* accounts are set up, such as Cost of Goods Sold, and Trading (an account which shows the gross profit for the period), and successive closings are made to these accounts. The purpose of these intermediate clearing accounts is to show separately some or all of the elements comprising Loss and Gain (e.g., cost of goods sold and gross profit). The ultimate effect, however, is the same as direct closing to Loss and Gain.

The closing process consists of transferring the balance of each temporary account to the same side of a clearing account. This is done by making a journal entry debiting the account to be closed if it has a credit balance (or crediting it if it has a debit balance) in an amount equal to the balance. This has the effect of reducing the balance in the account to zero, thereby closing it. Note that each entry is made on the opposite side from the side with the balance. The other half of this entry is made to Loss and Gain or to one of the intermediate clearing accounts.

> EXAMPLE: If the credit balance in the Sales account at the end of an accounting period is $174,000, the account is closed by the following entry:

```
dr.  Sales. . . . . . . . . . . . . . . . . . . .  174,000
     cr.   Loss and Gain. . . . . . . . . . . . . .          174,000
```

> EXAMPLE: If the Salaries and Wages expense account has a debit balance of $21,000, it is closed by the following entry:

```
dr.  Loss and Gain. . . . . . . . . . . . . . . .  21,000
     cr.   Salaries and Wages . . . . . . . . . . .          21,000
```

At the completion of the closing process, all temporary accounts have zero balances; the only accounts remaining open are the permanent accounts—the asset, liability, and owners' equity accounts.

Ruling and Balancing Accounts

At the end of the accounting period, each account is ruled and balanced so that it is in a convenient form for the preparation of financial statements and ready to begin accumulating entries for the coming period. A frequently followed procedure is as follows: First, a balancing amount is written in the appropriate column so as to make equal totals in both columns. The totals are then shown and double-ruled to indicate the end of the accounting period sequence. Finally, the new balance is "brought down" on the opposite side from that in which it was first written, as the initial figure for the new period.

The Trial Balance

The trial balance is simply a list of the account names and the balances in each account as of a given moment of time, with debit balances in one column and credit balances in another column. The preparation of the trial balance serves two principal purposes (1) it shows whether the equality of debits and credits has been maintained, and (2) it provides a convenient transcript of the ledger record as a basis for making adjusting and closing entries or in the preparation of financial statements.

To maintain the relationship "Total Assets = Total Liabilities + Owners' Equity," debits and credits must be kept in balance. Although the fact that totals on a trial balance are equal does indicate that the integrity of the accounting equation has been maintained, it does not prove that errors have not been made. Entries may have been omitted entirely; they may have been posted to the wrong account; counterbalancing errors may have been made; or the transaction may have been analyzed incorrectly. For example, when a debit for the purchase of a truck is made incorrectly to an expense account rather than correctly to a fixed asset account, the totals of the trial balance are not affected. Nevertheless, errors that result in unequal debits and credits are common, and the fact that such errors exist is evident when a trial balance does not balance; that is, when the debit column does not add to the same total as the credit column.

A trial balance may be prepared at any time. A *preadjustment* trial balance is one prepared after the original entries for the period have been posted, but prior to the adjusting and closing process. A *postclosing* trial balance is prepared after the closing process.

The Work Sheet

The work sheet is a preliminary compilation of figures that facilitates recording or analysis. A work sheet is often used as a preliminary to the formal journalizing and posting of the adjusting and closing process. Its use permits the accountant to make a "dry run" of the whole process. Since a pencil is ordinarily used, any errors detected on the work sheet can be easily corrected, whereas alterations to the formal records are to be avoided wherever possible. The work sheet also classifies account balances according to the financial statements in which they are to be used.

The form of the adjusting-and-closing work sheet varies depending upon the procedure followed in closing the books, the form of the statements to be prepared, and the preference of the accountant. The work sheet consists of several pairs of columns. In each pair, the first column is used for debits and the second column for credits. On most adjusting-and-closing work sheets the first pair of columns contains the preadjustment trial balance. The next pair of columns is used for the adjustments for the period. These are followed by a pair of columns for the income statement items, and another pair for the balance sheet items. In some cases there are additional pairs of columns for principal subdivisions of the income statement, such as the cost of goods sold section.

A work sheet is often used *in lieu of*, rather than as a preliminary to, the process of adjusting and closing the accounts. Many companies close their books only once a year, but nevertheless prepare monthly financial statements. These interim statements are prepared from a work sheet on which are listed the account balances at the end of the month together with the adjustments necessary to reflect revenue and expense in that month. Statements are prepared from the adjusted account balances that are developed on this work sheet. The income statement figures on such a work sheet would be cumulative for the year to date. An income statement for the current month can be derived from the cumulative figures simply by subtracting the corresponding figures on the work sheet for the preceding month.

A sample work sheet for a merchandising company is shown in Illustration 4–3. The five adjustments shown thereon reflect:

a) Cost of merchandise sold, $121,300 (dr. Cost of Goods Sold, cr. Inventory). During the period all purchases of merchandise had been debited to inventory, but no entries had been made to show the movement of merchandise out of inventory.

b) Expired insurance of $300 (dr. Insurance Expense, cr. Prepaid Insurance).

c) Accrued interest expense of $100 (dr. Interest Expense, cr. Accrued Interest Payable).

d) Accrued wages of $1,000 (dr. Salaries and Wages, cr. Wages Payable).

e) Accrued employer's tax on wages of $30 (dr. Social Security Tax Expense, cr. Withholding and Social Security Taxes Payable).

f) Estimated income tax for the year of $5,400 (dr. Income Tax Expense, cr. Income Tax Liability).

Note that additional accounts are added as needed at the bottom of the work sheet.

The last item on this work sheet, $13,100, is the net income for the period. It is found by subtracting the sum of the other debits to "Income Statement" from the sum of the credits to "Income Statement." Showing the same amount in the credit column of "Balance Sheet" has the effect of closing the net income to retained earnings. After this amount is entered, each column of a pair should add to the same total, which is a check on the arithmetic accuracy of the whole closing process.

So that the connection between the adjusting and closing process and the financial statements will be clear, financial statements prepared from Illustration 4–3 are shown in Illustration 4–4. All figures used are condensed and rounded in order to make the process easier to follow. These statements therefore do not indicate the amount of detailed work that is involved in an actual business situation.

Illustration 4-3

ILLUSTRATIVE WORK SHEET

(in round numbers)

	Trial Balance December 31 Dr.	Cr.	Adjustments Dr.	Cr.	Income Statement Dr.	Cr.	Balance Sheet Dr.	Cr.
Cash	18,600						18,600	
Inventory	156,300			121,300 (a)			35,000	
Prepaid insurance	900			300 (b)			600	
Accounts payable		8,700						8,700
Employee taxes payable		570		30 (e)				600
Notes payable		4,000						4,000
Capital stock		20,000						20,000
Retained earnings		1,300						1,300
Sales		174,000				174,000		
Rental and other space costs	8,300				8,300			
Salaries and wages	20,000		1,000 (d)		21,000			
Social security tax expense	670		30 (e)		700			
Advertising expense	2,100				2,100			
Miscellaneous expenses	1,900				1,900			
Nonoperating revenue		400				400		
Interest expense	200		100 (c)		300			
	208,970	208,970						
Cost of goods sold			121,300 (a)		121,300			
Insurance expense			300 (b)		300			
Accrued interest payable				100 (c)				100
Wages payable				1,000 (d)				1,000
Income tax expense			5,400 (f)		5,400			
Income tax liability				5,400 (f)				5,400
Net income to Retained earnings					13,100			13,100
			128,130	128,130	174,400	174,400	54,200	54,200

Illustration 4–4

FINANCIAL STATEMENTS PREPARED FROM DATA SHOWN IN ILLUSTRATION 4–3

Balance Sheet as of December 31

ASSETS			EQUITIES	
Cash.	$18,600	Accounts payable.		$ 8,700
Inventory	35,000	Employee taxes payable. . . .		600
Prepaid insurance . .	600	Wages payable		1,000
		Notes payable		4,000
		Accrued interest payable. . .		100
		Income tax lability		5,400
		Total Liabilities		$19,800
		Capital stock		20,000
		Retained earnings		14,400
Total Assets. . .	$54,200	Total Equities.		$54,200

Income Statement for the Year

Sales.		$174,000
Less: Cost of goods sold		121,300
Gross profit		$ 52,700
Expenses:		
Rental and other space costs	$ 8,300	
Salaries and wages	21,000	
Social security tax expense.	700	
Advertising expense.	2,100	
Insurance expense.	300	
Miscellaneous expense.	1,900	
Interest expense	300	34,600
		$ 18,100
Other revenue.		400
Profit before income taxes		$ 18,500
Provision for income taxes		5,400
Net Income		$ 13,100

Reversing Entries

Under some conditions, it is desirable to *reverse* the adjusting entries made to record accruals. This is done by making an entry, subsequent to the closing entries, which is the reverse of the adjusting entry. Consider the adjustment that recognizes $5 of interest expense accrued on transactions related to borrowing $1,000 for four months, one month of which is in one accounting period and the other three in the next period, the total interest cost of $20 to be paid when the loan is repaid (see p. 50). The adjusting entry at the end of the first period, which recognizes the interest expense of that period, is as follows:

```
dr.  Interest Expense. . . . . . . . . . . . . . . . . .      5
     cr.  Accrued Interest Payable. . . . . . . . . . . .        5
```

Now what happens in the next period when the loan and interest thereon is paid? A natural entry to make is the following:

```
dr.  Notes Payable . . . . . . . . . . . . . . . . . . . 1,000
dr.  Interest Expense. . . . . . . . . . . . . . . . . .     20
     cr.  Cash. . . . . . . . . . . . . . . . . . . . . .       1,020
```

But this overstates interest expense for the next period, which is in fact only $15, and also leaves the liability, accrued interest payable, outstanding on the books even though it no longer exists. Such an error is avoided if the adjusting entry is reversed before the accounting for the next period starts, thus:

```
dr.  Accrued Interest Payable. . . . . . . . . . . . . .      5
     cr.  Interest Expense. . . . . . . . . . . . . . . .        5
```

The credit to Interest Expense is made to offset a part of the debit entry that will be made in the normal course of bookkeeping in the next period. After this entry has been made, as above, the accounts will show the correct amount of interest expense for the period ($20 − $5 = $15). The following T account summarizes these entries for the two periods:

	Interest Expense		
Dec. 31 (Adjusting)	5	Dec. 31 (Closing)	5
Mar. 31 (Payment)	20	Jan. 1 (Reversing)	5
		Dec. 31 (Closing)	15
	20		20

The same result can be attained by omitting the reversing entry and recording the repayment of the loan as follows:

```
dr.  Notes Payable . . . . . . . . . . . . . . . . . . . 1,000
dr.  Interest Expense. . . . . . . . . . . . . . . . . .     15
dr.  Accrued Interest Payable. . . . . . . . . . . . . .      5
     cr.  Cash. . . . . . . . . . . . . . . . . . . . . .       1,020
```

This entry requires, however, that the bookkeeper remember the fact that part of the interest was an expense of the prior period.

Summary of the Accounting Process

1. The first, and by far the most important, part of the accounting process is the *analysis of transactions*, that is, the process of deciding which account or accounts should be debited, which should be credited, and in what amounts, in order to reflect events in the accounting records. This requires judgment.

2. Next comes the purely mechanical step of *journalizing original entries*, that is, recording the result of the analysis.

3. *Posting* is the process of recording changes in the ledger accounts, exactly as specified by the journal entry. This is another purely mechanical step.

4. At the ending of the accounting period, judgment is involved in deciding on the *adjusting entries*, and these are journalized and posted in the same way as are original entries.

5. The *closing entries* are journalized and posted. *Reversing entries*, if any, are also journalized and posted. These are purely mechanical steps.

6. *Financial statements* are prepared. This requires judgment as to the best arrangement and terminology, but the figures that are used result from the judgments made in Steps No. 1 and No. 4.

ACCOUNTING SYSTEMS

The simple journals, ledgers, and work sheets, together with the rules for using them, described in the preceding pages, constitute *an* accounting system, but such a system would not usually be the *best* system for an actual business. The best system is that which best achieves the following objectives:

1. To process the information efficiently, that is, at low cost.
2. To obtain reports quickly.
3. To insure a high degree of accuracy.
4. To minimize the possibility of theft, fraud, or misrepresentation.

Designing a good accounting system is a specialized job requiring a high degree of skill. Only a few of the principles and techniques are noted here.

Special Journals

The journal form illustrated on page 70 is called a *general journal*. This form requires that the title of each account affected by each entry be written down. If there are a large number of entries made to a single account, time can be saved, both in journalizing and in posting, by using a *special journal* or *register*. In the special journal there are several columns, each headed with the name of an account that is to be debited or credited plus, usually, a "miscellaneous" column in which entries to other accounts may be recorded. Entries to the accounts indicated by column headings are made simply by entering the proper amount in these columns. At the end of the accounting period, all the amounts in each column are added, and the total is posted as one figure to the appropriate account. Entries in the "miscellaneous" column are posted individually. Illustration 4–5 is an

Illustration 4–5

CHECK REGISTER

Date	To Whom Drawn	Cash Cr.	Accounts Payable Dr.	Miscellaneous Dr.	
				Account	Amount

example of a check register, which is a special journal used to record credits to Cash and debits to various accounts. Columns are provided for the accounts in which entries are likely to be made frequently (here, Cash and Accounts Payable), and a miscellaneous column is provided for other debits.

The special-journal device illustrates one of the important considerations in systems design: to keep to a minimum the amount of *manual copying* of information from one document to another. Copying not only requires effort, and hence costs money, but it also increases the likelihood of making errors. In the simple check register shown, the amount of copying required is reduced, as compared with the general journal, in that all the credits to Cash and all the debits to Accounts Payable are posted to the ledger as single totals. The special journal also reduces the amount of writing effort, since the name of the account at the head of the column does not have to be written for each entry.

The same idea can be extended further by the use of bookkeeping machines. In recording sales on credit, for example, the use of a machine makes it possible to make the journal entry and post the debit to the customer's ledger account in the same operation: the operator positions the journal form and the ledger account form properly in the machine, and the amounts are entered on both forms simultaneously by the use of carbon paper. Carrying the anticopying idea one step further, once information has been recorded on punched cards, magnetic tape, or in some other form that can be handled by automatic machines, it can be manipulated and recorded thereafter without any human intervention whatsoever.

Control Accounts and Subsidiary Ledgers

Most businesses use one or more *subsidiary ledgers,* which are groups of related accounts taken out of the general ledger. For example, all the separate accounts for individual customers may be kept in an accounts receivable ledger. One advantage of this practice is that several bookkeepers can be working on the ledger accounts simultaneously. Moreover, it facilitates the process of localizing errors, since each ledger can be made the responsibility of a specific individual. If there are three bookkeepers working on accounts receivable, for example, there can be three accounts receivable ledgers.

In order to keep the general ledger in balance, a *control account* takes the place of the individual accounts removed to the subsidiary ledgers. A control account shows in summary form debits and credits that are shown in detail in a subsidiary ledger. When subsidiary ledgers are used, each amount is, in effect, posted twice: it is posted, often daily, to the proper account in the subsidiary ledger, and it also becomes a part of the total which is posted at the end of the period to the control account in the general ledger. In a large business, most if not all of the general ledger accounts are control accounts.

The use of various *ledgerless bookkeeping* devices should also be noted. The accounts receivable "accounts," for example, may consist not of actual ledger records but rather of copies of the invoices themselves. Or, bills for vendors may be kept in an "accounts payable" file, with the accounting entry made when the bill is paid rather than when it is received. The total of bills in the file at the end of the accounting period constitutes the accounts payable liability for the balance sheet and is recorded by an adjusting entry, crediting Accounts Payable and debiting various expense and asset accounts. In the latter situation, work is saved, but the possibility of verifying the accounts against the invoices is sacrificed.

Imprest Funds

The imprest fund is another device for saving work. An imprest fund consists of cash advanced to a responsible person and periodically replenished by additional cash that equals the amounts expended by this person.

The operation of an imprest fund may be illustrated by its most common version, the *petty cash* fund. The fund is established by drawing a check on the regular bank account. The person responsible for the fund cashes the check and puts the money in a separate place, a petty cash box. This transaction is recorded by the following entry:

```
dr.  Petty Cash. . . . . . . . . . . . . . . . . .    50
    cr.   Cash. . . . . . . . . . . . . . . . . . . . .          50
```

The petty cash is used to pay small bills until it is nearly exhausted. At that time, these bills are summarized, and a check is drawn for the amount they total. The journal entry for this check debits the various expense or asset accounts represented by the bills, for example:

```
dr.  Office Supplies . . . . . . . . . . . . . . . . .    21
dr.  Miscellaneous Expense . . . . . . . . . . . . . .    25
    cr.   Cash. . . . . . . . . . . . . . . . . . . . .          46
```

Note that the credit is to the regular Cash account. Once established, the Petty Cash account is not touched unless the size of the fund is changed.

This procedure saves the effort involved in drawing checks and making separate journal entries for small bills. It also provides a safeguard, since the petty cash box should at all times contain cash and receipted bills which together total the amount shown in the Petty Cash account.

The imprest device is by no means limited to petty cash. Many government disbursing agencies operate on the same principle, but in amounts that run into millions of dollars. These agencies are advanced funds from the central treasury, they disburse these funds to pay properly authorized bills, and they submit these bills to the treasury as a basis for replenishing the fund. The accounting entries are essentially the same as those given above for petty cash.

Internal Control

Two of the objectives of an accounting system stated above—accuracy and protection against theft, fraud, or misrepresentation—cannot be attained absolutely without conflicting with the other two—speed and economy. A system that "can't be beaten" would be prohibitively expensive and time consuming. A basic principle of internal control therefore is that the system should make it *as difficult as is practical* for people to be dishonest or careless. This is significantly different from making the system absolutely foolproof. Such a principle is based not on a cynical view of people in general but rather on the realistic assumption that a small fraction of people will be dishonest or careless if it is easy for them to do so.

Some of the devices used to insure reasonable accuracy have been touched on—the idea of verifying one set of figures against another, for example. The idea of divided responsibility is another important one. Whenever feasible, no one person should be responsible for recording all aspects of a transaction, nor should the *custodian* of assets (e.g., the storekeeper or the cashier) be permitted to do the *accounting* for the assets. Thus, one person's work is a check on another's, and although this does not eliminate the possibility that two people will steal through collusion, the likelihood of dishonesty is greatly reduced.

The *voucher system* is another commonly used internal control device. Under this system, every incoming bill is inserted in a voucher, or folder, which contains spaces in which authorized people write their initials to signify their approval of the appropriateness of the charge and the accounting entries made. Under this system, all bills, even those that are paid immediately in cash, are credited to Accounts Payable (or to Vouchers Payable) and debited to the appropriate asset or expense account. For cash payments, putting the bill through Accounts Payable involves additional work, but this is often warranted in the interest of having a single, uniform procedure through which all bills must pass and a prescribed set of approvals to assure that the business makes only proper payments.

These brief comments indicate only the nature of the problem of internal control, which is a big subject. Furthermore, a study that focuses on accounting principles, as this one does, leads to incorrect impressions of the complexities involved in operating accounting *systems*. Cash transactions, for example, are very easy to analyze, whereas *Montgomery's Auditing* contains a 16-page list of questions that should be considered in connection with the internal control of the single item, cash.

THE EXPERT ACCOUNTANT

Some of the knowledge that the expert accountant has acquired through study and experience, beyond the material in this introductory treatment, is listed below:

1. The expert accountant knows the procedures for recording accounting transactions quickly, efficiently, accurately, and in a way that minimizes the opportunity for fraud or theft. Only a few of the techniques and mechanical or electronic aids for facilitating the bookkeeping process have been mentioned here.

2. The expert accountant knows techniques for summarizing, arranging, and presenting information so that it meets the needs of various types of users of the information.

3. The expert accountant knows the legal requirements that govern or influence certain types of transactions. These are especially important in transactions affecting owners' equity items.

4. The expert accountant knows, or knows how to find out about, tax laws and regulations. Although tax requirements should not govern financial accounting, tax considerations do play a major part in many business decisions.

5. The expert accountant knows, or can find by referring to accounting texts or handbooks, generally accepted ways of handling many specialized types of transactions. For example, whole books have been written on methods of valuing inventory, and even on the question, "What is a sale?"

6. The expert accountant has acquired knowledge about terminology and procedures that are customarily used by companies in the same industry as his company. Many industries tend to develop a more or less common pattern for handling certain types of transactions, and in some industries these common practices are set forth in industry accounting manuals.

7. The expert accountant knows a great deal about his own company, the type of information that management and others have found useful, the way in which recurring transactions have been handled—in short, all the matters that are connoted by the word "experience," for which no book or classroom is a satisfactory substitute.

SIGNIFICANT BOOKKEEPING IDEAS

At least two significant ideas should emerge from this description of the bookkeeping process.

The first is the idea of debit and credit equality—"every debit must have an equal credit." This idea is much more than a mechanical requirement of bookkeeping. It is a way of thinking that is extremely useful in analyzing what is going on in a business. There is a natural human tendency to think only about part of the consequences of a decision and to overlook some equally important part. For example, although a growing cash balance superficially looks good, this is only half of the story. It makes considerable difference whether the credits offsetting these debits to cash reflect income from profitable operations or whether they reflect emergency bank loans.

The second significant idea is that of *balancing*, the notion that one total should always equal some other total. Three balancing techniques have been described: (1) the fundamental debit-credit structure; (2) the control-subsidiary relationship, in which the total of the subsidiary items must always equal a control total; and (3) the imprest technique, in which the sum of cash and paid bills must always equal a predetermined total. As noted above, these devices provide a check on arithmetic accuracy, they lessen the risk of loss through dishonesty, and they lessen the chance that some part of a transaction will be overlooked.

These balancing techniques have a much wider applicability than in business accounting. In recent years economists have come to use the debit-credit idea to construct national income accounts which show, in balanced form, the impact of the main economic forces at work in a nation. Electronic computers are designed with built-in checks on accuracy which are derived from the control-subsidiary idea. Figures derived from a system that does *not* contain some balancing mechanism should be regarded skeptically; the likelihood of errors or omissions is great.

APPENDIX

Locating Errors Revealed by the Trial Balance

Following are four suggested aids in detecting errors revealed by differences in the totals of the trial balance:

1. If the difference between the totals is 1, 0.01, 1.00, 100, 1,000, etc., the error is probably in addition. Such an error is usually detected by re-adding the columns of the trial balance, or, if necessary, the columns in the ledger accounts.

2. When the discrepancy is an even number, the error may be the result of making a debit entry in a credit column, or vice versa. Divide the difference in totals by 2, and look, first, through the trial balance and, then, the ledger accounts for an amount corresponding to the quotient secured. The difference is divided by 2 because an item placed in the wrong column results in a difference of twice its amount.

3. If the difference is divisible by 9, the error is probably either a transposition or a transplacement, and the search can be narrowed down to numbers where these errors might have been made. A *transposition* occurs when 79 is written for 97, 318 for 813, and so on. A *transplacement* or *slide* occurs when the digits of the number are moved to the left or right, as when $6,328.00 is written as $632.80 or $63.28.

4. When the source of error is not readily discernible, it is advisable to check the trial balance against the ledger to determine whether all the account balances have been copied properly. This check may reveal that certain accounts have been omitted. As a last resort, it may be necessary to check all of the figures in the ledger with the journal and to check all additions and subtractions in the several accounts.

Care in making the entries, such as writing legibly, double-checking additions and subtractions as journalizing and posting proceeds, and making sure all entries are entered properly, will save much time otherwise spent in hunting for errors.

SUGGESTIONS FOR FURTHER READING ON SYSTEMS AND AUDITING

HOLMES, ARTHUR W. *Auditing: Principles and Procedures.* 6th ed.; Homewood, Ill.: Richard D. Irwin, Inc., 1964.

LENHART, NORMAN J., and DEFLIESE, PHILIP L. *Montgomery's Auditing.* 8th ed.; New York: Ronald Press Co., 1957.

MOORE, FRANCIS E., and HOWARD F. STETTLER. *Accounting Systems for Management Control.* Homewood, Ill.: Richard D. Irwin, Inc., 1963.

NEUSCHEL, RICHARD F. *Management by System.* New York: McGraw-Hill Book Co., Inc., 1960.

CHAPTER 5

FURTHER ASPECTS OF
INCOME MEASUREMENT

In Chapters 2 and 3 the basic concepts governing the measurement of income were described, and some of the problems involved in applying these concepts were outlined. As noted there, this class of problems is by far the most difficult in accounting. Also, it is the area in which there is the greatest disagreement among accountants.

Additional aspects of the income measurement problem are discussed in Chapters 5 through 9. Those treated in Chapter 5 include the following: deducing cost of goods sold; inventory pricing; accounts receivable and bad debts; other problems of revenue measurement; wages, salaries, and related costs; income tax allocations; and losses. The techniques and conventions described are basically derived from the concepts already given; that is, they are an application of these concepts, rather than new concepts.

DEDUCING COST OF GOODS SOLD

When a company's accounting system contains a record of the cost of each item it sells, the amount to be recorded as cost of goods sold can be determined simply by adding up these costs for all items sold in the accounting period. In many businesses, notably in retail stores, it is not practicable to keep track of the cost of each individual item that is sold, however. One can easily visualize the delay, and indeed the embarrassment, that would result in a supermarket if the cashiers attempted to record the cost, as well as the sales value, of each item the customer brought to the check-out station. In such situations, the cost of goods sold during an accounting period is determined by the process of *deduction*.

This process requires that a physical inventory, or count, be taken of the merchandise on hand at the end of each accounting period. The dollar amount of this inventory appears as an asset on the balance sheet as of the end of the period. Having established the amount of inventory, the cost of goods sold during a period is determined by the following reasoning process: The total amount of inventory available for sale during a period is what was on hand at the beginning of the period plus what was added (through purchasing additional merchandise) during the period; the difference between the total amount available for sale and the amount remaining at the end of the period is assumed to have been sold. Thus:

Beginning inventory	$ 4,000
Plus: Purchases	7,400
Equals: Goods available for sale	$11,400
Less: Ending inventory	2,000
Cost of Goods Sold	$ 9,400

The amount of beginning inventory in the above calculation is, of course, the amount found by the physical inventory taken at the end of the *preceding* period.

Some companies show such a calculation in the cost of goods sold section of the income statement itself. Others, although deducing cost of goods sold by the method shown above, do not present the details.

The amount of detail shown can be carried even further. For example, the cost of a product includes not only its invoice price but also the cost of delivering it to the premises, and the amount of this "freight-in" might be shown separately. Also, a separate record might be kept of purchased items that were subsequently returned. A calculation giving this detail follows:

Beginning inventory		$ 4,000
Plus: Purchases, gross	$7,000	
Freight-in	600	
	$7,600	
Less: Purchase returns	200	
Net purchases		7,400
Goods available for sale		$11,400
Less: Ending inventory		2,000
Cost of Goods Sold		$ 9,400

Accounts

When the cost of goods sold is deduced by the method described above, a separate account is established for each element in the calculation. Thus, a Purchases account is established, and the invoice cost of merchandise purchased is debited to this account, rather than directly to Inventory. Accounts are also established for Freight-In, Purchase Returns, and any other items involved in the calculation.

Rules for debiting and crediting these accounts can be deduced from their relationship to other accounts. Since Purchases shows additions to the asset account, Inventory, it increases on the debit side. Purchase Returns is a reduction in Purchases and hence must have the opposite rule; it increases on the credit side. Freight-In adds to the cost of purchases and therefore increases on the debit side. (The rules can also be deduced by thinking of the offsetting part of the transaction. Whenever possible, it is simplest to assume that the other account is Cash. Thus, a cash purchase involves a decrease in Cash, which is a credit; therefore, the entry to Purchases must be a debit.)

Adjusting and Closing

The accounts described above are temporary accounts which must be closed at the end of each accounting period. Furthermore, when these accounts are used, no entries are made during the accounting period to the Inventory account; therefore the amount shown in Inventory when the adjusting process begins will be the amount of *beginning* inventory. The Inventory account must be adjusted to show the proper inventory amount as of the end of the period. These adjusting and closing entries are customarily made in a certain order, which is more in the nature of a ritual than something of fundamental significance. It is as follows:

(1) Transfer the beginning inventory to Cost of Goods Sold.
(2) Close Freight-In, Purchase Returns, and similar accounts to Purchases, thereby showing the amount of net purchases in the Purchases account.
(3) Close Purchases to Cost of Goods Sold.
(4) Enter the ending inventory by debiting Inventory and crediting Cost of Goods Sold.
(5) Close Cost of Goods Sold to Loss and Gain.

Example: Using the figures given above, these entries would be as follows:

(1)

```
dr. Cost of Goods Sold . . . . . . . . . . . . . . . 4,000
    cr.  Inventory. . . . . . . . . . . . . . . . . .      4,000
```

(2)

```
dr.  Purchases. . . . . . . . . . . . . . . . . . . . .   600
     cr.   Freight-In . . . . . . . . . . . . . . . . .          600


dr.  Purchases Returns. . . . . . . . . . . . . . .   200
     cr.   Purchases. . . . . . . . . . . . . . . . . .          200*
```

* The entry is shown in this form for clarity. In practice, the two parts of this entry would be combined, thus saving some work, as follows:

```
dr.  Purchases.............................................................400
     Purchase Returns......................................................200
     cr.  Freight-In.......................................................        600
```

(3)

```
dr.  Cost of Goods Sold . . . . . . . . . . . . . . . 7,400
     cr.   Purchases. . . . . . . . . . . . . . . . . .        7,400
```

(4)

```
dr.  Inventory. . . . . . . . . . . . . . . . . . . . 2,000
     cr.   Cost of Goods Sold . . . . . . . . . . . . .        2,000
```

(5)

```
dr.  Loss and Gain. . . . . . . . . . . . . . . . . . 9,400
     cr.   Cost of Goods Sold . . . . . . . . . . . . .        9,400
```

If a work sheet is used, there might be a separate pair of columns labeled Cost of Goods Sold, and amounts corresponding to the above would be entered in these columns.

Limitation of the Deduction Process

Note that the validity of the reasoning behind the calculation described above rests on the *assumption* that if the merchandise is not found to be on hand at the end of the period, it must have been sold. This assumption is not necessarily correct because some of the goods may have been lost, or stolen, or thrown away, or overlooked when the physical inventory was taken. Usually, but not always, safeguards are set up to detect or avoid most of the shrinkages resulting from these causes. Nevertheless, in this system the physical inventory count must be used to determine the cost of goods sold, whereas in the perpetual inventory system, an actual count of the goods on hand can be used as a check on the accuracy of the inventory records.

Service Businesses

The cost of the services from which a service business derives its revenue is not as easily identifiable as the cost of the physical products sold by a retail store. Many service businesses do not attempt to measure the cost of the services they sell and hence do not develop a gross profit figure, since gross profit is the difference between sales revenue and cost of sales. Others do calculate a cost of sales, counting wages and salaries and other direct costs as their "cost of services."

> EXAMPLE: A plumbing business might show the wages of plumbers and the cost of pipes, fittings, and other material as its cost of sales, and list as operating expenses, below the gross profit figure, its management salaries, office costs, and other expenses.

INVENTORY PRICING

As is the case with other assets, the primary basis of accounting for inventories is cost, that is, the amount paid to acquire them. If, however, the goods are no longer worth as much as they cost, they are stated at what they are currently believed to be worth, that is, at their market value. Thus, the rule for pricing inventories is often stated as, "cost or market, whichever is lower."

Cost

As used in the above phrase, "cost" may or may not represent the actual cost of the specific items that are in the inventory. For one thing, the inventory of an item may consist of an intermingling of several lots purchased at different times and at different prices, in which case it may be literally impossible to determine the actual amount paid for the quantity remaining in inventory at the end of the period. In such cases, it is necessary to make some assumption about the flow of merchandise through inventory. Any of several assumptions is acceptable.

The most frequently used assumption is that the oldest items are used first, or "first-in, first-out." The opposite assumption, "last-in, first-out," is also acceptable; the reasons why some companies adopt this assumption, despite the undeniable fact that the oldest goods tend to be sold first, are given in Chapter 9. Use of an *average* cost is another acceptable practice.

> EXAMPLE: Assume 50 units priced at $1 each are in inventory at the beginning of the year; that during the year 100 units are purchased at $1.20 each and another 100 units at $1.40 each; and that 50 units remain in inventory at the end of the year. What is the amount of the ending inventory and the cost of the 200 units that were sold?
> Under *first-in, first-out*, the 50 units in inventory at the end of the year are priced at $1.40 each or $70, and cost of goods sold is $(50 \times \$1) + (100 \times \$1.20) + (50 \times \$1.40) = \$240$.
> Under *last-in, first-out*, the 50 units in inventory at the end of the

year are priced at $1 each, or $50, and cost of goods sold is $(100 \times \$1.20) + (100 \times \$1.40) = \$260$.

Under *average cost*, the average cost of the 250 units available for sale is $(50 \times \$1) + (100 \times \$1.20) + (100 \times \$1.40) \div 250 = \$1.24$. The 50 units in inventory are priced at $1.24 each, or $62, and cost of goods sold is $200 \times \$1.24 = \$248$.

Even if the cost of the specific items sold is known, one of the above assumptions as to flow, rather than this specific cost, may be used in inventory pricing.

Market

In the ordinary situation, inventory is reported at its cost. It is reduced below cost (i.e., "written down") only when there is evidence that the value of the items, when sold or otherwise disposed of, will be less than cost. Such evidence may reflect physical deterioration, obsolescence, changes in price level, or other causes. When this evidence exists, inventory is stated at "market."

Since the goods in inventory have not in fact been sold, their true market value is not ordinarily known and must therefore be estimated. The Accounting Principles Board states that this estimate should be the current *replacement* cost of the item; that is, what it would cost currently to purchase or manufacture the item. The APB further sets upper and lower boundaries on "market":

1. It should not be higher than the estimated selling price of the item less the costs associated with selling it. This amount is called the *net realizable value*.

2. It should not be lower than the net realizable value less a normal profit margin.[1]

ACCOUNTS RECEIVABLE AND BAD DEBTS

The main source of revenue in many businesses is the sale of merchandise to customers for credit, that is, "on account." This type of transaction gives rise to the asset, accounts receivable, and to an increase in sales revenue and hence in owners' equity. Let us assume that the Essel Company began operations in 1967 and that during the year the company made sales of $262,250, all on credit. In the interest of simplicity, let us further assume that none of the customers had paid their bills by the end of 1967. The record made of these transactions would show accounts receivable in the amount of $262,250 and sales of $262,250. It would be

---

[1] Paul Grady, *Inventory of Generally Accepted Accounting Principles* (AICPA 1965) pp. 246–49.

correct to report $262,250 as an asset on the balance sheet as of the end of 1967 and $262,250 as sales on the income statement for 1967 if, *but only if,* it is believed that the customers eventually will pay their obligations to the Essel Company. The unfortunate fact is, however, that some of these customers may never pay their bills; that is, their accounts may become *bad debts.*

Consider the extreme case: the person who purchases merchandise with no intention of paying for it and who in fact does not pay for it. In this case, the company has not actually made a sale at all. Although the fact was not known at the time, no revenue was actually earned and nothing valuable was added to the asset, Accounts Receivable, as a result of this transaction. If this event is recorded as an increase in Sales and as an increase in Accounts Receivable, both these accounts will be overstated.

In the more usual bad debt situation, the customer fully intends to pay his bill, but for one reason or another he never actually does make payment. The effect is the same as that in the extreme case. Such a sale is also recorded initially by debiting Accounts Receivable and crediting Sales at the sales value of the merchandise. In these situations, a subsequent entry must be made to show that the amount debited to Accounts Receivable does not represent a valid asset and that owners' equity has not in fact increased by the amount of the sale.

Accounting Recognition of Bad Debts

When the company made the sale, the fact that the customer would never pay his bill was not known; otherwise the sale probably would not have been made. Even at the end of the accounting period, the company probably does not know which of the obligations carried as accounts receivable will never be collected. An estimate of the amount of bad debts can nevertheless be made, and it is customary to adjust the accounting records at the end of each accounting period to reflect this estimate.

One method of making this adjustment is by a *direct write-off.* Accounts that are believed to be uncollectible are simply eliminated from the records by subtracting the amount of the bad debt from Accounts Receivable and showing the same amount as an expense item on the income statement. The entry to accomplish this would be as follows:

```
dr.  Bad Debt Expense. . . . . . . . . . . . . . . . .   200
   cr.   Accounts Receivable . . . . . . . . . . . . .        200
```

The direct write-off method, however, requires that the specific uncollectible accounts be detected, whereas this usually is not possible. An alternative procedure, therefore, is to estimate the *total* amount of uncollectible accounts, and to show this estimated amount as a deduction from accounts receivable on the balance sheet, and as an expense on the income statement. Instead of reducing the accounts receivable figure directly, the estimate is often shown as a separate figure on the balance sheet, so that the reader can observe both the total amount owed by customers and that portion of the amount which the company believes will not be collected.

An account used to record deductions in the amount shown in some other account is called a *contra* account. The balance sheet contra account for accounts receivable is often labeled *allowance for doubtful accounts* or *allowance for uncollectible accounts*. It may also be labeled "reserve for bad debts," but this is likely to cause confusion since the word "reserve" connotes to many people that a sum of money has been set aside, and such is not the case. The allowance for doubtful accounts is in the nature of a suspended credit to accounts receivable for specific, but as yet unknown, customers.

The corresponding item on the income statement is called *bad debt expense* or *loss on bad debts*. Ordinarily, this item appears as one of the miscellaneous operating expenses listed below the gross profit, on the grounds that this is an item that is an almost inevitable cost in any business that extends credit to its customers. Some companies show it as a subtraction from gross sales, reflecting the belief that bad debts represent sales that never actually resulted in revenue; still others show it as a nonoperating expense. This possible difference in treatment should be kept in mind when comparing the income statements of two companies in which bad debts are a significant item, since the gross profit of one may reflect the recognition of bad debt expense, while that of the other may not.

METHODS OF MAKING THE ESTIMATE.   Any one of several methods may be used to estimate the amount of bad debt expense in an accounting period. One method is to examine each of the customer accounts and to set up an amount that is large enough to equal those accounts that seem to be uncollectible. In companies with hundreds, or thousands, of customer accounts, an analysis of each individual account may not be feasible. A common practice, therefore, is to rely on some overall formula developed on the basis of experience over a period of years. Some of the methods commonly used are as follows:

1. Estimate bad debts expense as a *percentage of total sales* for the period. This method can logically be used only when cash sales are either negligible or a constant proportion of total sales, for bad debt expense is not, of course, related to cash sales.
2. Estimate bad debt expense as a *percentage of credit sales*.
3. Adjust the Allowance for Doubtful Accounts so that it equals a prescribed *percentage of accounts receivable* outstanding at the end of the period.

The percentage used in each case depends in part on what the records show as to experience in the past and in part on management's judgment as to the extent to which past experience reflects the current situation.

AGING ACCOUNTS RECEIVABLE. Sometimes different percentages are applied to accounts outstanding for various lengths of time. This requires the preparation of an *aging schedule*, which is also a useful device for analyzing the quality of the asset, accounts receivable. An example is shown in Illustration 5–1.

Illustration 5–1

AGING SCHEDULE FOR ESTIMATING BAD DEBTS

Status	Amount Outstanding	Estimated % Uncollectible	Allowance for Doubtful Accounts
Current.	$207,605	1	$2,076
Overdue:			
Less than 1 month.	26,003	1	260
1 up to 2 months .	10,228	5	511
2 up to 3 months .	7,685	10	768
3 up to 4 months .	3,876	20	775
Over 4 months. . .	6,853	40	2,741
Total.	$262,250		$7,131

THE ADJUSTING ENTRY. Once the amount has been determined, it is recorded as one of the adjusting entries made at the end of the accounting period. If Essel Company management estimated the Allowance for Doubtful Accounts on the basis of the above aging schedule, the entry would be as shown below:

```
dr.  Bad Debt Expense. . . . . . . . . . . . . . . . . .  7,131
    cr.   Allowance for Doubtful Accounts . . . . . . .        7,131
```

The accounts receivable section of the December 31, 1967, balance sheet would then appear as follows:

```
Accounts receivable. . . . . . . . . . . . . . .  $262,250
    Less: Allowance for doubtful accounts. . . . .      7,131
        Accounts Receivable, Net . . . . . . . . .  $255,119
```

The income statement for 1967 would show bad debt expense in the amount of $7,131.

For reasons to be described, the Allowance for Doubtful Accounts usually will have a balance even before the adjusting entry is made. In these circumstances the amount reported as bad debt expense on the income statement will be different from the amount reported as allowance for doubtful accounts on the balance sheet. (In the Essel Company example just given, this did not occur because the company was organized in 1967, and the above entry was the first one made to Allowance for Doubtful Accounts.)

When the Allowance for Doubtful Accounts has a balance, care must be taken in applying the formulas listed above. Formulas No. 1 and No. 2, which are related to sales, give the amount of bad debt *expense* for the period; this same amount is credited to whatever balance existed in Allowance for Doubtful Accounts prior to the entry. Formula No. 3, which is related to accounts receivable, gives the amount that is to appear as the Allowance for Doubtful Accounts; the journal entry is made in an amount that brings the Allowance for Doubtful Accounts *up to* the desired balance.

> EXAMPLE: If at the end of 1968, in the Essel Company, Allowance for Doubtful Accounts had a credit balance of $1,000, and if it was decided that the allowance should be 2 percent of accounts receivable, which at that time amounted to $300,000, the balance must be increased *to* $6,000, which is an increase of $5,000. The journal entry would therefore be the following:

```
dr.  Bad Debt Expense. . . . . . . . . . . . . . . . .  5,000
  cr.   Allowance for Doubtful Accounts . . . . . . .           5,000
```

The balance sheet as of December 31, 1968, would then show:

```
Accounts receivable. . . . . . . . . . . . . . . . . . $300,000
   Less: Allowance for doubtful accounts. . . . . . . .    6,000
      Accounts Receivable, Net . . . . . . . . . . . . $294,000
```

Write-Off of an Uncollectible Account

When the company decides that a specific customer is never going to pay his bill, Accounts Receivable is reduced by the amount he owes and a corresponding reduction is made in the Allowance for Doubtful Accounts. This entry is made whenever it is recognized that a specific account is bad, which may be either during the accounting period or at the end of the period. This event has *no* effect on Bad Debt Expense.

> EXAMPLE: If sometime in 1969 the Essel Company decided that John Jones was never going to pay his bill of $200, the following entry would be made:

```
dr.  Allowance for Doubtful Accounts . . . . . . . . .    200
    cr.  Accounts Receivable. . . . . . . . . . . . . .           200
```

A balance sheet prepared immediately after this transaction had been recorded (assuming no other changes since December 31) would appear as follows:

```
Accounts receivable. . . . . . . . . . . . . . . . .   $299,800
    Less: Allowance for doubtful accounts. . . . . . . .      5,800
    Accounts Receivable, Net . . . . . . . . . . . . .   $294,000
```

Note that the *net* amount of accounts receivable is unchanged by this entry.

Collection of a Bad Debt Written Off

If, by some unexpected stroke of good fortune, John Jones should subsequently pay all or part of his bill, cash would be increased (i.e., debited) and a corresponding credit would be recorded to have one of the following effects:

1. Increase retained earnings on the balance sheet.
2. Add back the amount to allowance for doubtful accounts on the balance sheet.
3. Show as bad debts recovered, a separate item of revenue on the income statement.
4. Decrease bad debt expense on the income statement.

The first method ordinarily is not used since it violates the "all-inclusive income" principle. The second method has the effect of reversing the previous entry, and it is often used. The third method is rarely used because the amount involved is ordinarily too small to warrant reporting it as a separate item. The fourth method is not entirely logical but is often used in practice since it provides a convenient way of handling the transaction.

Still another common procedure is, first, to reverse the entry by which the account was written off (i.e., debit Accounts Receivable and credit Allowance for Doubtful Accounts) and, then, to treat the collection just like any other payment on account (i.e., debit Cash and credit Accounts Receivable). This has the advantage of showing a complete record of the transaction in the account for the customer.

The allowance for doubtful accounts should be sufficient at all times to absorb the accounts that prove to be uncollectible. Because business conditions fluctuate, the amount may well turn out to be too large in some periods and too small in others. In practice, because of the doctrine of conservatism, it is common to find that the allowance is too large rather than too small. On the other hand, there have been some cases where the allowance for doubtful accounts turned out to be woefully inadequate.

Summary

Let us summarize the handling of events described above by showing the effect of hypothetical transactions in 1969 on the Essel Company accounts:

1. *Write-off of $5,000 more of bad debts during the year:*

```
dr. Allowance for Doubtful Accounts. . . . . . . . . .  5,000
    cr.   Accounts Receivable. . . . . . . . . . . . . .         5,000
          The balance in Allowance for Doubtful Accounts
          becomes $800.
```

2. *Recovery of $500 previously written off:*

```
dr. Cash . . . . . . . . . . . . . . . . . . . . . .  500
    cr.   Allowance for Doubtful Accounts* . . . . . . .          500
          The balance in Allowance for Doubtful Accounts
          becomes $1,300.
```

  * As mentioned, this is only one of several possible treatments.

3. *Adjustments at end of 1969* assuming allowance is to be maintained at 2 percent of accounts receivable, which are $400,000 as of December 31, 1969.

```
dr. Bad Debts Expense. . . . . . . . . . . . . . . . .  6,700
    cr.   Allowance for Doubtful Accounts. . . . . . . .        6,700
          This brings the allowance up to $8,000, which
          is 2 percent of accounts receivable.
```

OTHER PROBLEMS OF REVENUE MEASUREMENT

The rationale of the bad debt adjustment is that expense should be matched with revenue, regardless of the time of *discovery* that accounts are uncollectible. The same rationale applies to sales discounts, sales returns and allowances, and similar items. If the amounts involved are material, similar adjustments should be made for these items; for example, the amount of sales discounts that will be taken in future periods on sales counted as revenue in the current period should be estimated, and the sales discount expense adjusted accordingly. However, although the procedure of estimating bad debt expense on a reasonable basis is acceptable for income tax purposes, such a procedure is not acceptable with respect to sales discounts and similar items. For tax purposes, most types of sales discounts can be deducted only if the customer actually took the discount during the period in question.

For other reasons, the amount specified in the sales contract may not be the best estimate of the revenue that actually will be realized from the transaction. The possibility that the company might incur repair costs or make replacements in order to discharge its obligations under a warranty agreement, mentioned in Chapter 3, is an example. When such amounts are significant, the matching principle requires that these future costs be estimated and set up as deductions from the current period's revenue. The mechanics of doing this are similar to those described above for bad debts.

Long-Term Contracts

When, under a firm contract, a business works for several accounting periods on a single product, a portion of the revenue is often recognized in each of these periods rather than solely in the final period in which the product is completed and shipped. Shipbuilding and major construction projects are examples of situations in which this *percentage-of-completion* method is used. The revenue recognized for a period can easily be estimated when the product is constructed under a straight *cost-plus* contract, since the revenue is a specified percentage of the costs incurred in the period. In the case of fixed-price contracts or contracts with a fixed dollar amount of profit (i.e., cost-plus-fixed-fee contracts), the total amount of profit, and hence the amount applicable to each period, cannot be known exactly until the total costs have been determined at the completion of the job. In these situations, an estimated revenue may nevertheless be assigned to each of the accounting periods in the same proportion to the cost for the period that total revenue is expected to be of total cost, the proportion being estimated conservatively so as to avoid overstatement of interim profits.

In accordance with the matching principle, when revenue is measured by the percentage-of-completion basis, the expenses for the period are the costs associated with the revenue.

Installment Sales

Consumers who pay for their purchases on installments (so much a month or so much a week) are, as a class, not exceptionally good credit risks; a significant number of them do not complete their payments, and the seller accordingly repossesses, or tries to repossess, the merchandise. When this happens, the face amount of the installment contract overstates the amount of revenue that actually is earned on the transaction. One way of allowing for these defaults is to use the estimated bad debt mechanism already described. Another method used by many businesses is to recognize the revenue only as the installment payments are received, rather than when the sale is made; this is called the *installment method*. Either method is acceptable for income tax purposes, but the Accounting Principles Board states that sales revenue should "ordinarily" be accounted for when the sale is made, and that the installment method is acceptable only when "the circumstances are such that the collection of the sales price is not reasonably assured."[2] If the installment method is used in measuring revenue, the relevant expense is that fraction of the product's cost that corresponds to the fraction of installment payments received during the period.

Cash Basis

Despite the realization concept, a number of businesses, particularly small ones, recognize revenue only when cash is received. Many physicians and other professional people use this so-called *cash basis* rather than recording revenue as of the period when they render the service. This practice is conservative and is permitted under certain circumstances for income tax purposes, but it is not in accordance with generally accepted accounting principles. A business that uses the cash basis cannot measure its net income in the accounting sense of this term.

Consignments

Shipments on *consignment* are not sales.[3] The consignor, that is, the manufacturer, retains title to consignment merchandise, and the sale is not consummated until the consignee, who is usually a retailer, resells to the final customer. A consignment shipment therefore represents only the movement of the asset, inventory, from one place to another. In order to show the amount of merchandise out on consignment, it may be desirable to reflect this movement by a journal entry, at cost:

```
dr.  Inventory on Consignment . . . . . . . . . . . .   100
  cr.   Merchandise Inventory. . . . . . . . . . . .          100
```

In the period in which the goods are sold, the effect on the accounts would be as in the following entries (although these amounts would probably be recorded, in practice, as a part of other summary entries for revenues and expense):

---

[2] *Opinions of the Accounting Principles Board No. 10,* December, 1966.

[3] Nevertheless, some businesses treat consignment shipments as if they were sales on the grounds that they have learned through experience that the consigned merchandise ordinarily is not returned, and that the sale for all practical purposes is therefore consummated at the time of shipment.

```
dr.  Cost of Goods Sold. . . . . . . . . . . . . . . 100
   cr.   Inventory on Consignment. . . . . . . . . . .          100
         To record the cost of consigned goods sold.

dr.  Accounts Receivable . . . . . . . . . . . . . . 150
   cr.   Sales . . . . . . . . . . . . . . . . . . . .          150
         To record the sales value.
```

WAGES, SALARIES, AND RELATED COSTS

As a matter of custom, the word "wages" usually refers to the compensation of employees who are on a piece-rate, hourly, daily, or weekly basis; while the word "salaries" usually refers to compensation expressed in monthly, or longer, terms. Alternatively, the word "wages" may be related to employees who must be paid overtime when they work more than 40 hours in a week, as required by the Fair Labor Standards Act, and the word "salaries" may be related to employees who are exempt from this provision. (The latter are called *exempt* employees.) The effect on the accounting records of earning and paying wages and salaries is more complicated than merely debiting expenses and crediting cash, for when wages and salaries are earned or paid, certain other transactions occur almost automatically.

An employee is rarely paid the gross amount of wages or salary he earns since from his gross earnings there must be deducted—

1. An amount representing his contribution under the Federal Insurance Contribution Act (F.I.C.A.), which currently (1969) is 4.8 percent of the first $7,800 of wages earned each year.
2. The withholding deduction, which is an amount withheld from gross earnings to apply toward his income tax.
3. Deductions for pension contributions, savings plans, health insurance, union dues, and a variety of other items.

None of these deductions represents an expense to the business. In the case of the tax deductions, the business is acting as a collection agent for the government; the withholding of these amounts and their subsequent transfer to the government does not affect owners' equity. Rather, the withholding creates a liability, and the subsequent transfer to the government pays off this liability. Similarly, the business is acting as a collection agent in the case of the other deductions. The employee is paid the net amount after these deductions have been taken.

When wages and salaries are earned, other expenses are automatically created. The employer must pay a tax equal in amount to the employee's F.I.C.A. tax, and the employer must also pay an additional percentage of the employee's pay (the rate varies in different states) for the *unemployment insurance tax*. Collectively, F.I.C.A. and unemployment insurance are called *social security taxes*. The *employer's* share of these taxes *is* an expense of the business.

Thus, if an employee with three dependents earns $100 for his work in a given week in 1969, there would be deducted from his pay $4.80 for his F.I.C.A. tax contribution and $8.50 for withholding tax, and he would receive the balance, $86.70. This is his "take-home pay." (Other possible deductions are omitted for purposes of simplification.) The *business* would incur an expense of $4.80 for F.I.C.A. tax and an additional expense of, say, $3.20 for the federal and state unemployment insurance taxes, or a total of $8.00 for the two social security taxes.

The journal entries for these transactions are as follows:

1. *When wages are earned; wages expense:*

```
dr.  Wages Expense . . . . . . . . . . . . . . . . . .  100.00
     cr.  Wages Payable . . . . . . . . . . . . . . . . .       100.00
```

2. *When wages are earned; business tax expense.*[4]

```
dr.  Social Security Tax Expense . . . . . . . . . . .   8.00
     cr.  F.I.C.A. Taxes Payable. . . . . . . . . . . .         4.80
          Unemployment Taxes Payable. . . . . . . . . .         3.20
```

3. *When the employee is paid:*

```
dr.  Wages Payable . . . . . . . . . . . . . . . . . .  100.00
     cr.  Cash. . . . . . . . . . . . . . . . . . . . .        86.70
          F.I.C.A. Taxes Payable. . . . . . . . . . . .         4.80
          Withholding Taxes Payable . . . . . . . . . .         8.50
```

4. *When the government is paid:*

```
dr.  F.I.C.A. Taxes Payable. . . . . . . . . . . . . .   9.60
     Unemployment Taxes Payable. . . . . . . . . . . .   3.20
     Withholding Taxes Payable . . . . . . . . . . . .   8.50
     cr.  Cash. . . . . . . . . . . . . . . . . . . . .        21.30
```

In practice, the above entries would be made for all employees as a group rather than separately for each person. The government does require, however, that a record be kept for the amount of F.I.C.A. tax and withholding tax accumulated for each employee, and that he be furnished a copy of this record.

Pensions

The above transactions, although complicated, involve no new problem in the application of accounting principles. One matter related to wages

---

[4] This entry matches the tax expense with wages *earned* in the period, which is in principle the correct treatment. Some businesses compute the tax as of the period in which the wages are *paid*, on the grounds that this involves a much simpler calculation and that there is no material difference between the results of the two methods.

does involve a very difficult problem. This is the liability and related expense for pensions.

About 25 million Americans work for companies that agree to pay them pensions when they retire. All or part of the cost of these pensions is borne by the company; the remainder, if any, comes from contributions made by employees. Accounting for the company's cost for pensions is a particularly difficult matter because the expense is incurred during the years in which the employee works for the company, but the payments to him are made at some distant future time, and the total amount of the payment is uncertain, depending on how long he lives, on his final wage or salary, and possibly on other considerations.

The pension plans of many companies are *funded;* that is, an estimate is made of the amount that will be necessary to meet the future pension payments arising out of the employees' earnings in the current year, and this amount is either set aside in a trust fund or paid to an outside agency that guarantees to make the future pension payments. The amount paid into such a fund is a deductible expense for income tax purposes, provided certain other conditions are met, and is usually treated as an expense of the current year for accounting purposes. If the company retains the fund, the following entries are required each year:

```
dr. Pension Expense. . . . . . . . . . . . . . . . .   xxxx
    cr.   Pension Liability. . . . . . . . . . . . . .        xxxx
          To establish the expense and related liability.

dr. Pension Fund (a noncurrent asset). . . . . . . .   xxxx
    cr.   Cash . . . . . . . . . . . . . . . . . . .         xxxx
          To transfer cash to the fund.
```

When the pension is paid to the retired employee, the entry is as follows:

```
dr. Pension Liability. . . . . . . . . . . . . . . .   xxxx
    cr.   Pension Fund . . . . . . . . . . . . . . .         xxxx
```

If the plan is not funded, only the amount actually paid to retired employees is deductible for income tax purposes. This is *not*, however, an acceptable basis for measuring pension expense in accordance with generally accepted accounting principles. The accrual concept requires that the amount of expense in a year be computed on the basis of the pension obligation that was created in the year, which is related to employee earnings in the year, not to the pensions paid in the year. The amount of pensions paid in a year is, of course, a function of employee earnings in prior years.

When a pension plan is first adopted, an especially difficult problem arises: What shall be done about the liability created for employees who are entitled to benefits because of the years they have worked for the company up to the time of adoption of the plan? Although this liability arises as a result of work done in prior years, for income tax purposes the estimated amount thereof may be treated as a tax deduction over the next 10 or 12 *future* years. The Accounting Principles Board also requires that these *past-service benefits* be spread over the income of future years, not more than 40 years, nor less than 10 years.[5]

Even a careful estimate of the future liability under a pension plan may turn out to be wrong, partly because such factors as whether the employee will stay with the company until retirement and his length of life after retirement are quite uncertain, and also because there is a tendency to liberalize benefits as time goes on. Consequently, the actual amount of expense attributable to the work done in a given year cannot be known for many years later.

INCOME TAX ALLOCATIONS

In accordance with the matching concept, the income tax reported as an expense for a year should be related to the income reported for the year; that is, if the company reports an income of $1 million before taxes, and the tax rate is approximately 48 percent, the income tax expense should be approximately $480,000. If companies figured their taxable income exactly the same way they figured their net income on the income statement, there would be no matching problem. Many companies use different rules for tax purposes than they use for financial accounting purposes, however, and the income tax calculated for a given year will therefore be based on a different amount of income from that reported on the income statement. Under these circumstances, the income tax as calculated will not match the reported income. When there is a difference between net income measured in accordance with accounting principles and net *taxable* income calculated in accordance with tax regulations, a problem arises.

EXAMPLE: Assume that in 1968 a company spends $400,000 on research and development which results in a successful new product; that it decides for accounting purposes to charge this cost as an expense over the next five years, 1969–73, during which time the new product is expected to be producing revenue; but for tax purposes it deducts the $400,000 in the year of expenditure, thus postponing the payment of a corresponding amount of taxes. If its net income in 1968 prior to considering the research and development item is $1 million for both tax purposes and accounting purposes, its income subject to tax will be $600,000, and its income tax will be approximately 48 percent[6] of this, or $288,000. If the company regarded this $288,000 as its income tax

---

[5] *Opinions of the Accounting Principles Board No. 8*, November, 1966.

[6] In 1968, federal income taxes on ordinary corporations were 22 percent of the first $25,000 of taxable income and 48 percent of income in excess of $25,000 (exclusive of a temporary surtax). Many states also impose corporate income taxes.

expense for 1968, then its net income for accounting purposes would be $1,000,000 − $288,000 = $712,000. This, however, would be incorrect, because the $288,000 tax matches, or relates to, an income of $600,000, not of $1 million. The tax applicable to the $1 million is $480,000, and the net income should be reported as $1,000,000 − $480,000 = $520,000.

The opposite situation will arise in the next five years, for in each of them the company will charge $80,000 as research and development expense for accounting purposes, but it cannot deduct this amount again for tax purposes, so its accounting income will be lower than its taxable income. By the end of the fifth following year, 1973, the difference between taxable income and accounting income will have washed out.

When such differences between accounting income and taxable income in a year are material, the Accounting Principles Board states that the income tax actually calculated for the year should be adjusted so that it equals the income tax that would have been paid had the accounting income been taxable in that year.[7] The offsetting entry is made to a liability account, Deferred Income Tax Liability.

EXAMPLE: Carrying on the above illustration, the estimated amount of income tax actually payable for 1968 is recorded by this entry:

```
dr.  Income Tax Expense . . . . . . . . . . . . . . . 288,000
   cr.   Income Tax Liability . . . . . . . . . . . .        288,000
```

A second entry is then made to bring the income tax up to the amount applicable to the accounting income, which is $480,000.

```
dr.  Income Tax Expense . . . . . . . . . . . . . . . 192,000
   cr.   Deferred Income Tax Liability. . . . . . . .        192,000
```

Deferred Income Tax Liability appears on the balance sheet and is written off in each of the next five years by this entry:

```
dr.  Deferred Income Tax Liability. . . . . . . . . .  38,400
   cr.   Income Tax Expense . . . . . . . . . . . . .         38,400
```

In this way, the income tax expense figure is made to match the income as measured by accounting principles.

The practice described above is highly controversial. Some of the largest accounting firms disagree with it, and some of the government regulatory agencies prohibit its use for purposes of the financial statements required of the companies they regulate. This is the reason why the Union Pacific Railroad Company reports two figures for net income, as described on page 20.

---

[7] *Opinions of the Accounting Principles Board No.* 7, December, 1967.

LOSSES

A distinction is often made between an *expense*, which is made to benefit the operations of a period, and a *loss*, which is an expenditure that does not benefit anything. The destruction of an uninsured building by fire, or the theft of some asset, results in a loss. Since both expenses and losses are ordinarily charged to the accounting period to which they relate, there is no great need to draw a fine line between them.

CONCLUSION

As additional problems are discussed, it should become increasingly apparent that the goal of matching revenue and expense in an accounting period can never be exactly attained. This fact could easily lead to a sense of frustration, were it not for the concept of materiality. In this concept we have the practical solution: one does the best he can with the information and in the time available, realizing that despite his best efforts, a perfect matching is not likely to result.

CHAPTER 6

FIXED ASSETS
AND DEPRECIATION

This chapter discusses principles and procedures involved in recording the acquisition of fixed assets and in the subsequent amortization of their cost as expenses of the periods benefited.

ACQUISITION OF FIXED ASSETS

When an expenditure is recorded in the accounts as a fixed asset (rather than as an expense or a current asset), it is said to be *capitalized*. In accordance with the cost concept, the amount that is to be capitalized as the value of a newly acquired asset is its cost. In principle, this amount is the sum of all costs incurred in acquiring the asset, installing it, and getting it ready for service.

In many cases this amount can be determined easily. For example, the cost of a truck purchased for cash is simply the amount of cash paid. In other cases, the problem is more complicated. The cost of a parcel of land includes the purchase price, broker's commission, legal fees, and the cost of grading or tearing down existing structures so as to make the land ready for its intended use; and some of these items may be difficult to ascertain. The cost of machinery includes the purchase price, transportation costs to where the machinery is to be used, and installation costs.

Despite the principle stated above, many companies do not capitalize the costs incurred to make the asset ready to provide service. Instead they capitalize only the purchase price. They do this both because it is simpler and in order to minimize property taxes.

When the company constructs a machine or a building with its own personnel, the amount to be capitalized includes all the costs incurred in construction. If the actual cost of building a machine is unreasonably high (as would be the case if the machine was an experimental model and required a considerable amount of development work), the doctrine of conservatism dictates that the asset be "booked" (i.e., recorded in the accounts) at an amount not greater than the purchase price of a similar machine from an outside vendor or not greater than what the cost of building a duplicate machine would be if the "trial-and-error" cost involved in building the original machine could be avoided.

Occasionally a company acquires a fixed asset that turns out to be worth significantly more than the amount paid for it, as, for example, when valuable minerals are discovered on land that was acquired at low cost. These are called *fortunate acquisitions.* Under such circumstances, an exception is often made to the principle that assets are carried on the books at an amount not in excess of their cost, and the asset is recorded at its estimated current value. The difference between this recorded value and actual cost is credited directly to a special category of owners' equity called capital surplus.

Betterments and Replacements versus Maintenance

Repair and maintenance is work done to keep the asset in good operating condition or to bring it back to good operating condition if it has broken down. Repair and maintenance costs are ordinarily expenses of the accounting period in which the work is done; they are *not* added to the cost of the fixed asset.

A *betterment is* added to the cost of the asset. The distinction between maintenance expenses and betterments is simple to state: maintenance work keeps the machine in good condition, but in no better condition than when it was purchased; a betterment makes the machine better than it was when it was purchased. In practice, the line between the two is difficult to draw. A new accessory designed to make the machine operate more efficiently or perform new functions is a betterment; an overhaul during which worn-out parts are replaced with new ones is maintenance. In the interests of conservatism some work which strictly speaking should be considered as a betterment is charged as an expense of the current period.

Replacements may be either assets or expenses, depending on how the asset unit is defined. The replacement of an entire asset results in the writing off of the old asset and the booking of the new. The replacement of a component part of an asset is maintenance expense. Thus, if one company treats a complete airplane as a single asset unit and another company treats the airframe as one unit and the engine as another, then the replacement of an engine results in a maintenance charge in the first company and in a new asset in the second. In general, the broader the definition of the asset unit, the greater will be the amount of costs charged as "maintenance" and hence expensed in the year of acquisition.

Trade-Ins

When a new fixed asset is acquired in exchange for another, the old asset is part of the consideration given; therefore its trade-in value is part of the cost of the new asset. If the stated trade-in allowance differs from the actual value of the old asset, as is often the case with automobiles for example, then this artificial price should not be used in valuing the new asset; under these circumstances, the value is arrived at indirectly, often by estimating what the new asset would have cost if it had been purchased for cash.

> EXAMPLE: An automobile dealer offers to sell Company X a new automobile with a list price of $3,500 for $1,800 cash plus one of Company X's old automobiles for which the dealer says he will make a trade-in allowance of $1,700. Neither the fact that the list price is $3,500, nor the fact that the cash plus trade-in allowance totals $3,500 is conclusive evidence that the asset value of the new automobile is $3,500. Automobiles are customarily sold for less than their list price. Upon further inquiry, it may be discovered that the new automobile can actually be purchased for $3,300 cash; if so, its cost is $3,300.

DEPRECIATION

With the exception of land, most fixed assets have a limited useful life; that is, they will be of use to the company over a limited number of future accounting periods. A fraction of the cost of the asset is properly chargeable as an expense in each of the accounting periods in which the asset is used by the company. The accounting process for this gradual conversion of fixed assets into expense is called *depreciation*. It is described as follows by the Accounting Principles Board:

> The cost of a productive facility is one of the costs of the service it renders during its useful economic life. Generally accepted accounting principles require that this cost be spread over the expected useful life of the facility in such a way as to allocate it as equitably as possible to the periods during which services are obtained from the use of the facility. This procedure is known as depreciation accounting, a system of accounting which aims to distribute the cost or other basic value of tangible capital assets, less salvage (if any), over the estimated useful life of the unit . . . in a systematic and rational manner. It is a process of allocation, not of valuation.[1]

---

[1] Paul Grady, *Inventory of Generally Accepted Accounting Principles* (AICPA *Accounting Research Study No. 7*, 1965), p. 126.

The question is sometimes asked: Why is depreciation an expense? The answer is that *all* goods and services consumed by a business during an accounting period are expenses. The cost of insurance protection provided in a year is an expense of that year even though the insurance premium was paid two or three years previously. Depreciation expense is like insurance expense except that the fraction of total cost of a fixed asset that is an expense in a given year is difficult to estimate, whereas the fraction of the total cost of an insurance policy that is an expense in a given year can be easily calculated. This difference does not change the fundamental fact that both insurance policies and fixed assets provide service to the company over a *finite* number of accounting periods and must therefore be charged as expenses of each of these periods.

The useful life of an asset is limited for one of two reasons: *deterioration*, which is the physical process of wearing out; and *obsolescence*, which refers to loss of usefulness because of the development of improved equipment or processes, changes in style, or other causes not related to the physical condition of the asset. No distinction need be made between the two since depreciation relates to both of them.

The word "depreciation" is sometimes used as referring only to physical wear and tear; this usage is incorrect. In many cases, a machine becomes obsolete, and consequently is no longer useful, even though it is in good physical condition.

Judgments Required

In order to determine the depreciation expense for an accounting period, three judgments or estimates must be made for each fixed asset:

1. The *service life* of the asset; that is, over how many accounting periods will it be useful to the company?

2. *Salvage or resale value* at the end of its life. The net cost of the asset to the company is its original cost less any amount eventually recovered through sale or salvage, and it is this net cost that should be charged as an expense over the asset's life. In a great many situations, however, the estimated salvage or resale value is so small and uncertain that it is disregarded.

3. *The method of depreciation;* that is, the method that will be used to allocate a fraction of the net cost to each of the accounting periods in which the asset is expected to be used.

Businessmen, not being clairvoyant, cannot *know* in advance how long the asset will last or what its salvage value will be; and they usually have no scientific or strictly logical way of deciding the best depreciation method. The figure of depreciation expense that results from all these judgments is therefore an estimate, and often it is only a rough estimate.

Service Life

The most widely used basis for estimating the service life of assets is the *Depreciation Guidelines,* published by the Internal Revenue Service.[2] This publication contains estimates for the service lives of machinery and equipment used in all types of industries. Some examples are: petroleum drilling, 6 years; aerospace industry and electrical manufacturing industry, 8 years; shoe manufacturing and printing and publishing, 11 years; cement making, 20 years. The booklet also gives estimates for other assets without regard to industry. Examples are:

Office furniture, fixtures, machines, and equipment.................10 years
Automobiles.. 3 years
Light trucks... 4 years
Heavy trucks.. 6 years
Land improvements...20 years
Apartments, hotels, theatres.................................45 years
Dwellings, factories, garages, office buildings, machine shops.........40 years
Banks, loft buildings, stores.................................50 years
Grain elevators, warehouses.................................60 years

It should be emphasized that these figures are only *guidelines.* If a company has reason to believe that some other estimate is better, it should by all means use the better estimate.

Depreciation Methods

Consider a machine purchased for $1,000 with an estimated life of 10 years and estimated salvage value of zero. The problem of depreciation accounting is to charge this $1,000 as an expense over the 10-year period. How much should be charged as an expense each year?

This question cannot be answered by observing the amount of asset value physically consumed in a given year, for physically the machine continues to be a machine; usually, there is no observable indication of its decline in usefulness. Nor can the question be answered in terms of changes in the machine's market value during the year, for accounting is concerned with the amortization of cost, not with changes in market values. An indirect approach must therefore be used. Three conceptual ways of looking at the depreciation process are described below, together with the methods that follow from each.

STRAIGHT-LINE METHOD. One concept views a fixed asset as existing to provide service over its life, with its readiness to provide this service being equal in each year of life, just as a three-year insurance policy

---

[2] *Depreciation Guidelines and Rules,* Internal Revenue Service publication No. 456 (Washington, D.C.: U.S. Government Printing Office, 1962).

provides equal protection in each of the three years. This concept leads to the straight-line method, which is to charge an equal fraction of the cost each year. For a machine costing $1,000 with an estimated service life of 10 years, $\frac{1}{10}$ of $1,000 is the depreciation expense of the first year, another $\frac{1}{10}$ is the depreciation expense of the second year, and so on. Expressed another way, the machine is said to have a *depreciation rate* of 10 percent per year, the rate being the reciprocal of the estimated useful life.

ACCELERATED METHODS.   A second concept takes what is perhaps a broader view of the asset since it relates to the *amount* of service provided each year. Many fixed assets are more valuable in their youth than in their old age—because their mechanical efficiency tends to decline with age, because maintenance costs tend to increase with age, and because of the increasing likelihood that better equipment will become available and make them obsolete. It is argued, therefore, that when an asset was purchased the probability that the earlier periods would benefit more than the later periods was taken into account, and that the depreciation method should reflect this. Such a line of reasoning leads to a method which charges a larger fraction of the cost as an expense of the early years than of the later years. This is called an *accelerated* method.[3]

Accelerated methods have been widely adopted since their use was permitted for income tax purposes beginning in 1954. A survey of the 1968 annual reports of 360 manufacturing companies indicated that 9 percent of the companies used the straight-line method for both financial statements and for income tax purposes, 37 percent used principally accelerated methods for both purposes, 42 percent used principally accelerated methods for tax purposes and straight-line methods for their financial statements, and 12 percent used a variety of methods or did not disclose the method that they used. There seems to be a continuing trend toward the use of accelerated methods for tax purposes and straight-line depreciation for financial statements. In 1968, as compared with 1967, 5 percent of the companies in the study changed from accelerated methods for both purposes to this practice.[4]

The two methods specifically mentioned in the 1954 tax law, the double declining-balance method and sum-of-years'-digits (or simply "years'-digits") method, are described below. The effect of either of these methods is to write off approximately two thirds of the cost in the first half of the asset's estimated life, as contrasted with the straight-line method under which, of course, half the cost is written off in each half of the asset's estimated life. Thus, if an accelerated method is used,

---

[3] An argument can also be made for an opposite approach, that is, charging a smaller fraction of the cost to the early years and a larger fraction to the later years. This leads to an *annuity method*. It is relatively uncommon.

[4] Unpublished study by Charles H. Roush, Harvard Business School.

depreciation expense is greater in the early years and less in the later years as compared with the straight-line method.

In the *double declining-balance method,* the depreciation for each year is found by applying a rate to the book value of the asset at the beginning of that year rather than to the original cost of the asset. *Book value* is cost less total depreciation accumulated up to that time. If the declining-balance method is used, the tax law permits the company to take *double* the rate allowed under the straight-line method, hence the name, double declining balance.

In the *years'-digits method,* the numbers 1, 2, 3 . . . *n* are added, where *n* is the estimated years of useful life. The depreciation rate each year is a fraction in which the denominator is the sum of these digits and the numerator is for the first year, *n;* for the second year, *n − 1;* for the third year *n − 2;* and so on. Assume, for example, a machine with an estimated life of 10 years. The sum of the numbers 1, 2, 3 . . . 10 is 55. Depreciation in the first year would be $^{10}\!/_{55}$ of the cost; in the second year, $^{9}\!/_{55}$; in the third year, $^{8}\!/_{55}$; and so on.

Illustration 6–1 is an example of the way these three methods work out for a machine costing $1,000 with an estimated life of 10 years and no salvage value. Illustration 6–2 shows the same depreciation patterns graphically.

As an incentive to modernize, taxpayers are permitted to deduct in the

Illustration 6–1

Year	Straight-Line (10% Rate)		Declining-Balance (20% Rate)		Years'-Digits		
	Book Value, 12/31	Annual Depreciation	Book Value, 12/31	Annual Depreciation	Rate	Book Value, 12/31	Annual Depreciation
0.........	$1,000	$ ...	$1,000.00	$	....	$1,000.00	$ ....
First.......	900	100	800.00	200.00	10/55	818.18	181.82
Second.....	800	100	640.00	160.00	9/55	654.54	163.64
Third......	700	100	512.00	128.00	8/55	509.09	145.45
Fourth.....	600	100	409.60	102.40	7/55	381.82	127.27
Fifth.......	500	100	327.68	81.92	6/55	272.73	109.09
Sixth......	400	100	262.14	65.54	5/55	181.82	90.91
Seventh....	300	100	209.71	52.43	4/55	109.09	72.73
Eighth.....	200	100	167.77	41.94	3/55	54.54	54.55
Ninth......	100	100	134.22	33.55	2/55	18.18	36.36
Tenth.....	0	100	107.38	26.84	1/55	0	18.18
Eleventh...	....	...	85.90	21.48	....	....	....
Twelfth....	....	...	68.72*	17.18	....	....	....
		$1,000		$931.28*			$1,000.00

* Under the strict declining-balance method, depreciation continues until the asset is disposed of or until the book value declines to salvage value. Many companies, however, switch from the declining-balance method to the straight-line method in the later years of life, and thus write off the entire cost in a specified number of years. This is permitted for tax purposes.

Illustration 6–2

PATTERNS OF ANNUAL DEPRECIATION

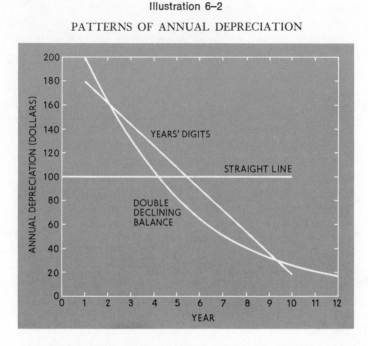

year of acquisition 20 percent of the cost of certain assets, in addition to regular depreciation for that year. This deduction is limited to a total of $2,000 per year. It is allowed only for tangible personal property (not buildings) with an estimated useful life of at least six years. It does not increase the total amount of depreciation that can be taken over the life of the asset; this remains equal to the net cost of the asset.

UNITS-OF-PRODUCTION METHOD. A third concept of depreciation views the asset as consisting of a bundle of service units, the cost of each unit being the total cost of the asset divided by the number of such units, and the depreciation charge for a period therefore being related to the number of units consumed in the period. This leads to the units-of-production method. If a truck has an estimated net cost of $12,000 and is expected to give service for 300,000 miles, depreciation would be charged at a rate of $0.04 per mile, the depreciation expense in a year in which the truck traveled 50,000 miles being $2,000.[5]

Choice of a Method

In deciding on the best depreciation method, tax considerations should be kept completely separate from financial accounting considerations. For

---

[5] An alternative method is to charge a decreasing rate as the number of miles increases, as in the accelerated methods.

tax purposes, the best method is that which minimizes the effect of taxes. Unless tax rates applicable to the business are expected to increase, this is usually one of the accelerated methods.

With respect to financial accounting, each of the concepts described above has its advocates. It should be emphasized that in a single business different methods can be used for different types of assets; for example, straight-line for buildings, accelerated for certain types of machinery and equipment, and units-of-production for other types. An essential require-ment also is that there *be* a method. The former practice of charging "whatever the income statement can stand" is indefensible.

If a company uses one depreciation method for income tax purposes and a different method for financial accounting, its taxable income will not match the income as measured by financial accounting. Under these circumstances, it must adjust its reported income tax expense, as explained on page 106.

Accounting for Depreciation

Assume that the Trantor Company purchased, on December 31, 1957, for $90,000, a building with an estimated useful life of 45 years and zero salvage value and that it has decided to depreciate this building on a straight-line basis, that is, $2,000 per year. Let us now consider how to record this depreciation on the accounting records.

It would be possible to reduce the asset value by $2,000 a year and to show on the balance sheet only the remaining amount, which at the end of 1958 would be $88,000; but this is *not* ordinarily done. Instead, a separate contra account is shown on the balance sheet for the accumulated amount of depreciation. This item is usually called *accumulated deprecia-tion*, or it may have some other name such as "allowance for deprecia-tion," "reserve for depreciation," and so on. (The last term is another example of a misleading use of the word "reserve"; the depreciation process does not "reserve" money or anything else.) Both the original cost and the accumulated depreciation figures appear on the balance sheet. The figures as of December 31, 1958, would look like this:

```
Building. . . . . . . . . . . . . . . . . . . . . . .   $90,000
   Less: Accumulated depreciation. . . . . . . . . . .     2,000
   Net . . . . . . . . . . . . . . . . . . . . . . . .   $88,000
```

As of December 31, 1959, another year's depreciation would be added, and the balance sheet would then show:

```
Building. . . . . . . . . . . . . . . . . . . . . . .   $90,000
   Less: Accumulated depreciation. . . . . . . . . . .     4,000
   Net . . . . . . . . . . . . . . . . . . . . . . . .   $86,000
```

The foregoing figures can be interpreted as follows:

Original cost of the building. $90,000
That portion of the cost charged to operations for all periods to date. . . .   4,000
That portion of the cost remaining to be charged to operations of future
    periods. $86,000

On the income statement, the expense item is usually labeled *depreciation expense*. In the income statement for 1958, this item for the Trantor Company would be $2,000 (disregarding depreciation on assets other than the building we are considering), and $2,000 would also appear in the income statement for 1959, 1960, and following years until either the building was disposed of or it was fully depreciated. Usually, the depreciation expense account includes depreciation for all types of fixed assets, but there must be a separate accumulated depreciation account for each category of fixed assets (building, machinery, office equipment, etc.) shown separately on the balance sheet, except for the category, land, since land does not depreciate.

The annual journal entry, which is one of the adjusting entries, would therefore be as follows:

```
Depreciation Expense. . . . . . . . . . . . . . . . .   2,000
      Accumulated Depreciation, Building. . . . . . . .            2,000
```

If the Trantor Company should use its building for more than 45 years, depreciation would cease to be accumulated at the end of the 45th year, since by then the total cost of the building would have been charged to expense. (If the fact that its life will be longer than 45 years became apparent earlier, the depreciation rate should be decreased so as to spread the remaining book value over the longer period.) Until the asset is disposed of, it is customary to continue to show the asset on the balance sheet. Thus, from December 31, 2002, onward, the balance sheet would show the following:

```
Building. . . . . . . . . . . . . . . . . . . . . . .   $90,000
      Less: Accumulated depreciation. . . . . . . . . . .    90,000
      Net . . . . . . . . . . . . . . . . . . . . . . . .   $     0
```

Often, half a year's depreciation is recorded in the year of acquisition and half a year's depreciation in the year of disposal no matter what the actual date of acquisition or disposal is, on the grounds that depreciation is a rough estimate and there is no point in attempting to figure it to exact fractions of a year. This practice, if followed consistently, is permitted for tax purposes. Similarly, if accounts are kept on a monthly basis, half a month's depreciation may be recorded in the month of acquisition.

Reporting in Financial Statements

The Accounting Principles Board requires that the income statement show the amount of depreciation expense as a separate item, and that the balance sheet show the balances of major depreciable assets by nature or function, accumulated depreciation by classes or in total, and a general description of the method(s) of computing depreciation for major classes of depreciable assets.[6]

The Investment Credit

In order to encourage purchases of machinery and equipment, the income tax statute (as of 1968) permits a credit against income tax of up to 7 percent of the cost of such assets, provided they are long-lived and meet certain other criteria. This is called the *investment credit*. The investment credit is a direct reduction in taxes; that is, if a company acquired $100,000 in equipment in 1968, it can deduct $7,000 from the income tax it would otherwise pay for 1968. Furthermore, the company can depreciate the full cost of the asset (less salvage value) over its useful life; it is not required to deduct the investment credit in calculating the amount to be depreciated.

The Accounting Principles Board approves either of two methods of handling the investment credit for accounting purposes. The first method, called the *cost-reduction* method, is to spread the effect of the investment credit over the useful life of the asset by making a reduction in the depreciation expense of each year of the useful life. The second method, called the *flow-through* method, reduces income tax expense, and hence increases net income, in the year in which the credit is taken.[7]

The accounting entries involved in both methods are shown in the following example:

> EXAMPLE: Assume that in December 1968 a company purchases $100,000 of machinery that qualifies for the investment credit, that the service life of these assets is 10 years and that (for simplicity) straight-line depreciation is to be used. The investment credit is $7,000, and this $7,000 is subtracted from the income tax liability in 1968.
>
> Under the cost-reduction method, the investment credit would be recorded, in effect, as:

```
Income Tax Liability. . . . . . . . . . . . . . . . .   7,000
    Machinery . . . . . . . . . . . . . . . . . . . . .         7,000
```

Note that net income for 1968 is unaffected by this entry. In 1969 and subsequent years depreciation expense would be calculated on a net cost of $93,000, rather than $100,000, and would therefore be $9,300 per year. This has the effect of increasing net income $700 in each of the next 10 years, as compared with what the net income would have been had the depreciation expense been $10,000 per year.

---

[6] *Opinions of the Accounting Principles Board No. 12,* December, 1967.

[7] Grady, *op. cit.,* pp. 137–47.

Under the flow-through method, the investment credit would be recorded in 1968 as:

```
Income Tax Liability. . . . . . . . . . . . . . . .    7,000
    Income Tax Expense. . . . . . . . . . . . . . .          7,000
```

This has the effect of increasing 1968 income by $7,000.

DISPOSAL OF FIXED ASSETS

Suppose that at the end of 10 years the Trantor Company sells its building. At that time, $1\%_{45}$ of the original cost, or $20,000, will have been built up in the Accumulated Depreciation account, and the net book value of the building will be $70,000. If the building is sold for $70,000 cash, the accounts are changed, as follows: Cash is increased by $70,000; the Building account is decreased by $90,000, and Accumulated Depreciation is decreased by $20,000, which is the amount of depreciation accumulated up to that time. The entry is as follows:

```
Cash. . . . . . . . . . . . . . . . . . . . . . .    70,000
Accumulated Depreciation. . . . . . . . . . . . .    20,000
    Building. . . . . . . . . . . . . . . . . . .          90,000
```

This has the effect of eliminating from the accounts both the original cost of the building and the accumulated depreciation thereon.

If the building were sold for less than $70,000, say $60,000, the transaction would be recorded as follows: Cash is increased by $60,000, the Building account is decreased by $90,000, Accumulated Depreciation is decreased by $20,000, and an account, Loss on the Sale of Fixed Assets, or some similar title, is set up, as in the following entry:

```
Cash. . . . . . . . . . . . . . . . . . . . . . .    60,000
Accumulated Depreciation. . . . . . . . . . . . .    20,000
Loss on Sale of Fixed Assets. . . . . . . . . . .    10,000
    Building. . . . . . . . . . . . . . . . . . .          90,000
```

Note that the effect on the Building and Accumulated Depreciation accounts is identical with that in the previous illustration: the amounts relating to this building disappear. The loss is a decrease in owners' equity, reflecting the fact that the total depreciation expense recorded for the preceding 10 years was less than what we now know to have been the actual net cost of the building over that period of time. The actual net cost turns out to have been $30,000, whereas the total depreciation expense charged has amounted to only $20,000.

Since the depreciation expense as originally recorded turns out to have been incorrect, the Retained Earnings account which reflects the net of all revenue and expenses is also incorrect, and there is therefore some logic in closing the Loss on Sale of Fixed Assets account directly to Retained Earnings, thus correcting the error contained therein. Nevertheless, the "all-inclusive income" principle requires that unless the loss is extraordinarily large, it be shown as an expense on the income statement of the current period.

If an asset is sold for more than its book value, the entries correspond to those described above. The account, Gain on the Sale of Fixed Assets, is usually classified as nonoperating revenue on the income statement.

A trade-in involves the disposal of an asset, and the asset traded in is treated in the accounting records exactly like the sale of the building described above; that is, both its cost and its accumulated depreciation are removed from the books. As mentioned in a preceding section, a problem may arise in determining the proper "sales" value to use in recording this transaction. For income tax purposes, however, a trade-in is treated quite differently. When one asset is exchanged for another of "like kind," no gain or loss is ordinarily recognized for tax purposes. The definition of "like kind" and the circumstances under which this principle is applicable are intricate, and expert tax advice is needed on all except the most routine fixed asset exchanges.

Debits to Accumulated Depreciation

If a machine is given an unusual major overhaul which makes it "as good as new," the cost of this overhaul is sometimes debited to Accumulated Depreciation rather than to Maintenance Expense on the ground that the overhaul has actually canceled or offset some of the accumulated depreciation. Or, it can be argued that the overhaul has extended the useful life of the machine, and that the depreciation accumulated up to the time of overhaul is therefore excessive. In theory, if the estimated useful life has changed, the depreciation rate should be recalculated and the accounts changed to reflect the new estimate of useful life; but in practice, charging the overhaul to Accumulated Depreciation may have approximately the same effect.

GROUP AND COMPOSITE DEPRECIATION

The procedure described above related to a single fixed asset, one building. To find the total depreciation expense for a whole category of assets, this procedure could be repeated for each single asset, and the total depreciation for all the assets in the category would then be recorded by one journal entry. This is the procedure used in many businesses.

An alternative procedure is to treat several assets together rather than making the calculation for each one separately. If similar assets with approximately the same useful life, such as all typewriters or all general-purpose lathes, are treated together, the process is called *group* depreciation. If dissimilar assets are treated together, the process is called *composite* depreciation.

The depreciation rate in composite depreciation is a weighted-average rate, the weights being the dollar amounts of assets in each of the useful-life categories. All the production equipment in a plant, for example, might be included in a single composite account, even though the useful lives of the various items of equipment were not the same. The *Depreciation Guidelines* referred to above give a single depreciation rate for all the machinery and equipment in most types of manufacturing plants (e.g., 11 years for the machinery and equipment in a chemical plant). These are composite rates.

The annual depreciation expense under group or composite depreciation is computed in a manner similar to that described above for an individual asset. If the straight-line method is used, for example, the depreciation rate is applied to the total cost of the whole group of assets.

The accumulation of depreciation does not stop when one item in the group reaches its estimated useful life, however, but continues indefinitely unless it becomes apparent that the accumulation is too large or too small for the whole group of assets. In this case, the depreciation rate is changed. For tax purposes, the Internal Revenue Service has established a set of maximum "reserve ratios" for various asset categories, and companies are penalized if they exceed these ratios. A reserve ratio is the ratio of accumulated depreciation to the cost of the assets in the group.

If a group or composite method is used, no gain or loss is recognized when an individual asset is sold or otherwise disposed of. The asset account is credited for the cost, and the difference between cost and the sales proceeds is simply debited to Accumulated Depreciation. This procedure assumes that gains on some sales are offset by losses on others.

SIGNIFICANCE OF DEPRECIATION

The amount shown as accumulated depreciation on the balance sheet does not represent the "accumulation" of any tangible thing; it is merely that portion of the assets' original cost that has been already charged off against income.

Occasionally a company does set aside money for the specific purpose of purchasing new assets, and this process is sometimes called "funding depreciation." This transaction is completely separate from the depreciation mechanism described above. If depreciation is funded, cash or securities are physically segregated; that is, they are set aside in such a way that they cannot be used in the regular operation of the business (for example, a special bank account may be created). This fact is reflected on the balance sheet by an asset titled "New Building Fund," or some similar name, the offsetting entry being a credit to Cash. This practice is not common and is mentioned here only to emphasize, by contrast, the point that the depreciation process itself is *not* a means of automatically creating a fund for the replacement of assets.

There is a widespread belief that, in some mysterious way, depreciation does represent money, specifically, money that can be used to purchase new assets. Depreciation is *not* money; the money that the business has is shown by the balance in its Cash account.

EXAMPLE: This quotation is from a well-known publication: "Most large companies draw much of the cash flow they employ for expanding and modernizing their operations from their depreciation reserves." This statement is not true in anything remotely approaching a literal sense. Possibly the author intended some figurative, rather than literal, meaning, but it is difficult to imagine how the statement could be true in even a figurative sense.

There is also a widespread belief that the book value of assets is related to their real value, and this is equally erroneous.

EXAMPLE: An auditor's report included the following statement: "Our inspection of insurance policies in force at the close of the year disclosed that the plant assets, on the basis of book values, were amply protected against fire." Such a statement has little if any significance. What the management wants to know is whether the insurance policies equal the *actual cash value* of the assets, and this is unlikely to correspond to their *book value*.

Concluding Comment

The key to a practical understanding of depreciation is a sentence from the AICPA statement quoted earlier: *Depreciation is a process of allocation, not of valuation.* Depreciation expense does *not* represent the shrinkage in real value during an accounting period; physically, the machine may be as useful and as valuable at the end of the period as it was at the beginning. Neither does the net book value represent the market value of the assets on hand. Depreciation expense is a write-off of a portion of the *cost* of the asset, and it follows that the net book value of fixed assets reported on the balance sheet represents only that portion of the original cost of the fixed asset which has *not yet* been charged to expense.

No one really knows how long an asset will last or what its residual value will be at the end of its life. Without this knowledge, the depreciation figure is necessarily an estimate.

OTHER ASPECTS OF TANGIBLE ASSETS

Depletion

Natural resources such as coal, oil, other minerals, and timber are called *wasting assets*. The process of writing off the cost of these fixed assets to expenses in the accounting periods benefited is called *depletion*. The objective is the the same as that for depreciation: to amortize the cost in some systematic manner over the asset's useful life. The unit-of-production method is ordinarily used. For example, if an oil property cost $500,000 and is estimated to contain 1 million barrels of oil, the depletion rate is 50 cents per barrel; the total depletion for a year in which 80,000 barrels of oil were produced would be $40,000.

For income tax purposes, however, the depletion allowance usually bears no relation to cost; rather, it is a percentage of revenue. The permitted percentage (as of 1969) varies from 5 percent on clay, gravel, and other common materials to 27½ percent on oil and gas. This is perhaps the most clear-cut example of an income tax provision that is inconsistent with generally accepted accounting principles. Advocates of this provision in the tax law claim that it stimulates exploration for and development of new supplies of natural resources and is therefore in the national interest.

Accretion and Appreciation

Accretion is the increase in value of timberland, cattle, and other agricultural products that arises through the natural process of growth. Since accretion does not represent realized revenue, it is ordinarily not recognized in the accounts, although the *costs* incurred in the growing process may be added to the asset value, just as is done in the case of costs incurred in the manufacture of products.

Appreciation is also an increase of value and is therefore *not* the opposite of depreciation, which is a write-off of *cost*. Appreciation of either fixed assets or inventory is recognized in the accounts only under highly unusual circumstances; for example, if a new owner took over a business and an appraisal disclosed that the current market value of fixed assets was substantially above their book value, it is conceivable that the asset values would be written up to their current value. Generally, however, increases in value are recognized in the accounts only when revenue is realized, whereas expiration of cost is recognized when it occurs.

INTANGIBLE ASSETS

Intangible long-lived assets, such as goodwill, organization cost (i.e., cost incurred to get a business started), trademarks, and patents are usually converted to expenses over a number of accounting periods. The periodic write-off is specifically called *amortization*, although the word "amortization" is also used in the broad sense of any write-off of a cost over a period of years. The amortization of intangible assets is essentially the same process as the depreciation of tangible assets. Amortizations is ordinarily recorded as a credit directly to the asset account, not to a separate account analogous to Accumulated Depreciation.

The Accounting Principles Board suggests that these intangibles be classified into two categories:

(a) Those having a term of existence limited by law, regulation, or agreement, or by their nature (such as patents, copyrights, leases, licenses, franchises for a fixed term, and goodwill as to which there is evidence of limited duration);

(b) Those having no such limited term of existence and as to which there is, at the time of acquisition, no indication of limited life (such as goodwill generally, going value, trade names, secret processes, subscription lists, perpetual franchises, and organization costs.)[8]

The treatment recommended for each category is as follows:

The cost of the type (a) intangibles should be amortized by systematic charges in the income statement over the period benefited, as in the case of other assets having a limited period of usefulness. . . .

When it becomes reasonably evident that the term of existence of a type (b) intangible has become limited and that it has therefore become a type (a) intangible, its cost should be amortized by systematic charges in the income statement over the estimated remaining period of usefulness.[9]

Although the above statement does not sanction such a treatment, many companies *do* write off "type (b)" intangibles (those that do not have a definitely limited life) over one or more accounting periods. Organization cost is frequently handled in this manner, for although the "benefit" of organizing a company may be said, in a sense, to extend over the whole life of the company, it would be a considerable bother, with little offsetting advantage to anyone, to hold this cost as an asset on the balance sheet year after year. There is, by definition, no logical way of determining over how many periods such assets should be written off. In some cases, they are written off as an expense in the year of acquisition. Other companies choose to write them off over some fairly short period, such as 5 or 10 years, with the choice of the time period depending on the amount that safely can be charged without having a material effect on income.

These practices have been heavily influenced by the doctrine of conservatism, although custom has a great deal to do with them also. Customarily, for example, advertising expenditures are not capitalized even though it may be quite clear that these expenditures benefit future rather than current periods. Often, these practices are justified on the grounds that the future benefits are so uncertain that an attempt to estimate them is unwarranted. With respect to the argument for conservatism, it should

---

[8] Grady, *op. cit.*, p. 262.
[9] *Ibid.*, p. 263.

be pointed out that a practice that understates asset values and current income inevitably overstates future income.

Incidentally, some companies emphasize their conservatism by showing intangible assets at a nominal amount on the balance sheet, thus:

Goodwill, patents, and other intangibles..................$1.00

This practice stems from the pre-1930's when some companies *watered* their assets by capitalizing a wide variety of intangibles of dubious value and hiding these values in with other asset items. Companies that followed the more conservative practice of writing off intangibles as acquired have indicated this fact to the reader of the balance sheet by the above wording. Since current practice requires that intangibles be reported as a separate item if they are material in amount, the absence of any such item means that no material amount of intangibles is being carried as an asset, and the above method of presentation is not as necessary as formerly.

The *useful* life of a "type (a)" intangible may be shorter than its legal life; if so, the cost of the asset is written off over the shorter period. For example, although a patent is legally valid for 17 years, the company may decide that technological change or other forces may make it obsolete within a shorter period of time; if such is the case, the patent may be written off over 15 years, 10 years, or even less.

Leasehold improvements are the costs incurred by the lessee to improve leased property. Since, as a matter of law, any remaining value of these improvements reverts to the owner when the leased property is given up, the benefits to the lessee automatically end when he gives up the leased property, and the cost must therefore be written off over the time he expects to have the use of the property.

SUMMARY

Fixed assets are originally recorded at their acquisition cost, including costs involved in making them ready to provide service. This cost is charged off as depreciation expense in some systematic manner over the periods in which the asset is expected to be useful. The method selected may charge an equal amount each year, a larger amount in early years than in late years, or an amount that depends on usage. A corresponding reduction is made in the asset amount. Upon disposition, both the cost and the accumulated depreciation are removed from the accounts, and any gain or loss is reported separately, usually on the income statement.

Intangible assets are amortized by a similar process. Although the write-off of intangibles that have no limited life is not officially approved, many companies do amortize such assets on the grounds of conservatism.

CHAPTER 7

INCOME MEASUREMENT IN MANUFACTURING COMPANIES

Manufacturing companies perform different functions from those performed by merchandise trading companies (e.g., retail stores, wholesalers, distributors), and there is a corresponding difference between methods of accounting for the cost of goods sold in the two types of companies. This chapter describes the measurement of cost of goods sold in manufacturing companies. A manufacturing company has as a major function the conversion of raw materials into finished goods. In any company, cost of goods sold is the total of the purchase price plus conversion costs, if any, of the products that are sold. The manufacturer, therefore, includes in cost of goods sold the cost of raw material used, the cost of labor, and other costs incurred in the manufacture of the goods that are sold. The difference between accounting for the cost of goods sold in a merchandising company and in a manufacturing company arises because the merchandising company usually has no conversion costs; thus, its cost of goods sold is practically the same as the price that the company paid for the products that it sells.

The measurement of cost of goods sold is therefore more complicated in a manufacturing company than in a merchandising company. In a merchandising company, this cost is normally obtained directly from invoices. In a manufacturing company it must be obtained by collecting and aggregating the several elements of manufacturing cost.

Both manufacturing and merchandising companies usually have general and administrative expenses. Generally, the manufacturer is also a merchandiser and incurs selling expenses in disposing of his goods. These selling expenses, along with general and administrative and financial costs, appear on the income statement of a manufacturing company in the same manner as in a merchandising firm, that is, below the gross profit figure.

FLOW OF COSTS

Elements of Cost

Illustration 7–1 shows elements of cost that are frequently considered in determining the total cost of a manufactured product. These are described below.

Illustration 7–1

ELEMENTS OF COST

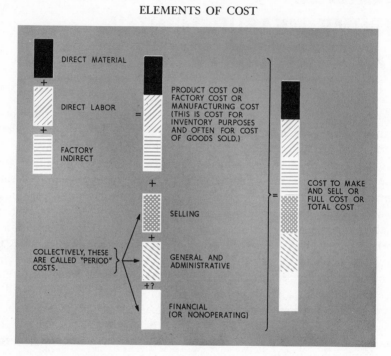

DIRECT MATERIALS. Direct materials (sometimes called "stores") are materials which actually enter into and become part of the finished product. They are to be distinguished from *supplies*, which are materials used in the operation of the business but not directly in the product itself. Direct material costs include the cost of inward freight, and many companies also include storage and handling costs. Purchase discounts are often deducted from the invoice price of goods purchased.

DIRECT LABOR. A second element of manufacturing cost is direct labor, which is labor applied to convert raw material into the finished product. Direct labor costs are those which can be specifically identified with a product or which vary so closely with the number of products produced that a direct relationship is presumed to be present. The wages and related costs of workers who assemble parts into a finished product, or who operate machines in the process of production, or who work on the product with tools would be considered as direct labor cost.

FACTORY INDIRECT. The third category of manufacturing costs is factory indirect, sometimes termed "burden," or, simply, "overhead." Factory indirect includes all manufacturing costs other than raw materials and direct labor. One such element is indirect labor, which represents wages and salaries earned by employees, such as foremen, truckmen, and janitors, who do not work directly on the product itself but whose services are related to the process of production. Factory indirect also includes such costs as heat, light, power, maintenance, supplies, and depreciation, taxes, and insurance on the assets used in the manufacturing process.

Selling costs or *distribution costs* or *marketing costs* are those incurred in an effort to makes sales and those costs incurred in storing the completed product and in transferring it to the customer. These costs incurred "beyond the factory door" include warehousing costs, billing costs, and transportation costs.

General and administrative costs is a catchall classification to cover items not included in the above categories. Such items are as follows: costs incurred in the general and executive offices; research, development, and engineering costs (which may be wholly or partly included in factory overhead); public relations costs (often included in selling); donations; and miscellaneous items.

Financial costs include interest and other costs incurred in connection with borrowed capital. Sometimes these costs are included in general and administrative costs, although they are often collected separately and treated as nonoperating expenses.

As Illustration 7–1 indicates, the cost figure which is used for inventory valuation and cost of goods sold is typically the factory cost, that is, the sum of direct material, direct labor, and factory indirect costs.

Product Costs and Period Costs

Elements of cost that are included in the cost of a product are called *product* costs; other elements of cost are called *period* costs. There is considerable disagreement among accountants as to where the line between these two types of costs should be drawn.

At one extreme there are those who view a business as performing only two functions, production and distribution. They therefore assign all costs to one of these functions, and thus assign a large fraction of general and administrative costs to product costs. Selling costs, however, are never included in product costs.

The great majority of companies define product costs as the sum of direct labor, direct material, and factory indirect, excluding general and administrative costs, as indicated in Illustration 7–1. Among these companies there are differences in the treatment of specific items. Some companies include the cost of such functions as manufacturing administration, personnel and industrial relations, plant protection, and accounting in factory indirect and hence in product costs; other companies include part of the cost of some or all of these functions; and still others exclude all of them.

At the other extreme are the advocates of "direct costing," a procedure in which all fixed indirect costs are excluded from product costs. Although a direct cost system may provide useful information for management, it is not an accepted procedure for financial accounting.[1]

The way in which a manufacturing company classifies its costs into period costs and product costs can have an important effect on its reported net income. Period costs are expenses in the accounting period in which they are incurred, whereas product costs add to the cost of the product and do not have an impact on net income until the product has been sold, which may well be a later accounting period than the period in which the costs were incurred. This point is discussed further in Chapter 13.

In view of these wide variations in practice, the reader of financial statements needs to know what types of cost a company has decided to include in its inventory if he is to understand what its statements mean.

Inventory Accounts

A manufacturing company typically has three types of inventory accounts: raw materials, goods in process, and finished goods. *Raw Materials Inventory* shows the cost of the raw materials on hand. *Goods in Process* (or *Work in Process*) *Inventory* shows the costs accumulated for those products on which production has been started but not yet completed as of the end of the accounting period. This includes the direct material, direct labor, and factory indirect costs assigned to such products. *Finished Goods Inventory* shows the cost of products that have been manufactured but not yet sold. This account is comparable to the Merchandise Inventory account in a trading company.

---

[1] AICPA *Accounting Research Bulletin No. 43* states: "As applied to inventories, cost means in principle the sum of the applicable expenditures and charges directly or indirectly incurred in bringing an article to its existing condition and location . . . the exclusion of all overheads from inventory costs does not constitute an accepted accounting procedure." Paul Grady, *Inventory of Generally Accepted Accounting Principles* (AICPA, 1965), pp. 245–46.

The Account Flow Chart

The flow of costs through the inventory accounts, ending with their appearance on the income statement as cost of goods sold, is described in the next section. As an aid in understanding this flow, the concept of the account flow chart is introduced. Such a flow chart consists of the accounts used in the system, shown in T account form, with lines indicating the flow of figures from one account to another.

Most of the accounts associated with the manufacturing process are either asset accounts (principally inventory accounts) or expense accounts. (For some purposes, the general term "cost account" is useful, but a cost account is always classifiable either as an asset, if the cost will benefit a future period, or as an expense, if the benefit has expired.) A characteristic of both asset and expense accounts is that increases are shown on the debit side and decreases are shown on the credit side. Since a line on a flow chart indicating a transfer "from" one account "to" another account signifies that the first account is being decreased and the second account is being increased, it follows that the typical line on a flow chart of the manufacturing process leads from the credit side of one account to the debit side of another. In addition to the lines designating "flow," other lines indicate debit and credit entries that are generated in the production process; an example is the entry for the acquisition of raw material, which is a debit to Raw Materials Inventory and a credit to Accounts Payable.

Flow of Costs

Illustration 7–2 illustrates the flow-chart concept and shows the essential cost flows in a manufacturing company. This flow chart contains a hypothetical set of figures for a month's operation in a small company manufacturing smoking pipes. The cycle of operations shown therein may be explained as follows:

1. During the month, $3,000 of raw material was purchased on open account, $4,200 of other assets were purchased, and $15,000 of accounts payable were paid.
2. During the month, raw material costing $4,000 (principally briar wood, hard rubber blanks for stems, and filters) was withdrawn from inventory and sent to the shop to be worked on. This decreased Raw Materials Inventory and increased Goods in Process.
3. During the month, men worked on this material and fashioned it into pipes. The amount which they earned, $2,500, was added to the value of the Goods in Process, and the resulting liability was credited to Wages Payable.

Illustration 7-2

FLOW CHART OF A PIPE COMPANY

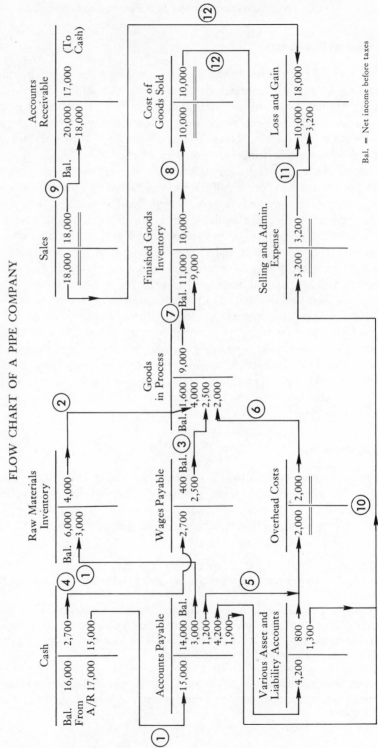

NOTE: Circled numbers refer to events described in the text.

4. The men were paid $2,700. This decreased the liability account, Wages Payable, and also decreased Cash. (The payment of wages also involved social security taxes, withholding taxes, and certain other complications; these matters have been omitted from this introductory diagram.)

5. Factory overhead costs were incurred during the month in the amount of $2,000. Of the total, $1,200 was ascertained from current invoices for such things as electricity and telephone bills, or current earnings of indirect labor and supervisors, so the offsetting credits were to Accounts Payable. The remaining $800 represented depreciation, the charge-off of prepaid expenses, and other credits to asset accounts or obligations credited to liabilities other than Accounts Payable. All of these items are here summed up in the general account, Overhead Costs, but in practice they are usually shown in separate overhead cost accounts, one for each type of cost.

6. Since the overhead cost is a part of the cost of the pipes that were worked on during the month, the total overhead incurred was transferred to Goods in Process.

7. Pipes whose total cost was $9,000 were completed during the month and were transferred to Finished Goods Inventory. This resulted in a decrease in Goods in Process and an increase in Finished Goods Inventory.

8. Pipes with a cost of $10,000 were sold during the month. Physically, these pipes were removed from inventory and shipped to the customer. On the accounting records, this was reflected by a credit to Finished Goods Inventory and a debit to Cost of Goods Sold.

9. At the same time, and for the same products, sales revenue of $18,000 was created, and this was shown on the books by a credit to Sales and a debit to Accounts Receivable. Later on, these receivables were paid, thus resulting in a debit to Cash and completing the accounting cycle. It should be particularly noted that the Sales transaction described here and the Cost of Goods Sold transaction described in Item 8 related to the same physical products, the same pipes. The difference between the balances in Sales and Cost of Goods Sold, $8,000, therefore represented the gross margin earned on products sold during the month.

10. During the month $3,200 selling and administrative expenses were incurred, $1,900 of which represented credits to Accounts Payable and $1,300 credits to various asset and liability accounts.

11. Since these were expenses applicable to the current period, Selling and Administrative Expense was closed to Loss and Gain.

12. The balances in Sales and Cost of Goods Sold were also closed to Loss and Gain, and Loss and Gain then showed the net profit for the period. (This is a somewhat oversimplified statement, for income taxes and certain nonoperating and financial items which would appear in many income statements have not been considered.)

A manufacturing company can find its cost of goods sold in either of two ways: (1) directly, or (2) by deduction.

In the direct method, the company keeps track of the costs that are accumulated on each product as it moves through the factory, and the total cost thus accumulated becomes the cost of goods sold in the accounting period in which the product is sold. The techniques for arriving at this cost are part of the branch of accounting that is called *cost accounting*. Since cost accounting data are also used for purposes other than the preparation of financial statements, a description of cost accounting is deferred to Chapter 13.

The process of deduction used to find the cost of goods sold in a manufacturing company is essentially similar to, but more complicated than, the corresponding process in a merchandising company that was described in Chapter 5. The increased complexity can readily be seen by comparing the income statement for a merchandising company in Illustration 7–3 with the income statement for a manufacturing company in Illustration 7–4.

Illustration 7–3

MALONE STORES, INCORPORATED

Income Statement, 1968

Net sales.			$666,720
Cost of goods sold:			
Beginning inventory, January 1		$184,350	
Merchandise purchases.	$454,920		
Freight and express.	30,210	485,130	
Cost of goods available for sale		$669,480	
Less: Ending inventory, December 31. . . .		193,710	
Cost of goods sold			475,770
Gross profit			$190,950
Selling, administrative, and general expenses:			
Salaries and wages		$ 88,170	
Employment taxes and benefits.		4,623	
Rent		24,390	
Light, heat, and power		8,840	
State and local taxes and licenses		5,130	
Depreciation		4,140	
Repairs.		2,110	
Other expenses		16,677	154,080
Profit from operations			$ 36,870
Other revenue.			5,810
Net income before, taxes.			$ 42,680
Provision for income tax			15,120
Net Income			$ 27,560

In order to deduce cost of goods sold, the amounts for each inventory account as of the end of the period must be determined on the basis of a physical inventory. In the description that follows, these amounts are merely stated. In practice, however, the problem of assigning a reasonable value to the partially completed items in Goods in Process Inventory and to the completed items in Finished Goods Inventory without a cost accounting system can be formidable.

Illustration 7–4

ALFMAN MANUFACTURING COMPANY

Income Statement, 1968

et sales.			$669,100
ost of goods sold:			
Raw materials cost:			
Raw materials inventory, January 1		$154,300	
Purchases.	$263,520		
Plus: Freight-in	9,400		
Total purchases.		272,920	
Total inventory and purchases.		$427,220	
Less: Raw materials inventory, December 31		163,120	
Cost of materials used			$264,100
Direct labor cost.			150,650
Manufacturing overhead cost:			
Indirect labor		$ 23,750	
Factory heat, light, and power		89,500	
Factory supplies used.		22,100	
Insurance and taxes.		8,100	
Depreciation--plant and equipment.		35,300	
Total manufacturing overhead cost. . . .		178,750	
Total manufacturing costs.		$593,500	
Add: Goods in process inventory, January 1 .		18,800	
Total.		$612,300	
Less: Goods in process inventory, December 31		42,600	
Cost of goods manufactured		$569,700	
Add: Finished goods inventory, January 1 . .		69,200	
Cost of goods available for sale		$638,900	
Less: Finished goods inventory, December 31.		66,400	
ost of goods sold			572,500
ross profit			$ 96,600
elling and administrative expenses:			
Selling expense.		$ 38,500	
Depreciation--selling.		3,200	
Administrative expense		32,200	73,900
et operating profit			$ 22,700
ther revenue.			15,300
et income before taxes.			$ 38,000
rovision for income tax			12,640
et Income			$ 25,360

In order to find the cost of goods sold by the deduction process, two other costs must be deduced first—the cost of raw materials used and the cost of goods manufactured. A set of journal entries for finding these costs is given and explained below. They relate to the income statement in Illustration 7–4 and are diagrammed in a flow chart, Illustration 7–5.

Raw Materials Used

In determining the cost of raw materials used, the assumption is made that the amount of raw materials used is the difference between the materials available for use during the period (which is the total of the

Illustration 7-5

FLOW OF FIGURES THROUGH THE ACCOUNTS

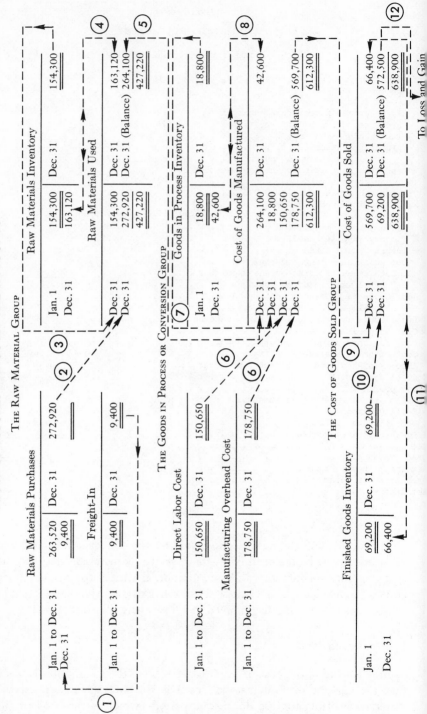

beginning inventory and the net purchases) and the ending inventory. This assumption does not take into account any waste or spoilage of material that might have occurred. In practice, waste and spoilage is either disregarded or is collected separately and removed from material costs by crediting Raw Materials Inventory and debiting a manufacturing cost account.

This calculation can be made in a temporary account, Raw Materials Used. The journal entries that bring the necessary data to this account are as follows:

(1)

```
Raw Materials Purchases . . . . . . . . . . . . . . .    9,400
     Freight-In. . . . . . . . . . . . . . . . . . . .            9,400
     To find net purchases.
```

(2)

```
Raw Materials Used. . . . . . . . . . . . . . . . . 272,920
     Raw Materials Purchases . . . . . . . . . . . .          272,920
     To transfer net purchases.
```

(3)

```
Raw Materials Used. . . . . . . . . . . . . . . . . 154,300
     Raw Materials Inventory . . . . . . . . . . . .          154,300
     To add the beginning inventory.
```

(4)

```
Raw Materials Inventory . . . . . . . . . . . . . . 163,120
     Raw Materials Used. . . . . . . . . . . . . . .          163,120
     To deduct ending inventory from raw material used
     and to set up this inventory as an asset.
```

These entries can be read as follows: (1) The net amount of purchases for the year is found by closing related accounts into the purchases account. (2) Net purchases is closed to Raw Materials Used. (3) The beginning inventory of raw material is added, thus giving the total amount of raw material available for use. (4) The amount of raw material on hand at the end of the period is subtracted, and the balance in Raw Material Used is assumed to have been used in the manufacturing process.

Cost of Goods Manufactured

The sum of raw materials used, direct labor, and manufacturing overhead, together comprise the total amount of cost added to Goods in Process Inventory during the period. Given the amount in Goods in Process Inventory at the beginning of the period and the amount remaining at the end of the period, the *cost of goods manufactured,* that is, the goods completed and transferred to Finished Goods Inventory, can be deduced. Again, the assumption is made that if the goods are no longer in

Goods in Process Inventory, they must have been completed and transferred to Finished Goods Inventory. To apply this line of reasoning, another temporary account, Cost of Goods Manufactured, is created, and the following journal entries are made:

(5)

```
Cost of Goods Manufactured. . . . . . . . . . . . . 264,100
     Raw Materials Used. . . . . . . . . . . . . . .           264,100
   To transfer raw materials used.
```

(6)

```
Cost of Goods Manufactured. . . . . . . . . . . . . 329,400
     Direct Labor Cost . . . . . . . . . . . . . . .           150,650
     Indirect Labor. . . . . . . . . . . . . . . . .            23,750
     Factory Heat, Light, and Power. . . . . . . . .            89,500
     Factory Supplies Used . . . . . . . . . . . . .            22,100
     Insurance and Taxes . . . . . . . . . . . . . .             8,100
     Depreciation--Plant and Equipment . . . . . . .            35,300
   To add direct labor and manufacturing overhead.
```

(7)

```
Cost of Goods Manufactured. . . . . . . . . . . . .  18,800
     Goods in Process Inventory. . . . . . . . . . .            18,800
   To add the beginning inventory.
```

(8)

```
Goods in Process Inventory. . . . . . . . . . . . .  42,600
     Cost of Goods Manufactured. . . . . . . . . . .            42,600
   To deduct the ending inventory from Cost of Goods
   Manufactured and to set up this inventory as an
   asset.
```

Cost of Goods Sold

Having determined the cost of goods manufactured, the cost of goods sold is found by adding this to the beginning Finished Goods Inventory so as to find the total amount available for sale, and then subtracting the ending Finished Goods Inventory. As with a merchandising company, the assumption is that if the merchandise is not in inventory, it has been sold. The following journal entries are made:

(9)

```
Cost of Goods Sold. . . . . . . . . . . . . . . . . 569,700
     Cost of Goods Manufactured. . . . . . . . . . .           569,700
   To transfer goods completed.
```

(10)

```
Cost of Goods Sold. . . . . . . . . . . . . . . . .  69,200
     Finished Goods Inventory. . . . . . . . . . . .            69,200
   To add the beginning inventory.
```

(11)

```
Finished Goods Inventory. . . . . . . . . . . . . . 66,400
    Cost of Goods Sold. . . . . . . . . . . . . . . .          66,400
    To deduct the ending inventory from Cost of Goods
    Sold and to set up this inventory as an asset.
```

The balance in the Cost of Goods Sold account is the cost of goods sold during the year, and this is now closed to Loss and Gain:

(12)

```
Loss and Gain . . . . . . . . . . . . . . . . . . . 572,500
    Cost of Goods Sold. . . . . . . . . . . . . . .            572,500
```

Condensed Closing Process

The form of closing process that has just been described in detail was chosen so as to make it possible to relate the accounting entries to the actual events that occur in a manufacturing company: the acquisition of raw material, the conversion of this material into a manufactured product, the temporary storage of this finished product, and its eventual shipment to customers. The identical end result would be achieved if all the separate entries described were compressed into three entries which (1) closed all beginning inventory balances; (2) set up new inventory balances; and (3) closed purchases, direct labor, and manufacturing overhead accounts. The three entries would be as follows:

(1)

```
Cost of Goods Sold. . . . . . . . . . . . . . . . . 242,300
    Raw Materials Inventory . . . . . . . . . . . . .          154,300
    Goods in Process Inventory. . . . . . . . . . . .           18,800
    Finished Goods Inventory. . . . . . . . . . . . .           69,200
    To close beginning inventories.
```

(2)

```
Raw Materials Inventory . . . . . . . . . . . . . . 163,120
Goods in Process Inventory. . . . . . . . . . . . .  42,600
Finished Goods Inventory. . . . . . . . . . . . . .  66,400
    Cost of Goods Sold. . . . . . . . . . . . . . .            272,120
    To enter ending inventories.
```

(3)

```
Cost of Goods Sold. . . . . . . . . . . . . . . . . 602,320
    Purchases . . . . . . . . . . . . . . . . . . . .          263,520
    Freight-In. . . . . . . . . . . . . . . . . . . .            9,400
    Direct Labor. . . . . . . . . . . . . . . . . . .          150,650
    Indirect Labor. . . . . . . . . . . . . . . . . .           23,750
    Factory Heat, Light, and Power. . . . . . . . . .           89,500
    Factory Supplies Used . . . . . . . . . . . . . .           22,100
    Insurance and Taxes . . . . . . . . . . . . . . .            8,100
    Depreciation--Plant and Equipment . . . . . . . .           35,300
    To close costs.
```

The transfer of the Cost of Goods Sold to Loss and Gain would be made exactly as before:

```
Loss and Gain . . . . . . . . . . . . . . . . . . . . 572,500
    Cost of Goods Sold. . . . . . . . . . . . . . . .           572,500
```

Alternative Income Statement Format

The income statement given in Illustration 7–4 is useful in showing the steps involved in calculating the cost of goods sold. It is, however, a cumbersome and complicated looking set of figures. Illustration 7–6 re-

Illustration 7–6

ALFMAN MANUFACTURING COMPANY

Income Statement, 1968
(Alternative Format)

Net sales			$669,100
Manufacturing costs:			
Raw material costs:			
Purchases	$272,920		
Increase in raw materials inventory	8,820		
Cost of materials used.		$264,100	
Direct labor cost		150,650	
Manufacturing overhead cost:			
Indirect labor.	$23,750		
Factory heat, light, and power. . .	89,500		
Factory supplies used	22,100		
Insurance and taxes	8,100		
Depreciation--plant and equipment .	35,300		
Total manufacturing overhead cost		178,750	
Total manufacturing cost. . . .		$593,500	
Changes in inventory:			
Increase in goods in process.	$23,800		
Decrease in finished goods.	2,800		
Net increase in inventory		21,000	
Cost of goods sold.			572,500
Gross profit.			$ 96,600
Selling and administrative expenses:			
Selling expense		$ 38,500	
Depreciation--selling		3,200	
Administrative expense.		32,200	73,900
Net operating profit.			$ 22,700
Other revenue			15,300
Net income before taxes			$ 38,000
Provision for income tax.			12,640
Net Income.			$ 25,360

casts this information in a form that is both shorter and better suited for analysis. Instead of showing separately the figures for beginning and ending inventories, this statement shows only the *changes* in inventory. These changes account for the difference between the costs incurred in manufacturing and the cost of goods sold. It is suggested that the reader think out for himself the reason why inventory increases are subtracted and why inventory decreases are added.

Entries with a Cost Accounting System

Since in a cost accounting system the cost of raw materials used, the cost of goods manufactured, and the cost of goods sold are found directly rather than by the roundabout process of deduction, the entries required under this system are even fewer than above. They would be:

(1)

```
Raw Materials Inventory . . . . . . . . . . . . . . . 272,920
    Accounts Payable. . . . . . . . . . . . . . . . .          272,920
    To record inventory purchased.
```

(2)

```
Goods in Process Inventory. . . . . . . . . . . . . . 593,500
    Raw Materials Inventory . . . . . . . . . . . .           264,100
    Direct Labor. . . . . . . . . . . . . . . . . .           150,650
    Manufacturing Overhead. . . . . . . . . . . . .           178,750
    To show material, labor, and overhead costs put into
    process.
```

(3)

```
Finished Goods Inventory. . . . . . . . . . . . . . . 569,700
    Goods in Process Inventory. . . . . . . . . . .           569,700
    To transfer completed products to finished goods
    inventory.
```

(4)

```
Cost of Goods Sold. . . . . . . . . . . . . . . . . . 572,500
    Finished Goods Inventory. . . . . . . . . . . .           572,500
    To record cost of goods sold and reduce inventory.
```

SIGNIFICANCE OF THE PROCESS

For the objective of this book, there is no particular reason why the reader should memorize the details of the procedures described in this chapter; he can easily refer back to them as needed. He should, however, understand thoroughly the nature of the process, for without such an understanding, events that are reflected on the income statement of a manufacturing company can easily be misinterpreted.

A fundamental difference between a manufacturing company and a merchandising company is illustrated by the procedures described. In a merchandising company, costs of labor, supplies, depreciation, and so on affect net income *in the accounting period in which these costs are incurred*. In a manufacturing company, on the other hand, those labor and other costs that are associated with the manufacturing process affect, initially, the value of inventory; they affect net income only *in the accounting period in which the products containing these costs are sold*. This may be a later accounting period than that in which the product was manufactured. The larger the inventory in relation to sales, the longer the time interval that elapses between the incurrence of a cost and its impact on net income.

Consider, for example, a wage increase amounting to $50,000 per year. In a merchandising company, net income would be reduced $50,000 in the year in which the increase becomes effective, other things being equal. In a manufacturing company, however, that part of the increase paid to manufacturing employees would first go to increase the inventory value of the products they worked on, and net income would not receive the full impact of the increase until these products were sold. You may find it interesting to explore this phenomenon by tracing through the impact of a $50,000 increase in wages on the two companies whose statements are shown in Illustrations 7–3 and 7–4, assuming (so that the effect of the wage increase can be isolated) that selling prices are not changed.

CHAPTER 8

LONG-TERM EQUITIES

The treasurer and other executives who are responsible for financial affairs in a company need a considerable store of technical knowledge regarding the various means of raising money, the legal and tax rules relating to financing, and so on. Other members of management should have some understanding of these matters, even though they scarcely can be expected to be conversant with all the details.

This chapter discusses the accounting aspects of these financial matters at a level that is intended to provide literacy to the nonfinancial manager. To cover the subject at the detailed level appropriate for the specialist would require a whole book, and a selection of such books is listed in the suggestions for further reading at the end of this chapter. The topics all relate to items listed on the equities side of the balance sheet: bonds and other long-term liabilities, the capital stock and surplus of corporations, and the owners' equity of unincorporated businesses. The principles underlying the preparation of consolidated financial statements are described briefly.

In the typical company, events of the type discussed in this chapter occur infrequently, but when they do occur they are likely to have a major impact on the financial statements. Thus, the nonfinancial manager can postpone acquiring a detailed knowledge of the accounting for these transactions until the need arises, but at that time he is well advised to acquire such a knowledge.

NATURE OF LIABILITIES

In Chapter 2, a liability was defined as a claim against assets by an outside party, as distinguished from a claim by the owners. This definition is approximately correct; however, not all legal obligations to outside parties are liabilities in the accounting meaning of this word, and not all liabilities are legally enforceable claims.

As an example of a claim that is not a liability, consider the case of an employee who has a written contract guaranteeing him employment at a stated salary for the next two years (e.g., professional athletes, coaches, executives). Such a contract is a legally enforceable claim against the business, but it is *not* a liability; in fact, this transaction is not recorded in the accounts at all until the man actually performs the work.

What distinguishes such a contract from those that do give rise to liabilities? Essentially, the distinction is determined by whether or not there is an asset or expense debit to offset the liability credit. When an employee works, the offsetting debit to the liability Accrued Wages Payable is Wages Expense. But when a contract is signed covering *future* employment, no expense account in the current period is affected, nor is an asset created. A liability is not created until the services have been performed.

For the same reason, a lease agreement, even though it may be just as binding and cover just as long a time period as a first-mortgage bond, is not a liability because the leased property is not owned by the lessee and hence is not an asset.[1] Similarly, the amount of interest on notes and bonds that is to accrue subsequent to the date of the balance sheet is not a liability.

An estimated allowance for future costs under a warranty agreement mentioned in Chapter 3 is an example of a liability that is not a definite obligation at the time it is set up. Liabilities of this type arise out of attempts to match revenue and costs. As explained in Chapter 3, revenue is ordinarily recognized when products are shipped; but when a warranty agreement applies, some of the costs associated with the transaction will not be incurred until later on when customers obtain repairs or replacement of products that turn out to be defective. The liability account is set up in the period in which the revenue is recognized, the offsetting debit being to an expense account of that period, such as Estimated Warranty Expense.

Contingent Liabilities

A *contingent liability* exists when a current situation may result in a liability upon the occurrence of some future event, but the amount, if any, of the liability cannot reasonably be predicted as of the balance sheet date. The situation must exist currently; hence, possible future losses from

---

[1] However, a long-term, noncancelable lease may create substantially the same equity in the property covered by the lease as if the property had been purchased on an installment basis. Such a lease should be capitalized; that is, both the asset and liability amounts should be shown on the financial statements. These amounts are calculated by discounting the stream of lease payments to which the company is committed. Also, other noncancelable leases, if material in amount, should be disclosed in a footnote to the balance sheet. (See *APB Opinion No. 5*, in Paul Grady, *Inventory of Generally Accepted Accounting Principles* [AICPA, 1965], pp. 171–80.)

fire, natural catastrophies, and war are not contingent liabilities. The amount must depend upon some future event, such as the settlement of a law suit; if the amount can be reasonably estimated now, it is not a contingent liability. Examples of contingent liabilities are possible penalties, fines, or damages from pending litigation; possible assessments of additional taxes; possible payments from default on debts which the company has guaranteed; possible refund resulting from renegotiation of contracts; and possible additional payments to employees for services they have already performed.

Contingent liabilities are not recorded in the financial statements themselves; however, they must be disclosed in a footnote if they are material in amount.[2] By contrast, an obligation whose amount can be reasonably estimated *is* a liability, and is so recorded, even though the precise amount is not now known.

Distinction between Liabilities and Owners' Equity

The exact dividing line between liabilities and owners' equities is a difficult one to draw. Although a distinction based on whether the claim is that of an owner or that of an outside creditor is satisfactory for most situations, in borderline cases fine-spun philosophical arguments can often be made for either treatment. A practical approach is to ask whether the claim involves a definite promise to pay; if so, the claim is a liability. If, on the other hand, the business does not incur a definite obligation to pay—definite in the sense that failure to make payment would be grounds for legal action—the item is part of owners' equity.

The problem of defining the dividing line has become acute in recent years because interest on a liability is a tax-deductible expense, whereas a dividend paid to owners is not; therefore companies have an incentive to make agreements that are sufficiently like liabilities to qualify for tax purposes but which impose as slight an obligation as possible.

BONDS

The most common form of long-term liability is a bond, which is a certificate, usually negotiable, promising to pay the holder a specified sum of money, usually $1,000, plus interest at a stated rate. Bonds may be sold to the general public through investment bankers, or they may be sold directly to an insurance company or other financial institution.

Recording the Issue

To illustrate the entries typically made to record the sale of an issue of bonds, assume the Mason Corporation sells an issue of 100 bonds, each

---

[2] See Grady, *op. cit.*, pp. 290–93.

with a face or *par* value of $1,000, with an interest rate of 5 percent, payable in 20 years, and secured by a first mortgage on certain Mason Corporation assets. (Such a bond would be called a "5 percent, 20-year, first mortgage bond.") If the corporation receives $1,000 each for the sale of these bonds, the following entry would be made:

```
Cash. . . . . . . . . . . . . . . . . . . . . . . 100,000
    Bonds Payable . . . . . . . . . . . . . . .        100,000
```

Frequently bonds are sold for less than their par value, that is, at a *discount*, or for more than their par value, that is, at a *premium*. This happens when the prevailing interest rate at the time of sale is different from the *nominal* interest rate, i.e., the rate printed on the bond.

> EXAMPLE: If the prevailing rate of interest in the bond market is 5.5 percent for bonds with a risk similar to those issued by the Mason Corporation, buyers will be unwilling to pay $1,000 for Mason Corporation 5 percent bonds. They would be willing to pay an amount such that the $50 annual interest on these bonds would be 5.5 percent of this amount. This amount (neglecting brokers' fees and other costs) works out to approximately $909. The bond would therefore be sold at a discount of $91.

The words "discount" and "premium" carry no connotation of "bad" or "good." They reflect simply a difference between the nominal interest rate for the issue and the going rate of interest at the time of issuance. The stated rate may be made intentionally different from the going market rate in the belief that this makes the bonds more attractive.

The sale of a bond issue is usually undertaken by an investment banking firm which charges a fee for this service. Determination of bond premium or discount is based on the net amount the corporation receives after this fee has been deducted, not on the price at which the bonds are sold to the public. In addition to this fee, the corporation also incurs printing, legal, and accounting costs in connection with a bond issue. These issue costs are usually taken into account when determining the net amount of discount or premium, but in some cases they are set up separately as an asset and amortized over the life of the issue.

If, because of a difference between the market rate and the nominal rate of interest, and taking into account the costs of issuance, the Mason Corporation received $88,000 from the issuance of $100,000 face amount of bonds, the following entry would be made:

```
Cash. . . . . . . . . . . . . . . . . . . . . . .  88,000
Bond Discount . . . . . . . . . . . . . . . . . .  12,000
    Bonds Payable . . . . . . . . . . . . . . . . .       100,000
```

If the corporation received more than the face amount, the corresponding entry would be:

```
Cash. . . . . . . . . . . . . . . . . . . . . . . . 110,000
    Bond Premium. . . . . . . . . . . . . . . . .          10,000
    Bond Payable. . . . . . . . . . . . . . . . .         100,000
```

If bonds are sold after the bond contract date (i.e., the date on which interest starts to be earned), the purchaser pays both the price of the bond itself and the interest that has accrued up to the date of the transaction. This is done because the corporation, for reasons of convenience, will pay to all bondholders the interest earned for the full period (usually six months) beginning with the contract date, and the purchaser is clearly not entitled to interest for the period prior to the time he purchased the bonds.

> EXAMPLE: If the Luton Corporation sold a $1,000 6 percent bond three months after the contract date, at a price that netted par value to the corporation, the purchaser would pay one quarter of a year's interest, or $15.
>
> The following entry would be made:

```
Cash. . . . . . . . . . . . . . . . . . . . . . . 1,015
    Bonds Payable . . . . . . . . . . . . . . . .           1,000
    Bond Interest Payable . . . . . . . . . . . .              15
```

In this case, when the semiannual interest payment is recorded, part of it will be debited to Bond Interest Payable, and the remainder to Bond Interest Expense; thus Bond Interest Expense will reflect the net interest expense of the period.

Balance Sheet Presentation

Bonds payable are shown in the long-term liabilities section of the balance sheet until one year before they mature, when ordinarily they become current liabilities. The description should give the principal facts about the issue, e.g., "5 percent first mortgage bonds due 1989." When a bond issue is to be refunded, however, it is not shown as a current liability in the year of maturity since it then will not require the use of current assets. If the bonds are to be retired in installments (as with *serial bonds*), that portion to be retired within a year is shown in the current liabilities section.

Bond discount is preferably shown on the balance sheet as a deduction from, and bond premium as an addition to, the face amount of bonds payable so as to reflect the net amount of the liability.

Bond Interest

An accounting entry is made to record the semiannual interest payments to bondholders and at the same time to amortize a portion of the bond premium or discount. The effect of this entry is that the *net* debit to

Interest Expense reflects, not the stated amount of interest actually paid to bondholders (unless the bonds are sold at par), but rather the effective rate of interest, which is larger or smaller than the stated rate, according to whether the bonds were sold at a discount or at a premium. The existence of bond discount in effect increases the interest expense, while the existence of bond premium decreases it.

Bond discount or premium may be amortized in one of two ways: by the straight-line method, in which the discount is debited (or the premium is credited) to Interest Expense in equal installments over the life of the issue; or by the compound interest method in which the discount or premium is written off in such a way that the net interest expense bears a constant ratio to the book value of the bonds over the whole life of the issue. This ratio is the effective interest cost of the borrowed funds.

The following entry records the semiannual bond interest payment and amortization of discount on a straight-line basis for the 5 percent Mason Corporation bonds that were assumed to have been sold at $880 each:

```
Interest Expense. . . . . . . . . . . . . . . . . . .    2,800
     Bond Discount . . . . . . . . . . . . . . . . . .            300
     Cash. . . . . . . . . . . . . . . . . . . . . . .          2,500
```

The cash that is paid out as interest is $2,500, which is 5 percent × $100,000 × ½ year. The $300 credit to Bond Discount is $\frac{1}{40}$ of the $12,000 that is to be amortized over 40 semiannual periods. The interest expense is the sum of these amounts.

If the interest payment date does not coincide with the closing of the company's books, an adjusting entry is made to record accrued interest expense and the amortization of discount or premium. Assuming that the Mason Corporation bonds are sold at $880 each on September 30, that the interest dates are September 30 and March 31, and that the fiscal year ends on December 31, the following entries would be made:

1. *Adjustment on December 31:*

```
Bond Interest Expense . . . . . . . . . . . . . . . .    1,400
     Bond Discount . . . . . . . . . . . . . . . . . .            150
     Accrued Interest Payable. . . . . . . . . . . . .          1,250
```

2. *Payment of semiannual interest on March 31:*

```
Bond Interest Expense . . . . . . . . . . . . . . . .    1,400
Accrued Interest Payable. . . . . . . . . . . . . . .    1,250
     Bond Discount . . . . . . . . . . . . . . . . . .            150
     Cash. . . . . . . . . . . . . . . . . . . . . . .          2,500
```

3. *Payment of semiannual interest on the following September 30:*

```
Bond Interest Expense . . . . . . . . . . . . . . . .    2,800
     Bond Discount . . . . . . . . . . . . . . . . . .            300
     Cash. . . . . . . . . . . . . . . . . . . . . . .          2,500
```

In the above examples, bond issuance costs were assumed to have been included in calculating the discount. If recorded separately, issuance costs would be amortized by debits to Interest Expense over the life of the issue, in the same manner as shown for bond discount.

Retirement of Bonds

Bonds may be retired in total, or they may be retired in installments over a period of years. In either case the retirement is recorded by a debit to Bonds Payable and a credit to Cash, or to a sinking fund which has been set up for this purpose. The bond discount or premium will have been completely amortized by the maturity date, so no additional entry is required for discount or premium at that time.

Bonds are sometimes retired at maturity out of a sinking fund which has been created in installments over the life of the issue. Bond sinking funds may be controlled by the originating corporation, or they may be controlled by a trustee under specified contractual arrangements. In either case, such funds usually appear in the investment section of the assets side of the balance sheet.

The company may decide to retire bonds earlier than the date originally specified. If such bonds were sold at a discount, an unamortized discount will exist as of the date of early retirement because the schedule of amortization was originally set up so as to charge off the discount over the specified life of the issue. Correspondingly, an unamortized premium will exist if the bonds were sold at a premium. Under the all-inclusive income concept, this unamortized balance is shown on the current income statement, as an item of extraordinary loss (if a discount) or gain (if a premium).

EXAMPLE: If the Mason Corporation bonds are retired at the end of 10 years (i.e., half their scheduled life) by paying the face amount to each bondholder, half the bond discount would not have been amortized. The entry would be as follows:

```
Bonds Payable . . . . . . . . . . . . . . . . . . . . . 100,000
Loss on Retirement of Bonds . . . . . . . . . . . . .     6,000
    Cash. . . . . . . . . . . . . . . . . . . . . . . .           100,000
    Bond Discount . . . . . . . . . . . . . . . . . . .             6,000
```

Refunding a Bond Issue

The terms of some bond issues state that the bonds can be called, or retired before maturity, by paying for them at a premium, that is, by paying more than the par value. In this case, a schedule of *call prices* is included in the terms of the issue. In periods when interest rates have declined, a company may consider it advantageous to *refund* a bond issue, that is, to call the old issue and float a new one with a lower rate of interest. Problems then arise in accounting for the call premium (the difference between the call price and par value) and any unamortized issue costs and discount (or premium) on the old bonds.

The preferred treatment is to write off these costs over the remaining life of the issue being retired. Since for tax purposes these costs are a deductible expense in the year of refunding, thereby decreasing income taxes in that year, it is appropriate to report a fraction of the unamortized costs, equal to the income taxes saved, as an expense of the year of refunding and to spread only the remainder of the cost over the future years. This is consistent with the treatment of income taxes discussed in Chapter 5.

It is also in accordance with accounting principles to write off all the unamortized costs and the call premium in the year of refunding, as an extraordinary expense on the income statement.

The alternative of writing off the unamortized costs and call premium of the *old* issue over the life of the *new* bond issue is also permitted under certain circumstances (see Opinion No. 6).

Generally, if the alternative of amortizing over the remaining years of the old bond issue is chosen, the balances of all accounts which refer to the refunded issue, such as call premium, unamortized premium or discount, and issue costs, are closed into a single account, for example, "Unamortized Charges on 5 Percent Series A Mortgage Bonds." This single account is carried on the books and amortized over the remaining years of the old bond issue.

SHAREHOLDERS' EQUITY

The *shareholders' equity* (or *owners' equity*, or *stockholders' equity*) section of the balance sheet consists of two parts: (1) the amount contributed by the shareholders, and (2) retained earnings. The amount contributed by shareholders is called *contributed capital* or *invested capital*, and is further divided into (*a*) the par value or stated value of the stock, and (*b*) capital surplus. This section describes transactions related to these amounts.

Types of Capital Stock

Capital stock may be either *common* or *preferred*. Preferred stock has preference, or priority, over common as to the receipt of dividends, as to assets in the event of liquidation, or as to other specified matters. There is no substantial difference in the accounting treatment of these two types of stock, however, so no distinction is here made between them.

Stock may be either *par value* or *no-par value*. Par value stock appears in the accounts at a fixed amount per share (often $1, $10, or $100), which is specified in the corporation's charter or bylaws. Except by coincidence, the par value of the stock in a going concern has no relation either to the stock's market value or to its book value. *Market value* is what people will pay for the stock. *Book value* is the total shareholders' equity as reported on the balance sheet, that is, the sum of capital stock plus capital surplus plus retained earnings (or, stated another way, assets minus liabilities).

No-par value stock has a *stated value*, which is either specified in the corporation's charter or bylaws or fixed by the board of directors. The stated value governs the amounts to be entered in the Capital Stock account just as if it were a par value. The distinction between par value and no-par value stock is therefore of little practical significance.

Recording the Issue

To illustrate the issuance of stock, let us consider the Carroll Corporation, which received a charter from the state authorizing the issuance of 20,000 shares of $10 par value common stock. If 1,000 shares of this stock are issued at par ($10) and immediately paid for, the following entry would be made:

```
Cash. . . . . . . . . . . . . . . . . . . . . . . .  10,000
     Common Stock. . . . . . . . . . . . . . . . . .          10,000
```

Stock is often sold for more than its par or stated value; that is, it is sold at a *premium*. In such situations the Common Stock account still reflects the par or stated value, and the premium is shown separately, usually in the account, Paid-In Surplus (or Capital Surplus). If 1,000 shares of Carroll Corporation $10 common stock were sold at $12 a share, the following entry would be made:

```
Cash. . . . . . . . . . . . . . . . . . . . . . . .  12,000
     Common Stock. . . . . . . . . . . . . . . . . .          10,000
     Paid-In Surplus . . . . . . . . . . . . . . . .           2,000
```

Unlike bonds, stock is almost never sold at a discount. In most states and under most circumstances, this is illegal. Even where sale at a discount is permitted, individual shareholders would be required to contribute the amount of the discount in cash if the company should go bankrupt, and such a possibility makes discount stock unattractive to investors. Corporations therefore set the par value or stated value low enough so that the stock can be sold at a premium.

The sale of an issue of stock is often handled by an investment banking firm which receives a fee or "spread" for this service. Logically, the corporation should record only the net amount received from the investment banker, that is, the price paid by the public less the banker's spread, since this is the only amount that the corporate entity receives. Many companies, however, record the stock at the price paid by the public, and show the banker's spread as an expense. When this is done, the ultimate effect on shareholders' equity is the same as if only the net amount were recorded, since the expense item winds up as a decrease in shareholders' equity. The practice of recording the spread separately provides a useful piece of information, namely, the size of the spread, which is not revealed in the alternative treatment.

In connection with the issuance of stock, the corporation itself incurs issue costs over and above the banker's spread. These amounts may also be deducted from the amount received from the issue. The facts are perhaps more clearly shown, however, if these costs are recorded separately either as an expense of the current period or, if they are material, as an asset, such as organization cost.

> EXAMPLE: The Dorith Corporation issued 10,000 shares of $10 par value common stock and the public bought these shares at $13. The investment banker's spread was $2 per share and the issue costs incurred by the Dorith Corporation were $4,000. The following entries would be made:

1. *Entry for issue costs:*

```
Stock Issue Costs . . . . . . . . . . . . . . . . . . .    4,000
        Cash (or Accounts Payable). . . . . . . . . . . .            4,000
```

2. *Entry when payment is received from investment bankers:*

```
Cash. . . . . . . . . . . . . . . . . . . . . . . . . .  110,000
        Common Stock. . . . . . . . . . . . . . . . . . .          100,000
        Paid-In Surplus . . . . . . . . . . . . . . . . .           10,000
```

3. *Possible entry closing stock issue costs:*[3]

```
Paid-In Surplus . . . . . . . . . . . . . . . . . . . .    4,000
        Stock Issue Costs . . . . . . . . . . . . . . . .            4,000
```

Note that the amount actually paid by the public does not appear in the company's accounts. Note also that these transactions are between the company and its shareholders. When one shareholder sells his stock to another shareholder, the amounts in the company's accounts are not affected in any way; the only change is in the secretary's detailed record of the identity of shareholders.

---

[3] This entry not made if stock issue costs are capitalized or charged to expense.

Treasury Stock

Treasury stock is a corporation's own stock that has been issued and subsequently reacquired by purchase or donation but not canceled. Although a few corporations show treasury stock as an asset on their balance sheet, this practice is not generally accepted since treasury stock is clearly not a "valuable thing or property right owned by the business"; a corporation can't own a claim against itself. The preferable practice is to treat treasury stock as a reduction in shareholders' equity, that is, as a reduction in the number and value of the shares outstanding, which is what it is.

In many companies, treasury stock purchased is debited to the Treasury Stock account at its cost, regardless of its par or stated value. It continues to be shown at cost until it is canceled or reissued, at which time adjustments are made in shareholders' equity to dispose of any differences between this cost, the paid-in value (i.e., the net proceeds at the time the stock was originally issued), and, in the event of reissuance, the amount then received.

Any excess of selling price above cost is credited to a surplus account (such as Capital Surplus from Treasury Stock Transactions), which may be shown as a separate item in the capital surplus section of the balance sheet. If treasury stock is sold at a price below cost, the loss may be deducted from the related surplus account if such an account already exists from prior transactions; otherwise the loss is debited to Retained Earnings.

If the capital stock was originally issued over a period of time at varying prices, there may be no way of determining the amount originally received from the issuance of the specific shares later reacquired as treasury stock. In this situation the "average paid-in value" becomes the base against which the costs of reacquisition are compared. The average paid-in value is determined by dividing the total number of shares outstanding at the time of the treasury stock transaction into total stated value less discounts or plus premiums.

None of these transactions enter into the determination of net income, nor are gains or losses from such transactions recognized for tax purposes.

Capital Surplus

As noted in Chapter 2, the Accounting Principles Board has recommended that the word "surplus" not be used in financial statements. The term "retained earnings" avoids the prohibited word for that part of shareholders' equity that results from the earning of net income, but the phrase suggested for another type of what was formerly labeled "surplus"

—"capital contributed in excess of the par or stated value of shares"—is cumbersome. Thus, although language that avoids the word "surplus" is used on many corporate balance sheets, the term "capital surplus" will be used here, simply as a matter of convenience.

The most common source of capital surplus is proceeds from the issuance of stock which exceed the par or stated value of the stock. This is the *paid-in surplus* described on page 151. Capital surplus also includes *donated surplus*, arising from gifts made to the corporation, and *appraisal surplus*, arising when the book value of assets is increased as a result of an appraisal. Appraisal surplus, however, is recorded only under highly unusual circumstances. As an example of its rarity, 1,800,000 acres of land owned by Kern County Land Company was carried on its books for some 70 years at its acquisition cost of less than $10 per acre, although its market value in 1967, when this company merged with Tenneco, was many tens of times this amount.

Cash Dividends

Dividends are ordinarily paid to shareholders in cash, but they sometimes are paid in other assets—the whiskey distributed by a distillery corporation to its shareholders being a noteworthy example.

Dividends are debited to retained earnings in the period in which they are declared, that is, voted, by the board of directors, even though payment is made at a later date. For example, if the Carroll Corporation declared a $5,000 dividend on December 15 to be paid on January 15, the entries would be as follows:

```
                     Dec. 15

Dividends (an owners' equity account). . . . . . . . .  5,000
    Dividends Payable (a liability account). . . . . .        5,000

                     Dec. 31

Retained Earnings. . . . . . . . . . . . . . . . . . .  5,000
    Dividends. . . . . . . . . . . . . . . . . . . . .        5,000
  A closing entry.

                     Jan. 15

Dividends Payable. . . . . . . . . . . . . . . . . . .  5,000
    Cash . . . . . . . . . . . . . . . . . . . . . . .        5,000
```

Stock Dividends and Stock Split-Ups

Some shareholders, in the mistaken belief that the amount reported as surplus is "their money," put pressure on the directors to authorize cash dividends equal to, or almost equal to, the amount of retained earnings. Clearly, retained earnings are not money at all, and for any of a number of reasons, cash may not be available for dividend payments even though the balance sheet shows a large amount of retained earnings. These same shareholders may be quite satisfied with a *stock dividend,* which actually does not change their equity in the corporation. As Mr. Justice Pitney said in *Eisner* v. *Macomber* (252 U.S. 189):

A stock dividend really takes nothing from the property of the corporation and adds nothing to the interests of the stockholders. Its property is not diminished and their interests are not increased . . . the proportional interest of each shareholder remains the same.

From an accounting standpoint, a stock dividend is recorded as a debit to retained earnings and as a credit to capital stock; the total owners' equity remains unchanged. The amount transferred from retained earnings to capital stock is usually calculated on the basis of the current market price of the stock.

EXAMPLE: The Bruce Corporation has 10,000 shares of common stock outstanding. Suppose that the directors voted a 5 percent stock dividend. Each shareholder would receive ¹⁄₂₀ of a share of new stock for every share he then held. If the stock currently had a stated value of $12 a share, the common stock item on the balance sheet would increase by $6,000 (500 shares at $12 per share), and retained earnings would decrease by $6,000, but the *total* shareholders' equity would remain exactly as before.

As a matter of custom, a stock dividend is ordinarily not more than 25 percent of the number of shares issued, and usually it is 5 or 10 percent.

Since a stock dividend reduces retained earnings, and since the amount of cash dividends that can be legally declared is related to the amount of retained earnings, the declaration of a stock dividend reduces the maximum amount of dividends that henceforth can be paid. By declaring a stock dividend, therefore, the directors signal their intention that this amount will be invested permanently in the company. The converse does not apply, however, for failure to declare a stock dividend is by no means an indication that the directors do plan to distribute all the retained earnings.

An advantage of a stock dividend is that a shareholder may realize cash by selling his dividend stock while preserving the number of his owned shares intact; but if he does this, he should recognize that he is in fact selling a fraction of his equity in the business.

A *stock split-up* merely increases the number of shares of stock outstanding, with no change in the total stated value of the stock and no change in surplus. As with a stock dividend, it has no effect on shareholders' equity; its effect is solely to repackage the evidence of ownership in smaller units. A stock split automatically reduces the market price of a share of stock. Often, however, the reduction is not quite proportional to the split since stock with a fairly low market price per share tends to be more attractive than stock with a high market price per share. Thus, if a stock selling at $150 is split "3-for-1," the new shares often will sell for somewhat more than $50 each.

The stock referred to in the preceding paragraphs is the company's own stock. If the company distributes to its shareholders the shares of some other corporation's stock which it owns, this distribution is similar to a regular cash dividend, and is recorded in the same manner except that the credit is to the Investments account rather than to Cash. Such a transaction is called a *spin-off*.

Surplus Reserves

In an attempt to explain to shareholders why they do not receive dividends that are equal to the amount shown as retained earnings plus other forms of surplus, a corporation may show on its balance sheet an appropriation, or reserve, as a separate item that is subtracted from surplus. Some of the terms used to describe the reasons for such an appropriation are as follows: *reserve for bond sinking fund*, which indicates a restriction on dividends in accordance with agreements made to bondholders; *reserve for contingencies*, indicating management's belief that funds may be required for an unusual purpose or to meet a possible obligation that does not yet have the status of a liability (such as settlement of a pending lawsuit, or a retroactive wage increase); *reserve for future inventory price decline*, indicating the possibility that inventory may be sold at a price less than the value reported on the balance sheet; and *reserve for expansion*, indicating an intention to use funds for the acquisition of new assets.

None of these reserves represents money, or anything tangible; the assets of a business are reported on the assets side of the balance sheet, not in the shareholders' equity section. The accounting entry creating the reserve involves a debit to Retained Earnings (or some other surplus account) and a credit to the reserve. This entry obviously does not affect any asset account, nor does the reserve represent anything more than a segregated portion of surplus.

Earnings per Share

In analyzing the financial statements of a corporation, investors pay particular attention to the ratio called "earnings per share." This is computed by dividing net income applicable to the common stock by the number of shares of common stock outstanding. The Accounting Principles Board requires that earnings per share be reported on the income statement, and in its *Opinion No. 9* (December, 1966) and *Opinion No. 15* (May 1969) provided detailed guidelines for making the calculation.

If the corporation has a simple capital structure, with only one class of stock, the net income used in this ratio is the same as the net income shown on the income statement.

> EXAMPLE: The 1968 income statement of McLean Corporation showed net income of $5 million. The corporation had one million shares of common stock outstanding in 1968. It therefore earned $5 per share.

The various classes of stock that a corporation might issue can be divided into one of two categories: (1) *senior securities*, and (2) *common stock* and its equivalent. Senior securities are those that have a claim on net income ahead of the claim of the common stockholders. The income figure used in the calculation of earnings per share is the amount that remains after the claims of the senior securities have been deducted from net income.

> EXAMPLE: The Nugent Corporation in 1968 had net income of $5 million. It had outstanding 100,000 shares of $6 preferred stock (which means that each share of preferred is entitled to an annual dividend of $6 before any dividends can be paid to common stockholders), and one million shares of common stock. Its earnings per share were therefore ($5,000,000 − $600,000) ÷ 1,000,000 shares = $4.40 per share.

If the number of shares of common stock outstanding fluctuates within a year, then a weighted average number of shares is computed.

> EXAMPLE: The Optel Corporation in 1968 had net income of $5 million. It had outstanding on January 1, one million shares of common stock, and on July 1 it issued an additional 500,000 shares, which were therefore outstanding for half of the year. Its average number of common shares outstanding was 1,000,000 + (500,000 × ½) = 1,250,000. Its earnings per share was $5,000,000 ÷ 1,250,000 = $4.

A *common stock equivalent* is a security which, although not in form a common stock, contains provisions that enable its holder to become a common stockholder and which, because of its terms and the circumstances under which it was issued, is in substance equivalent to a common stock. The value of a common stock equivalent is derived in large part from the value of the common stock to which it is related. One example is convertible bonds, which are bonds that can be exchanged for a prescribed amount of common stock if the bondholder elects to do so. Stock options and warrants, which permit their owners to buy common stock at a specified price, are other examples.

When a corporation has securities that are common stock equivalents, the Accounting Principles Board requires that the amount of such securities be taken into account in calculating earnings per share.

> EXAMPLE: Peter Corporation in 1968 had net income of $3,300,000. It had outstanding 1,000,000 shares of common stock and also convertible bonds which could be converted into 100,000 shares of common stock. When these bonds were issued, their market price was significantly higher than the price that would have reflected the going rate of interest, which indicates that they were common stock equivalents. Peter Corporation earnings per share was $3,300,000 ÷ (1,000,000 + 100,000) = $3.

The detailed criteria for deciding whether a security is a common stock equivalent and if so how the equivalent number of shares should be calculated are much too lengthy to be given here. APB *Opinion No. 15*, which states these criteria, is by far the longest opinion issued by the Accounting Principle Board.

APB *Opinion No. 15* also states that if a corporation has securities that *may*, under certain circumstances, have a claim on common earnings— even though these securities are not equivalent common shares—then the corporation should report two figures for earnings per share: (1) *primary earnings per share*, which is net income divided by the number of common and common equivalent shares, as above; and (2) *fully diluted earnings per share*, in which it is assumed that the maximum amount of potential conversion, exercise of warrants, and the like has taken place.

Significance of Shareholders' Equity

A study of the shareholders' equity section may provide some clues as to the methods used to obtain capital, as to transactions involving the purchase or sale of treasury stock, or as to the occurrence of unusual events not reflected in the income statement that result in changes in the shareholders' equity. An analysis of the growth in retained earnings in relation to net income may indicate the extent to which the company has obtained capital by "plowing back" its earnings.

In some states, dividend payments cannot exceed the amount shown as retained earnings, while other state laws allow dividend payments to equal retained earnings plus certain types of capital surplus. In still other states, however, dividend payments can be made if there are earnings in the current year, even though a deficit is shown from prior years. Banks or other lenders may impose other restrictions on the amounts that can be paid as dividends.

Whatever the legal restriction on dividend payments may be, factors other than the amount reported as retained earnings or surplus are likely to have a much more important bearing on dividend decisions in the ordinary situation. These factors include the amount of cash available, the funds required for expansion, the anticipated effect of dividends on stock prices and on the sale of new securities, the desire to maintain an unbroken record of dividend payments, a sense of fairness to shareholders, and so on.

Some accountants advocate that shareholders' equity be reported as a single figure rather than showing separate amounts for stock and for various types of surplus. Although this is not in accordance with generally accepted accounting principles, the suggestion does emphasize the difficulty of obtaining useful information from the separate figures that appear in the shareholders' equity section of the balance sheet.

Balance Sheet Presentation

In the shareholders' equity section of the balance sheet (or in a separate note, if presentation of all the detail would make the balance sheet itself too long), the following detail is presented:

1. For *each* class of stock, the par or stated value, the capital surplus attributed to that class, the number of shares authorized and issued and outstanding, rights and preferences as to dividends and as to amounts received in liquidation, and amount of treasury stock.

2. The amount of retained earnings, in total, and a note as to any portion of this amount that cannot be distributed as dividends (such as a restriction arising under the terms of a bank loan).

Thus, the basic distinction is maintained between (1) the capital contributed by shareholders, and (2) the equity resulting from net income that has been retained in the business.

The dollar amounts shown for each class of stock relate to the shares issued, not to the shares authorized.

In many balance sheets, the capital surplus is shown as one item, rather

Illustration 8–1

CARROLL CORPORATION

Owners' Equity Section of Balance Sheet

Shareholders' Equity:

Preferred stock, $0.60 dividend; par value $10, authorized and issued 2,900 shares	$ 29,000
Common stock, $10 par value; authorized 20,000 shares, issued 10,000 shares	100,000
Add: Paid-in surplus	4,000
	$133,000
Less: 100 common shares in treasury at cost	1,200
Contributed capital	$131,800
Retained earnings	10,000
Total Shareholders' Equity	$141,800

than being divided among the several classes of stock. In some balance sheets, the treasury stock item is listed below retained earnings, but this treatment is not preferred by the Accounting Principles Board.

The company must also report the details on all *options* to purchase capital stock. Such options are often granted to executives. They permit the holder to purchase stock at a stated price, and thus are valuable if the market price of the stock subsequently increases. The amount of stock options outstanding does not affect the balance sheet itself, so disclosure is by means of a separate note.

Illustration 8–1 shows the shareholders' equity section of a hypothetical corporation.

ACQUISITIONS AND MERGERS

In recent years there has been in the United States a surge in the urge to merge, a significant increase in the number of occasions on which two or more corporations join together to become one. These combinations take one or two forms; they are an *acquisition* or a *merger*.

In an acquisition, Corporation A buys either the assets or the stock of Corporation B, either by paying cash or other assets or by issuing bonds or preferred stock to Corporation B or to its shareholders. The shareholders of Corporation B therefore no longer have an interest in the activities heretofore carried on by that corporation, and in most cases Corporation B disappears.

In a merger, the shareholders of Corporation B exchange their stock for stock in Corporation A (or occasionally, the shareholders of both A and B receive stock in a newly organized Corporation C.) Corporation B usually disappears, and its business is henceforth conducted by Corporation A (or Corporation C, if such is organized). Occasionally Corporation B will continue in existence as a subsidiary of Corporation A.

Many difficult problems arise in accounting for a merger or acquisition. Basically, the transaction can be accounted as either a *purchase* or a *pooling of interests*.

If a purchase, the assets of Corporation B are recorded on the books of Corporation A at either their book value as shown on the books of Corporation B or at their current fair market value. The difference, if any, between this amount and the amount that Corporation A paid for Corporation B is recorded as goodwill. The fair market value may be difficult to estimate, and if the consideration for the purchase was other than cash, problems also arise in measuring the amount of goodwill. Acquisitions are always recorded as purchases, and so are mergers unless the merger meets certain criteria outlined below.

If the transaction is recorded as a *pooling of interests*, the book values of the assets and the retained earnings of Corporation B are simply added to those of Corporation A. No amount for goodwill is shown. Conceptually, a merger is treated as a pooling of interest when it resembles "two streams converging into a single river"; that is, when the relative rights of the shareholders of A and B are substantially the same in the merged entity as they were in the former separate entities. More specifically, there is a presumption that the transaction should be treated as a purchase, rather than as a pooling of interest, if the shareholders of Corporation B have significantly different voting rights or other rights in Corporation A than they formerly had; if a significant part of B's business is to be sold; if the shareholders of Corporation A clearly dominate the new entity; or if there is other evidence that the transaction was a disguised purchase.

The importance of the distinction between a purchase and a pooling of interest is that if the latter form is used improperly, the subsequent financial statements of the surviving corporation may not convey a realistic story of what has happened. One obvious possibility is that the comparisons with prior years may be distorted.

> EXAMPLE: The 1967 annual report of "Automatic" Sprinkler Corporation contains the statement, "Earnings after taxes rose from $4,425,000 reported in 1966 to $9,193,000 in 1967." The 1966 figure excludes the earnings of companies that were merged into "Automatic" Sprinkler in 1967. If the 1966 earnings of these companies had been included, the 1966 earnings would have been $10.8 million, and the 1967 earnings would then be less, rather than more, than 1966. (Reported in the *Wall Street Journal*, August 5, 1968, p. 1)

Such distortions can be avoided by restating the prior year balance sheet and income statements to include amounts for all the companies currently included in the corporation.

A more subtle problem arises when the assets of the acquired company are carried on the books at considerably less than their market value. In these circumstances the surviving corporation can add significantly to its income by selling some of these assets and reporting the gain as income.

CONSOLIDATED FINANCIAL STATEMENTS

A "company," as it is thought of by its management, its employees, its competitors, and the general public, may actually consist of a number of different corporations, created for various legal, tax, and financial reasons. The existence of a family of corporations is by no means peculiar to "big business." A fairly small enterprise may consist of one corporation that owns the real estate and buildings, another that primarily handles production, another for marketing activities, and over them all a *parent* corporation which is the locus of management and control. Each of these corporations is a legal entity, and each therefore has its own financial statements. The "company" itself may not be a separate legal entity, but it is an important *business* entity, and a set of financial statements for the whole business enterprise may be more useful than the statements of the separate corporations of which it consists.

Such statements are called *consolidated financial statements.* They are prepared by first adjusting and then combining the financial statements of the separate corporations; usually, no separate journals or ledgers are kept for the consolidated entity.

Basis for Consolidation

The legal tie that binds the other corporations, or *subsidiaries,* to the parent is the ownership of their stock. A subsidiary is not consolidated unless more than 50 percent of its common stock is owned by the parent; some companies use an even higher percentage as the criterion.

Even though it is 100 percent owned by the parent, a subsidiary may not be consolidated if its business is so different from that of the other companies in the family that including it in the consolidation would result in financial statements that do not well describe the family as a whole. General Motors Corporation does not consolidate the statements of General Motors Acceptance Corporation with those of its other corporations because GMAC is a huge financial corporation dealing principally in installment payments on automobiles, and its assets and liabilities are quite unlike those of an industrial company. Many companies do not consolidate their foreign subsidiaries.

If a subsidiary is not consolidated, the amount of the parent's investment in it appears as an asset on the consolidated balance sheet. *Opinion No. 10* of the Accounting Principles Board requires that for domestic subsidiaries the amount of the asset be the cost of the acquisition plus the parent's share of any retained earnings (or minus the amount of losses) that have been booked subsequent to the date of acquisition. Note that this is a departure from the basic concept that assets are reported at cost.

Consolidation Procedure

Illustration 8–2 shows the consolidation process in the simplest possible situation, consisting of the parent company and one subsidiary company, named "Parent" and "Subsidiary," respectively. Parent owns 100 percent of Subsidiary's stock; this is an asset which is shown on its balance sheet as Investment in Subsidiary. The investment is recorded at cost, and it is assumed here that Parent purchased Subsidiary's stock at its book value as of the time of acquisition.

In the illustration, the separate balance sheets of Parent and Subsidiary are given in the first two columns. The "combined" balance sheet in the third column is simply the sum of the figures in the first two columns

Illustration 8–2

CONSOLIDATION WORK SHEET

	Separate Statements		Com-bined	Eliminations		Consoli-dated Balance Sheet
	Parent	Sub-sidiary		Dr.	Cr.	
Debit Balances						
Accounts receivable.....	40,000	11,000	51,000		(1) 5,000	46,000
Inventory.............	30,000	15,000	45,000		(2) 1,000	44,000
Other current assets....	45,000	12,000	57,000			57,000
Fixed assets, gross......	405,000	65,000	470,000			470,000
Investment in Subsidiary	55,000		55,000		(3) 55,000	
	575,000	103,000	678,000			617,000
Credit Balances						
Accumulated deprecia-tion................	160,000	20,000	180,000			180,000
Accounts payable.......	20,000	13,000	33,000	(1) 5,000		28,000
Other current liabilities..	25,000	9,000	34,000			34,000
Long-term liabilities....	100,000		100,000			100,000
Capital stock..........	100,000	40,000	140,000	(3) 40,000		100,000
Retained earnings.......	170,000	21,000	191,000	(2) 1,000 (3) 15,000		175,000
	575,000	103,000	678,000			617,000

This combined balance sheet contains some items which, so far as the consolidated entity is concerned, are counted twice, and the effect of this double counting is eliminated by the adjustments made in the next two columns and explained below. Essentially, these adjustments eliminate the effect of transactions that have occurred between the two corporations as separate legal entities. Since the consolidated financial statements should report only assets owned by the consolidated entity and the equities of parties *outside* the consolidated entity, these internal transactions must be eliminated. The consolidated balance sheet that results from these adjustments appears in the last column. The adjustments are as follows:

1. INTERCOMPANY FINANCIAL TRANSACTIONS. The consolidated balance sheet must show as accounts receivable and accounts payable only amounts owed by and owed to parties outside the consolidated business; therefore, amounts that the companies owe to one another must be eliminated. Assuming that Parent owes Subsidiary $5,000, this amount is eliminated from Accounts Payable and Accounts Receivable. The effect is as in the following journal entry (although it should be remembered that no journal entries actually are made in the books of either corporation):

```
Accounts Payable. . . . . . . . . . . . . . . . .    5,000
     Accounts Receivable . . . . . . . . . . . . . . .         5,000
```

Interest on intercompany loans would also be eliminated in a similar manner.

The payment of dividends by the subsidiary to the parent is a financial transaction that has no effect on the consolidated entity. In the separate statements, this was recorded on Parent's books as a credit to Other Income (which was closed to Parent's Retained Earnings), and on Subsidiary's books as a debit to Dividends (which was closed to Subsidiary's Retained Earnings). Since this transaction affected only the two retained earnings accounts, adding to one the same amount that was subtracted from the other, the act of combining the two of them automatically eliminated its effect; therefore, no further adjustment is necessary.

2. INTERCOMPANY PROFIT. In accordance with the realization principle, the consolidated company does not earn revenue until sales are made to the outside world. The revenue, the related costs, and the resulting profit for sales made between companies in the consolidated entity must therefore be eliminated from the consolidated accounts.

The sales and cost of sales on intercompany transactions are subtracted from the total sales and cost of sales figures on the consolidated income statement; if this were not done, the figures would overstate the volume of business done by the consolidated entity with the outside world. In order to do this, records must be kept that show both the sales revenue and the cost of sales of shipments made within the family.

On the balance sheet, these intercompany transactions may affect the Inventory account of the company receiving the goods and the Retained Earnings account of the company selling them, and adjustments to these accounts are required. Assume that during a year, Subsidiary shipped products with a sales value of $60,000 to Parent. During the year, Parent sold three fourths of these products to outside customers, and the other one fourth remains in Parent's inventory at the end of the year at its cost to Parent of $15,000. The products sold to the outside world present no problem, since they have disappeared from inventory and the revenue has been realized. If these products were sold by Parent for more than $45,000, the excess will wind up in Parent's Retained Earnings as profit. When Parent's Retained Earnings is added to Subsidiary's Retained Earnings, the total profit on this part of the transaction will be included, and properly so.

The $15,000 remaining in Parent's inventory, however, is regarded by Subsidiary as a sale, the profit on which appears in Subsidiary's Retained Earnings. This portion of the profit must be eliminated from the consolidated balance sheet. This is done by reducing Retained Earnings and Inventory by the amount of the profit, assumed to be $1,000, as in the following entry:

```
Retained Earnings . . . . . . . . . . . . . . . . . .   1,000
    Inventory . . . . . . . . . . . . . . . . . . . . .          1,000
```

3. ELIMINATION OF THE INVESTMENT. The Parent company's investment in the Subsidiary's stock is strictly an intrafamily matter and must therefore be eliminated from the consolidated balance sheet. Since it is assumed here that the stock was purchased at book value, the $55,000 cost shown on Parent's books must have equaled Subsidiary's Capital Stock plus Retained Earnings at the time of purchase. We know that Capital Stock is $40,000, and the difference, $15,000, must therefore equal the balance of Retained Earnings at that time. The additional amount of retained earnings now shown on Subsidiary's books has been created subsequent to the acquisition by Parent. To eliminate the investment, therefore, the entry in effect is as follows:

```
Capital Stock . . . . . . . . . . . . . . . . . . . . .   40,000
Retained Earnings . . . . . . . . . . . . . . . . . . .   15,000
    Investment in Subsidiary. . . . . . . . . . . . . .          55,000
```

The necessary eliminations having been recorded, the figures for the consolidated balance sheet can now be obtained by carrying each line across the page.

In the preceding example, two of the most difficult problems in preparing consolidated statements did not arise because of simplifying assumptions that were made. These problems are described below.

Asset Valuation

In the example, it was assumed that Parent purchased Subsidiary's stock at its book value. Quite often, a subsidiary's stock is purchased at a figure other than its book value. Under these circumstances, the first step is to examine the value of Subsidiary's underlying assets; if their fair value differs from the amount at which they appear in Subsidiary's accounts, the accounts are adjusted to show the fair value, but not to exceed the purchase price. If after this revaluation, book value is still less than the price paid for the stock, the difference appears on the consolidated statement as Goodwill.[4] In the above illustration, if Parent had paid $65,000, rather than $55,000, for Subsidiary's stock, and if Subsidiary's assets were found to be recorded at their fair value, there would be goodwill of $10,000, and the adjustment marked (3) above would have been:

```
Goodwill. . . . . . . . . . . . . . . . . . . . . . . .   10,000
Capital Stock . . . . . . . . . . . . . . . . . . . . .   40,000
Retained Earnings . . . . . . . . . . . . . . . . . . .   15,000
    Investment in Subsidiary. . . . . . . . . . . . . .          65,000
```

---

[4] As explained in the preceding section, if the merger were treated as a pooling of interest, no goodwill would arise.

Minority Interest

In the illustration above, it was assumed that Parent owned 100 percent of the stock of Subsidiary. If, instead, it owned less than 100 percent, the *minority interest*, which is the equity of the other owners in Subsidiary's assets, would appear as an equity item on the consolidated balance sheet. In measuring this equity, the matter of intercompany profits discussed in the second entry above raises a problem to which there is no completely satisfactory answer. From the standpoint of the minority shareholders of Subsidiary, products sold to Parent result in realized income, while from the standpoint of the consolidated entity these same products result in income only when they are sold to an outside party. This problem is often solved by eliminating the intercompany profit from the minority interest. In other words, the adjustment to inventory described in item (2) above would still be $1,000. Such a solution results in some understatement of the equity of the minority owners, but an attempt to show their equity correctly would inevitably result in an offsetting distortion of either the inventory or the retained earnings items on the consolidated balance sheet.

If in the above illustration, Parent purchased only 80 percent of Subsidiary's stock at book value of $44,000, adjustment (3) to eliminate the investment would be 80 percent of the figures given above, or:

```
Capital Stock . . . . . . . . . . . . . . . . . . . .   32,000
Retained Earnings . . . . . . . . . . . . . . . . . .   12,000
    Investment in Subsidiary. . . . . . . . . . . . .            44,000
```

The remaining 20 percent of Subsidiary's Capital Stock plus 20 percent of Subsidiary's Retained Earnings after the elimination of intercompany profits would be set up as the equity of the minority interest on the consolidated statement, as follows:

```
Capital Stock . . . . . . . . . . . . . . . . . . . .    8,000
Retained Earnings . . . . . . . . . . . . . . . . . .    4,000
    Minority Interest . . . . . . . . . . . . . . . .            12,000
```

Retained Earnings on the consolidated balance sheet would then be $174,000. The minority interest, $12,000, would appear just above the owners' equity section.

Concluding Comment

The preceding brief discussion of consolidated statements is by no means adequate as a basis for actually preparing consolidated financial statements. A great many problems in addition to those discussed above arise in practice. The illustration given does, however, indicate the main types of problems and the principles applied in solving them, and thus should help the user, as distinguished from the preparer, in understanding how the figures on a consolidated statement were derived.

UNINCORPORATED BUSINESSES

Single Proprietorships

Not much more need be said about the owner's equity accounts in a single proprietorship than the comments already made in Chapter 2. There may be a single account in which all entries affecting the owner's equity are recorded, or a separate *drawing account* may be set up to handle periodic withdrawals made by the owner. If a drawing account is used, it may either be closed into the capital account at the end of the accounting period, or it may be kept separate so as to show the owner's original contribution of capital separate from the effect on his equity of subsequent events. As far as the ultimate effect is concerned, it is immaterial whether the owner regards his withdrawals as salary or as a return of profit; but if he wishes to compare his income statement with that of a corporation, he will undoubtedly treat a certain part of his withdrawals as salary (although in a corporation that is managed by its owners, the distinction between salary and dividends may also be quite fuzzy in practice).

Partnerships

A partnership has the problem of showing in the accounts the equity of the individual partners, and this varies depending on the terms of the partnership agreement. The accounts are set up to facilitate the computation of each partner's equity, in accordance with whatever the agreement may be. In the absence of a specific agreement, the law assumes that net income is to be divided equally among the partners, and this is also common in written partnership agreements. If such is the case, in a three-man partnership the capital account, or the drawing account, of each partner is credited with one third of net income. It is debited with the actual amount of his withdrawals.

If the agreement is that profits are to be divided in proportion to the capital originally contributed by each partner, then the capital account is maintained to show the amount of that contribution, and other transactions affecting the partners' equity are debited or credited to separate drawings or personal accounts. If one of the partners made a temporary loan to the partnership, it would be shown in a liability account (but separate from loans made by outside parties) rather than in the partner's equity account.

Partnership agreements may also provide that the partners receive stated salaries and a stated share of residual profits after salaries, or a stated percentage of interest on the capital they invested and a stated share of residual profits, or a combination of salary and interest. The accounting required in connection with such arrangements depends on the specific terms of the agreement.

EXAMPLE: The partnership agreement of Paine and Webber provided that Paine (who worked half time) would receive a salary of $10,000 and Webber a salary of $20,000; that each would receive 6 percent interest on the capital they contributed; and that they would share equally in the remainder. In 1969 the average balance in Paine's capital account was $50,000 and in Webber's, $10,000. The partnership net income was $40,000.

The income of each partner would be computed as follows:

	Total	Paine	Webber
Salary	$30,000	$10,000	$20,000
Interest	3,600	3,000	600
Remainder	6,400	3,200	3,200
Total	$40,000	$16,200	$23,800

Whatever the partnership arrangement, the law does not regard salaries or interest payments to the partners as being different from any other type of withdrawal, since the partnership is not an entity legally separate from the individual partners. Neither does the partnership as such ordinarily pay a federal income tax; the income of the partnership, regardless of whether it has been withdrawn, is taxable income to the individual partners. A partnership can, however, elect to be taxed as if it were a corporation, and certain small corporations can elect to be taxed as partnerships; special rules apply in these cases.

SUMMARY

Long-term equities consist, in general, of bonds and of shareholders' equity.

The liability arising from the sale of bonds is shown at its face amount, and the difference between this amount and the net proceeds received is recorded as bond premium or discount. Premium or discount is amortized over the life of the issue. This amortization is combined with the periodic interest payments to give the effective interest expense of each period.

In a corporation, shareholders' equity consists of two parts which should always be reported separately: (1) the amount paid to the corporation by each class of shareholders, which may be further divided into (*a*) the par or stated value of stock, and (*b*) capital surplus; and (2) retained earnings, representing the cumulative amount of net income that has not yet been paid out as dividends. In unincorporated businesses, the distinction between the original contribution of capital and subsequent changes in shareholders' equity may or may not be set forth on the balance sheet.

A business may consist of more than one corporation. If so, consolidated financial statements are prepared for the whole enterprise as a single entity. This is done by eliminating the effect of intercompany transactions from the accounts of the separate corporations and then combining them.

SUGGESTIONS FOR FURTHER READING

BACKER, MORTON (ed.). *Modern Accounting Theory.* 2d ed.; New York: Prentice-Hall, Inc., 1968.

FINNEY, HARRY A. and MILLER, H. E. *Principles of Accounting, Intermediate.* 6th ed.; New York: Prentice-Hall, Inc., 1965.

WELSCH, GLENN A.; ZLATKOVICH, CHARLES T.; and WHITE, JOHN ARCH. *Intermediate Accounting,* chaps. xv and xvi. Homewood, Ill.: Richard D. Irwin, Inc., 1968.

WIXON, RUFUS (ed.). *Accountants' Handbook.* 4th ed.; New York: Ronald Press Co., 1966.

CHAPTER 9

THE PRICE LEVEL PROBLEM

The accountant measures the goods and services that enter into his calculation of net income essentially at their acquisition cost, that is, at the prices paid when these goods and services were originally acquired by the company. The economist, however, often measures cost not in terms of the price originally paid for the goods and services but rather in terms of "real prices"; that is, he adjusts acquisition prices to allow for changes in purchasing power or in the economic significance of the specific good or service. In periods when there are substantial changes in prices, such as the downward movement in the early 1930's or the inflationary movement which began in the 1940's, the difference between the accounting concept of income and the economist's concept of income can be substantial.

This difference arises because the purchasing power of the monetary unit of measurement is different at different times. Thus, the measuring stick used in accounting is unlike the yardstick used to make linear measurements; a yardstick is always 36 inches long. A balance sheet prepared at one moment of time contains some items, such as cash, that are stated at current purchasing power; other items, such as inventory, that may be stated in monetary units that reflect purchasing power of the recent past; and still other items, such as plant and equipment, stated at amounts that reflect purchasing power of several years previous to the current date.

Several proposals have been advanced for dealing with this problem, and three are described in this chapter. One of these, the Lifo method of inventory measurement, has become a generally accepted accounting principle and is also allowed for tax purposes. The second, depreciation on replacement cost, is not a generally accepted accounting principle in the United States. The third, price level adjustments, involves the preparation of supplementary financial statements rather than a change in the principles underlying the regular balance sheet and income statement. All

170

are important to know about, partly because they are widely discussed, and partly because they demonstrate, by contrast, some limitations of the figures developed under conventiona! principles.

THE LIFO METHOD

Lifo, which stands for "last-in, first-out," is a method of measuring inventory costs. In this method, inventory is costed *as if* the units most recently added to inventory (last-in) were the first units sold (first-out) *even though this is in fact not the case.* Ending inventory is therefore assumed to consist of the oldest units and is measured at the cost of these oldest units. If the number of physical units in inventory remains constant from period to period, the accounting measurement of the inventory will also remain constant, regardless of what happens to the market replacement price of the inventory items. It follows that under the Lifo method, cost of goods sold tends to reflect the cost of the items most recently purchased.

The Lifo inventory method normally does not correspond to the physical flow of material, nor do its advocates claim that it has any relation to physical flow. Physically, material moves out of inventory on approximately a Fifo, or first-in, first-out, basis; that is, the oldest stocks normally are used up first. Advocates of Lifo contend, however, that in certain industries Lifo does match the *economic* flow of values since, they claim, the profit margin that actually influences business pricing decisions is the margin between sales prices and *current* costs, not the margin between sales prices and cost levels that existed at the time the inventory was purchased.

If this contention is correct, the conventional Fifo system results in the reporting of false "inventory profits" during periods of rising cost prices. During these periods goods are sold at sales prices commensurate with current costs, while cost of goods sold reflects earlier, lower costs rather than current costs. (Lifo only *approximates* current costs since it shows the cost of *most recent* purchases, and this is not necessarily the same as current cost.)

Arguments For and Against Lifo

A frequently used example of what is meant by this economic flow is the following excerpt from the Report of the Special Committee on Inventories of the AICPA (1936), a report which had much to do with the adoption of Lifo as a generally accepted principle:

A wagon maker has a wagon in stock which cost him $50, the selling price of which is $65 to yield him his desired profit of $15 per wagon. Before he sells the wagon he learns from the concern supplying him with his material of a price increase, the result of which is to make the reproduction cost of his wagon $60. By reason of this knowledge the wagon maker "marks up" his wagon to $75, at which figure he sells it for cash and builds a new wagon costing him $60. The net change resulting from the whole transaction is that his till shows $15 more cash than he had before.

Now the advocate of "reproduction cost of sales" says to the wagon maker:

The profit you made is $15, and the proper inventory price for the present wagon you have in stock is $50. That is the number of dollars of your capital invested in your stock-in-trade; the only change that you have effectively realized in that investment is the substitution of one wagon for another exactly like it—the same wagon, in fact, except only as regards physical identity.

On the other hand, the advocate of "first-in, first-out" says to the wagon maker: Your profit is $25, although you may have only $15 more in cash to show for it. The other $10 is contained in the increased cost and value of the new wagon—$60 as against the old one at $50. You must not fail to recognize and to give effect to the price level change.

Considering the other side of the problem, let us assume that after the above transaction the price level reverted to its original status, thus consummating the economic cycle; accordingly the wagon at present in stock, which actually had cost $60 to build (but was inventoried at either $50 or $60, according to the procedure followed) is sold for $65 and replaced in stock by one which cost $50 to build. Now, under either procedure the latest wagon will be inventoried at $50. The profit on the second transaction, however, will have been $15 according to the "reproduction cost of sales" advocate, or $5 according to the "first-in, first-out" advocate. The aggregate profit on the two transactions, of course, will be the same in either case but the periodic distribution will differ.

One virtue of the Lifo method is its tendency to limit the amount of reported net income to an amount which might be made available to shareholders without imparing the scope and intensity of the operations of a going concern. Advocates also argue that such restrictions in reported income serve to conserve funds by reducing income taxes.

Opponents of Lifo, while agreeing that it is not good management policy to regard funds needed to maintain the level of operations as representing disposable income, attack the Lifo argument on the grounds that it confuses two distinct processes: (1) the measurement of income, and (2) the utilization of income. They argue that income may be realized and valid even though such income is to be subsequently invested in inventories or other assets. They also point out that the Lifo method falls short of achieving the underlying objective in that costs of only the most recent acquisitions are charged against revenue rather than the total cost of replacing all the items sold.

No one argues that Lifo is applicable to every company; rather it is recommended only when there is a definite relationship between selling price and *current* cost. For example, if a retailer sets his selling price by adding a fixed markup to the invoice cost of specific units of merchandise, and if he usually can sell the merchandise at this price, his profit is based not on replacement cost but rather on his invoice cost, and he should not use the Lifo system. If, on the other hand, he finds it necessary or possible to change his retail prices as soon as, or shortly after, a change in wholesale prices occurs, his cost may be considered to be the replacement or Lifo cost.

A close correspondence between changes in selling prices and changes in current costs may reflect a general change in the value of money in the economy. If this is the case, it is argued that it makes little sense to state the revenue component of profit at the current value of the dollar while stating the principal expense component, cost of goods sold, in terms of a different kind of dollar. On the other hand, if the facts are that in a particular company the profit margin has really changed, for reasons having nothing to do with fluctuations in price levels, the use of Lifo may conceal such changes.

In addition to companies whose selling prices are related to invoice costs rather than to current costs, Lifo is also not appropriate for companies which eliminate inventory profits or losses by the practice called "hedging," nor for companies which are in the business of speculating on price changes, as are certain companies that trade in grain and other commodities.

The relative importance of inventory profits varies among companies, and Lifo has a more important influence on profits when—

1. Material cost constitutes a relatively large part of total cost.
2. The inventory is relatively large.
3. The manufacturing process is relatively long (which is a variation of No. 2, because a long manufacturing process means a large work in process inventory).

Example

Illustration 9–1 illustrates the effect of the Lifo method on profit and on inventory valuation, as contrasted with the Fifo method. The situation illustrated is the simplest possible, namely, where—

1. Selling price is immediately and exactly adjusted for changes in material cost.
2. There is no change in inventory quantity, that is, as soon as a unit is sold, it is replaced in inventory by another unit.
3. Sales *volume* each year is constant (at 1,000 units).
4. One hundred percent of the product cost is material cost.
5. Inventory turnover is 1; that is, inventory consists of 1,000 units.

Illustration 9–1

GROSS PROFIT CALCULATION UNDER FIFO AND LIFO

	(1) Inventory, January 1	(2) Purchases	(3) Inventory, December 31	(4) Cost of Sales*	(5) Sales†	(6) Gross Profit
		UNDER FIFO				
19X1.........	1,000 at $1.00	1,000 at $1.00	1,000 at $1.00	$1,000	$2,000	$1,000
19X2.........	1,000 at 1.00	1,000 at 1.50	1,000 at 1.50	1,000	2,500	1,500
19X3.........	1,000 at 1.50	1,000 at 2.00	1,000 at 2.00	1,500	3,000	1,500
19X4.........	1,000 at 2.00	1,000 at 0.50	1,000 at 0.50	2,000	1,500	(500)
19X5.........	1,000 at 0.50	1,000 at 1.00	1,000 at 1.00	500	2,000	1,500
				Total Five-Year Profit........$5,000		
		UNDER LIFO				
19X1.........	1,000 at $1.00	1,000 at $1.00	1,000 at $1.00	$1,000	$2,000	$1,000
19X2.........	1,000 at 1.00	1,000 at 1.50	1,000 at 1.00	1,500	2,500	1,000
19X3.........	1,000 at 1.00	1,000 at 2.00	1,000 at 1.00	2,000	3,000	1,000
19X4.........	1,000 at 1.00	1,000 at 0.50	1,000 at 1.00	500	1,500	1,000
19X5.........	1,000 at 1.00	1,000 at 1.00	1,000 at 1.00	1,000	2,000	1,000
				Total Five-Year Profit........$5,000		

* Beginning inventory, plus purchases, less ending inventory, each being assumed in this example to be 1,000 units. With an inventory turnover of 1, cost of sales under Fifo will equal the value of the beginning inventory, since it is assumed that the units sold were the oldest units on hand and equal in units to purchases. Under Lifo, cost of sales will equal the value of purchases, since it is assumed that the units sold were the units most recently purchased.
† 1,000 units times sales price per unit, which is assumed to be the current purchase price +$1.

In the example, prices are assumed to go through a complete cycle; that is, they rise and then fall back to the starting point. The following points can be noted from these calculations:

1. There is no difference in total profits under Lifo and under Fifo over the complete cycle.
2. Under the conventional Fifo method profits are high in years of high prices and low in years of low prices, even though the quantity sold and the margin between selling price and current material cost remains constant; also inventory values fluctuate widely, and inventory is at its highest price at the very top of the cycle.
3. Under the Lifo method, profit and inventory values are the same in each year; in one year 19X4, inventory was valued at more than "market."

Basic Arguments

A more generalized argument in favor of Lifo goes beyond the limitation of exact agreement of cost and selling price, as was presumed in the example given above. The real issue, from this point of view, is whether or not the company has properly counted its current costs against its current revenue in figuring its net income. In periods of rising prices the company does have increased costs in maintaining its inventory position, and current sales should be charged with a cost of goods sold that reflects these current costs. To do otherwise, this argument runs, is to count a cost as a profit and to pay stiff taxes on the amounts so reported.

This broader view of Lifo looks on inventory as a necessary stock in trade, just as essential to operations as are plant or facilities. Accordingly, such an investment ought *not* to be revalued on the balance sheet with every cyclical swing of prices any more than plant is revalued. As Illustration 9–1 demonstrates, the Lifo method tends to stabilize both profits and the reported value of inventory as prices change.

Opponents of Lifo argue that one of management's primary responsibilities is effective utilization of the economic resources at its disposal. They admit that over sustained periods of price level changes, conventional accounting fails to reflect the economic values of such resources as plant and inventory, but they claim that Lifo confuses, rather than clarifies, the picture. Under Lifo, inventory is valued forever in terms of whatever the price level happened to be at the time Lifo was introduced. As time goes on and price levels change, the inventory figure under Lifo departs further and further from reality, becoming neither a reflection of actual purchase costs nor of current costs. Thus Lifo may make the inventory figure on the balance sheet of dubious usefulness to management or to others who attempt to appraise the financial status of the business.

Advocates of Lifo are thinking primarily of its effect on the income statement and are willing to accept the fact that the usefulness of the balance sheet inventory figure may be impaired. Opponents of Lifo emphasize its effect on the balance sheet; they admit that the conventional Fifo income statement may not reflect the flow of economic values, although they do not grant that this is necessarily bad.

Dollar Value Method

Originally, Lifo was used only by companies whose inventory consisted of fungible products, such as wheat, each unit of which is physically like every other unit. Other companies, however, argued that this was unfair to them, and Lifo may now be used for almost any kind of inventory. It is applied to an inventory of physically unlike items by the so-called *Lifo dollar value method*. In this method, items whose prices tend to move together are grouped into an *inventory pool*. A pool may consist of all the items in the hardware department of a department store, for example, or it may consist of a store's entire inventory. The dollar amount invested in such a pool is treated as a unit in figuring the Lifo inventory value and cost of goods sold, and changes in the value of the dollar during the accounting period are allowed for by the application of index numbers of price changes.

As an illustration, assume that the beginning inventory in a pool had an actual invoice cost of $780,000, and that the inventory at the end of the year had an actual invoice cost of $880,000. Without additional information, we do not know how much of the $100,000 increase in the amount of inventory represents an increase in the *physical size* of the inventory and how much results from the same quantity being valued at a higher price because of inflation. By the use of an index number of price changes, the change associated with size can be separated from the change associated with price movements. Thus, if an appropriate price index increased from 100 at the beginning of the year to 110 at the end of the year, the year-end inventory can be *deflated* to the beginning price level by multiplying it by the ratio of the index change, or $^{100}/_{110}$. The value of the ending inventory expressed in beginning prices is therefore $^{100}/_{110}$ of $880,000, or $800,000. Since $800,000 exceeds the beginning inventory of $780,000 by $20,000, we estimate that the physical size of the inventory has increased by $20,000 during the year. This $20,000 is expressed in beginning prices, however, and under the Lifo method it must be added to inventory at the most recent prices, so it is *reinflated* by multiplying by the ratio $^{110}/_{100}$, to give $22,000. The ending inventory thus is valued at $802,000, which is the sum of the beginning inventory, $780,000, plus the increase in physical inventory, $22,000. Cost of goods sold is then found by the deduction formula—beginning inventory, plus purchases, less ending inventory—which results in a difference of $78,000 between the invoice cost and the Lifo cost of ending inventory going into cost of goods sold.

In applying the dollar value method, department stores use price indexes especially computed for this purpose by the government. Other companies compute their own index from the movement of prices of all, or a sample of, items in inventory.

Decreases in Inventory

When the physical size of the inventory increases, in a Lifo system the inventory account is increased by the current cost of the units added. During a period of growth, the inventory account will therefore consist of a number of *layers*, a new layer being added each year. If subsequently the physical inventory should decrease in size, these layers in effect are stripped off, taking the most recently added layer first, in accordance with the basic Lifo rule. This process can have a peculiar effect on the income statement. If, for example, inventory is decreased even below its original size when the Lifo system started, inventory items will be moving into cost of goods sold at costs established several years previously; and if there has been constant inflation during the interim, such a shrinkage in inventory can result in a significant increase in reported income. Some people assert that in a recession some companies deliberately eat into their Lifo inventories in order to increase reported income in a lean year.

Variations

In applying the general idea of Lifo to a particular situation, several alternatives are possible:

1. Lifo may be applied to all inventories, or only to the raw materials inventory, or only to certain items in inventory.
2. Products may be run through the cost accounting mechanism at Lifo values, or the detailed cost records may show Fifo or specific invoice values, with an adjustment to Lifo being made only at the end of the accounting period.
3. Inventory changes may be calculated annually, or monthly, or even daily.

Usually the differences in results between the several methods of applying Lifo are small compared with the basic difference between Lifo and Fifo, but the fact that these differences in the application of Lifo exist is one reason why Lifo is criticized. It is difficult to compare the earnings of a company that uses Lifo with the earnings of a company that uses Fifo; variations within the general Lifo idea make "confusion worse confounded."

Tax Considerations

A company that wishes to use Lifo for income tax purposes must make application to do so, and once having been granted permission, it must continue to use Lifo thereafter unless it receives special permission to change again; such permission is not easily obtained.

If the company uses Lifo for tax purposes, it must also use Lifo in its annual financial statements (although not necessarily in monthly or quarterly statements). Incidentally, this is the only instance of a statutory requirement that the same method be used for financial accounting purposes as is used for tax purposes.

A company using Lifo cannot use the "lower of cost or market" rule for tax purposes; that is, it cannot write down its inventory to market if market values are below Lifo cost. On its financial statements, however, the company is permitted to show a write-down to market.

Although it is easy to calculate whether or not tax savings will result in the year in which Lifo is adopted, it is impossible to determine whether the net effect over a number of years will be a savings or not. The existence and amount of any future tax savings depends largely upon future price movements, fluctuations in tax rates applicable to the business, and variations in the amounts and kinds of physical inventories held at the end of each taxable year. Although over a period of years total income computed under either the Lifo or Fifo method may be the same, it does not follow that total income taxes will also be the same. Generally, total income taxes tend to be greater under Fifo than under Lifo if the following conditions exist: if income tax rates are progressive, if income tax rates are higher in years of rising prices than in years of falling prices, or if there is no provision for carry-back of losses. There is a permanent deferment of taxes, of course, if prices continue upward indefinitely; that is, if inflation is always with us. Although tax savings under Lifo are likely in periods of rising prices, they are by no means certain if prices are near their peak when the change to Lifo is made, for tax losses after prices begin to fall may be greater than the initial tax savings when prices were rising.

Base Stock Method

Another method of recognizing the impact of price changes on inventory, the *base stock method*, actually antedates Lifo in practice. It accomplishes approximately the same result as the Lifo method and indeed reflects current costs more closely than Lifo, but since its use is not permitted for tax purposes, it has not become widely adopted.

DEPRECIATION ON REPLACEMENT COST

Since the fixed assets of a company may have been purchased at various times extending many years into the past, price fluctuations cause the expense and asset amounts associated with these items to deviate even farther from current cost than is the case with inventory. The American Appraisal Company index of construction costs has more than quadrupled in the period from 1940 to 1968, and it doubled in the period from 1950 to 1968. This means that a dollar spent on construction in 1968 would buy only about half as many physical units of assets as a dollar spent in 1950, or that a 1968 dollar is a "50-cent dollar" in terms of its 1950 purchasing power.

Conventional accounting does not differentiate between 50-cent dollars and 100-cent dollars. If a company, for example, purchased an 80,000 square-foot factory building for $500,000 in 1950, this building, exclusive of accumulated depreciation, would appear on the balance sheet at $500,000; and if the building was replaced with a physically identical 80,000 square-foot factory building for $1 million in 1968, this would appear at $1 million. Although the balance sheet figure for the new building is double that of the old, the company actually has the same amount of factory space as it had before.

Moreover, the annual depreciation charge for fixed assets, being based on the actual cost of the asset, is not expressed in the same kind of dollars as the revenue item on the income statement. In periods of inflation, depreciation expressed in past dollars of relatively high purchasing power is matched against revenue expressed in current dollars of relatively low purchasing power.

Although the depreciation mechanism charges off the cost of the asset over its useful life, it does not, and is not designed to, provide for the replacement of the asset. Suppose, for example, that a company actually set aside a cash fund equal to its depreciation charge, paying out all its net income as dividends. Some might believe that a company could operate indefinitely on such a plan, using this fund to buy new assets as the old assets required replacement. If prices were steady this would be possible, but in periods of inflation the replacement fund could not purchase the same quantity of assets as those discarded, and the company would gradually shrink and eventually disappear.

The impact of income taxes increases the severity of the replacement problem. If the company recognizes the inadequacy of depreciation as a replacement medium and tries to earn additional income to add to its "replacement fund," it must, at a 50 percent rate, earn $2 of income before taxes for every $1 it wishes to put into a fund; the other $1 will be siphoned off in taxes.

Replacement Cost Proposal

In view of these problems, some people argue that depreciation should be calculated on the estimated replacement cost of an asset rather than on its original cost. The most famous attempt to do this is that of the United States Steel Corporation in the 1940's. This attempt did not succeed in obtaining either a change in accounting principles or a change in income tax regulations.

A change to a replacement cost basis of figuring depreciation would represent a fundamental modification in the concepts of accounting, since it would be a departure from the basic idea that balance sheet and expense amounts are based on monetary cost, and not on purchasing power or economic values. Even the Lifo inventory method uses monetary costs as obtained from actual transactions. The advantages of the cost basis of measurement—certainty, uniformity of interpretation, objectivity—have been discussed in earlier chapters. The question is whether an accounting system based on the attempt to measure the existence and flow of economic values has additional advantages that more than offset these.

A further question is whether assets should in fact be replaced by funds generated by current operations. Should selling prices be high enough so that net income will provide for both an adequate profit and the replacement of assets? Or should selling prices only provide for profits plus recovery of the costs actually incurred? Stated another way: Who should pay for the future machines, the current customers or the future customers who buy products made on the future machines? If operations do not generate enough funds for replacement, it is argued, the difference can and should be raised through borrowing or issuing new stock.

Accelerated Depreciation

Calculating depreciation on replacement cost is to be distinguished from *accelerated depreciation,* such as the double declining-balance or sum-of-years'-digits methods. Accelerated depreciation does mitigate somewhat the income tax problem discussed above since it permits depreciation to be written off faster than under the straight-line method, but accelerated depreciation is nevertheless restricted to actual cost. A replacement cost mechanism would, in periods of inflation, write off as expense *more than* the actual monetary cost of the asset.

Investment Policy

Although depreciation calculations in accounting are based on original cost rather than on replacement cost, the management of a company takes into account the effect of inflation in its decisions relating to the replacement of fixed assets. This is one reason why the Retained Earnings account tends to increase during an inflationary period. Management recognizes that the accounted amount of depreciation is likely to be inadequate as a measure of the amounts that must be provided to replace plant and equipment and that for this reason (as well as for other reasons) it is not prudent to declare dividends equal to the amount of net income reported on the income statement. The difference between recorded depreciation and the higher amounts that are likely to be required to replace assets may therefore be retained in the business.

This is a matter of management policy, not of accounting. There is no assurance that this policy is being followed in a given company, and even when it is followed, there is no way of estimating precisely what the actual cash needs for replacement will be since these needs depend partly on what the level of prices is at the time the assets are replaced and partly on changes in technology. Because of technological changes, new fixed assets are unlikely to cost the same as those they are replacing, even if there were no change in the general level of prices.

PRICE LEVEL ADJUSTMENTS

In studies sponsored by the AICPA, by the American Accounting Association, and by a few university groups, procedures have been devised for expressing each item on the balance sheet and the income statement in dollars that have the same purchasing power. Usually, these procedures are advocated as a supplement to, not a replacement of, the conventional procedures. In other words, the conventional statements would continue to be the "official" reports, and the adjusted statements would be given separately.

The process of making such adjustments is a fairly long and complicated one, and it requires information as to the approximate date on which each asset was acquired, which usually involves considerable searching of old records. Essentially, an index number of prices is selected and each item is converted to current prices by multiplying its original cost by the ratio of the current price index to the index value at date of acquisition. (The best index for this purpose is probably the "Gross National Product Implicit Price Deflator," prepared by the U.S. Department of Commerce.) Thus, if an asset were purchased when the index was 100, and currently the index is 200, the dollar amount of the asset value would be doubled. If this were a depreciable asset, depreciation would be recalculated on the basis of the doubled amount.

In a period of inflation, the effect of these adjustments is to increase the book value of the assets and to decrease the reported income for the year. The decrease in income results primarily from the increased depreciation charge but also from upward adjustments in other expense items.

The Reece Corporation is one of the few that reported net income on both a "historical dollars" basis and on a "uniform dollars" basis. In its 1957 annual report, management pointed out that although on the conventional basis net income for 1956 was the largest ever reported in the company's 76 years of existence, on a uniform dollars basis 1956 net income was actually less than that of 1955. Its 1961 annual report showed net income as 225 percent of that in 1943 when reported on a conventional basis, but only 130 percent of 1943 on a uniform dollar basis. Reece did not compute net income in 1962 on a "uniform dollars" basis, giving the severe illness of its office manager as the reason. It has not resumed the practice.

Advocates of the price level adjustment process point to this shrinkage of income as a measure of how much the company may be fooling itself by relying on conventional accounting as a measure of economic progress. Those who do not prepare these adjusted statements say that they are not in fact misled; they can recognize the approximate impact of price level changes without going through all the calculations.

Instead of adjusting all items, some accountants advocate that only depreciation expense be adjusted for changes in prices. Such a procedure would not give the same end result as the calculation of depreciation based on replacement costs since the underlying procedures are different. In both cases, however, the adjustment grows out of a desire to recognize the effect of inflationary forces on the accounts.

The AICPA Studies

In April, 1961, the Accounting Principles Board of AICPA took the action summarized in the following excerpt from its minutes:

. . . the Board . . . agreed that the assumption in accounting that fluctuations in the value of the dollar may be ignored is unrealistic, and that therefore the Director of Accounting Research should be instructed to set up a research project to study the problem and to prepare a report in which recommendations are made for the disclosure of the effect of price-level changes upon the financial statements. In this study, special attention should be paid to the use of supplementary statements as a means of disclosure.

The report on this research project, published in October, 1963, is an excellent presentation of all facets of the problem.[1] Some of the highlights of this study are quoted below:

1. [There is] clear evidence of the widespread concern of businessmen and accountants with the need for changes in financial reporting to reflect the effects of inflation and deflation.
2. The examples quoted from financial statements around the world are sufficient to demonstrate that recognition of price-level changes in financial statements is practical, and not misleading or dangerous to investors.
3. The study of the index number problem indicates that at least one index of the general price level is available in the United States and is reliable enough for use in financial statements.
4. The effects of price-level changes should be disclosed as a supplement to the conventional statements. This disclosure may take the form of physically separate statements, or of parallel columns in a combined statement, or of detailed supporting schedules (including charts and graphs), or some combination of these.
5. In the supplementary data, all elements of the financial statements (e.g., balance sheet, income statement, analysis of retained earnings) should be restated by means of a single index of the general price level as of the

---

[1] AICPA Accounting Research Division, *Reporting the Financial Effects of Price-Level Changes* (Accounting Research Study No. 6) (New York, 1963). For earlier studies, see Ralph C. Jones, *Price Level Changes and Financial Statements* (American Accounting Association, 1955); Perry Mason, *Price-Level Changes and Financial Statements* (American Accounting Association, 1956); and H. W. Sweeney, *Stabilized Accounting* (New York: Harper & Bros., 1936).

balance-sheet date so that all the financial data will be expressed in terms of dollars of the same purchasing power.

In June 1969, the Accounting Principles Board published a new statement on the subject.[2] The Board's position is that although financial statements adjusted for price-level changes provide useful information, these statements should be regarded as supplements to, rather than as substitutes for, the basic financial statements prepared in the conventional way. The Board gave detailed instructions for the preparation of such statements.

Holding Gains and Operating Gains

Some people propose that instead of recasting the financial statements to reflect price level changes, the income statement should be redesigned so that it distinguishes between (1) that part of net income which results from the physical process of manufacturing and selling products, and (2) that part which results from inflation. The former is called *operating gains*, and the latter *holding gains*, the word "holding" suggesting that the gain results from holding assets that were acquired at a cost that is lower than their current cost.

As an illustration, consider the second year (19X2) of the situation shown in Illustration 9–1. In that year, 1,000 units of goods that cost $1,000 were sold for $2,500, so the gross profit, measured on the Fifo basis, was $1,500. The current cost of these goods, however, was $1,500, and the gross profit on the Lifo basis was therefore $1,000 = ($2,500 − $1,500). Since the selling price in this situation was assumed to be set at $1 per unit above the current cost, it can be said that the *operating gain* was 1,000 units × $1, or $1,000, the same amount as measured on the Lifo basis. The difference between this amount and the $1,500 measured on the Fifo basis, i.e., $500, is a *holding gain;* it arises because goods bought at $1 were held until the selling price increased. Both the operating gain and the holding gain would be shown on the income statement, the latter as an extraordinary item appearing below the operating net income.

A similar separation can be made for depreciation on fixed assets. The operating gain would be calculated using depreciation based on replacement costs, and the holding gain would be the difference between this amount and the amount of depreciation based on historical costs.

This proposal is in accordance with generally accepted accounting principles, since it involves no change in the final figure for net income. Nevertheless, few companies follow it for their published financial statements, although some make this separation for purposes of internal analysis.

---

[2] Accounting Principles Board, *Financial Statements Restated for General Price-Level Changes*, Statement No. 3 (New York, 1969).

EXAMPLE: UNITED STATES STEEL CORPORATION[3]

United States Steel Corporation is the nation's largest steel producer. Its postwar changes in depreciation accounting policies are described here in some detail as an example of how some companies try to take account of the effect of price level changes.

The 1947 Change

For several years prior to 1947 the management of United States Steel Corporation had been concerned with the effects upon the company's capital replacement program of the steady rise in the general price level since the late 1930's. This concern, shared by a major segment of American business management, arose chiefly from the realization that the amounts being deducted from earnings to cover the depreciation and amortization of plant and equipment were not sufficient to provide for the replacement of such facilities when they were worn out or became obsolete.

As a step toward stating depreciation in an amount which would recover in current dollars of diminished buying power the same purchasing power represented by the original plant expenditure, the company deducted, in arriving at net income for 1947, an amount of $26.3 million over and above its regular depreciation charge (based on the straight-line method.) Although the federal tax authorities would not allow the extra depreciation as a deduction in arriving at taxable income for that year, the company's executives considered it essential that they recognize this element of cost in arriving at a measure of income to be used in other matters of company management.

In its 1947 annual report the management stated that "while awaiting accounting and tax acceptance, U.S. Steel believed that it was prudent for it to give some recognition to increased replacement costs rather than to sit idly by and witness the unwitting liquidation of its business should inadequate recording of costs result in insufficient resources to supply the tools required for sustained production."

In its opinion on the 1947 financial statements, the company's independent auditors stated that the corporation had included in costs additional depreciation of $26.3 million "in excess of the amount determined in accordance with the generally accepted accounting principle heretofore followed of making provision for depreciation on the original cost of facilities."

Carman G. Blough, director of research of the American Institute of

---

[3] Copyright © by the President and Fellows of Harvard College.

Certified Public Accountants (at that time the American Institute of Accountants), commented on this practice as follows:

There can be no argument but that a going concern must be able to replace its productive assets as they are used up if it is to continue to do business. It is also important for management to understand that the difference between cost and estimated replacement value may be significant in determining production and pricing policies. It does not follow, however, that the excess of the cost of replacement over the cost of existing assets should be accounted for as current charges to income. All who have dealt with appraisal values know how very difficult it is just to determine current replacement costs, but the most striking difficulty in this respect is the impossibility of predicting what will be the eventual cost of replacing a productive asset. How many men are prepared to state what the price level will be two years from today, to say nothing of trying to guess what it will be five or ten years hence when many of those assets are to be replaced.[4]

The AICPA Committee on Accounting Procedure issued, in late 1947, *Accounting Research Bulletin No. 33* (later restated as *ARB No. 43*, Chapter 9, Section A, paragraphs 4–9), in which it stated that it disapproved "immediate write-downs of plant cost by charges against current income in amounts believed to represent excessive or abnormal costs occasioned by current price levels."

The 1948 Retreat

In its annual report for 1948, U.S. Steel announced that it was abandoning the policy adopted in 1947 and was substituting in its place a method of charging "accelerated depreciation on cost," which was explained as follows in the annual report:

The accelerated depreciation is applicable to the cost of postwar facilities in the first few years of their lives when economic usefulness is greatest. The amount thereof is related to the excess of current operating rates over U.S. Steel's long-term peacetime average rate of 70% of capacity. The annual accelerated amount is 10% of the cost of facilities in the year in which the expenditures are made and 10% in the succeeding year, except that this amount is reduced ratably as the operating rate may drop, no acceleration being made at 70% or lower operations. The accelerated depreciation is an addition to the normal depreciation on such facilities, but the total depreciation over their expected lives will not exceed the cost of the facilities.

This method was made retroactive to January 1, 1947, and there was included, in the $55,335,444 deducted for accelerated wear and exhaustion

---

[4] "Replacement and Excess Construction Costs," *Journal of Accountancy*, Vol. LXXIV (October, 1947), p. 335.

of facilities for 1948, an amount of $2,675,094 to cover a deficiency in the $26,300,000 sum reported in 1947 as "depreciation added to cover replacement cost." In other words, the new method when applied to the 1947 situation resulted in a deduction that exceeded the figure actually reported in 1947. It was again pointed out at this time that the accelerated depreciation was not "presently deductible for federal income tax purposes."

The company's independent auditors stated in their report to the shareholders for 1948 that they "approved" the new policy.

The management's convictions on the change in policy were, however, clearly set forth by the chairman of the board of directors in the following quotation from the company's annual report for 1948:

> U.S. Steel believes that the principle which it adopted in 1947 and continued in 1948 is a proper recording of the wear and exhaustion of its facilities in terms of current dollars as distinguished from the dollars which it originally expended for those facilities. However, in view of the disagreement existing among accountants, both public and private, and the stated position of the American Institute of Certified Public Accountants, which is supported by the Securities and Exchange Commission, that the only accepted accounting principle for determining depreciation is that which is related to the actual number of dollars spent for facilities, regardless of when or what buying power, U.S. Steel has adopted a method of accelerated depreciation based on cost instead of one based on purchasing power recovery.

The 1953 Change

United States Steel Corporation continued its policy of charging accelerated depreciation through 1952. Deductions for accelerated depreciation for 1947 through 1952 totaled slightly more than $201 million; none of this sum, however, had been allowed in computing taxable income during that period.

During and after the Korean War, U.S. Steel was granted Certificates of Necessity which permitted amortization of designated facilities over a 60-month period for tax purposes regardless of the facilities' probable economic life. Management decided to depreciate these facilities in the corporate accounts over the 60-month period.

In 1953, U. S. Steel changed its accelerated depreciation policy, as explained in this note to the 1953 financial statements:

> Since 1946 U.S. Steel has followed the policy of reflecting accelerated depreciation on the cost of new facilities in the first few years of their lives when the economic usefulness is greatest. The amounts charged to income for accelerated depreciation have been related to U.S. Steel's rate of operations.

Under the Internal Revenue Code, that portion of the cost of facilities certified by the Defense Production Administration as essential to the defense effort is covered by a Certificate of Necessity and can be written off for tax purposes at the rate of 20% per year. The effect of amortization of these facilities is to charge to income a greater portion of their cost in the earlier years of life, and therefore, follows the principle of accelerated depreciation.

U.S. Steel has included in wear and exhaustion in 1953, as a measure of the accelerated depreciation for the year, $105,137,893, representing amortization on its facilities covered by Certificate of Necessity.

In commenting on the effect of accelerated amortization and the tax laws, management pointed out that it had to be regarded as a temporary expedient, since "for many companies the addition of amortization on new facilities to so-called regular depreciation on old facilities may approximate, temporarily, a truer total of wear and exhaustion on all facilities based on current dollar value. But it automatically guarantees something of a future crisis." As an example of this, management cited the recently constructed Fairless Works. A portion of this plant's cost was amortized over five years, thus partially offsetting "inadequate" depreciation charges for other facilities. It was stated that this situation would naturally change when the five-year amortization was completed.

Management noted in 1954 that the new methods of accelerated depreciation, first allowed for tax purposes in 1954, would ease the future crisis, but even these provisions, applicable to new assets only, would fall far short of providing adequate depreciation on the relatively more numerous and older existing facilities.

1956

In its 1956 report, U.S. Steel included a chart (see Illustration 9–2) comparing "wear and exhaustion recorded" with "wear and exhaustion needed." To calculate "total wear and exhaustion needed," as shown in the chart, the following statistical procedure was followed: Excluding the amount of nontax-deductible accelerated depreciation from 1947 through 1952, and including only regular depreciation on emergency facilities, the amount of wear and exhaustion previously recorded for *each year* included in the chart was subdivided according to the acquisition years of the assets being depreciated. Each yearly subdivision was then adjusted to reflect the change in the *Engineering News-Record*'s index of construction cost from the various earlier acquisition years to any given year included in the chart. The sum of that year's adjusted depreciation amounts gave the "total wear and exhaustion needed" for that year. The process was repeated for every year in the chart. Notice that each year's deficiency is in dollars of the buying power that prevailed in *that* year.

Illustration 9–2

WEAR AND EXHAUSTION RECORDED VERSUS WEAR AND
EXHAUSTION NEEDED

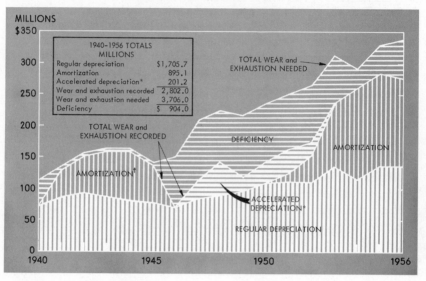

* Not deductible for tax purposes.
† Additional amortization due to ending of emergency period allocated to years 1941–1945.

Inflation in Cost of Facilities*

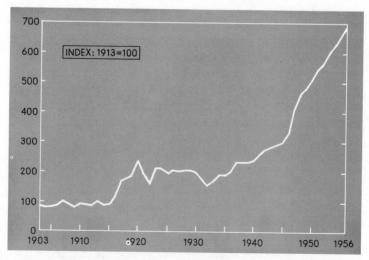

* From *Engineering News-Record* Construction Cost Index.
Source: *United States Steel Corporation Annual Report*, 1956. Used by permission.

The 1959 Strike

In 1959, management noted the approaching exhaustion of emergency amortization:

This (depreciation) deficiency has been aggravated by the running out of 5-year amortization permitted on varying percentages of the total costs of certain defense and defense-supporting facilities covered by Certificates of Necessity. The need for revision of the tax laws as they relate to depreciation . . . continues to be most vital to the maintenance of existing and the addition of new productive capacity.

In the spring of 1959, the representatives of the United Steelworkers of America and the major steel companies met to negotiate a new wage contract to replace the contract expiring in June. The union requested sizable increases in wages and fringe benefits, contending that large steel profits would permit these increases without affecting the prices of finished steel. The steel industry spokesmen argued this was not possible; any *sizable* wage increase would have to be passed along in the form of higher prices. There was considerable government pressure for a settlement without the need for a price increase in order to avoid the threat of further inflation.

A full-page newspaper advertisement in May 1959, paid for by the union, read in part:

STEELWORKERS SHARE OF
STEEL INDUSTRY'S INCOME HAS
NOT INCREASED SINCE 1952

True, there have been wage increases, but because fewer men are making more steel, the total labor costs have remained the same.

Please examine these LABOR COSTS:

1952. . . . . .42.1¢ of each sales dollar
1958. . . . . .42.8¢ of each sales dollar

(notice they are about the same)

Now examine the NET PROFITS:

1952. . . . .$143,678,740
1958. 301,558,231

(profits have DOUBLED)

A nationwide steel strike lasted from July until mid-November.

On December 8, 1959, J. S. Seidman, president of AICPA released to the press a statement explaining the issues in the steel strike:

The industry's contention was that under conventional accounting, depreciation is calculated based on the original dollar cost, and that this is inadequate because it fails to give effect to the tremendous change that has taken place in the purchasing power of the dollar, as a result of which it would cost many more dollars today to replace the plant than were originally spent. The industry maintains that realistic profits should be figured by reference to replacement figures. On that basis, the industry's profits are one half of what the financial statements show.

The labor officials contend that original cost is all that should be recovered, and that anything in excess of that is a profit. Furthermore, they say that the original cost should be spread over the expected period in which the plant will be used. However, the companies have been following the tax laws in the way they write off depreciation, and the tax laws have allowed a higher write-off to be bunched in early years and counterbalanced by a lower write-off in later years. The figures presented by the steel industry cover the earlier years where there is the higher write-off. The labor people say that the depreciation amounts should be reduced by this excess write-off in the early years. Reducing the depreciation would result in an increase in profits.

. . . All of this raises a question as to whether the conventional accounting use of historical dollars is meaningful in an inflationary period.

Investment Credit

By 1962, the inflationary pressures on the economy had diminished. Also in 1962, U.S. Steel benefited from two changes in the system of federal income taxation: adoption of the new guideline procedures for depreciation lives set forth in Revenue Ruling 62–21 added $44 million to the wear and exhaustion amounts previously determined; and the use of the investment tax credit resulted in a $8.2 million reduction in federal income taxes.

The investment tax credit provided by the Revenue Act of 1962 was intended to stimulate capital investment. It allowed a credit directly against the company's federal income tax liability of 7 percent of the cost of "qualified" depreciable property.

Shift to Straight-Line

During 1968, economic pressure increased on companies within the steel industry. The contract with the United Steelworkers was due to terminate and there was a widespread expectation that a strike would be called on August 1. As a result, steel users stockpiled inventories heavily. The high volume of orders during the first half of the year resulted in capacity operations by steel mills, including the use of less efficient, marginal production equipment. In addition, foreign imports of steel had increased substantially during the first half of 1968. To meet the stiff price competition, many domestic producers engaged in price "discounting" to customers despite general acceptance of standard prices by the industry.

The labor dispute was settled without a strike on July 30. Production fell sharply as customers reduced excess inventories. It was anticipated that the normal ordering pattern would not be resumed until January 1969.

Under these conditions (the high costs of cutting back production, the generally higher wage levels; and production pegged near the break-even point) third quarter earnings were sharply reduced. U.S. Steel's 1968 third quarter profits fell 70 percent below those of the corresponding quarter of 1967. Bethlehem Steel Corporation reported a decline of 0.6 percent, Republic Steel 31 percent, National 21 percent, Jones and Laughlin 86 percent, and Youngstown Sheet and Tube 57 percent. Only Armco Steel and Inland reported profit increases over the previous year.

The effect of the profit decline would have been more severe, except that many of the companies switched from accelerated to straight-line depreciation in the third quarter. The exact method of change varied among the steelmakers: some applied the change only to equipment purchased after 1967, others applied it to all depreciable property on hand. Several companies also switched from deferring to flowing through their investment tax credits.

Despite these changes, U.S. Steel continued to follow its policy of accelerated depreciation. It announced, however, that if it had changed to straight-line depreciation, profits would have increased $33 million, or $0.61 per share, for the third quarter, and $205.6 million, or $3.80 per share, for the first three quarters of the year.

One factor considered by some to have a bearing on the accounting changes of some steel companies was the takeover of Jones and Laughlin by Ling-Tempco-Vought. Many of the smaller steel manufacturers were also considered attractive acquisitions because of their high cash flows, understated assets, and low earnings per share and price earnings ratios.

As an admitted direct response to this potential problem, Armco Steel had changed to straight-line depreciation methods in the first half of 1968. This change had added $0.46 to earning per share in the first two quarters of the year. By consolidation of European operations, an additional $0.19 per share had been obtained. As a result, earnings for the first half of 1968 ran 25 percent above the comparable period in 1967.

Financial statistics for the corporation are given in Illustration 9–3.

CONCLUSION

Of the techniques discussed in this chapter, only Lifo is currently (1969) in accordance with generally accepted accounting principles. In fact, *either* Lifo or Fifo is acceptable, although they are completely inconsistent with one another. Depreciation on replacement costs may

Illustration 9–3

U.S. STEEL CORPORATION

Selected Financial Statistics 1946–1967
(millions of dollars)

Year	Net Income	Depreciation	Capital Expenditures	Investment Tax Credit Taken	Amortization of Emergency Facilities
1967............	$172.5	$354.7	$547.7	$33.4	13.7
1966............	249.2	344.3	440.7	20.8	22.2
1965............	275.5	324.5	353.6	13.7	57.2
1964............	236.8	335.8	292.6	.6	115.8
1963............	203.5	307.8	244.7	.6 (est.)	140.2
1962............	163.7	265.9	200.6	.4 (est.)	147.7
1961............	190.2	210.5	326.8	...	142.8
1960............	304.2	208.4	492.4	...	105.1
1959............	254.5	189.9	366.1	...	46.2
1958............	301.5	204.9	448.1	...	12.8
1957............	319.4	276.0	514.9	...	...
1956............	348.1	277.6	311.8	...	...
1955............	348.1	285.2	239.8	...	...
1954............	195.4	261.8	227.4	...	...
1953............	222.1	236.6	361.4	...	...
1952............	143.6	176.9	469.2	...	...
1951............	184.3	162.1	352.4	...	...
1950............	215.5	143.9	179.3	...	...
1949............	165.9	119.7	179.1	...	...
1948............	129.6	146.0	275.2	...	...
1947............	127.1	114.0	206.6	...	...
1946............	88.6	68.7	201.0	...	...

become accepted either as in accordance with accounting principles, as a basis of income taxation, or both, although acceptance seems less likely now than was the case in the 1950's. The overall adjustment of all financial statement items to current prices is likely to remain as a supplementary report rather than as a substitute for figures based on historical cost.

PART II

Using Information on Financial Statements

CHAPTER 10

UNDERSTANDING FINANCIAL STATEMENTS

In the preceding chapters the basic concepts of accounting were discussed, accounting terms were defined, and conventions and procedures were described. This was done from the point of view of the user of accounting information, rather than that of the accountant. The user is primarily interested in the end products of the accounting process, which are the balance sheet and the income statement. This chapter discusses the uses and the limitations of these statements.

CRITERIA AND BASIC CONCEPTS

In Chapter 2 it was suggested that accounting concepts and principles gain acceptance according to how well they meet three criteria: relevance, objectivity, and feasibility. Others list these criteria somewhat differently. For example, an American Accounting Association publication, *A Statement of Basic Accounting Theory*, 1966, lists the two criteria of "verifiability" and "freedom from bias" rather than the single criterion of "objectivity."

Conflict among Criteria

Brief mention was also made in Chapter 2 of the inevitable conflict between the criterion of relevance on the one hand and the criteria of objectivity and feasibility on the other. Accounting principles in general use reflect a workable compromise between these opposing forces.

Of the many examples that have been discussed in the intervening chapters, perhaps the most clear-cut is that relating to the measurement of fixed assets. In general, the most relevant rule for stating fixed assets, the rule that would provide readers of financial statements with what they really want to know, would be: state fixed assets at their market value, what they are really worth. But such a rule would be neither objective nor feasible in most situations. The market value of assets in a going concern depends upon the future earnings that will be generated with these assets. In special circumstances, outside experts, i.e., appraisers, can be relied upon to make estimates of future earnings, but there are by no means enough appraisers in the country to make such estimates annually for all companies. Even if there were enough of them, the appraisers would be forced to rely heavily on the judgment of the management, which is in by far the best position to know about future earnings prospects. To rely on the opinions of management, however, would introduce a highly subjective element. Shareholders, prospective shareholders, banks, and others use financial statements, in part, to find out how well management has done. It would be highly unrealistic to expect that management would make unbiased estimates under these circumstances.

At the other extreme, the most objective and feasible rule for measuring fixed assets would be: state fixed assets at the price paid for them, i.e., at their cost, and hold them at cost until they are disposed of (or, alternatively, write them off the books immediately). In most cases such a rule would be perfectly simple to apply and would involve little, if any, judgment. But such a rule would prohibit accounting from reflecting on the income statement the expense called depreciation, which represents an estimate of the amount of asset cost that is properly charged to the operations of each accounting period. A net income figure that includes such an estimate of fixed asset expiration is much more useful for most purposes than one that omits depreciation altogether.

So accounting takes a middle ground. Assets are originally booked at cost, which is an objectively determined amount in most cases, and this cost is charged against income over the useful life of the asset. The annual depreciation charge is an estimate, and any of several ways of making this estimate are permitted, but the number of permitted alternatives is small, and freedom to tamper with the estimates is further restricted by the concept of consistency.

A similar conflict among objectives arises in the case of many other principles. As will be discussed further below, failure to appreciate this fact is behind the feeling of many of the uninitiated that "accounting doesn't make sense."

Currently (1969) the Securities and Exchange Commission is proposing that companies should report a breakdown of revenue and expenses for each of their major product lines. Unquestionably, the income by product lines is relevant information, especially in diversified or conglomerate companies; investors would like very much to have this information. Some oppose this requirement, on the grounds that the principles governing the allocation of costs to product lines are so vague that the resulting data would not be meaningful. Thus, the conflict between relevance and objectivity/feasibility continues.

Concepts

Ten concepts that are basic to accounting were described in Chapters 2 and 3. Since no set of concepts has been adopted as such by any authoritative body, others would classify and describe them somewhat differently. For example, Paul Grady in his highly respected *Inventory of Generally Accepted Principles for Business Enterprises* lists 10 concepts, a majority of which are similar to, but not identical with, those given in this book. In the early 1960's the Accounting Principles Board gave some thought to approving a set of concepts, but it has not done so. Until it, or some other authoritative group, does so, the concepts must be deduced from practice.[1]

The many conventions and procedures described in Part I were amplifications to and applications of the basic concepts, rather than additions to them. As a matter of convention, for example, accumulated depreciation is shown in a separate account rather than being credited directly to the asset account, but the basic idea of depreciation accounting is nevertheless in accordance with the concepts that assets are recorded at cost and costs are matched against revenue in the period benefited.

Any conceivable transaction, provided that it is clearly described, can be analyzed in terms of its effect on the assets and equities of the business in accordance with the basic accounting concepts. For an extremely large fraction of the transactions in a typical business, the answer is simple and unequivocal: for a cash sale, debit Cash and credit Sales; for receipts from a credit customer, credit Accounts Receivable and debit Cash.

In a relatively small number of transactions, real analysis is required. For some of these, a correct answer can be found. For example, a number of transactions involve a credit to Cash or Accounts Payable for the purchase of something. The question is whether the offsetting debit is to an asset account or to an expense account, and the answer to this question depends on whether the business has, or has not, acquired a property right that has material value beyond the end of the accounting period. In still other cases, there is no unique "right" answer: accounting principles permit any of several treatments. In these cases, one simply uses his best judgment.

Many of these situations that require judgment do so because of inevitable uncertainties about the future. How long will the building

---

[1] The American Accounting Association publication, "A Statement of Basic Accounting Theory," is a statement of what accounting concepts *should be,* not what they *are.*

really last? Will this expenditure for research really result in future profits, and if so, how much? Is a decline in the market value of inventory only temporary, or should the inventory be written down? There are no unequivocal answers to such questions, and hence no way of arriving at a result with which everyone would agree.

Misconceptions about Concepts

Some of the basic concepts are intuitively sensible: for example, the idea that accounting data are expressed in monetary terms. Certain concepts, however, are rather different from the impression that the typical layman has about them. As Professor Walter F. Frese puts it:

. . . Generally, the character of accounting is not fully understood either by the people who use it as a means of communicating the results of operations for which they are responsible (business managers) or by people to whom such results are communicated (stockholders, investors, labor, general management and others). Those at both ends of this communication process often believe that somewhere in the middle the accountant, through application of mysterious specialized techniques, can translate the facts and judgments underlying business transactions into quantitative terms, predigest them, and come out at the end of the process with figures which precisely measure the results of business operations.[2]

Undoubtedly the greatest misconception on the part of laymen relates to the cost concept. To the layman, it seems only reasonable that the accountant should report the *value* of assets—what they are really worth—rather than merely to trace the flow of costs. The layman finds it difficult to believe that the balance sheet is not, even approximately, a statement showing what the business is worth, especially when he sees on many balance sheets an item labeled "net worth." And even if he eventually recognizes that the balance sheet does not in fact report values, he criticizes accounting and accountants for not being able to devise a way of doing this.

The root of the layman's difficulty is his failure to appreciate the importance of the criteria of objectivity and feasibility. A balance sheet that set forth the real value of the assets would of course be more relevant to the reader than a balance sheet based on cost. But there simply is no objective and feasible way of ascertaining true values under most circumstances. As noted above, a reasonable estimate of the value of the assets can be made only by the management, but the financial statements are supposed to be reports of management's stewardship. To base them on management's own estimates would be equivalent to letting the batter call his own balls and strikes.

[2] Walter F. Frese, in the Foreword to *Contemporary Accounting Problems* by Leonard Morrissey (Englewood Cliffs, N.J.: Prentice-Hall, Inc., 1963).

A related misconception is the layman's failure to appreciate the significance of the going-concern concept. If one accepts the idea that the productive assets are held not for sale but rather for their future usefulness, then one sees that there is no necessity for determining the current sales value of these assets.

The layman also finds the accrual concept—the matching of costs and revenues—a difficult one to comprehend. In his personal life, he knows that when he makes an expenditure to the grocer, to the service station, and so on, he is that much "out of pocket." He has difficulty in understanding the fact that many business expenditures are merely the exchange of one asset for another, with the business getting as much as it gives up. Expenses occur in the time period when costs expire—when they are used up—and this time period is not necessarily the same as the time period in which the expenditure is made.

Those who do understand the basic concepts do not necessarily agree with all of them. The accounting profession is constantly involved in debates over one or another of the currently accepted principles. Since they are not laws of nature, they are subject to change, and occasionally they are changed. At the same time, the *user* of accounting information must do the best he can with the situation as it exists. He may wish that the principles were different, but as he reads an accounting report he needs to know how it *was* prepared, not how it might have been prepared.

LIMITATIONS OF ACCOUNTING

Although the person who understands the basic concepts of accounting can make an acceptable record of any accounting transaction, this knowledge does not, unfortunately, equip him fully to understand the financial statements that have been prepared by others. The rules governing the preparation of financial statements vary considerably from one company to another, for at least three reasons: (1) there is no general agreement as to what the principles are; (2) not everyone applies even those principles that are generally agreed upon, and (3) principles are not applied uniformly.

Absence of a Complete Set of Principles

The most authoritative source of accounting principles is the Accounting Principles Board of the American Institute of Certified Public Accountants. Its pronouncements have been relied on heavily in the preceding chapters. (The Securities and Exchange Commission also makes authoritative pronouncements, but these usually follow, or are at least consistent with, those of the Accounting Principles Board.) These pronouncements, however, do not comprise a complete, consistent body of principles. Instead, they are statements on specific topics, usually topics about which a controversy arose at some time in the past.

Lack of Agreement on Principles

The pronouncements of the Accounting Principles Board are not binding, even on the members of the AICPA. Its members are required to so state when they have departed from the Board's pronouncements, but an auditor can, and does, in good conscience, state that a certain practice is "in accordance with generally accepted accounting principles" if he knows of a number of reputable companies that follow the practice, even though the practice is not consistent with pronouncements of the Accounting Principles Board. For example, in 1963 the APB recommended that the "investment credit" allowed under the 1962 Revenue Act be treated as affecting income in the years over which a fixed asset is depreciated, rather than the year in which the asset is acquired. Nevertheless, three of the eight largest accounting firms approved financial statements which followed the opposite practice. (As noted in Chapter 6, the APB now permits either practice.)

Moreover, certain groups of companies are required to adhere to principles that are not necessarily consistent with those recommended by AICPA. Railroads and other common carriers follow rules prescribed by the Interstate Commerce Commission; public utilities, by the Federal Power Commission; banks and insurance companies, by state regulatory agencies. Government agencies, colleges and universities, hospitals, and other not-for-profit organizations follow practices that in important respects are inconsistent with AICPA recommendations. In approving the financial statements of such bodies, the auditor does not state that the statements are prepared in accordance with "generally accepted principles"—rather, he says they are "consistent with practice followed in the industry," or words to that effect.

INCOME TAX PRINCIPLES. We should note at this point that the principles governing the calculation of income for federal income tax purposes are basically the same as the principles of financial accounting; that is, in general, taxable income is the difference between realized revenue and expired cost. There are, however, some important differences, which are as follows:

First, taxpayers may, if they wish, disregard the accrual concept and elect to be taxed on the difference between cash receipts and cash expenditures. Many small businesses do this.

Second, the depletion allowance computed for tax purposes bears no relation to the principles of financial accounting.

Third, in taxation, a distinction is made between ordinary income and capital gains, with the latter being taxed less heavily than the former. In financial accounting, the distinction, although present, is not so important since both ordinary income and capital gains usually enter into the measurement of net income.

Finally, as already pointed out, although the principles are basically the same, a company usually applies them differently in its tax accounting and its financial accounting, respectively. It does this primarily by changing the *timing*, rather than the *amount*, of revenues and expenses. Thus, for tax purposes, a company usually reports costs as early as it legitimately can and defers revenue until as late as it legitimately can. For accounting purposes, it tends to report costs in later time periods and revenues in earlier time periods.

Differences in the Application of Principles

In his *Inventory*,[3] Grady lists some 35 topics on which alternative treatments are permitted within generally accepted accounting principles, and gives from two to eight alternatives for each. These topics range in importance from cash discounts on sales which may be taken either at the time the sale is made or the time the receivable is collected, to the basic question of whether a merger is to be recorded as a purchase or a pooling of interest.

Andrew Barr, the Chief Accountant of the Securities and Exchange Commission, has listed the following areas of accounting where alternative practices could produce materially different results under generally accepted accounting principles: valuation of inventories, depreciation and depletion, income tax allocation, pensions, research and development costs, goodwill, time of recognizing income, "all-inclusive" versus "current operating performance" income statement, intercorporate investments, long-term leases, principles of consolidation, business combinations, income measurement in finance and small loan companies, and intangible costs in the oil and gas industries. Even this list is set forth as "illustrative" rather than complete. Note that the topics mentioned affect the income statement and practically every balance sheet asset item except cash.[4]

There is also considerable latitude in applying principles. Examples that have been mentioned in earlier chapters are as follows: inventory can be recorded at Lifo, at Fifo, or some parts of inventory may be handled one way and some the other; inventory cost may or may not include inward transportation, storage costs, handling costs, or cash discounts on pur-

---

[3] Paul Grady, *Inventory of Generally Accepted Accounting Principles* (AICPA *Accounting Research Study No. 7*, 1965), pp. 373–79.

[4] Testimony before the Subcommittee on Commerce and Finance of the Committee on Interstate and Foreign Commerce, House of Representatives, February 19, 1964.

chases; research and development costs, organization costs, goodwill, advertising costs, and the like may be charged to expense as incurred or they may be capitalized as an asset; if capitalized, they may or may not be written off over future periods; and if written off, the number of periods over which they are written off and the proportion written off each period may vary from company to company.

In part, these differences reflect differences in personal judgment as to what is or is not *material* and as to the importance that should be attached to the *conservatism* concept. In attempting to describe a complex situation, such differences are inevitable. In part, the differences reflect customs that have grown up in particular companies or industries.

Mr. Leonard Spacek, managing partner of Arthur Andersen and Company, illustrates this point with the following comparison between the reported earnings of two hypothetical companies, with the same revenue ($10 million) and the same physical operations.[5] Company A reports a net income of $480,000, and Company B reports a net income of $1,076,000. The difference of $596,000 is explained entirely by differences in accounting practices, as follows:

1. Company B uses Fifo in pricing inventory; Company A uses Lifo............$192,000
2. Company B uses accelerated depreciation; Company A uses straight-line.....   48,000
3. Company B capitalizes research costs and amortizes over five years; Company A expenses on incurrence...   38,000
4. Company B charges the present value of pensions vested; Company A expenses actual current pension costs..   72,000
5. Company B grants stock options to executives, which are not an expense; Company A pays a cash bonus...   96,000
6. Company B credits capital gains to income; Company A credits them directly to retained earnings...   150,000
   Total...$596,000

Example: Nudoll Company

A company, here called the Nudoll Company, spent three years and some $90,000 developing a new product. By October, 1964, the product was ready for market and seemed to have a promising future. Of the funds used up to that point, $30,000 had been contributed by the management, in exchange for common stock, and $60,000 had been loaned by a friend of the principal owner, payable on demand. The balance sheet at that time, in round numbers, was as shown in Illustration 10–1. According to this balance sheet, current assets were about one ninth of current liabilities and the company had a substantial deficit.

The Nudoll Company needed additional capital, which the management planned to raise by selling stock. An advisor pointed out that the

---

[5] Quoted in Myles L. Mace and George G. Montgomery, Jr., *Management Problems of Corporate Acquisitions* (Boston: Division of Research, Harvard Business School, 1962), pp. 178–80.

Illustration 10–1

NUDOLL COMPANY

Balance Sheet as of October 31, 1964
(As Originally Prepared)

ASSETS		EQUITIES		
Cash...................	$1,000	Accounts payable.............		$ 2,000
Inventory...............	6,000	Notes payable..............		60,000
Total Current Assets...	$7,000	Total Current Liabilities..		$62,000
		Capital stock...............	$30,000	
		Less: Deficit.............	−85,000	−55,000
Total Assets.......	$7,000	Total Equities........		$ 7,000

balance sheet shown in Illustration 10–1 would look unattractive to prospective investors. Two steps were therefore taken: (1) the person who had loaned the $60,000 agreed to sign a five-year note, with the informal understanding that he would be repaid as soon as funds were available (this understanding was the same as his understanding when he made the loan, even though technically the original note was payable on demand); and (2) the expenditures to develop the new product were set up as an asset on the grounds that these costs were incurred in order to benefit future periods. These changes produced the balance sheet shown in Illustration 10–2. According to this revised balance sheet, current assets were 3.5 times current liabilities, total assets were 14 times as large as those shown on the first balance sheet, and the company had retained earnings (which had resulted from the profitable sale of trial lots of the new product).

Arguments can be made to support the view that both these balance sheets were prepared in accordance with generally accepted accounting principles. Each statement shows certain useful information: that the company has some cash and a little inventory, that it is probably going to have difficulty meeting its bills unless it obtains more cash quickly, and

Illustration 10–2

NUDOLL COMPANY

Balance Sheet as of October 31, 1964
(As Adjusted)

ASSETS		EQUITIES		
Cash.....................	$ 1,000	Accounts payable...........		$ 2,000
Inventory.................	6,000	Total Current Lia-		
Total Current Assets.....	$ 7,000	bilities..............		$ 2,000
Unamortized development		Long-term debt............		60,000
costs..................	90,000	Capital stock..............$30,000		
		Retained earnings...........	5,000	35,000
Total Assets.........	$97,000	Total Equities.......		$97,000

that it owes someone $60,000. Neither one describes the overall status of this company, for its status depends almost entirely on the excellence of the new product, and this will not be known until the product is marketed.

Implications of These Differences

No one can state reliably what the "general practice" is or how the majority of companies handle any specific problem. There are at least four million accounting entities in the United States, of which about one million are corporations. No report on the accounting practices of these companies exists. The best source, *Accounting Trends and Techniques,* an annual publication of the AICPA, reports the practices of approximately 600 of the largest corporations. A person who has a personal knowledge of the detailed procedures of as many as 100 companies has an unusually broad experience. Thus, generalizations about what "the majority of companies" do with respect to detailed accounting matters should not be taken too seriously.

It follows that a detailed comparison of the items reported in the financial statements of two companies is a difficult problem. Useful comparisons can often be made in terms of rough approximations, but precise statements are rarely possible.

The existence of diversity in accounting practice should not be considered as a reason for criticizing accountants or accounting. The fundamental fact is that a business is a complex organism. There is no conceivable way of prescribing a uniform set of rules by means of which the significant facts about that organism can be reduced to a few pages of figures, any more than there is any way of formulating a standard set of rules for biographers. Standard procedures for listing physical characteristics, birth dates, marital status, and certain other information about a person can easily be specified, but these details do not really describe the person completely. The accuracy and usefulness of the "picture" of a person that emerges from a biography depends on the author's skill and judgment in the collection, analysis, and presentation of information about his subject. So it is with financial statements.

Nor should the existence of diversity lead to frustration on the part of the user. The *consistency* concept prevents diversity from becoming chaos. Although Company A may follow practices that differ from those of other companies, Company A ordinarily follows the same practices year after year, or if it changes, the doctrine of consistency requires that it disclose the change. Thus its statements are likely to be comparable with one another from year to year. Also, although railroads use rules that are different from those used by industrial companies, railroad A is likely to use approximately the same rules as railroad B, and thus the two can be compared (with some notable exceptions).

Inherent Limitations

In addition to the points noted above, it is important to remember that accounting has inherent limitations. A business is such a complex organism that no one should expect that accounting, or any device, can record a complete and accurate picture of its activities. The two most important limitations—limitations which no foreseeable change in accounting can overcome—are (1) accounting reports are necessarily monetary, and (2) they are necessarily influenced by estimates of future events.

Accounting reports are limited to information that can be expressed in monetary terms. Nothing in the accounts explicitly describes personalities, the impact of outside forces, or other nondollar information that is vital to the complete understanding of a business.

Some accounting figures are influenced by future events which cannot conceivably be foreseen; these figures are necessarily estimates. The depreciation expense of the current period, for example, depends partly on how long the assets will be used in the future. The real significance of accounts receivable and the related item of sales revenue cannot be assessed until the number of credit customers who will not pay their bills is known. The actual value of inventory depends on what the merchandise can be sold for in the future. The possible impacts of contingent future events, such as the results of pending or threatened litigation, retroactive agreements on wage rates, and redetermination of profits on contracts, are not shown in the financial statements, although if material they should appear in a footnote. Incidentally, the very fact that footnotes, which may be numerous, are labeled as being an "integral part of the financial statements" is an indication of the limitation of the statements themselves.

Attempts to Reduce Diversity

The AICPA Accounting Principles Board is working vigorously to reduce the diversity in accounting practice, and it has made great progress since its establishment in 1959. It is discussing a number of proposals to resolve currently controversial accounting issues. If these efforts of the APB do not bear fruit, it is quite possible that the government will promulgate accounting principles, as is done in several European countries. The Securities and Exchange Commission has the statutory authority to do this under the Securities Act of 1933, the Securities Exchange Act of 1934, the Public Utility Holding Company Act of 1935, and the Investment Company Act of 1940, but to date the SEC has been most cautious about exercising this authority.

ROLE OF THE AUDITOR

All companies whose securities are listed on an organized stock exchange, nearly every company that sells its securities to the public, most other corporations, and a great many unincorporated businesses have their financial statements and the accounting records from which they are produced examined by independent, outside public accountants called auditors. Usually, these are certified public accountants (CPA's), who meet prescribed professional standards and who have received a certificate or license to practice from the state in which they do business.

When financial statements are examined by auditors, the results of this examination are reported in a letter that should be studied carefully by the reader of the statements. This letter ordinarily consists of two paragraphs. The first, or *scope,* paragraph reads as follows:

We have examined the statement of financial position of . . . Company as of (date) and the related statements of income and retained income for the year then ended. Our examination was made in accordance with generally accepted auditing standards and accordingly included such tests of the accounting records and such auditing procedures as we considered necessary in the circumstances.

The key words in this paragraph are: *such tests . . . as we considered necessary.* They signify that the auditor, not the management, is responsible for deciding on how thorough a job is required. The management cannot ask the auditor, for example, to "make as much of an audit as you can for $10,000." If the auditor's freedom is abridged in any material way, he is required to indicate this fact by adding to the above paragraph, "except. . . ." Such exceptions are rare.

The second, or *opinion* paragraph reads as follows:

In our opinion, the accompanying statements of financial position, of income, and of retained income present fairly the financial position of . . . Company at (date) and the results of its operations for the year then ended, in conformity with generally accepted accounting principles applied on a basis consistent with that of the preceding year.

There are three significant points in this opinion, indicated by the words: (1) *present fairly,* (2) *in conformity with generally accepted accounting principles,* and (3) *applied on a consistent basis.*

The word *fairly* should be contrasted with the word *accurately.* The auditor does not say that the reported net income is the only, or the most accurate, figure that could have been reported. He says, rather, that of the many alternative principles that could have been used, those actually selected by the management do give a fair picture in the circumstances relevant to the particular company. This contrast between "fairness" and "accuracy" is further emphasized by the fact that the auditor's report is called an "opinion" rather than a "certificate." The auditor does not certify the accuracy of the report; instead, he gives his professional opinion that it is fair.

The second phrase means that each of the accounting principles used in preparing the statements is "generally accepted." As noted in the preceding section, for many transactions there are several generally accepted principles, and the auditor's opinion merely states that the management has selected one of these.

If the Accounting Principles Board has issued an *Opinion* on a certain point, this, by definition, constitutes a generally accepted principle. However, an alternative principle is also regarded as being generally accepted if it has "substantial authoritative support." Evidences of such support are pronouncements of regulatory bodies or the practices of a number of other bodies. When a company uses a principle that is inconsistent with APB opinions, even though this principle has substantial authoritative support, the auditor is required to disclose this fact and to show, if practicable, the amount of decrease or increase in net income and retained earnings that would have resulted had the Accounting Principles Board *Opinion* been followed.

The third point, *consistency*, refers, it will be noted, to *the preceding year*. It does not mean *internal* consistency, that is, it does not mean that the principle used to measure fixed assets is consistent with that used to measure inventory, or even that each corporation in a consolidated enterprise follows practices that are consistent with those of other corporations in the same enterprise. The consistency doctrine is nevertheless of great significance because it does mean that the figures for one year are comparable with those of the preceding year, and assurance of such comparability is essential if meaningful comparisons are to be made to show the changes that have occurred in the company's financial position and earning performance.

The paragraphs quoted above constitute a *clean* opinion. If the auditor cannot make these statements, he adds in the appropriate place, "except that . . . ," and the opinion is then called a *qualified* opinion. Before making a qualified opinion, the auditor will of course discuss the situation with the management of the company, and in many cases the management is willing to change the financial statements rather than to have an exception reported.

Many people have the impression that the auditor is responsible for *preparing* the financial statements. This is not so. Preparation of the statements is the responsibility of the management, not of the auditor. When two or more alternative practices are permitted by generally accepted accounting principles, and either is "fair" (which is of course an ambiguous criterion), management, not the auditor, decides which one is to be used. In his opinion, the auditor does not state that management has necessarily made the *best* choice among alternative principles, but only that the choice made by management was an acceptable one.

It should also be noted that the auditor's opinion relates only to the financial statements, including the footnotes thereto, and not to other material that may appear in a company's annual report.

In making their examination, auditors no longer rely primarily on a detailed rechecking of the analysis, journalizing, and posting of each transaction; rather, they satisfy themselves that the accounting system is designed to ensure that the data are processed properly. This reliance on the internal control system is relatively new. As late as 1949, the U.S. General Accounting Office received a copy of every one of the millions of accounting documents generated annually in the federal government and, theoretically at least, checked each of them for propriety and accuracy. When the General Accounting Office changed its emphasis to a reliance on properly designed accounting systems, it not only was able to release several *thousand* employees but also was able to do a better auditing job by concentrating its efforts on checking the reliability of accounting systems and by examining the relatively few important or unusual transactions which previously had tended to be buried in the detail.

In addition to the examination of the adequacy of the accounting system, the auditors make test checks of how well it is working, they verify the existence of assets (for example, they usually are present at the taking of physical inventory, they ask a sample of customers to *confirm* or verify the accuracy of the accounts receivable shown for each of them, they check bank balances, and so on), and they make sure that especially important or nonroutine transactions are recorded in conformity with generally accepted accounting principles. The observation of inventories and the confirmation of receivables is regarded as being so important that the omission of either of these tests must be specifically mentioned in the "scope" paragraph of the opinion.

SIGNIFICANCE OF THE FINANCIAL STATEMENTS

The limitations mentioned above must be taken into account when one tries to understand a set of financial statements. The existence of these limitations should not, of course, lead to a complete rejection of accounting. After all, accounting does provide a way of summarizing numerous, complicated, and heterogeneous events into two brief documents, the balance sheet and the income statement. This is a remarkable achievement.

It is useful at this point to balance the limitations with the virtues, and attempt to describe their net effect in terms of the principal categories on the financial statements.

The Balance Sheet

It is not possible to define the whole balance sheet in anything other than vague terms. The AICPA definition of the balance sheet as a "list of balances in the asset, liability, or net worth accounts" is like the statement that "a rose is a rose"; it is accurate but not meaningful. A more meaningful statement is the following: the balance sheet shows the sources from which funds currently used to operate the business have been obtained (i.e., liabilities and owners' equity) and the types of property and property rights in which these funds are currently locked up (i.e., assets). This statement regards the balance sheet as essentially a report of management's *stewardship;* that is, what management has done with the funds entrusted to it.

In appraising the significance of individual balance sheet items, it is useful to make a distinction between *monetary items* and *nonmonetary items,* since items in the former category have a more clear-cut meaning than those in the latter.

Monetary items include not only cash itself, but also other assets that represent a specific monetary claim on some external party and liabilities that represent the specific monetary claim by some external party. Accounts Receivable is a monetary asset. The amount that each customer owes is definite, and it is usually possible to estimate the amount of uncollectible accounts within fairly close limits. Short-term investments held in lieu of cash also represent a definite claim, and although fluctuations in interest rates can affect the market value of these claims, such fluctuations are often not significant for the types of investments in this category.

Inventory, by contrast, is not a monetary asset. Its value depends ultimately on the result of a sales transaction that will occur at some future time, rather than on an agreement that already has been made.

On the liabilities side, accounts payable, notes payable, various accruals such as wages or interest payable, and bonds payable are all monetary items. They represent specific, measurable claims against the assets. Deferred liabilities, such as deferred income taxes, and the whole of the owners' equity section are in the nonmonetary category.

The analyst can use the amounts shown for the monetary items with reasonable assurance that they represent the current value of property rights in the case of assets, or the actual amount of claims against the business in the case of liabilities. He has much less confidence in the significance of the amounts shown for the nonmonetary items. He does know that the amounts for nonmonetary assets are based on cost, but he ordinarily has no way of relating these amounts to current market values.

In examining the balance sheet, the analyst usually makes a basic distinction between the working capital items and the other items. (Working capital equals the total current assets minus the total current liabilities.) Current assets are normally converted into cash within a year or a single operating cycle, and current liabilities are those that are payable within a year. Thus, items in the current section reflect reasonably recent transactions, and are more likely to reflect current market conditions than items in the other sections, which may reflect transactions that occurred many years previously.

Working capital items also tend to have more flexibility than other items; that is, management has more frequent opportunities to make decisions on the recommitment of funds in the case of current items than in the case of noncurrent items. Management can, for example, add an item to or delete an item from inventory on relatively short notice, but it cannot change the amount of investment in fixed assets as frequently or in as short a time after the decision to do so has been made. This flexibility relates to the individual items that make up the category more than it does to the total. Even though individual items flow through inventory rapidly, the inherent characteristics of the business may dictate that the total investment in inventory be relatively constant. In this sense, the amount of inventory may be as "fixed" as the amount of so-called fixed assets.

The *fixed asset* section of the balance sheet is a statement of unexpired costs; that is, it shows costs that have not yet been charged against operations. Ordinarily, the amounts listed bear no relation to market value, and no inference as to such value should be attempted solely on the basis of balance sheet information.

Interpretation of the *liabilities* section involves a subtle point. The items included there are indeed "claims against the assets," but they are only those claims which are recorded with an offsetting debit to an asset or another equity account, and these are not necessarily all the obligations which the company knows it must pay. For example, if an automobile is purchased on December 31 for $2,000 and if the business signs a note agreeing to pay the $2,000 at the rate of $50 per month for 40 months, the note appears as a liability (notes payable) on the December 31 balance sheet, and the automobile appears as an asset. On the other hand, if, instead, the business *rents* an automobile on December 31 and signs an agreement to pay $50 a month rent for 40 months, no record of this obligation appears as a liability (although it may be indicated in a footnote to the balance sheet).

One other important point about the liabilities section is that the amounts are usually definite, more so than the amounts in any other section. The amount shown as accounts payable *is* the amount owed to creditors; and the amounts shown as notes payable or bonds payable *are* the amounts owed to banks and to the bondholders. Even the tax liability and the other accruals, although estimated, are likely to be close estimates.

The *owners' equity* section gives some useful bits and pieces of information, such as the number of outstanding shares of stock of various types, clues as to dividend policy, and so on. Dividends may be limited to the amount shown as surplus, although considerations other than this accounting relationship are usually more important. In the event of liquidation or other crises, the amounts recorded as capital and surplus are important in determining the relative claims of the shareholders, and especially of each class of shareholders if there are several classes. In the usual situation, however, the amount shown as owners' equity in no way indicates the actual "worth" of the shareholders' equity, except in those rare instances where a company's assets consist entirely of cash or readily marketable assets.

The Income Statement

What is the meaning of "net income," the final item on an income statement? It is correct to say that net income is the difference between revenues and expenses, but this statement begs the question because there is no general agreement on the precise definitions of "revenue" and "expense" or on the method of measuring each of them. In the absence of such an agreement, there is room for considerable difference of opinion about the real meaning of net income.

How reliable is the estimate of the net income for an accounting period? Reliability depends primarily on (1) the length of the accounting period chosen, (2) the extent to which events relating to the current period are separated from events affecting prior or future periods, (3) the amount of long-lived assets owned by the company, and (4) the stability of prices.

Estimates of net income for a day or a month are likely to be much less reliable than estimates for a year, and estimates for a year less reliable than estimates covering a longer period.

Although the expenses assigned to a period are supposed to relate to the revenues realized in that period, it usually is not practicable to attempt a precise matching. For example, advertising is typically "bread cast upon the waters" in the hope of generating sales revenue in future periods, yet advertising is usually charged as an expense in the period in which the advertising is done rather than in the periods in which the revenues are earned. The difficulty of estimating the portion of the cost of a long-lived asset applicable to a given accounting period has already been described. The manner in which fluctuations in prices influence the income statement was discussed in Chapter 9.

For all these reasons, the net income reported on the income statement is unlikely to correspond exactly to the true increase in the owners' equity during an accounting period. The true *monetary* income of an enterprise can be known only after the enterprise has been completely terminated and its assets disposed of. The nonmonetary "income"—personal satisfaction, service rendered to society, and so on—are not determined from accounting reports even then. Any attempt to measure income for a shorter interval of time is necessarily inexact.

Nevertheless, certain of the individual items on an income statement may be highly reliable. The sales revenue figure is usually a close approximation to actual sales revenue, and the amounts for many expense items, such as wages, supplies, light, and power, are close approximations to actual expenses. Depreciation, on the other hand, is usually only a rough approximation, while some special adjustments reported as nonoperating expenses may be little more than informed guesses.

CONCLUSION

Perhaps the best way to summarize the intent of the discussion in this chapter is to point out that in accounting, one refers to the *measurement* of income rather than to the *determination* of income. To determine is "to fix conclusively and authoritatively"; accounting cannot do this. A measurement, on the other hand, is an approximation, according to some agreed-upon measuring stick, and this is what accounting sets out to do.

A person can and should find out about the particular rules that govern the accounting for the company in which he works. He usually cannot do this for other companies, and when he is using financial statements prepared in these companies, he must recognize, even though he cannot allow precisely for, the probable existence of differences in the preparation of these statements.

SUGGESTIONS FOR FURTHER READING

EDWARDS, EDGAR O., and PHILIP W. BELL. *The Theory and Measurement of Business Income.* Los Angeles: University of California Press, 1961.

MOONITZ, MAURICE. *The Basic Postulates of Accounting.* AICPA Accounting Research Study No. 1, 1961.

MORRISSEY, LEONARD E. *Contemporary Accounting Problems.* Englewood Cliffs, N.J.: Prentice-Hall, Inc., 1967. This text focuses on a number of current problems faced by the accounting profession, the need for generally accepted accounting principles, and the difficulty encountered in defining and applying such principles.

SPROUSE, ROBERT T., and MAURICE MOONITZ. *A Tentative Set of Broad Accounting Principles for Business Enterprises.* AICPA Accounting Research Study No. 3, 1962.

CHAPTER **11**

FINANCIAL STATEMENT ANALYSIS

The amount of time that an analyst spends on a set of financial statements depends on the nature of his interest in the company. At one extreme, the investor who wants to see what has happened in one of the several companies in which he owns stock may do little more than compare current earnings per share with last year's earnings per share. At the other extreme, the banker who has made, or who is considering making, a sizable loan will use every scrap of information that he can find. This chapter describes the more common, but by no means all, of the devices that are used in financial statement analysis.

All analyses of accounting data involve comparisons. An absolute statement, such as "X Company earned $1 million profit" is, by itself, not useful. It becomes useful only when the $1 million is compared with something else. The comparison may be quite imprecise and intuitive. For example, if we know that X Company is an industrial giant with tens of thousands of employees, we know intuitively that $1 million profit is a poor showing because we have built up in our minds the impression that such companies should earn much more than that. Or, the comparison may be much more formal, explicit, and precise, as is the case when the $1 million profit this year is compared with last year's profit. In either case, it is the process of comparison that makes the figure meaningful.

In general terms, the process of analysis can be described as one of comparing what actually happened with a *standard. A standard is a measure of what should have happened under the circumstances prevailing.*

BUSINESS OBJECTIVES

In order to decide the types of comparisons that are useful, we need first to consider what business is all about—what its objectives are—for the comparisons are essentially intended to shed light on how well business is achieving its objectives. As a generalization, it may be said that *insofar as it can be measured quantitatively, the overall objective of a business is to earn a satisfactory return on the funds invested in it, consistent with maintaining a sound financial position.*[1] It should be noted that this statement is limited to facts that can be expressed numerically. Personal satisfaction, public responsibility, ethical considerations, and other nonmeasurable objectives may be important and must be taken into account wherever relevant in appraising the overall success of the enterprise.

The foregoing statement of objectives has two aspects: (1) earning a satisfactory return on its investment, and (2) maintaining a sound financial position. Each aspect is discussed briefly below.

Return on Investment

The fact that return on investment is the broadest measure of overall performance can be seen from Illustration 11–1, which shows how return on investment is calculated and relates it to the main categories of items appearing on the balance sheet and income statement. The assets side of a balance sheet shows the categories to which investors' funds are committed. A portion of the current assets is offset by current liabilities, and investors must furnish only the remainder, which is called *working capital*.[2] They must also furnish the funds for noncurrent assets.

The return-on-investment measure is used in two senses: (1) the return on shareholders' investment, in which "investment" means assets less all liabilities; and (2) the return on total investment, in which "investment" includes both the stockholders' investment and that of bondholders and other long-term creditors. Illustration 11–1 is based on the latter meaning.

Investors who commit their funds to an enterprise do so because they expect to earn a return on these funds. The diagram shows how a change in any single category affects this return. Thus, an increase in gross profit, or a decrease in expenses, or a decrease in income taxes, increases net income and hence increases return on investment IF these changes are not accompanied by an offsetting change in some other category. On the other hand, if an increase in gross profit is accompanied by a correspond-

---

[1] This statement is not consistent with the *profit maximization* assumption often made in economics. The techniques in this chapter are equally applicable under a profit maximization assumption, however, so there is no point in arguing here whether the profit maximization assumption is valid and useful. Discussion of this point is deferred to Chapter 18.

[2] Occasionally, "working capital" is taken to mean total current assets. This is of course confusing and is unnecessary since "total current assets" is a perfectly good term. In order to avoid any possibility of confusion, the term "net working capital" is sometimes used for the difference between current assets and current liabilities.

ing increase in working capital (as can happen, for example, when a growth in sales volume is accompanied by a corresponding increase in inventories and accounts receivable), there will be no change in the overall percent return. It is therefore important that the relationships among the various categories be studied; this is done by the use of ratios as described in the next section. Illustration 11–2 shows the average return on owners' equity for various industry classes. Note the great differences among industries.

Illustration 11–1

FACTORS AFFECTING RETURN

ON INVESTMENT

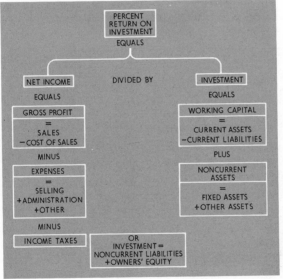

Sound Financial Position

In addition to desiring a satisfactory return, the investor expects that his capital will be protected from more than a normal amount of risk. The return on the *shareholders'* investment could be increased if a larger proportion of the investment came from low-cost, long-term liabilities and net income remained unchanged. This move, however, would increase the shareholders' risk of losing their investment, since the interest charges and principal repayments on the long-term liabilities are fixed obligations, and failure to make these payments when due could throw the company into bankruptcy. The degree of risk in a situation can be measured in part by the relative amounts of various types of liabilities

Illustration 11–2

RETURNS OF LEADING CORPORATIONS

	% Return on Equity		% Return on Sales	
	1967	1968	1967	1968
Dairy products	11.8	11.4	3.2	3.0
Meat packing	9.2	8.2	1.0	1.0
Other food products	12.3	12.5	4.0	4.1
Soft drinks	23.3	23.2	7.6	7.4
Distilling	10.5	9.5	4.7	4.3
Tobacco products	14.8	14.3	5.8	5.4
Textile products	8.8	9.6	3.6	3.7
Clothing and apparel	13.6	15.3	3.7	3.9
Shoes, leather, etc.	13.6	14.7	3.6	3.8
Rubber and allied products	10.8	12.7	4.1	4.7
Lumber and wood products	9.4	13.1	4.8	6.1
Paper and allied products	9.5	10.0	5.2	5.1
Printing and publishing	15.4	14.6	6.4	6.2
Chemical products	11.5	11.4	6.5	6.3
Drugs and medicines	20.3	20.0	9.8	9.5
Soap, cosmetics	19.4	18.7	6.7	6.6
Petroleum prod. and refining	12.8	12.9	9.1	9.0
Glass products	11.1	11.6	6.1	6.1
Other stone and clay products	7.3	8.7	4.8	5.3
Iron and steel	7.4	8.3	5.0	5.2
Nonferrous metals	11.4	11.0	7.2	6.6
Other metal products	13.8	13.3	5.1	4.9
Farm, constr, mat-hdlg, equip.	10.9	8.9	4.8	4.0
Office and computing equip.	17.8	19.1	8.3	8.5
Other machinery	14.7	13.4	5.5	5.2
Electr. equip. & electronics	15.4	14.2	4.5	4.3
Household appliances	14.7	15.0	4.6	4.7
Autos and trucks	12.0	16.6	4.9	5.8
Automotive parts	11.4	12.7	4.4	4.7
Aircraft and space	13.4	13.9	2.7	2.8
Instruments, photo goods, etc.	20.3	18.9	9.0	8.7
TOTAL MANUFACTURING	12.6	13.1	5.6	5.7
TOTAL MINING	16.2	15.1	12.6	12.6
TOTAL TRADE	13.2	13.5	2.5	2.5
Class I railroads	3.0	3.3	5.3	5.5
Common carrier trucking	15.7	19.1	3.2	3.6
Air transport	18.5	9.3	6.3	3.6
TOTAL TRANSPORTATION	5.4	4.9	5.6	4.8
TOTAL PUBLIC UTILITIES	11.0	10.5	13.9	13.0
TOTAL SERVICES	15.9	16.4	5.1	5.4
TOTAL FINANCE	6.0	5.6	..	..
GRAND TOTAL	10.6	10.6	5.9	5.8

Equity is stockholders' equity, i.e., the excess of total assets over total liabilities.
Source: Adapted and condensed from First National City Bank *Monthly Economic Letter*, April 1969. Data are for 3,928 companies.

and of the funds available to discharge them, and this also involves the use of ratios.

SOME COMMON RATIOS

A *ratio* is simply one number expressed in terms of another. It is found by dividing one number, the base, into the other. A *percentage* is one kind of ratio, in which the base is taken as equaling 100 and the quotient is expressed as "per hundred" of the base.,

Dozens of ratios can be computed from a single set of financial statements, but usually only a few are helpful in a given situation. Thus, although many frequently used ratios are described below, the best analytical procedure is not to compute all of them mechanically but rather to decide first which ratios might be relevant in the particular type of investigation being made and then to compute these, and only these, ratios.

Financial ratios can be grouped loosely into four categories: (1) tests of profitability, (2) tests of liquidity, (3) tests of solvency, and (4) overall ratios. The ratios listed under each category are illustrated by figures drawn from Illustrations 11–3 and 11–4, which show a simplified balance sheet and income statement for a hypothetical company.

Since the balance sheet figures refer to one instant of time while the income statement figures refer to events over a period of time, care must be taken in calculating ratios that use amounts from both statements. For many purposes, the income statement figure is best compared to the *average* of the balance sheet figures. In the examples below, such an average is necessarily computed as one half the sum of the amounts on the beginning and ending balance sheets. When other information is available, a more representative average is often preferable, such as the average of the 12 monthly balance sheet figures.

1. Tests of Profitability

Illustration 11–4 shows each of the items on the income statement expressed as a percentage of sales, which is a commonly used method of examining them. Usually, net sales is taken as 100 percent, as in the illustration. Of the percentages shown, gross profit (40 percent), the operating profit (14 percent), and net income, either before taxes (13.3 percent) or after taxes (6.7 percent), are perhaps the most important.

The *gross profit percentage* indicates the average mark-on or margin obtained on products sold. Since it is an average, it does not necessarily represent the mark-on on individual products, and these may differ widely from the average.

Illustration 11–3

ARLEN COMPANY

Balance Sheets
(in thousands of dollars)

	December 31 1968	1967
ASSETS		
Current Assets:		
Cash...	30	30
Accounts receivable.................................	42	32
Less: Allowance for bad debts..........................	2	2
Accounts receivable, net..............................	40	30
Merchandise inventory...............................	60	50
Prepaid expenses....................................	10	10
Total Current Assets...........................	140	120
Fixed Assets:		
Land...	30	30
Buildings and equipment..............................	120	120
Less: Accumulated depreciation.......................	70	60
Net buildings and equipment..........................	50	60
Total Fixed Assets.............................	80	90
Other Assets:		
Goodwill and patents.................................	10	0
Total Assets.................................	230	210
EQUITIES		
Current Liabilities:		
Accounts payable....................................	30	25
Accrued wages and taxes..............................	10	10
Estimated income taxes payable.........................	20	15
Total Current Liabilities........................	60	50
Fixed Liabilities:		
Mortgage bonds, 5 percent............................	40	40
Total Liabilities..............................	100	90
Shareholders' Equity:		
Common stock (5,000 shares outstanding).................	60	60
Retained earnings...................................	70	60
Total Shareholders' Equity.......................	130	120
Total Equities...............................	230	210

Gross margin percentages vary widely among industries, but within an industry the percentages for individual companies tend to be similar.

The *net income percentage* is a measure of overall profitability. This measure is also referred to as the *return on sales* or the *profit percentage*. Some people, particularly critics of a given industry or company, treat this measure as if it were the most important single measure of performance. This is erroneous, because net income, considered by itself, does not take into account the assets employed to produce that income. The steel

Illustration 11–4

ARLEN COMPANY

Condensed Income Statement, 1968
(in thousands of dollars)

	Dollars	Percentage
Gross sales................................	303	101.0
Less: Returns and allowances...............	3	1.0
Net sales..................................	300	100.0
Less: Cost of sales........................	180	60.0
Gross profit...............................	120	40.0
Operating expenses.........................	78	26.0
Operating profit...........................	42	14.0
Interest...................................	2	0.7
Income before taxes........................	40	13.3
Provision for income taxes..................	20	6.7
Net Income................................	20	6.7

industry, which is a favorite whipping boy, has a relatively high return on sales, but its investment is also high. The following example illustrates this point.

EXAMPLE: Company A operates a supermarket, and Company B operates a department store. Operating results of each are summarized below:

	A Super-market	B Department Store
Sales..................................	$10,000,000	$10,000,000
Net income............................	200,000	1,000,000
Total investment......................	1,000,000	5,000,000
Return on sales.......................	2%	10%
Return on investment..................	20%	20%

Supermarkets typically operate on a low gross margin, and therefore have a small profit on each dollar of sales, but they also have a much smaller investment per dollar of sales than do department stores. Thus an investor in Company A earns just as high a return on each dollar of his investment as an investor in Company B, even though Company A has a much smaller profit per dollar of sales.

2. Tests of Liquidity

Liquidity refers to the company's ability to meet its current obligations. The liquidity ratios therefore have to do with the size and relationships of current liabilities, which are the obligations soon coming due, and current assets, which presumably provide the source from which these obligations will be met. A company's financial position is not sound unless it has adequate liquidity. The ratios listed below help to answer the question: "Will the business probably be able to meet its obligations when they become due?"

CURRENT RATIO.

$$\frac{\text{Current Assets}}{\text{Current Liabilities}} = \frac{\$140,000}{\$60,000} = 2.3 \text{ Times, or 2.3 to 1.}$$

In other words, current assets are 2.3 times current liabilities.

The current ratio is the most commonly used of all balance sheet ratios. It is not only a measure of the company's liquidity but also is a measure of the margin of safety that management maintains in order to allow for the inevitable unevenness in the flow of funds through the current asset and liability accounts. If this flow were absolutely smooth and uniform each day (so that, for example, money coming in from customers exactly equaled maturing obligations), the requirements for such a safety margin would be small. Since a company rarely can count on such an even flow, it needs a supply of liquid funds to be assured of being able to pay its bills when they come due. The current ratio indicates the size of this buffer.

In interpreting the current ratio, consideration of the proportion of various types of current assets is important. A company with a high percentage of its current assets in the form of cash is more liquid than one with a high percentage in inventory, even though the companies have the same current ratio.

ACID-TEST RATIO.

$$\frac{\text{Quick Assets}}{\text{Current Liabilities}} = \frac{\$70,000}{\$60,000} = 1.2 \text{ Times, or 1.2 to 1.}$$

Quick assets include cash, temporary investments held in lieu of cash, and current accounts and notes receivable. Presumably, these items can be converted into cash quickly and at approximately their stated amounts, unlike inventory which is the principal current asset excluded. The acid-test ratio, or *quick ratio*, is therefore a measure of the extent to which liquid resources are immediately available to meet current obligations.

RECEIVABLES TO SALES.

$$\frac{\text{Receivables (Net)}}{\text{Net Sales}} = \frac{\$40,000}{\$300,000} = 13.3 \text{ Percent.}$$

If available, the base should be net *credit* sales, which is of course more closely related to accounts receivable than is total sales. Sometimes *average* accounts receivable ($35,000) is used as the numerator, but attention is more properly focused on the year-end figure. Receivables include trade accounts receivable plus trade notes receivable.

COLLECTION PERIOD. This is derived from the preceding ratio:

Receivables to Sales × Days in the Period = Collection Period.
13.3%   ×   365   =   49 Days.

The collection period can be related roughly to the credit terms offered by the company. A rule of thumb is that the collection period should not exceed 1⅓ times the regular payment period; that is, if the company's typical terms call for payment in 30 days, it is said that the average collection period should not exceed 40 days. Like all rules of thumb, this one has a great many exceptions. Changes in the ratio indicate changes in the company's credit policy or changes in its ability to collect its receivables.

INVENTORY TURNOVER.

$$\frac{\text{Cost of Sales}}{\text{Average Inventory}} = \frac{\$180,000}{\$55,000} = 3.3 \text{ Times.}$$

Inventory turnover is an indication of the velocity with which merchandise moves through the business. An increase in the absolute size of inventory, for example, may represent the additional stocks required by an expanding business, or it may represent an accumulation of merchandise because sales volume has recently declined. In the latter case, the inventory turnover will decrease. A decrease in the inventory turnover ratio may therefore be a significant danger signal.

If the cost of sales figure is not available, a turnover ratio may be computed using the sales figure instead. Such a ratio does not then show literally how many times the inventory turned over during the year because the numerator contains the profit margin while the denominator does not, and the two numbers therefore are not precisely comparable. Nevertheless, if profit margins remain roughly constant, a comparison of this ratio for several years may be useful.

3. Tests of Solvency

As liquidity refers to current obligations, *solvency* refers to a company's ability to meet the interest costs and repayment schedules associated with its long-term obligations.

EQUITY RATIOS. The division of equities among current liabilities, long-term liabilities, and owners' equity has an important bearing on solvency. These relationships are shown in the following condensed 1968 data of Arlen Company, derived from Illustration 11–3.

EQUITIES

	Percent
Current liabilities	26
Long-term liabilities	17
Equity capital	57
Total Equities	100

Of the ratios apparent in the above tabulation, the most important are those showing the relationship between *debt capital* and *equity capital*.

Debt capital is another name for liabilities. From the point of view of the company, debt capital is risky because if bondholders and other creditors are not paid promptly, they can take legal action to obtain payment which can, in extreme cases, force the company into bankruptcy. Equity capital is much less risky to the company because stockholders receive dividends only at the discretion of the directors.[3] Because the stockholders have less certainty of receiving dividends than the bondholders have of receiving interest, stockholders usually are unwilling to invest in a company unless they see a reasonable expectation of making a higher return than they could obtain as bondholders; that is, they would be unwilling to give up the relatively certain prospect of receiving 5 percent or 6 percent interest on bonds, unless the probable, but less certain, return on an equity investment were considerably higher, say 10 percent or more.

From the company's standpoint, the greater the proportion of its capital that is obtained from stockholders, the less worry the company has in meeting its fixed obligations; but in return for this lessened worry, the company must expect to pay a higher overall cost of obtaining its capital. Conversely, the more funds that are obtained from bonds, the more the company can *trade on the equity;* that is, it can use funds obtained at relatively low interest rates in the hopes of earning more on these funds for the stockholders. A company with a high proportion of bonds is said to be highly *leveraged.* The equity ratio shows the balance that the management of a particular company has struck between these forces.

Unfortunately, the equity ratio (often called the *equity/debt ratio* or the *capital/equity ratio* or simply the *debt ratio*) is defined in two quite different ways; the user must always be careful to ascertain which meaning is intended in a given situation. One definition includes the current liabilities, and the other excludes them. Including current liabilities, the equity/debt ratio for Arlen Company is 57 to 43, or 1.3 to 1. Excluding current liabilities, the corresponding figures are 57 to 17, or 3.4 to 1. This difference in meaning is confusing in general, but in particular situations it is less so, because a company or an industry usually settles on one meaning or the other, and those who use the ratios then have a common basis of understanding.

TIMES INTEREST EARNED.

$$\frac{\text{Operating Profit}}{\text{Bond Interest}} = \frac{\$42,000}{\$2,000} = 21 \text{ Times.}$$

The numerator of this ratio is the amount of earnings available to meet the fixed obligation of bond interest. In the example, interest requirements

---

[3] Note that "risk" is here viewed from the standpoint of the company. From the standpoint of investors, the opposite view prevails. Thus bondholders have a relatively low risk of receiving their payments, and stockholders have a relatively high risk. From this latter standpoint, equity capital is called "risk capital."

are said to be *covered* 21 times. This ratio is a measure of the level to which income can decline without impairing the company's ability to meet interest payments on its fixed liabilities. Income is taken before income taxes because if income declined, income taxes would decline proportionately. The ratio implies that net income is equivalent to additional cash, which is not necessarily the case, of course.

If preferred stock is outstanding, a similar coverage ratio can be computed for the preferred stock dividends, but here the numerator is income after taxes and after interest charges ($20,000).

A company may have fixed obligations in addition to its interest payments, as, for example, when it has rental commitments on leased property. In such a case coverage is properly computed by adding these other obligations to the amount of interest. The ratio is then labeled "Times Fixed Charges Earned."

4. Overall Measures

RETURN ON INVESTMENT. This is the grand, overall measure described earlier in this chapter. It can be expressed in several ways. From the viewpoint of the shareholders, it is the *return on shareholders' investment:*

$$\frac{\text{Net Income}}{\text{Average Shareholders' Equity}} = \frac{\$20,000}{\$125,000} = 16 \text{ Percent.}$$

In computing the average shareholders' equity, a simple average of the beginning and ending figures should not be used if additional equity funds were obtained and put to use at other than the middle of the year. New funds obtained near the end of the year, for example, might well be excluded from the denominator of the fraction because the income in the numerator did not arise from the use of these funds.

A variation of the above, called the return on *tangible net worth,* eliminates intangible assets from the shareholders' equity, thus:

$$\frac{\text{Net Income}}{\text{Avg. Net Worth} - \text{Avg. Intangibles}} = \frac{\$20,000}{\$125,000 - \$5,000} = 16.7 \text{ Percent.}$$

Return on total investment looks at income in relation to the total of the permanent funds invested in the enterprise. These permanent funds consist of shareholders' equity plus noncurrent liabilities; or the same figure may be found by subtracting current liabilities from total assets. The earnings on these funds are usually taken as net income before income taxes, plus interest on noncurrent liabilities. The ratio is as follows:

$$\frac{\text{Operating Profit}}{\text{Average Equity} + \text{Average Fixed Capital} \quad \text{Liabilities}} = \frac{\$42,000}{\$125,000 + \$40,000} = 25.5 \text{ Percent.}$$

If the interest expense on the income statement included interest on current borrowings as well as bond interest, the interest on current liabilities would be subtracted from operating profit. Sometimes an after-tax figure is used.

The return-on-total-investment ratio is a measure of how well management has used all the permanent funds entrusted to the business. Or, put another way, this ratio is intended to measure the earning power of the net assets (net working capital plus other assets) of the business.

For many purposes, especially for comparing one division of a company with another division, return on investment is best figured on the basis of *gross assets*, which means working capital plus fixed assets at cost but with no deduction for accumulated depreciation.

Return on investment can be calculated in another manner which, although it is longer and gives the same result, is often more illuminating. Two subsidiary ratios, *investment turnover* and *operating profit on sales*, are calculated first. Investment turnover is as follows:

$$\frac{\text{Sales}}{\text{Equity Capital} + \text{Fixed Liabilities}} = \frac{\$300,000}{\$125,000 + \$40,000} = 1.82 \text{ Times.}$$

The operating profit ratio, 14.0 percent, is given on Illustration 11–4. Then:

Investment Turnover × Op. Profit Ratio = Return on Investment.

1.82 Times   ×   14.0 Percent   =   25.5 Percent.

Many consider this to be the most useful way of looking at the overall performance of a business. It shows that performance can be improved either by generating more sales volume per dollar of capital employed or by increasing the profit margin on each sales dollar generated. It shows that a supermarket earning 2 percent on sales may be doing as good a job for its investors as a department store earning 10 percent on sales when the supermarket has an investment turnover of 10 and the department store a turnover of 2.

MARKET TESTS.   Persons who study the financial statements of companies as a basis for deciding where to invest their funds may use any of a number of other ratios in addition to those already listed. Some of these are mentioned below.

Earnings per share:

$$\frac{\text{Net Income}}{\text{Shares Outstanding}} = \frac{\$20,000}{5,000} = \$4 \text{ per Share.}$$

The calculation is more complicated when the company has preferred stock or convertible bonds, and these complications were discussed on page 157. Earnings per share is usually the most important single ratio for the investor. He watches changes in this ratio from year to year and also uses it, as explained below, to appraise the market price of the stock.

Price-earnings ratio:

The price-earnings ratio is based on the average market price of the stock. Assuming the market price for Arlen Company's stock is $36, the ratio is as follows:

$$\frac{\text{Market Price per Share}}{\text{Earnings per Share}} = \frac{\$36}{\$4} = 9 \text{ to } 1.$$

Turning this ratio upside down gives the *capitalization rate,* the rate at which the stock market is apparently capitalizing the value of current earnings:

$$\frac{\text{Earnings per Share}}{\text{Market Price per Share}} = \frac{\$4}{\$36} = 11 \text{ Percent.}$$

The price-earnings ratio is influenced heavily by how rapidly the company is growing and by its policy with respect to retained earnings, as well as, of course, the market's overall judgment as to the company's soundness. A P/E ratio as low as 10 to 1 is found for stable companies that pay out most of their income as dividends. The ratio can be as high as 25 to 1, and occasionally as high as 100 to 1, for "glamour" companies, those that are growing rapidly, that are expected to continue this growth, and that retain most of their net income.

The average price-earnings ratio of a selection of industrial stocks listed on the New York Stock Exchange was 15:1 in 1968, and it ranged from 14:1 to 21:1 in the period 1957 to 1968.

Yield:

The yield, or more properly the *dividend yield,* is based on dividends declared during the year. Assuming the Arlen Company declares a $2 dividend, the ratio is as follows:

$$\frac{\text{Dividends per Share}}{\text{Price per Share}} = \frac{\$2}{\$36} = 5.6 \text{ Percent.}$$

The yield on stocks is often compared with the yield, or interest, on bonds, but such a comparison is not valid. This is because the earnings of bondholders consist entirely of their interest, whereas the earnings of stockholders consist not only of their dividends, but also of retained earnings. Although stockholders have no guarantee that they will receive retained earnings, the fact that part of the net income has been retained in the business and presumably invested in income-producing assets should enhance the value of the stockholders' investment.

DIFFICULTIES IN MAKING COMPARISONS

Reasonably accurate reports of actual performance often can be obtained (although the problems involved in obtaining them may be by no means trivial). Finding an adequate standard against which these actuals can be measured, however, is often a perplexing and difficult matter.

Some of the problems are described below. Financial statement analysis is used as an example, but the same problems arise in analyzing other types of quantitative data. When a person says that performance is "good" or "poor," "better" or "worse," he is, either implicitly or explicitly, comparing actual performance to some standard that he believes is relevant.

1. Deciding on the Proper Basis for Comparison

Subject only to minor qualifications, a boy who runs a mile in six minutes (or, expressed as a rate, 10 miles per hour) is a better miler than a boy who runs a mile in seven minutes. In business, there are many situations in which one cannot tell whether a higher number represents better performance than a lower number, or whether it represents poorer performance.

A high current ratio is by no means necessarily better than a low current ratio. For example, the current ratio for the Arlen Company on December 31, 1968, was 2.3 to 1. Suppose that $40,000 of the current liabilities came due the very next day and that the company in fact paid these liabilities, using every dollar of its available cash and liquidating other current assets as well. A balance sheet prepared subsequent to this transaction would show $100,000 of current assets and $20,000 of current liabilities, and the current ratio would accordingly be 5 to 1, which is more than double the ratio of the previous day. Yet one could scarcely say that a company that had used up all its cash was in an improved financial condition. Or, conversely, consider what happens when a company expands, as illustrated by the Arlen Company balance sheet at the end of 1968 compared with its balance sheet for the end of 1967. Current assets have increased by $20,000, and current liabilities have increased by only $10,000; the current ratio has dropped from 2.4:1 to 2.3:1. The decrease may indicate no worsening of the company's liquid position at all; rather, it may reflect the result of a well-carried-out expansion program.

In some comparisons the direction of change that represents "good" or "better" is reasonably apparent. Generally, a high net profit percentage is better than a low one, and a high return on investment is better than a low one. Even these statements have many qualifications, however.

Many standards can usefully be thought of as a *quality range* rather than as a single number. When actual performance is within this range, it may be regarded as satisfactory. When it begins to go outside the range, *in either direction*, there is an indication of an unsatisfactory situation. For a certain company, the current ratio may be considered satisfactory if it is within the range 2:1 to 3:1. Below 2:1, there is the danger of being unable to meet maturing obligations. Above 3:1, there is an indication that funds are being left idle rather than being efficiently employed. As another example, a too-high profit ratio may indicate that the company is only "skimming the cream" off the market; a deeper penetration may increase sales and total return on investment even if the ratio of profit to sales is reduced.

2. Differences in the Situations Being Compared

No reasonable person would expect a 9-year-old boy to run as fast as a 19-year-old athlete; in judging the boy's performance, we attempt to compare his speed with that of other boys of the same age and with similar training. Differences in the factors that affect one company's performance this year as compared with those that affect the same company's performance last year, or the performance of another company, are complex and difficult to evaluate. Nevertheless, some attempt must be made to allow for these differences. In general, this task is least difficult when all the figures being compared pertain to the same company (although even here changes in size, in the functions performed by the company, in outside influences, and so on, may make comparisons of tenuous validity). The task is more difficult when attempting to compare one company with another, even if they are both of the same size and in the same industry, and it becomes exceedingly difficult if the two companies are in different industries or if they are of substantially different size.

3. Changes in the Dollar Measuring Stick

Accounting figures are expressed in historical dollars. A change in the value of a dollar, that is, a change in price levels, may therefore seriously lessen the validity of comparisons of ratios computed for different time periods. Also, a ratio whose numerator and denominator are expressed in different kinds of dollars may have no useful meaning.

The fact that asset amounts are stated as unexpired historical dollar costs causes particular difficulty in making comparisons of ratios calculated from such amounts. Two companies, for example, might have facilities that are physically identical in all respects except age, and they might operate exactly the same way and earn exactly the same net income. If, however, the buildings and equipment of one company had been purchased at a time when prices were low or if they had been almost fully depreciated, and if the buildings and equipment of the other company had been purchased at a time of higher prices or if they were relatively new, then the return-on-investment ratio for the company that carried its assets at a low book value would be much higher than the ratio for the other company.

4. Differences in Definition

The terms "one mile" and "six minutes" used to measure the runner are precisely defined and easily measured, but the individual elements making up such terms as "current assets" and "current liabilities" are by no means precisely defined, and there is considerable diversity in practice as to how they should be measured. Some of the many differences have been described in earlier chapters.

Similar differences affect the standards against which actual performance is compared. For example, the following are estimates of the "profits as a percent of sales of U.S. manufacturing companies in 1960" as reported by various agencies:[4]

	Percent
First National City Bank	5.5
Federal Trade Commission—SEC	4.5
Department of Commerce	3.3
Internal Revenue Service	2.7

The highest figure is twice as high as the lowest. The differences result both from differences in the way "profits" are defined and from differences in the data collected.

5. Hidden Short-Run Changes

A balance sheet may not reflect the average or typical situation. A balance sheet is prepared as of one moment of time, and it tells nothing about short-term fluctuations in assets and equities that have occurred within the period bounded by the two balance sheet dates. Many department stores, for example, end their fiscal year and publish annual balance sheets as of January 31. By that date, Christmas inventories have been sold out and many of the Christmas receivables have been paid, but Easter merchandise has not started to arrive and payables for this merchandise have not yet been generated. Current assets (other than cash) and current liabilities as reported on the January 31 balance sheet are therefore likely to be lower than at other times of the year; as a result, ratios such as merchandise turnover and the average collection period may be distorted, and other ratios may not be representative of the situation at other seasons. A company that is analyzing its own data can study the seasonal movements by using monthly, rather than annual, balance sheets, but these are ordinarily not available to the outsider.

The analyst should also recognize that companies have been known to

---

[4] Estimated from charts in *First National City Bank Letter,* January 1963, which gives some explanation of the differences.

take deliberate steps to "clean up" their balance sheets. They may, for example, pay off loans just before the end of the year, which usually increases the current ratio; they then borrow again early in the next year. Such transactions, which are called *window dressing*, may not be discernible on the balance sheet.

6. The Past as an Indication of the Future

Financial statements are historical documents, and financial ratios show relationships that have existed in the past. The analyst is, of course, interested in what is happening now and what is likely to happen in the future rather than what did happen in the past. Often the analyst has no choice but to rely on past data as an indication of the current situation, but he should not be misled into believing that the historical ratios necessarily reflect current conditions, and much less that they reflect future conditions.

POSSIBLE BASES FOR COMPARISON

There are four types of standards against which an actual figure can be compared: (1) experience; (2) a goal; (3) a historical figure; and (4) an external figure, that is, a figure for performance in another company, or other companies.

1. Experience

The analyst gradually builds up his own idea as to what constitutes "good" or "poor" performance. One of the important advantages that an experienced analyst has over inexperienced ones is that he possesses a feeling for what are "right" relationships in a given situation, developed on the basis of his knowledge about similar situations. (Of course, if he is not competent, his feeling may well be incorrect). These subjective standards of a competent analyst are more important than standards based on mechanical comparisons.

2. Goals

Many companies prepare *budgets,* which show *what performance is expected to be under the circumstances prevailing.* If actual performance corresponds with budgeted performance, there is a reasonable inference that the performance is good. There are two important qualifications that affect this inference, however. First, the budgeted figures may not have been set very carefully in the first instance, and the comparison can of course be no more valid than the goal figures themselves. Secondly, the goals were necessarily set on the basis of certain assumptions as to the conditions that would be prevailing during the period, and if these assumptions turn out to be incorrect, the goal figures are also incorrect as a measure of results "under the circumstances prevailing." If, because of a recession or other economic phenomenon outside the control of management, profits are lower than the amount budgeted, it cannot fairly be said that the difference between actual and budgeted profit indicates "poor" performance. Nevertheless, the budget is a type of standard that has fewer inherent difficulties than either the historical standards or the external standards.

3. Historical Standards

A comparison of current performance with past figures for the same company usually does not run into the problem of differences in accounting practice. If practices have changed, the change is presumably known to the analyst. Moreover, the analyst can also recollect, or find out from supplementary data, some of the circumstances that have changed between the two periods and thus allow for these changes in making his comparison. At best, however, a comparison between a current figure and a historical figure in the same company can show only that the current period is "better" or "worse" than the past. In many cases this does not provide a sound basis for judgment, for the historical figure may not have represented an acceptable standard. If a company increases its return on investment from 1 percent to 2 percent, it has improved, but it nevertheless is not doing very well.

4. External Standards

When one company is compared with another, the environmental and accounting differences affecting the two sets of figures may raise serious problems of comparability. If, however, the analyst is able to allow for these differences, even approximately, he obtains an outside check on performance that has the advantage, over a standard derived from internal sources, of being independently arrived at. Moreover, the two companies may well have been affected by the same set of economic conditions, so this important cause of noncomparability may not be operating.

Corporations whose stock is traded on organized security exchanges file annual reports with the U.S. Securities and Exchange Commission, and these "Form 10–K" reports are likely to be more useful for comparisons than the annual reports sent to shareholders, both because the SEC prescribes a uniform format and terminology and because the 10–K reports usually contain more detailed information than reports to shareholders.

Many sources contain *average ratios* for groups of companies in the same industry or of similar size. Perhaps the best known are those published by Dun & Bradstreet, Inc. For each of 125 industry groups, the following ratios are published (starred items have been described above; the derivation of the others should be apparent):

*Current ratio.
*Net profit as a percentage of net sales.
*Return on tangible net worth.
Net profit as a percentage of net working capital.
*Net sales as a percentage of tangible net worth.
Net sales as a percentage of net working capital.
*Collection period.
*Net sales to inventory.
Fixed assets to tangible net worth.
Current debt to tangible net worth.
*Equity ratio.
Inventory to net working capital.
Current liabilities to inventory.
Funded debt to net working capital.

Ratios are also prepared by Robert Morris Associates for their members. A variety of ratios will also be found in *Moody's Manual of Investments, Standard and Poor's Corporation Records,* and other publications prepared for investors.

Standard and Poor's Corporation has available a COMPUSTAT service which consists of magnetic tapes containing pertinent financial and statistical information for 1,800 industrial, 100 utility, and 200 insurance companies in the United States, and 350 industrial companies in Canada. The information is available on an annual basis for the past 7 to 20 years, depending on the file being used. The financial information consists of 19 balance sheet items, 22 income statement items, 19 additional statistical items including stock prices, dividends, and a variety of ratios computed from the above, etc. All companies are grouped and coded by industry classifications.

Use of these industrywide ratios involves all the difficulties of using ratios derived from one other company plus the special problems that arise when the figures for several companies are thrown together into a single average. Nevertheless, they may give some worthwhile impressions about the average situation in an industry.

Many trade associations and other groups collect and publish figures for the companies in an industry. In some instances, the association prescribes in detail the accounting definitions and concepts to be used in reporting these figures, and the resulting figures are therefore much more comparable than those compiled by the sources mentioned above, which must use the basic data in whatever form the company chooses to report it.

USE OF COMPARISONS

The principal value of an analysis of financial statement information is that it suggests questions that need to be answered; such an analysis rarely provides the answers. An unfavorable difference between actual performance and whatever standard is used, if it is large, indicates that something *may be* wrong, and this leads to an investigation. Even when the analysis indicates strongly that something *is* wrong (as when one company's profits have declined while those of comparable companies have increased), the analysis rarely shows what the *cause* of the difficulty is. Nevertheless, the ability to pick from the thousands of questions that *might* be asked those few that are really worth asking is an important one.

It is well to keep in mind the basic relationships shown in Illustration 11–1, or some variation of these applicable to the situation being analyzed. The only number that encompasses all these relationships is a return-on-investment ratio. A change in any less inclusive ratio may be misleading as an indication of better or worse performance unless possible compensating changes in factors not covered by the ratio are taken into account. An increase in dollars of net income indicates improved performance only if there was no offsetting increase in the investment required. An increase in the net profit ratio indicates improved performance only if there was no offsetting decrease in sales volume or increase in investment. An increase in the gross profit percentage indicates improved performance only if there was no offsetting decrease in sales volume, increase in investment, or increase in expenses.

In short, the use of any ratio other than return on investment, taken by itself, implies that all other things are equal. This *ceteris paribus* condition ordinarily does not prevail, and the validity of comparisons is lessened to the extent that it does not. Yet the return-on-investment ratio is so broad that it does not give a clue as to which of the underlying factors may be responsible for changes in it. It is to find these factors, which if unfavorable indicate possible trouble areas, that the subsidiary ratios of profitability are used. Furthermore, the return-on-investment ratio tells nothing about the financial condition of the company; liquidity and solvency ratios are necessary for this purpose.

In addition to, or in place of, the simple ratio of one number to another, many businessmen develop a more complicated set of interrelationships that they find useful in isolating the key factors that affect good performance. An automobile dealer may say: "If the gross profit on service and parts sales is large enough to cover total general and administrative expenses, and if we break even on used car sales, then we will earn an adequate profit for the whole business from the gross margin less selling costs on new car sales." Usually, there is no way of demonstrating that these relationships are logically correct—there is no logical reason why gross profit on one part of the automobile dealer's business should just equal general and administrative costs for the whole business—but the fact is that they do work out.

SUMMARY

The figures on financial statements are usually most useful for analytical purposes when they are expressed in relative terms in the form of ratios and percentages. Although a great many ratios can be calculated, only a few are ordinarily necessary in connection with a given problem.

The essential task is to find a standard or norm with which actual performance can be compared. In general, there are four types of standards: (1) subjective standards derived from the analyst's experience; (2) goals, or budgets, set in advance of the period under review; (3) historical figures, showing performance of the same company in the past; and (4) the performance of other companies, as shown by their financial statements, or by averages compiled from the financial statements of a number of companies. None of these is perfect, but a rough allowance for the factors that cause noncomparability often can be made.

The comparison may then suggest important questions that need to be investigated; it rarely indicates answers to the questions.

APPENDIX

Comparisons Involving Percentages

Two of the technical matters involved in making a comparison of percentage figures are discussed below: (1) the choice of a base, and (2) averaging.

CHOICE OF A BASE. Suppose that sales in a company were $1.5 million in 1967 and $1.8 million in 1968. The change can be expressed in any one of four ways: (1) sales in 1968 were 120 percent of sales in 1967 (1.8/1.5 [100] = 120); (2) sales in 1968 were 20 percent higher than 1967 sales (120 − 100 = 20); (3) sales in 1967 were 83 percent of 1968 sales (1.5/1.8 [100] = 83); and (4) sales in 1967 were 17 percent lower than 1968 sales (83 − 100 = − 17). All these statements are true, but the first two statements imply the use of the 1967 sales figure as a base while the third and fourth refer to 1968 sales as a base. So long as the particular base chosen is clearly indicated, either base may be used. When statements about the percentage choice do not clearly indicate what figure is used as the base, misunderstandings can easily be created. In order to lessen these misunderstandings, it has become conventional when comparing one time period with another to *use the earlier period as the base*. This practice should be followed as a matter of course, unless there is a compelling reason to make an exception to it. In the example above, then, the better choices would be "1968 sales were 120 percent of 1967," or "1968 sales were 20 percent higher than 1967 sales."

Another convention customarily followed is the one for expressing "mark-on," which is a relationship between cost and selling price. Mark-on is ordinarily expressed as a percentage of selling price, *not* as a percentage of cost. Thus, if an article has a cost of $0.60 and a selling price of $1, its mark-on is said to be 40 percent, not 66⅔ percent.

The following type of difficulty arises when the base is unconsciously shifted: Suppose the number of employees in a company is reduced 50 percent, that subsequently it is increased 30 percent, and still later it is increased another 20 percent. Is the number of employees now the same as at the beginning? Not if each change is figured from the base existing at the time of the change, for a quick calculation will show that the two increases have brought the labor force back to only 78 percent of its original size. This illustrates the general point that if a number is decreased by a certain percentage, the resulting number must be increased by a larger percentage to get back to the original number. For example, if the number 10 is decreased by 40 percent, the result, 6, must be increased by 66⅔ percent (rather than 40 percent) to get back to the original number, 10.

Another problem in using the correct base arises when percentages are compared with one another. If the net profit on Product A is 2 percent of sales and on Product B, 3 percent, B's profit ratio is 50 percent, *not* 1 percent, higher than A's, since 3 is 150 percent of 2. It is, however, a common and correct practice to describe B's profit as one *percentage point* higher than A's.

AVERAGING PERCENTAGES.   Suppose that the divisional income statements of a company with three divisions show the following percentages of net profit to sales:

Division	Profit Percentage
A	3
B	7
C	5

Can it be said that the average profit for all divisions is 5 percent (i.e., 3 + 7 + 5 divided by 3)? Unless the divisions are the same size, the answer is "no." A simple average is valid only when the separate percentages have the same relative importance. If the percentages are of varying importance, either the overall percentage must be computed from the totals for the three divisions or a *weighted average* must be used. Assume the following performance of the three divisions:

Division	Sales (thousands of dollars)	Profit	Profit Percentage
A......................	1,000	30	3
B......................	300	21	7
C......................	700	35	5
Total.................	2,000	86	

One way of finding the profit percentage of the company is to divide total profit (86) by total sales (2,000), giving an overall profit percentage of 4.3 percent. This procedure is simple if sales and profit data are available for the three divisions, but there are situations where the aggregates cannot be determined from the available data. In these situations, an overall percentage may be found by taking a *weighted average* of the individual percentages. Weights may be expressed either in *absolute* terms (e.g., sales dollars) or in *relative* terms (e.g., the proportion of each plant's sales to the whole). Both methods are shown below. Although the weighting procedure is not actually necessary in this case, since the answer has already been found from the aggregates, the figures illustrate the method:

Division	A. Absolute Weights			B. Relative Weights		
	Weight (Sales in Thousands of Dollars)	Profit Per- centage	Weighted Percentage	Weight (Sales Relative)	Profit Per- centage	Weighted Per- centage
A............	1,000	3	3,000	50	3	150
B............	300	7	2,100	15	7	105
C............	700	5	3,500	35	5	175
	2,000		8,600	100		430

$$\text{Average} = \frac{8,600}{2,000} = 4.3 \qquad\qquad \text{Average} = \frac{430}{100} = 4.3$$

Note that the sum of the weighted values is divided by the sum of the weights, not by the number of items being averaged.

Rounding

Rounding is dropping some of the digits at the right-hand portion of a number. Thus, on highway sign posts 22.16 miles would be reported as 22, and we often say an automobile cost $2,800, even though its exact price was, perhaps, $2,793.55.

The customary rules for rounding are as follows:

1. In rounding numbers, a digit *less than 5* or a *fraction less than one half* is discarded; a digit *greater than 5* or a *fraction more than one half* adds 1 to the digit next to the left. For example, 12.6 is rounded to 13; 12.4 to 12; and 12,501 to 13,000.
2. When an *even 5* or the *fraction ½* is to be dropped, the digit to the left, if *even*, is unchanged; if *odd*, it is raised by one. Under this rule, all numbers which have been rounded by dropping an even 5 or the fraction ½ will be reported as even numbers: thus 11½ is rounded to 12; 12½ to 12; 13½ to 14; 87½ to 88; and 12,500 to 12,000. Some people follow the practice of raising all numbers ending in 5 or ½ by one. This rule introduces a slight upward bias in the rounding process, and its use as a general rule of rounding is therefore not recommended.

Rounding is a process which can be of great help in the use and interpretation of figures. Most people find it difficult to think in terms of large numbers. For example, a speaker may state that a certain expenditure was two billion, one hundred ninety-one million, four hundred thirteen thousand, two hundred seventy-six dollars and twenty-three cents. By the time he has finished, the strongest impression remaining with his audience is "23 cents," the least important part of the entire figure. It is much more effective to report such a figure as "two billion dollars" or "two point two billion dollars."

In other circumstances, limits of accuracy call for rounding. Where digits included in a number are not known to be correct, they should be dropped and the remaining figures which are known to be correct should be rounded, as described below.

Significant Digits

The significant digits in a number are the digits known to be correct (although the digit farthest to the right may often be only an approximation). In considering the problem of determining how many significant digits should be reported, it is helpful to remember that there are two kinds of numbers: (1) those which represent a *count*, and (2) those which represent a *measurement* or estimate. Examples of the first type are "three children," "1,067 students," "12 months." These numbers are said to be discontinuous or discrete; that is, there is a gap or space between each number (e.g., there cannot be "three and a fraction" children; the next number has to be four). Counts, or discrete numbers, are completely significant; that is, every digit has significance.

On the other hand, most of the numbers used in accounting are *measurements*, and all measurements are approximations. Their significance is limited by the accuracy of the measuring rod or of the observer. When a man views a tower from a distance and judges its height to be 500 feet, he may mean that in his opinion the tower is closer to 500 than to either 400 or 600 feet. When this is the intended meaning, the number 500 has only one significant digit, 5; the zeros were inserted merely to locate the decimal point.

A second man might estimate the tower's height as 520 feet, by which he means that it is closer to 520 than to either 510 or 530 feet. The degree of reported uncertainty has been considerably reduced in this estimate, and this is shown by the fact that the number now has two significant digits, 5 and 2. The zero once again does not represent a measurement but is used only to locate the decimal point. If the second man is in fact a keener observer than the first, his measurement is more precise; it has more significant digits. The use of even better observers and more refined measuring instruments can increase the accuracy in successive stages, for example: 500, 520, 523, 522.8, 522.81. The number of significant digits thus increases from 1 to 5. However, there is always some limit to accuracy; even radar, which measures the timing of electronic impulses in terms of millionths of a second, is not precisely accurate.

The following rules are helpful in counting the significant digits in a number, subject to the qualification explained in the next paragraph:

1. All digits other than *zeros* are significant.
2. Zeros are not significant when—
    a) They are at the extreme left of a number (0.0019); or
    b) They are at the extreme right of a number *and* at the left of the decimal point (19,000).

Thus, the number 0.0019 and the number 19,000 each have two significant digits. The number 4,203 has four, and 500.00 has five significant digits. Note that a zero to the right of the decimal point, as above, indicates that all digits to the left are significant. Zeros at the left of a whole number (e.g., 0019) are meaningless and should be omitted.

These rules are not sufficient for all cases. A person might give a measurement as 500 feet and really mean "closer to 500 than to 499 or 501." In this context, 500 has three significant digits. In situations of this kind, the significance can be inferred only from the context and not solely from the number and location of zeros.

Rules for Significant Digits. The following rules for treatment of significant digits are worth noting:

1. In *multiplication and division* the number of significant digits in a product or quotient is not more than the number of significant digits in the less precise of the two numbers entering into the calculation. That figure is less precise which has the smaller number of significant digits. For example, 91,100 tons per year is equal to 7,590 tons per month since 91,100 (with three significant digits) divided by the whole number 12 gives an answer with three significant digits. Although 91,100 divided by

12 equals 7,591.6666⅔, the final figure should not be reported as more significant than 7,590. Note that in the above example, 91,100 is the less significant of the two figures since the other number, 12, is significant to an infinite number of places. (There are exactly 12.000 . . . months in a year.)

2. In *addition and subtraction* the answer contains no more correct decimal places than those in the least precise of the numbers. Thus, in addition and subtraction it is the number of significant digits with reference to the decimal place that governs. For example, $25,000 plus $1,000 (both estimates) equals $26,000; and $25,000 (an estimate) plus $1,312.21 (six significant digits) equals $26,000.

Following these rules will still not guarantee the same degree of precision as a scientist would require; however, they are adequate for most business purposes.[5]

USE OF THE RULES. Application of these rules does not require that digits without significance always be dropped, especially in intermediate stages of the calculation. It is usually desirable to retain one and perhaps two digits beyond the number that is significant. At each stage of the work, however, all digits that have no influence on the final result should be rejected. In the final answer all digits that are not significant should be eliminated by the process of rounding.

In the application of the above rules, some sticky problems arise. Fortunately, most of these are of academic, rather than practical, importance. In a practical situation, reporting one digit more or less than those that actually are significant makes little real difference. The important thing is to recognize that no amount of calculating can make a number more precise than it was to begin with.

Some people are overly impressed by a number that appears to contain many significant digits, and conversely they may believe that a number with only two or three significant digits indicates sloppy work on the part of the person who prepared it, rather than the inherent roughness of the estimates. When such misconceptions exist, the person preparing the numbers may decide to change an estimate from, say, $25,000,000 to an arbitrary number such as $25,008,526. This process is called *unrounding*.

SUGGESTIONS FOR FURTHER READING

FOULKE, ROY A. *Practical Financial Statement Analysis.* 6th ed.; New York: McGraw-Hill Book Co., Inc., 1968.

---

[5] For some purposes, the significance of an answer is determined by using the maximum *percentage* of error in each figure in the calculation. This is a more precise statement of the rule than that given here, but it is also more complicated to apply. Considering zeros as insignificant, as is done here, will usually give satisfactory results.

GRAHAM, BENJAMIN; DAVID L. DODD; and SIDNEY COTTLE. *Security Analysis: Principles and Technique.* 4th ed.; New York: McGraw-Hill Book Co., Inc., 1963.

KENNEDY, RALPH DALE, and STEWART YARDWOOD McMULLEN. *Financial Statements: Form, Analysis, and Interpretation.* 4th ed.; Homewood, Ill.: Richard D. Irwin, Inc., 1962.

CHAPTER 12

FUNDS FLOW ANALYSIS

A *flow statement* explains the changes that occurred in an account or a group of accounts during an accounting period. The income statement is a flow statement; it explains the changes that occurred in retained earnings in connection with the operation of the business by summarizing the increases (i.e., revenues) and decreases (i.e., expenses) during the period. Another report, the *funds flow statement,* summarizes the events of the period from a different standpoint; it describes the sources from which additional funds were derived and the uses to which these funds were put. This statement is also called "statement of sources and applications of funds," "funds statements" and a variety of other names.

The funds flow statement is essentially derived from an analysis of changes that have occurred in asset and equities items between two balance sheet dates. It is *not* prepared directly from the accounts, as is the balance sheet itself.

THE CONCEPT OF FUNDS FLOW

Illustration 12–1 depicts the flow of financial resources in a typical business. As indicated by the "pipes" at the upper right, resources flow into the business from shareholders and from banks and other sources of borrowed capital. Some of these resources flow initially into the cash "reservoir," where they are held until needed; some of them flow directly to plant facilities and inventory. Valves on the pipes indicate the places where the flows can be turned off or on by management action. As resources are needed in operations, they are permitted to flow out of the cash reservoir, and these resources, together with material furnished by suppliers, are used in the manufacturing and selling process. At the end of this process, the cash reservoir is replenished by receipts from customers. The receivables reservoir indicates that cash is not replenished as soon as

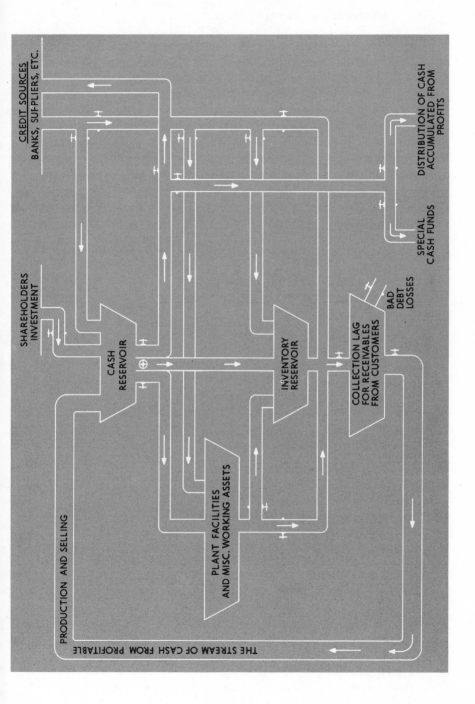

goods are shipped to customers, but rather that there is a lag until customers pay the amounts they owe. Cash also flows to suppliers and others to reimburse them for the resources they have provided.

The funds flow statement describes these flows, but it does not describe all of them. The flows in the left-hand section of the diagram are the result of the constantly recurring process of manufacturing and selling goods and collecting receivables from customers. The funds flow statement does not show the details of this more or less continuous movement of resources. Instead, it focuses on more basic changes. These changes are associated with the *permanent capital* of the business.

Permanent capital consists of resources supplied by long-term creditors and by shareholders, including both their original investment and the resources they have supplied by permitting earnings to be retained in the business. On the balance sheet, the amount of such resources is the sum of noncurrent liabilities plus owners' equity; in other words, it is the total of the right-hand side of the balance sheet, less the current liabilities.

Part of the permanent capital is invested in buildings, equipment, and other noncurrent assets. The remainder is invested in current assets, but only a fraction of the current assets has to be financed from permanent capital, since vendors and short-term creditors provide the remainder. The amount that is financed from permanent capital is the difference between the total current assets and the total current liabilities. This difference, as we have already seen, is called working capital.

The funds flow statement shows changes in permanent capital and the assets in which this permanent capital is invested. Changes in the sources of permanent capital and the uses to which it is put are likely to be of more than ordinary interest both to management and to outsiders since these changes reflect the results of the important financial decisions that have significant long-run consequences. The funds flow statement shows these changes. In order to focus on this "big picture," the funds flow statement disregards the recurring circulation of resources among the individual current asset and current liability accounts. It does this by lumping all these accounts into a single item, working capital.

The funds flow statement therefore shows changes in the total amount of working capital, but not fluctuations in the individual items comprising working capital, much like national population statistics show births, deaths, immigration, and emigration for the country as a whole rather than complicating the picture by showing the continual movement of people from one house to another within the country.

It can be seen that the word "funds" in this context has a specialized meaning. It is not synonymous with "cash," for cash is only one of the items comprising working capital. Rather, it is associated with permanent capital, and the assets in which permanent capital is invested, one of these assets being working capital.

Basic Relationships

Illustration 12–2 summarizes the total flow of funds for American industrial and commercial companies for an average year in the 1950's. Collectively, American companies generated $34 billion of funds from operations (that is, from the excess of operating revenue over operating expenditures); they obtained $6.1 billion of new permanent capital from the sale of stocks and bonds to investors; and they obtained $2.2 billion from other long-term creditors, a total of $42.3 billion. They used this $42.3 billion to acquire $23.7 billion of new plant and equipment, to increase working capital by $10 billion, and to pay $8.6 billion in dividends.

Our present task is to construct a similar picture for an individual company. We can do this by working with the information shown on its balance sheets.

Illustration 12–2

FLOW OF FUNDS IN NONFINANCIAL BUSINESS FIRMS

Average Year in 1950's
(billions of dollars)

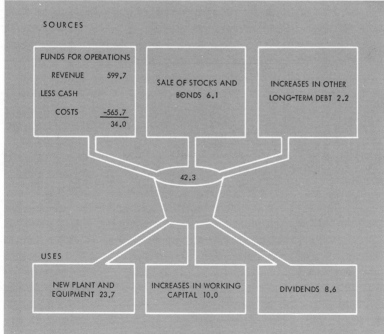

SOURCE: Adapted from Claude Robinson, *Understanding Profits* (Princeton, N.J.: D. Van Nostrand Co., Inc., 1961), p. 137.

A balance sheet shows the net effect of all the funds transactions from the beginning of the business to the balance sheet date. The equities side shows the sources from which funds have been obtained, and the assets side shows the way in which these funds have been used. The balance sheet in Illustration 12–3 shows that as of the end of 1967, long-term creditors have furnished $145,000 of capital, and shareholders have furnished $394,000. Of the latter, $211,000 represents their original contribution and $183,000 represents earnings that they have permitted the company to retain in the business. The total amount of funds provided is therefore $539,000, of which $125,000 is used for working capital and $414,000 is in fixed assets.

If all earnings were paid out in dividends and if replacements of fixed assets exactly equaled the annual depreciation charge, the amounts shown on Illustration 12–3 could remain unchanged year after year. Although there would be numerous changes in the several current asset and current

Illustration 12–3

CONDENSED BALANCE SHEET

December 31, 1967

NET ASSETS		NET EQUITIES	
Current assets.................	$233,000	Long-term debt.................	$145,000
Less: Current liabilities........	108,000	Capital stock...................	211,000
Working capital...............	$125,000	Retained earnings..............	183,000
Fixed assets...................	414,000		
Net Assets..............	$539,000	Net Equities.............	$539,000

liability accounts, these could offset one another so that the total working capital could remain constant. Under these circumstances, the business would not need additional financing. But of course the balance sheet items do change; additional funds are provided; and these are put to use.

From this simple balance sheet, we can see the possible ways in which the company can obtain additional funds. If it wished to buy a new plant, for example:

1. It could borrow, thus increasing long-term debt.
2. It could sell more stock, thus increasing the Capital Stock account.
3. It could forego dividends, which would show up as an increase in Retained Earnings.
4. It could use available cash, thus decreasing Working Capital.
5. It could sell some of its existing fixed assets, thus decreasing Fixed Assets.

The first, second, and third possibilities would be reflected on the balance sheet as an increase in equities; the fourth and fifth would show up as a decrease in assets. We can therefore generalize as follows: *sources of funds are indicated by increases in equities and decreases in assets.*

Looking at the other side of the coin, what uses could the company make of additional funds that it acquired? The possible uses are as follows:

1. It could add new fixed assets.
2. It could add to working capital.
3. It could pay off existing debt.
4. It could pay additional dividends to the shareholders, which decreases Retained Earnings.
5. It could repay capital to the shareholders.

The first two possibilities would show up as an increase in assets, and the next three as a decrease in equities. We can therefore generalize as follows: *uses of funds are indicated by increases in assets and decreases in equities.* (In describing both sources and uses, the reference is to *non-current* assets and equities since current items are lumped together in working capital.)

In accordance with the dual-aspect concept, total sources of funds must equal total uses of funds. The following relationships therefore exist:

1. Sources = Uses.
2. Increases in Equities + Decreases in Assets

$$= \text{Increases in Assets} + \text{Decreases in Equities.}$$

These same relationships can be explained in terms of debit and credit. Increases in equities and decreases in assets are both credits; increases in assets and decreases in equities are both debits. Thus, the above equation follows from the fact that changes in debits must equal changes in credits.

CONSTRUCTING THE FUNDS FLOW STATEMENT

The raw materials used for preparing a funds flow statement are the balances in asset and equities accounts, since these balances show the net effect of funds transactions. For example, if the company borrowed $26,000 from a long-term creditor, the following entry would be made:

```
Cash. . . . . . . . . . . . . . . . . . . . . . . .   26,000
    Long-Term Debt. . . . . . . . . . . . . . . . .            26,000
```

The increase in cash, which is an item of working capital, indicates that the business has obtained additional funds, and the credit part of the entry shows that the source of these funds was an increase in long-term debt.

Similarly, if the business purchased new fixed assets, the following entry would be made:

```
Fixed Assets. . . . . . . . . . . . . . . . . . . . . 61,000
    Cash (or a liability) . . . . . . . . . . . . .        61,000
```

The decrease in working capital indicates that the business has used funds, and the debit part of the entry shows that these funds have been used to acquire additional fixed assets.

Not all transactions involve a flow of funds, however, and those that do not must be eliminated before the funds statement is prepared. The most common of these is the entry to record annual depreciation, for example:

```
Depreciation Expense. . . . . . . . . . . . . . . . 29,000
    Accumulated Depreciation. . . . . . . . . . . .        29,000
```

This entry, made in accordance with the accrual concept, records the write-off of a portion of the cost of fixed assets as a charge against current operations, but it did not involve a flow of funds. It involves neither the receipt of additional capital, nor the use of capital. Funds were used in the period in which the fixed assets were acquired, not the period in which they are written off.

In order to construct a funds flow statement, the effect of these nonfund transactions must be eliminated.

The account balances may lump together the effect of certain transactions which are individually important in understanding what has happened during the year. For example, the Retained Earnings account is typically (1) increased by net income earned in the year and (2) decreased by dividends declared. The balance in the account shows the net effect of these transactions, but it is desirable that the effect of each be shown separately. Adjustments are therefore necessary to show the separate effect of these transactions.

Following is a procedure for making these adjustments.

Comparative Balance Sheets

A first approximation of the flow of funds during a period is obtained by finding the changes in the balance sheet amounts between the beginning and end of the period. This is done in Illustration 12-4, where *comparative balance sheets* for the beginning and end of the year 1968 are given, and the differences between amounts on the two balance sheets are computed. Note that increases in asset accounts are debits, that decreases in asset accounts are credits, and that increases in equities are credits. (Although not shown, it is apparent that decreases in equities would be debits.) Note also that, in accordance with the basic accounting equation, the sum of the debit increases equals the sum of the credit increases.

If it were not for the fact that some accounting transactions do not involve a flow of funds, it could be said that during the year funds were obtained from an increase in long-term debt, $26,000, and in retained earnings, $20,000, and that these funds were used to finance additional fixed assets, $21,000, and working capital, $25,000. These changes are only first approximations of the flow of funds, however, for they do include the effect of nonfund transactions. Also, they mask certain important fund flows, by lumping together individual flows in a single account.

Illustration 12–4

BALANCE SHEET USED FOR FUNDS FLOW ANALYSIS

(in thousands of dollars)

	Balances as of Dec. 31		Change in 1968	
	1968	1967	Debit	Credit
Current Assets...................................	262	233		
Less: Current Liabilities.........................	112	108		
Working Capital................................	150	125	25	
Plant and Equipment, Cost........................	648	601	47	
Accumulated Depreciation........................	(227)	(204)		23
Intangible Assets...............................	14	17		3
Net Assets...............................	585	539		
Long-Term Debt................................	171	145		26
Capital Stock..................................	211	211		
Retained Earnings..............................	203	183		20
Net Equities.............................	585	539		
Total Change................................			72	72

Adjustments

The balances must therefore be adjusted. The job of making these adjustments is difficult because it involves a clear understanding of the distinction between transactions that involve the flow of funds and those that do not. One approach is to think of the word "funds" as being synonymous with "working capital," since most individual funds transactions do involve an increase or decrease in some working capital item (i.e., a current asset or a current liability). The key questions then become: (1) Did this transaction, taken by itself, result in an increase in working capital? (If so, it was a source of funds.) (2) Did this transaction, taken by itself, result in a decrease in working capital? (If so, it was a use of funds.) (3) Did this transaction have no effect on working capital? (If so, it was neither a source nor a use of funds and must be eliminated.)

Of the several mechanical methods of keeping track of these adjustments, perhaps the most common is the work sheet, as shown in Illustration 12–5 and described below. The procedure is as follows:

1. Changes in balances in the balance sheet items are copied in the first two columns. (In the illustration, the changes are those derived from the comparative balance sheets shown in Illustration 12–4.)

2. Important funds flows that are concealed in the net balances are disentangled. This is done by making an entry in the account in which the amount was originally entered, so as to remove it from that account, and making a corresponding entry in a new account set up for that purpose. Since we want to remove the amount from the account in which it was originally recorded, the entry to this account must be the opposite of the entry originally made. Thus, if the original entry was a credit to the account, the adjusting entry would be a debit. The entry to the new account would be in this case a credit, because every entry must have debit-credit equality. These entries are made in the "adjustments" pair of columns.

3. Transactions that do not involve a flow of funds are discovered, and the balances are adjusted to remove the effect of these transactions. This is done by *reversing* the original transaction, that is, by making entries that are opposite to those that were made originally. These entries are also made in the "adjustments" pair of columns.

4. Each account balance is increased or decreased by the amount in the adjustment column opposite the item, and the adjusted amount is entered in the third pair of columns. The amounts in the debit column are uses of funds, and the amounts in the credit column are sources of funds.

Illustration 12–5

FUNDS FLOW WORK SHEET

(in thousands of dollars)

	Changes in Account Balances		Adjustments		Changes Affecting Funds	
	Debit	Credit	Debit	Credit	Debit (Uses)	Credit (Sources)
Working Capital..........	25				25	
Plant and Equipment, Gross..	47		(e) 14		61	
Accumulated Depreciation....		23	(d) 29	(e) 6		
Intangible Assets..........		3	(c) 3			
Long-Term Debt..........		26				26
Capital Stock.............						
Retained Earnings.........		20	(b) 42	(a) 22		
Dividends...............			(a) 22		22	
				(b) 42		
Funds from Operations......			(e) 2	(c) 3		72
				(d) 29		
Disposition of Fixed Assets				(e) 10		10
Total....................	72	72	112	112	108	108

Illustration of the Procedure

The adjustments shown in Illustration 12–5 are the most common type of adjustments that are made in constructing a funds flow statement. Each is described below. Information used as a basis for these adjustments can come from any of a number of sources. Most of them are derived from information shown on the income statement, and the income statement used for this purpose is shown in Illustration 12–6.

Illustration 12–6

INCOME STATEMENT, 1968

(in thousands of dollars)

Sales..........................		$1,080
Costs and expenses:		
Cost of goods sold..............	$890	
Selling and administrative.........	68	
Depreciation....................	29	
Amortization of goodwill.........	3	
Interest.......................	7	997
Operating income................		$ 83
Gain on disposal of fixed assets......		2
Income before taxes..............		$ 85
Income taxes....................		43
Net income.....................		$ 42
Dividends......................		22
Added to Retained Earnings........		$ 20

DIVIDENDS. From the income statement we learn that the net change in Retained Earnings, which was $20,000, was the result of two offsetting factors. There was an increase of $42,000, which was the net income of the year, and a decrease of $22,000 from the declaration of dividends. It would be useful to show these two elements separately, and this is done by reversing the entries originally made to Retained Earnings and setting up new accounts. In the case of dividends, the actual entry to Retained Earnings was a debit, so to reverse this, we credit Retained Earnings. The offsetting debit is to a new item set up on the work sheet below the balance sheet items. Thus, this adjustment is:

(*a*)

```
Dividends  . . . . . . . . . . . . . . . . . . . .   22,000
     Retained Earnings  . . . . . . . . . . . . . . .         22,000
```

FUNDS FROM OPERATIONS. A corresponding adjustment is made for the other entry that affected Retained Earnings, the $42,000 net income for the period. Since the original entry was a credit to Retained Earnings, it is reversed by a debit. The offsetting credit is to another new item set up on the work sheet. Rather than labeling this item "Net Income," however, it is labeled "Funds from Operations" because when we finish making other adjustments to it, its balance will no longer be the net income for the year, but rather the new funds that have been provided from the operations of the business. The adjustment is:

(*b*)

```
Retained Earnings . . . . . . . . . . . . . . . . .   42,000
    Funds from Operations . . . . . . . . . . . . .            42,000
```

These two adjustments were simply for the purpose of highlighting important funds flows. We shall now turn to the adjustments that are necessary in order to eliminate the transactions that did not involve a flow of funds at all.

AMORTIZATION OF INTANGIBLES. The income statement shows an expense labeled "amortization of goodwill" in the amount of $3,000, and the comparative balance sheet shows that Intangible Assets has decreased by the same amount. We can deduce that these items resulted from the write-off during 1968 of a portion of the intangible asset, Goodwill, by means of an entry debiting the expense item and crediting the asset.

This transaction did not involve a flow of funds in 1968. When the Goodwill was originally set up on the balance sheet in some previous year, a flow of funds was involved, but in 1968 the transaction reflects neither an inflow of resources to the business nor the use of resources. The entry was made in accordance with the accrual concept, which provides for a systematic write-off of such costs to the income of the periods benefited. To reverse it, the following adjustment is made:

(*c*)

```
Intangible Assets . . . . . . . . . . . . . . . . .    3,000
    Funds from Operations . . . . . . . . . . . . .             3,000
```

The credit is made to Funds from Operations since the original debit was to an expense account, which had the effect of decreasing net income. The amount of net income now appears on the line "Funds from Operations," so the credit to reverse the transaction appears on the same line.

DEPRECIATION. The income statement shows that depreciation expense for the year was $29,000. We know that the credit part of such an entry is always to the Accumulated Depreciation account. As already noted, this entry did not represent a flow of funds. At the time the assets were purchased, funds were used, but the subsequent write-off of the asset cost by means of the depreciation mechanism involves neither a source nor a use of funds. The entry must therefore be reversed, and the adjustment to accomplish this is:

(*d*)

```
Accumulated Depreciation. . . . . . . . . . . . . .   29,000
    Funds from Operations . . . . . . . . . . . . .            29,000
```

The credit is made to Funds from Operations for a reason similar to that given for the amortization of Goodwill, above.

DISPOSAL OF FIXED ASSETS. We note that the income statement contains an item, "gain on disposal of fixed assets, $2,000," and from this we know that fixed assets were sold for more than their book value. In order to find the facts about this transaction, we must go to the underlying accounting records (e.g., the general journal). Assume that these show that the gain on disposal arose in connection with the following transaction:

```
Cash. . . . . . . . . . . . . . . . . . . . . . . .  10,000
Accumulated Depreciation. . . . . . . . . . . . . .   6,000
    Plant and Equipment . . . . . . . . . . . . . .          14,000
    Gain on Disposal of Fixed Assets. . . . . . . .           2,000
```

This transaction means that the fixed assets being disposed of had a cost of $14,000 and accumulated depreciation of $6,000, so their net book value was $8,000. They were sold for $10,000, so there was a gain of $2,000.

The funds flow involved in this transaction was the $10,000 proceeds of the sale. The other items did not involve a flow of funds; they merely removed the asset and its accumulated depreciation from the books and recorded the gain. Note particularly that the amount of funds generated by this transaction was $10,000, not the $2,000 appearing on the income statement. An adjustment is therefore necessary, both to remove the nonfund items from the accounts and also to show the $10,000 as a source of funds. This adjustment is essentially the reverse of the original transaction. The reversal of the gain of $2,000 is made against Funds from Operations since that is where the net income, of which this item was a part, is now recorded. A new item, "Disposition of Fixed Assets," is set up on the work sheet. The adjustment is as follows:

(e)

```
Plant and Equipment . . . . . . . . . . . . . . . .  14,000
Funds from Operations . . . . . . . . . . . . . . .   2,000
    Accumulated Depreciation. . . . . . . . . . . .           6,000
    Disposition of Fixed Assets . . . . . . . . . .          10,000
```

ACQUISITION OF FIXED ASSETS. Refer again to the item on the work sheet labeled "Plant and Equipment, Gross." The comparative balance sheets showed an increase of $47,000 in the year, but to this, we have added $14,000 from adjustment (*e*) above, representing the write-off of plant that was sold. In order to show a net increase of $47,000, an entry must have been made during the year debiting Plant and Equipment for $14,000 more than this, or $61,000. Since the only debit entries to Plant and Equipment are those recording the acquisition of plant and equipment, we now know that fixed assets in the amount of $61,000 must have been acquired during the year, and this represented a use of funds.

PREPARATION OF THE STATEMENT. Having adjusted the amounts for all the nonfund transactions that we can discover, we are now in a position to compute the funds flows. This is done simply by extending the amounts on each line of the work sheet to the last pair of columns. The adjustments are added algebraically to the amounts in the first pair of columns. For example, for Accumulated Depreciation the calculation is $23 + 6 - 29 = 0$. Debit amounts in the last pair of columns now show uses of funds, and credit amounts show sources.

These amounts are used to prepare the funds flow statement, as shown in Illustration 12–7.

Illustration 12–7

FUNDS FLOW STATEMENT, 1968

Sources of Funds:
Funds provided by operations	$ 72,000
Proceeds from sale of fixed assets	10,000
Additional long-term debt	26,000
Total	$108,000

Uses of Funds:
New plant and equipment	$ 61,000
Dividends	22,000
Increase in working capital	25,000
Total	$108,000

Other Transactions

The nonfund transactions described above had to do with: (1) depreciation, (2) amortization of intangible assets, and (3) disposition of fixed assets. Other transactions that did not involve a flow of funds may occur, including: (4) amortization of bond discount or premium, (5) declaration of a stock dividend, and (6) creation of surplus reserves. When such transactions are found, the comparative balance sheet changes are adjusted in the same manner as described above, that is, by finding out what the original transaction was and then making an adjustment that is the reverse of it.

Hidden Transactions

The foregoing description assumed that the analyst had access to the company's accounting records, for the procedure required him to consult these records. An outside analyst may wish to construct a funds flow statement, even though he has only the information contained in the company's annual report, principally the balance sheet and income statement. (For example, he may be interested in a competitor's fund flow).

He often can do a reasonably good job of deducing what transactions *probably* caused the change in balance sheet items even without access to the underlying records.

In some cases, the exact nature of the transaction cannot be deduced, but an approximation can be derived that is better than nothing. The fixed asset transactions discussed above will be used as an example of what can be done.

After the depreciation adjustment (*d*) had been recorded, the "Accumulated Depreciation" line shows a debit balance of 6 (29 − 23 = 6). Since the Accumulated Depreciation item never involves a flow of funds per se, some other nonfund transaction must have affected it. The most likely type of transaction is the removal of accumulated depreciation when fixed assets are disposed of. From the fact that "gain on disposal of fixed assets, $2,000" appears on the income statement, we know that there was such a transaction, and that proceeds exceeded book value by $2,000. We therefore can reconstruct part of the entry that must have been made:

```
Cash. . . . . . . . . . . . . . . . . . . . . . . . . .        ?
Accumulated Depreciation. . . . . . . . . . . . . . .      6,000
    Plant and Equipment . . . . . . . . . . . . . . .              ?
    Gain on Disposal. . . . . . . . . . . . . . . . .          2,000
```

We cannot complete the entry without more information, but we do know that the credit to Plant and Equipment must have been *at least* $6,000, since the accumulated depreciation on an asset never exceeds its cost. Accepting this minimum amount, the original entry becomes:

```
Cash. . . . . . . . . . . . . . . . . . . . . . . .      2,000
Accumulated Depreciation. . . . . . . . . . . . . .      6,000
    Plant and Equipment . . . . . . . . . . . . . .              6,000
    Gain on Disposal. . . . . . . . . . . . . . . .              2,000
```

If the indicated adjustment of $6,000 is made to Plant and Equipment on the work sheet, the total amount of this item becomes 47 + 6 = 53. We can therefore deduce that funds were used to acquire plant and equipment costing *at least* $53,000. Reference back to the facts obtainable from the accounting records shows that this number understates the actual amount. Nevertheless, the deduction process brought us closer to the true facts than relying on the comparative balance sheet, which implies fixed asset additions of only $47,000.

Compound Transactions

A single transaction may involve the simultaneous source and use of funds. If so, it is usually more informative if the source is separated from the use. For example, if a $100,000 building was purchased and if $80,000 of this was financed with a mortgage loan, one could argue that the funds required for this transaction were only $20,000. Regardless of the theoretical merit of this argument, the reader of a funds flow statement undoubtedly wants to know about the two separate facts, the acquisition of the building and the incurrence of an additional liability. Such a transaction should therefore be shown on the funds flow statement as two separate items, a use of $100,000 for the building and a source of $80,000 from the mortgage loan.

Even in the case of a bond refunding, which involves only the exchange of one liability for another, with possibly no net change in the Bonds Payable account, it may be helpful to show separately the retirement of the old issue as a use of funds and the sale of the new issue as a source of funds.

Funds Provided by Operations

The $72,000 "funds from operations" that was developed from our analysis of funds flow differs considerably from the net income figure on the income statement, which was only $42,000. The work sheet shows that the $72,000 was arrived at by adding to net income the nonfund transactions involved in the net income calculation, principally the depreciation charge; that is,

Net income......................................	$42,000
Plus depreciation and other nonfund items...........	30,000
Equals funds provided by operations...............	$72,000

Many funds flow statements in fact show such a breakdown of "funds provided by operations," or, as it is often called, "internally generated funds."

Exactly the same result could have been obtained by subtracting expense items requiring the use of funds from revenue items that were a source of funds. The income statement (Illustration 12–6) shows these expense items as cost of goods sold, selling and administrative expense, interest expense, and income taxes. Each of these items is associated with either a decrease in a current asset (cash, inventory, prepaid expenses) or an increase in a current liability (accounts payable, taxes payable, accrued liabilities), both of which are decreases in working capital. The revenue item, Sales, is associated with an increase in cash or accounts receivable and hence with an increase in working capital. Operations generate funds to the extent that revenue which brings in funds exceeds expenses which require the use of funds, or—

Sales revenue................................	$1,080,000
Less expenses using funds.....................	1,008,000
Equals funds provided by operations............	$ 72,000

This calculation shows more clearly how the funds were actually generated than the method of adding back depreciation and other nonfund items to net income. The "funds from operation" sections of some funds flow statements are prepared in this way.

The choice of methods is relatively unimportant; they give identical results. It is important, however, to appreciate the fact that *depreciation is not a source of funds*. In the first method, depreciation is added to net income to find the funds provided by operations, but it is operations, not depreciation, that provides the funds. Depreciation is neither a source nor a use of funds.

The Funds Flow Statement

There is no prescribed format for the funds flow statement. The items are arranged and described in whatever way seems most clearly to show the important financial events of the period. Minor items should be combined in order to emphasize the major changes.

Incidentally, reporting working capital as a source or use of funds may

Illustration 12–8

BOISE CASCADE CORPORATION

Sources and Application of Funds
(in thousands of dollars)

	Year Ended December 31	
	1968	1967
Sources:		
Net income................................	$ 45,390	$ 29,544
Depreciation and depletion........................	31,437	29,419
Total from Operations........................	$ 76,827	$ 58,963
Borrowing under notes...........................	30,397	78,499
Sale of property and equipment....................	17,196	8,293
Exchange of timber and operating properties..........	86,107	. . .
Increase in deferred income taxes...................	25,635	2,876
Exercise of stock options........................	1,305	2,858
Issuances of common stock.......................	22,817	. . .
Miscellaneous.................................	1,812	(1,911)
Total Sources............................	$262,096	$149,578
Applications:		
Property and equipment..........................	$ 45,564	$ 52,093
Timber and timberlands..........................	17,365	40,977
Capital expenditures........................	$ 62,929	$ 93,070
Investments in companies and realty................	91,981	18,710
Increase in other noncurrent assets.................	3,520	23,327
Purchase of common stock for the treasury..........	. . .	3,061
Cash dividends declared.........................	8,606	7,525
Reduction of timberland rental obligations...........	30,779	
Reduction of long-term notes and other obligations.....	71,877	23,599
Total Applications...........................	$269,692	$169,292
Decrease in working capital......................	$ 7,596	$ 19,714

SOURCE: Condensed from 1968 annual report.

seem to involve a contradiction of terms. How can we regard uses of funds as "events that result in a decrease in working capital" and at the same time treat an increase in working capital itself as a use of funds? Actually, there is no contradiction if it is recalled that all transactions have two aspects. In a funds flow statement, increases in noncurrent assets and decreases in noncurrent equities are uses of funds, and the other aspect of each such change is a decrease in working capital; working capital *used* for the items stated is not available for other purposes. An increase in the working capital item itself represents management's decision to *use* this additional amount in the various working capital items rather than for some other purpose, such as paying it out as dividends.

In any event, the possible confusion can easily be avoided by treating the change in working capital as a residual item. This is done by arranging the funds flow statement in the following form:

$$\text{Source} - \text{Uses} = \text{Working Capital Change.}$$

The funds flow statements for Boise Cascade Corporation in Illustration 12–8 have such an arrangement. These statements show, for 1967, the financing of a major capital expenditure program (three times the annual depreciation charge) by funds generated from operations supplemented by long-term borrowing; and, for 1968, the financing of an even larger capital expenditure and investment program by funds generated from operations, from exchange of timber and operating properties, and from the issuance of common stock.

CASH FLOW STATEMENTS

Instead of lumping all current assets and current liabilities together as working capital, it may be desirable to consider changes in some or all of these items separately. A statement that has such a purpose is technically called a *cash flow statement*. Except that changes in individual current asset and liability items are treated separately, the procedures for analyzing transactions are the same as those described above. Increases in assets and decreases in equities indicate uses of cash; decreases in assets and increases in equities indicate sources of cash. Transactions that do not involve a flow of cash are eliminated.

Some people use the word "funds" as synonymous with "cash," as in statements such as, "We borrowed funds to increase our inventory," or, "We obtained funds by speeding up the collection of receivables." These people refer to the cash flow statement as a funds flow statement. This difference in terminology is unimportant, since the content of the statement will indicate which concept is used.

Illustration 12–9 shows a cash flow statement. This particular statement describes the effects of an expansion program, and since the expansion involved an increase in inventory and receivables as well as additional fixed assets, it was informative to show these current asset items on the statement rather than combining them into the single item, working capital. The unimportant changes, principally prepaid expenses and accrued liabilities, are lumped together as "miscellaneous changes."

Another cash flow statement, using a format suggested by Professor Almand R. Coleman of the University of Virginia, is shown in Illustration 12–10.

Illustration 12–9

BALDWIN MARKET COMPANY

Cash Flow Statement for the Year 1967

What We Did		*How We Financed It*		
Expanded:		Reduced cash		$ 2,453
Accounts receivable.	$ 67,477	Sold security holdings. .		100,000
Inventories.	61,586	Borrowed:		
Acquired new fixed assets.	255,861	Accounts payable. . . .		43,185
Paid dividends.	78,315	Bank loan.		26,000
Miscellaneous changes.	1,653	Mortgage.		175,000
		Obtained funds from operations:		
		Net income.	$95,679	
		Depreciation.	22,575	118,254
	$464,892			$464,892

Illustration 12–10

ALTERNATIVE FORM OF CASH FLOW STATEMENT

(in millions of dollars)

In 1963, sales revenue amounted to.		$150.6
Whereas cost of goods sold and operating "cash" expenses (exclusive of $7.2 depreciation) was.		128.8
So net income before noncash charges was.		$ 21.8
And there would have been a net inflow of cash of this amount from operations, except that—		
A. The company collected less from customers than it billed.	$(14.1)	
B. The company bought and manufactured more than the cost of goods it shipped.	(2.9)	
C. The company paid out less cash than the costs it incurred.	0.8	
The net effect of these items being.		(16.2)
So that operating activities resulted in an "internally generated" cash inflow of.		$ 5.6
There were inflows from—		
Sale of common stock.	$ 12.6	
Increase in short-term loans.	5.0	
Increase in long-term debt.	2.4	20.0
		$ 25.6
Outgo of cash was required for—		
Dividends.	$ 3.0	
Property, plant, and equipment acquired in excess of dispositions. . .	30.8	
Increase in investments and other assets.	2.0	35.8
So that the net decrease in cash during 1963 was.		$(10.2)

Although not usually contained in published financial reports, a cash flow statement is essential to management in examining short-run financial movements. It is frequently prepared for monthly or weekly time intervals. The amount of cash required to finance peak seasonal needs is obscured in an annual statement.

USES OF THE STATEMENT

The funds flow and cash flow statements are used for two principal purposes: (1) as a means of analyzing what has happened in the past, and (2) as a means of planning what is going to happen in the future.

As a tool of historical analysis, the statements shed light on the financial policies that the company has pursued. Of particular interest is the policy with respect to the acquisition of new fixed assets. To what extent were new assets financed by internally generated funds, and to what extent by borrowing or other external sources? For financial resources obtained externally, what proportion was from debt and what from equity? Some companies deliberately limit their growth to an amount that can be financed from internally generated funds. Others do not hesitate to go to the capital market for funds. For these, the balance selected between risky, low-cost debt and less risky, higher cost equity is of considerable interest, as discussed in Chapter 11.

As a tool of planning, a projected funds flow statement is an essential device for planning the amount, timing, and character of new financing. Estimated uses of funds for new fixed assets, for working capital, for dividends, and for the repayment of debt are made for each of several future years, usually at least two or three years, but in some cases 10 years or more. Estimates are made of the funds to be provided by operations, and the difference, if it is positive, represents the funds that must be obtained by borrowing or the issuance of new equity securities. If the indicated amount of new funds required is greater than management thinks it is feasible to raise, then the plans for new fixed asset acquisitions and the dividend policies are reexamined so that the uses of funds can be brought into balance with anticipated sources of financing them.

For shorter term financial planning, a cash budget is essential. The cash budget is a cash flow statement, similar to those shown above except that amounts are estimates of the future rather than those recorded in the past. Projections are made for each of the next several months or several quarters. One way to prepare such a budget is to list all the estimated uses of cash and all the sources other than from additional financing. The difference between these totals is the amount that must be obtained by borrowing or selling additional stock if the planned program is to be carried out. If it is believed that this amount cannot be raised, the indication is that the estimated uses of cash must be cut back. In other respects, the technique is the same as that already described.

In making a cash budget, special attention is paid to the timing of the flows; that is, to the anticipated need for cash in each month or each quarter of the period covered. Particularly in businesses subject to seasonal fluctuations, there are likely to be heavy, but temporary, cash needs in months when inventories are being built up, and these needs may be concealed in a statement that is not broken into short intervals of time.

MISUSES OF THE STATEMENT

In recent years, the number of companies publishing funds flow or cash flow statements has increased rapidly. As is often the case with a newly popular idea, a great deal of misunderstanding, and hence misuse is prevalent. Basically, the misunderstanding results from a tendency to think that sources of funds are synonymous with increases in owners' equity. This is not so. For reasons examined in detail in Part I of this book, increases in owners' equity must be measured in accordance with the accrual concept; there is not necessarily a correspondence between the earning of net income and changes in working capital. The using up of fixed assets is a real cost, a real decrease in owners' equity, even though no change in funds flow is involved.

The Accounting Principles Board of the AICPA, alarmed at the misunderstandings, published a useful clarification, part of which is quoted below:[1]

In recent years a new concept (or more correctly, an old concept with a new name) has become increasingly important in the analysis of the flow of funds. The term "cash flow" has been used to refer to a variety of concepts, but its most common meaning in financial literature, and to a lesser extent in accounting literature, is the same as "funds derived from operations" in a statement of source and application of funds. . . . Synonyms which are sometimes used include "cash earnings," "cash income," and "cash throw-off."

Many of the comments made in connection with "cash flow" analysis leave the reader with the erroneous impression that "cash flow" or "cash earnings" is superior to net income as a measure of a company's real earning power. Calculations of the Price/Cash Flow ratio are sometimes made and presented as a substitute for or supplement to the Price/Earnings ratio in evaluating a company's stock. The amount of "cash flow" or the "cash flow per share" has often been presented in the president's letter, the financial review, or the statistical section of the annual report of a corporation apart from or in the absence of a complete statement of source and application of funds in the report. In other words, there has been a growing tendency on the part of some people to single out one of the items on the statement of source and application of funds, thereby implying that this figure is more important

---

[1] Accounting Principles Board, AICPA, Opinion No. 3, *The Statement of Source and Application of Funds*, October 1963; cited in Paul Grady, *Inventory of Generally Accepted Accounting Principles* (AICPA *Accounting Research Study No. 7*, 1965), p. 314.

than other information regarding the flow of funds and often carrying the implication that "net income plus depreciation" is the best measure of the company's profitability. There is a strong implication running through the comments in the literature, including those in the annual reports of some corporations, that the total "cash flow" can be considered available for the payment of dividends.

Misconceptions about Depreciation

Most of the difficulty referred to above stems from the misconception that depreciation is a source of funds; for example, the following quotations:[2]

Most people pay too little attention to depreciation reserves as a contributor to corporate health. In some years depreciation actually exceeds net profit.

Company X shifted to accelerated depreciation last year, thus increasing its depreciation charge and its cash flow earnings by $6 million.

Depreciation money is cash. In your bank account, depreciation dollars and profit dollars look alike.

The most charitable thing that can be said about such quotations is that they are half truths. Some are in no sense true; the statement that an increase in depreciation results in an increase in "cash flow earnings" overlooks the fact that such an increase in depreciation is exactly offset by a decrease in net income. As Gaa has put it: "Depreciation should be sued for nonsupport; it does *not* provide funds or any other assets for the replacement of property."[3] And Robert C. Tyson, chairman of the Finance Committee of U.S. Steel, puts it this way:[4]

. . . For the security analyst the sum of profits plus depreciation may provide a measure of management discretion to choose between paying dividends, paying off debt or spending money to replace depreciated facilities. But as a measure of corporate success it is just as fallacious to add these two items as it is to add back taxes to profits.

The misuse of this type of measurement may be partly attributable to the vocabulary quirks in which the financial fraternity indulges when speaking of depreciation as a source of funds. If those supposed to know of what they speak say that depreciation is a source of funds, then those less well-informed can say, "The bigger the source, the better." So perhaps we had "better mind our language," as mothers used to admonish. The fact is, of course, that the only continuing source of cash that any firm has out of which to cover all its

---

[2] Adapted from quotations collected by William J. Vatter and reported by him in "Operating Confusion in Accounting," *Journal of Business,* University of Chicago, July 1963, pp. 290–301.

[3] Charles J. Gaa, "Depreciation—the Good Provider?", *Business Topics,* Michigan State University, Winter 1962.

[4] Speech before the Eastern Area Conference of the Financial Executives Institute, June 14, 1963.

costs is its sales receipts from customers. Among those costs are the prepaid expenditures for facilities. It takes a long time to get them covered. Depreciation is the record of their cost slowly being covered. To hold that big depreciation cost in the guise of big cash flow is good for a company is the same as saying that the bigger its costs the better off it is. And that is plain nonsense! Here, then, is another area in which clarification of public understanding is necessary for establishment of prudent public policy.

Finally, from the opinion of the Accounting Principles Board of AICPA:[5]

The amount of funds derived from operations cannot be considered as a substitute for or an improvement upon properly determined net income as a measure of results of operations and the consequent effect on financial position. Misleading implications can result from isolated statistics in annual reports of "cash flow" which are not placed in proper perspective to net income figures and to a complete analysis of source and application of funds. "Cash flow" and related terms should not be used in annual reports in such a way that the significance of net income is impaired, and "cash earnings" or other terms with a similar connotation should be avoided. The Board regards computations of "cash flow per share" as misleading since they ignore the impact of cash expenditures for renewal and replacement of facilities and tend to downgrade the significant economic statistic of "earnings per share."

SUMMARY

A funds flow statement shows the sources from which funds were provided and the uses to which these funds were put during an accounting period. The term "funds" is equivalent to "working capital." The net effects of funds flows are indicated by changes in noncurrent asset and equities accounts between the beginning and ending balance sheets of the periods. Increases in noncurrent assets and decreases in noncurrent equities indicate uses of funds; decreases in noncurrent assets and increases in noncurrent equities indicate sources.

The actual flows are found by reconstructing the transactions that resulted in these changes. In this process, transactions which affected balance sheet items but which did not involve a flow of funds are eliminated. When the analyst has access to the company's accounting records, all transactions can easily be identified. Even when he has only the incomplete information obtainable in published statements, he often can make a good approximation of the funds flow by deducing what transactions probably caused the balance sheet changes.

The amount of funds provided by operations of the period is by no means the same as the reported net income of the period. In a sense, funds provided by operations is net income adjusted for depreciation and other

---

[5] APB Opinion No. 3, *op. cit.*, paragraph 15.

nonfund expenses and revenues, but this adjustment should not lead to the inference that depreciation is itself a source of funds.

A cash flow statement is the same as a funds flow statement except that important current asset and current liability changes are identified separately rather than combined in the single item, working capital.

In recent years, there has been a widespread tendency to use "cash flow earnings" as an indicator of corporate health that is equal to or superior to the indication provided by the net income figure. This is erroneous.

SUGGESTIONS FOR FURTHER READING

SPROUSE, ROBERT T., and ROBERT K. JAEDICKE. *Income, Funds and Cash.* Englewood Cliffs, N.J.: Prentice-Hall, Inc., 1965.

PART III

Accounting in Management Control

CHAPTER 13

ESSENTIALS OF COST ACCOUNTING

Up to this point, attention has been focused on financial accounting, that is, on the type of accounting whose purpose is to produce balance sheets and income statements for use by parties external to the business. We now turn to the subject of management accounting, that is, to the accounting whose purpose is to provide information useful to the management.

MANAGEMENT ACCOUNTING AND FINANCIAL ACCOUNTING

Whereas financial accounting has been written about for over 400 years, little was written about management accounting until well into the 20th century. The actual practice of management accounting goes back much further; many of the techniques to be described here were used by Josiah Wedgwood and Sons, Ltd., in the 18th century, for example. The need for a type of accounting that was not aimed primarily at the preparation of financial statements is set forth in this 1875 memorandum by Thomas Sutherland, a British business executive:[1]

The present system of bookkeeping in the Accountant's Department is admirably suited for the end it has in view, viz., that of ascertaining once a year or oftener the profits upon the company's transactions; but it is evident that in a business of this kind much detailed information is necessary regarding the working of the Company, and this information should be obtainable in such a practical form, as to enable the Directors to see readily and clearly the causes at work in favor of or against the success of the Company's operations.

[1] This memorandum was called to my attention by Professor Lyle E. Jacobsen, who saw it reprinted in the London *Economist* in 1960.

In contrast with financial accounting, management accounting:

1. Has more than one purpose.
2. Is not governed by generally accepted accounting principles.
3. Is optional.
4. Focuses on segments as well as on the whole of a business.
5. Has less emphasis on precision.
6. Is part of other processes, rather than an end in itself.

Multiple Purposes

The governing objective of financial accounting is to furnish information to outsiders in order to report on stewardship. A single set of principles and a single system is adequate to meet this single objective. The governing objective of management accounting is to furnish information that is useful to management. Management needs information for several different purposes, among which are: as an aid in planning, as an aid in measuring and appraising performance, as an aid in setting selling prices, and as an aid in analyzing alternative courses of action. The information that is relevant for one of these purposes is often not relevant for another, and management accounting information must therefore be put together in several different ways, according to the purpose for which it is to be used. The concept of "cost," for example, may mean one thing in connection with planning and quite a different thing in connection with performance measurement.

Not Governed by Generally Accepted Principles

Financial accounting information must be prepared in accordance with generally accepted accounting principles. Outsiders, who usually have no choice but to accept information just as the company provides it, need assurance that this information is prepared in accordance with a mutually understood set of ground rules. Otherwise, they could not make sense out of the figures. Management, by contrast, can make and enforce whatever rules and definitions it finds most useful for its own needs, without worrying about whether these conform to some outside standard. Thus, in management accounting there may well be information on sales orders received, even though these are not financial accounting transactions; fixed assets may be stated at appraisal values, overhead costs may be omitted from inventories, or profits may be recorded before revenue is realized, even though each of these concepts is inconsistent with generally accepted accounting principles. The basic question in management accounting is the pragmatic one: "Is the information useful?" rather than, "Does it conform to generally accepted principles?"

Optional

Financial accounting *must* be done. Enough effort must be expended to collect data in acceptable form and with an acceptable degree of accuracy, whether or not the accountant regards this information as useful. Management accounting, by contrast, is entirely optional. No outside agency specifies what must be done, or indeed that anything need be done. Being optional, there is no point in collecting a piece of information for management purposes unless its value is believed to exceed the cost of collecting it.

Focus on Segments

The balance sheet and income statement relate to the business as a whole. Most management accounting information relates to segments of the organization, that is, to departments or other organizational segments, to products, or to individual functions. As we shall see, the necessity for dividing the total costs of the business among these individual segments creates some problems in management accounting that do not exist in financial accounting.

Less Emphasis on Precision

Management needs information rapidly, and is often willing to sacrifice precision in order to gain speed in reporting. Thus, in management accounting, approximations are often as useful as, or even more useful than, figures that are worked out to the last penny.

A Part, Rather than an End in Itself

Financial accounting is a complete, self-contained entity. Management accounting information is usually only part of a larger system. The monetary data of accounting are often used in conjunction with non-monetary data (such as pounds of material, hours of labor, units of product), and the historical accounting data are used in relation to estimates of the future (such as budgets and forecasts).

Similarities

The criteria by which management accounting practices should be judged are essentially the same as those already discussed for financial accounting: relevance, objectivity, and feasibility. Application of these criteria may lead to different practices, however. For example, imputed costs, which are costs not evidenced by an exchange transaction, are not ordinarily included in financial accounting, but it is not uncommon to find such costs recorded in management accounting records.

EXAMPLE: A trade association of retail hardware stores collecting records of expenses from its member firms may specify that the report include as rent expense an amount equivalent to what rental costs would have been even if the building were owned and no rent as such were actually paid. This would put the reports of members who owned buildings on a basis comparable with those who rented buildings, and thus increase the comparability of the data. Such a practice would not be permitted in financial accounting; in accordance with the cost concept, only the actual costs incurred in occupying the building could be shown.

The inclusion of imputed rent in the above example would increase the relevance of the report, would make it more useful. There would be a corresponding reduction in the objectivity of the information, but members of the trade association are not likely to introduce a deliberate bias into figures prepared for their mutual benefit, so on balance it probably is safe to relax the objectivity criterion in order to obtain more relevant data. By contrast, if financial accounting permitted the reporting of imputed rent, the possibility of manipulation would be increased.

Although differences do exist, most elements of financial accounting are also found in management accounting. There are two reasons for this. First, the same considerations that make these principles sensible for the purposes of financial accounting are likely to be present for purposes of management accounting. For example, management cannot base its reporting system on unverifiable, subjective estimates of profits submitted by lower echelons, which is the same reason that financial accounting adheres to the cost and realization concepts. Second, the internal accounting system must furnish the information used in preparing the financial statements. There is a presumption, therefore, that the basic data will be collected in accordance with generally accepted financial accounting principles, for to do otherwise would require two separate systems.

SYSTEMS FOR COST ACCUMULATION

Management accounting encompasses the same categories of data that have been described in Part I, namely, assets, liabilities, owners' equity, expenses, and revenues. In this chapter, the description will be limited to costs. Costs, it will be recalled, can be either expenses or assets, depending on whether the cost transaction does or does not decrease owners' equity in the current accounting period.

As already noted, management needs accounting information for several different purposes, and the type of information that is required varies with the purpose. Although there are many possible purposes, some of which (such as data for use in defense of an antitrust action) may not even be foreseeable when a system is being designed, most, if not all, of these purposes can be satisfied with two types of cost information: (1) costs accumulated in terms of products or programs, and (2) costs accumulated in terms of management responsibility. The first is called *product cost accounting,* and the second is called *responsibility accounting.*

In product costing, costs are accumulated for each product or groups of related products. If an organization performs services or carries out programs, rather than making a physical product, the procedure is called *program costing.* Product costs are used in determining the amounts to be reported as goods in process inventory, finished goods inventory, and cost of sales, and thus are a part of financial accounting. Many products or services are sold at a price that includes cost plus a predetermined allowance for profits. Such transactions range from the multibillion-dollar "cost-plus-fixed-fee" contracts for the development and production of complete weapons systems down to an order for printing 500 letterheads or repairing an automobile. Such transactions require the collection of costs by products or programs. Product costs are also used as an aid in setting selling prices, and in making other decisions related to products that will be discussed in Chapter 19.

In responsibility accounting, costs are accumulated by responsibility centers. A *responsibility center* is an organization unit headed by a responsible person. Since organizations function through the actions of human beings, it is important that costs be accumulated in such a way that they can be associated with the persons who manage each of the subdivisions into which the organization is divided. Responsibility accounting information is used as an aid in planning and controlling the activities of responsibility centers and in motivating the persons responsible for carrying out these activities.

In addition to these two main streams of cost information, some companies have a third type because they are required by an outside regulatory body to report costs in a certain way. These companies include gas companies, electric companies, water companies, trucking companies, railroads, airlines, bus companies, pipeline companies, telephone companies, broadcasting companies, banks, and investment trusts. Some government agencies that must report costs to legislative bodies require a separate stream of cost information for this purpose. Conceptually, the product or program cost information that a company collects for its own needs should also satisfy the needs of outside agencies, but the fact is that some regulatory bodies require reports that are of little or no use to company management. The essential reason for this discrepancy is that requirements of the regulatory bodies were promulgated many years ago, and they have not been modernized in accordance with more recent developments in cost accounting practice. These requirements differ with each regulatory body, and they will not be discussed further here.

Although a company has two, and sometimes three, streams of cost information, it has, or at least should have, only a single cost system; that is, product costs, responsibility costs, and regulatory costs can be viewed as end products that are produced by different ways of accumulating the same underlying data. Nevertheless, product costing and responsibility accounting are described separately here because this facilitates an understanding of each of them.

PRODUCT COSTING

The reader is asked to refer back to the flow chart in Illustration 7–2 (p. 180), which sketched the flow of costs as products (in this case, smoking pipes) moved through goods in process inventory to finished goods inventory, and then out to the customer. (It will be helpful, before going further, if the reader traces through each entry in Illustration 7–2 in order to refresh his memory.) Brief mention was made in Chapter 7 of the problem of assigning material, labor, and factory overhead costs[2] to the partially completed pipes in goods in process inventory, to the completed pipes in finished goods inventory, and to cost of goods sold when the pipes are shipped. This is the problem of product costing. Consider the transaction that recorded the transfer of pipes from Goods in Process Inventory to Finished Goods Inventory. (This was Transaction No. 7 in Illustration 7–2 in the amount of $9,000.) The number and types of physical units (pipes) involved in this transfer can be ascertained readily, but in order to assign dollar amounts corresponding to these physical units, a cost per unit must be established.

If the company manufactured only one style of pipe, it would be possible to divide the total amount of debits to Work in Process by the total number of units worked on to obtain an approximation of the cost per unit; this figure could then be used to calculate the amount to be transferred from Goods in Process Inventory to Finished Goods Inventory. If the factory made more than one kind of product, however, such a simple calculation would not give results that fitted the facts, since one product probably used more material, labor, or overhead—that is, it cost more—than another. If the entry transferring completed products from Goods in Process to Finished Goods Inventory is to reflect the facts of

---

[2] For the purpose of determining inventory amounts and cost of goods sold, it is not necessary to determine the selling, general, and administrative costs applicable to a particular unit of product; nevertheless, such a breakdown is useful for some pricing and other decisions relating to the product. Some cost accounting systems therefore do provide for the collection of these costs by units of product.

the situation, there must be some means of taking these differences into account.

Cost Principle

Basically, there is only one principle of product costing: the cost assigned to a product should be the sum of (1) the direct costs incurred in producing it, and (2) a fair share of the indirect costs. As will be seen, there are differences of opinion both as to what constitutes a direct cost and as to what is a fair or equitable share of the indirect costs. Thus, two companies making identical products with identical manufacturing techniques can come up with markedly different costs for these products simply because of differences in the way they interpret the basic principle.

The total costs to be assigned to the various products manufactured are measured in accordance with the principles of financial accounting, at least for those product costs that are used in measuring inventory and cost of sales on the published financial statements. Thus, the accrual concept, the distinction between costs that are to be capitalized and those that are to be expensed, the various methods of depreciation, and similar topics described in Part I, apply equally here. Product cost information is used for purposes other than the preparation of financial statements, however, and for these other purposes, the principles of financial accounting do not necessarily apply. For example, in accumulating costs as a basis for setting selling prices, a company may decide to figure depreciation on the replacement cost of fixed assets, rather than on original cost, or it may decide to omit depreciation altogether under certain circumstances.

Job Costing and Process Costing

There are two main methods of accumulating product costs, called, respectively, job costing and process costing. Each is described below.

Essentially, a job cost system collects costs for each physically identifiable job or batch of work as it moves through the plant, regardless of the accounting period in which the work is done, while a process cost system collects costs for all products worked on in an accounting period.

JOB COSTING. The "job" in a job cost system may consist of a single unit (e.g., a turbine or a house), or it may consist of all units of identical or similar products covered by a single production order (e.g., 1,000 printed books or 10 dozen white shirts).[3] Usually each job is given a number and costs are collected on a separate record that is set up for that number. This *job cost record* contains spaces to record the individual

---

[3] When the job consists of more than one unit of product, the system is often called "job-lot costing," or simply "lot costing."

elements of cost charged to that job, and these costs are recorded as the job moves through the various departments in the factory. Thus, when the job is completed, its costs can be readily totaled. The sum of all the costs charged to all the jobs worked on in the factory during an accounting period is the basis for the entries debiting Goods in Process and crediting Raw Materials Inventory, Wages, and Overhead accounts. When each job is completed, the total cost recorded on the job cost record is the basis for the entry transferring the product from Goods in Process to Finished Goods Inventory, and this same cost is the basis for the entry transferring the product from Finished Goods Inventory to Cost of Goods Sold when the product is sold. The total cost recorded on all job cost records for products still in the factory as of the end of an accounting period equals the total of the Goods in Process Inventory account at that time.

In summary:

1. A separate job cost record is established for each job or job lot.

2. Costs chargeable to the job are recorded on this sheet, and are also debited to Goods in Process Inventory.

3. When the job is completed and transferred out of the factory, the total cost accumulated on the job cost record is the amount used to debit Finished Goods Inventory and to credit Goods in Process Inventory (unless the job is immediately sold, in which case the debit is to Cost of Goods Sold.)

4. The balance in Work in Process Inventory at the end of the accounting period is therefore the sum of the costs accumulated on all jobs still in the factory.

PROCESS COSTING. In a *process cost system*, all the costs for a time period, such as a month, are collected, with no attempt to attach these costs to specific units of product. This system is used in a factory making only one product, such as cement, or in a factory where the difference between various types of products is not substantial, that is, where the products are relatively homogeneous. Essentially, in a process cost system the total cost incurred during the period and the total number of units of products worked on during the period are collected. By dividing total costs by total units, one derives the cost per unit; and this cost per unit is used as the basis of valuing the units transferred to Finished Goods Inventory and, later on, from Finished Goods Inventory to Cost of Goods Sold.

The units *worked on* in a period include the following: (1) units that were both started and completed during the period; plus (2) units that were started but not completed; plus (3) units that were started in prior periods and completed in this period. Since 100 percent of the costs of the first type were incurred in the current period, but only a portion of the costs of the second and third types, production activity for the period cannot be determined simply by adding up the number of units worked on. The three types of units must be converted to a common base, called *equivalent production*, that is, the equivalent of one completed unit. In order to convert the number of uncompleted products into their equivalence in terms of completed units, the assumption is often made that units still in process at the end of the period are 50 percent complete, and similarly that units in process at the beginning of the period were 50 percent complete at that time. Thus, in order to calculate the labor and overhead costs per unit worked on, each unit completed would be given a weight of one, each unit in process at the end of the period would be given a weight of one half, and each unit in process at the beginning of the period also would be given a weight of one half.[4]

> EXAMPLE: If 200 units were completed, 50 units were in process at the end, and 10 were in process at the beginning, the number of equivalent production units worked on would be $200 + 50/2 - 10/2 = 220$. If total costs incurred were \$2,200, costs per equivalent unit would be \$10, and each of the 50 partially completed units in process at the end of the month would be costed at \$5.

Raw material would be costed according to its physical flow (unless the Lifo system was used). If material was added evenly throughout the production process, it could reasonably be costed by use of the 50 percent assumption described above. If, as is perhaps more common, all the raw material for a unit is issued at the beginning of the process, material cost per unit would be obtained by dividing the total cost of material used by the number of units *started* during the period.

In any event, some reasonable assumption has to be made. In a process cost system, there is no precise way of determining the amount of costs attributable to partially completed units.

In summary:

1. Costs incurred during the accounting period are accumulated as debits to Goods in Process Inventory.

2. Production is measured in terms of the number of equivalent units of production.

3. A cost per unit is found by dividing total costs by the number of equivalent units.

4. Finished Goods Inventory is debited and Goods in Process Inven-

---

[4] A more precise procedure would be to estimate the actual stage of completion, but this involves more effort. At the other extreme, some companies disregard the units in process and show no Goods in Process Inventory account. If the goods in process inventory is small, or if it remains relatively constant in size, no serious error is introduced. Another variation is to apply the 50 percent assumption separately to each department through which the product passes rather than to the factory as a whole.

tory credited by an amount equal to the number of units completed in the period multiplied by this cost per unit.

5. The balance in Goods in Process Inventory at the end of an accounting period is the material cost of the units still in the factory plus an appropriate share (say, 50 percent) of the labor and overhead cost of these units if they had been completed.

CHOICE OF A SYSTEM.   Since a process cost system requires less record keeping than a job order system, there is a tendency to use it even though the products manufactured are not strictly homogeneous. Thus, many shoe manufacturers use a process cost system, even though there are considerable differences in cost among the various sizes, styles, and colors of shoes manufactured; for pricing purposes, these companies measure the approximate effect on cost of these differences by calculations made outside the accounting system itself.

If there are important reasons for keeping track of the differences between one product and another, or between one production lot of the same type of product and another, then a job cost system is more appropriate. For example, a job cost system would invariably be used if the customer paid for the specific item or production order on the basis of its cost (as is often the case in so-called "job shop production"). Also, use of a job cost system makes it possible to examine actual costs on specific jobs, and this may help one to locate trouble spots; whereas in a process cost system costs cannot be traced to specific units in this fashion.

For our purposes, there is no need to study differences in the detailed records required for the two types of systems. Both systems are essentially devices for collecting information. Either furnishes the information required for the system shown in Illustration 7–2. In practice, there are many systems that have job costing in some departments or for some types of cost, and process costing in other departments or for other types of cost.

Variations in Practice

The accounting system outlined in Illustration 7–2 will probably never be precisely duplicated in actual practice since it is a schematic representation of underlying structures. Companies build on the basic structure by adding accounts that collect the data in more detail so as to meet their particular needs for information. A company may, for example, set up several raw material inventory accounts, each one covering a different type of material, instead of the single account shown in Illustration 7–2. Another common variation is to have several goods in process accounts, one for each main department or "cost center" in the factory. A system using several goods in process accounts is shown in Illustration 13–1. It will be noted that such a system is essentially like that shown in Illustration 7–2 except that work is transferred from one department to another. The finished goods of one department become, in effect, the raw material of the next department.

Problems of Cost Accumulation

Three problems must be solved in the accumulation of an equitable product cost:

1. *Assignment of costs to accounting periods.* This problem is one of measuring costs incurred, in accordance with the accrual concept. Since this problem was discussed at length in Part I, nothing additional needs to be said here.
2. *Measurement of direct costs.*
3. *Accumulation and allocation of indirect, or overhead, costs.*

The second and third problems will be discussed in the following sections.

Direct Costs

Direct costs are those that are specifically traceable to or caused by the manufacture of a product or the carrying out of a program. These costs are also called *separable* costs since they can be separately identified with individual products or programs, in contrast with *joint* costs which cannot be so traced. For a product, direct costs are usually classified as either direct material or direct labor. For a program, direct costs may also include other elements of cost that are specifically traceable to the program.

DIRECT LABOR. Direct labor costs are the labor costs that can be specifically identified with a product or that vary so closely with the number of products produced that a direct relationship is presumed to exist. There are essentially two problems in the measurement of direct labor cost: (1) measuring the *quantity* of labor effort expended on the product (e.g., the time spent), and (2) ascertaining the *price* per unit of quantity.

Measuring the quantity of labor effort is relatively easy. In a job-cost system, there is often a time card, or comparable record, for each direct worker, and on it a record is made of the time he spends on each job. Or, if direct workers are paid a piece rate, the record shows the number of pieces completed. In a process cost system, all that is needed is the total of the time spent by all employees on activities directly related to production; these times appear on their time cards. (Actually, the matter is not quite this simple, for problems arise about the treatment of idle time,

Illustration 13–1

COST SYSTEM WITH DEPARTMENTAL ACCOUNTS

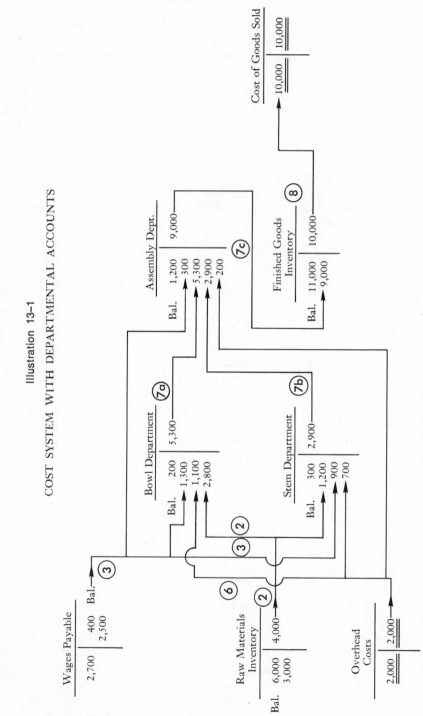

NOTE: Circled numbers refer to events described in Chapter 7 (pp. 179–81).

personal time, overtime, and so on. These are mostly beyond the scope of this introductory treatment.)

Deciding on the best way to price these labor quantities is conceptually more difficult. The great majority of companies have a simple solution, which is to price direct labor at the amounts actually earned by the employees concerned (so much an hour if employees are paid on a day-rate basis; so much a piece if they are paid on a piece-rate basis). There may be either a separate rate for each employee, or an average rate for all the employees in a section or department.

EXAMPLE: Assume that a certain job is worked on in four departments, and that the time worked in each department (as shown by time cards) and the labor rate is as indicated below. The direct labor cost of the job would be computed as follows:

Department	Hours on Job	Hourly Rate	Total
A	20	$3.00	$ 60.00
B	3	2.50	7.50
C	6	2.80	16.80
D	40	2.00	80.00
Total direct labor cost of job			$164.30

Some companies add *labor-related* costs to the basic wage rate. They reason that each hour of labor effort costs the company not only the wages paid to the employee but also the social security taxes, pension contributions, and other fringe benefits that are an inevitable part of the real cost of each employee. In some cases, they even add in a share of the costs of the personnel department and employee welfare programs. Using such a higher figure gives a more accurate picture of true labor costs. It also involves additional record keeping, however, and many companies do not believe the gain is worthwhile.

DIRECT MATERIAL. The measurement of direct material cost (or "raw materials cost") also has the two aspects of the quantity of material used and price per unit of quantity. The quantity is often determined from requisitions or similar documents that order material out of the storeroom and into production. The question of pricing this material is analogous to that already discussed under direct labor. It may be priced at solely its invoice cost, or there may be added some or all of the following *material-related* costs: inward freight, inspection costs, moving costs, purchasing department costs, and interest and space charges associated with holding material in inventory.

Indirect Costs

Indirect, or overhead, costs are those costs not associated directly with the products worked on; included are all manufacturing costs other than those classified as direct material and direct labor. Some costs are classified as indirect because it is *impossible* to associate them directly with products. Who can say how much of building depreciation or of a factory superintendent's salary actually belongs to each unit of product manufactured? Other costs are classified as indirect because it is *not convenient* to trace them directly to products, even though it would be possible to do so. Wage-related costs, as mentioned above, are one example.

Since, by definition, indirect costs are not associated directly with products, it is impossible to measure precisely how much indirect cost should be charged to a given product. Nevertheless, total indirect cost is properly part of the cost of the total products worked on, and some reasonable part of the total indirect costs incurred must therefore be charged to each unit of product. The procedure for doing this is called *allocation.*[5]

DISTINCTION BETWEEN DIRECT AND INDIRECT COSTS. Problems arise in attempting to define the precise line between costs that are "traceable to" or "caused by" a product and those that are not. For example, a cost may not be caused by a product even though it is incurred at the same time as the product is being manufactured.

> EXAMPLE: In a certain factory, Products A, B, and C were manufactured during regular working hours, and Product D was manufactured after regular hours. Overtime wages were paid to the men who worked on Product D. These overtime wages might, or might not, be a direct cost of Product D. If the factory worked overtime because of a general press of business, then the overtime was attributable to all the products worked on, and was an indirect cost. If, on the other hand, the overtime work on Product D was occasioned by a special request of the customer for Product D, then the overtime was a direct cost of Product D. It could also happen that the overtime was occasioned by a special need to make Product C quickly, and in order to meet this need, Product D was rescheduled from the regular work period to the overtime; in this case, the overtime was truly a direct cost of Product C, even though overtime was not in fact paid during the hours in which Product C was being manufactured.

Moreover, there are differences of opinion as to how close the causal relationship must be in order to classify a cost as direct. In many production operations, such as assembly lines of all types, refineries, and similar continuous process operations, a basic work force is required no matter what products are manufactured. Some would argue that the labor cost of this work force constitutes a cost that is required to operate the plant in general, much like depreciation on the machinery, and that it is therefore not properly considered as being direct to the specific products that are

---

[5] In Great Britain the name used for this procedure is *apportionment,* and the word "allocation" refers to the charging of *direct* costs to products. This is another example of semantic confusion.

manufactured. Nevertheless, most companies consider such costs as direct labor.

STEPS IN INDIRECT COST ALLOCATION. The steps in the process are as follows:

1. Estimated indirect costs are accumulated in cost centers.
2. Costs accumulated in service cost centers are transferred to product cost centers.
3. The total cost accumulated in each product center is divided by a measure of activity, giving an overhead rate.
4. Indirect costs are allocated at this rate to each product passing through the cost center.

Usually, the first three steps leading to the determination of an overhead rate are carried out annually, prior to the beginning of the year, although the overhead rate may be changed more than once a year or even less than once a year, depending on the volatility of the underlying factors. The figures used, therefore, usually are estimates of what the costs will be, rather than historical records of what they actually were. These steps apply to both job and process costing, except that in process costing there is no need to calculate overhead rates for individual units of product.

These steps are described in the following paragraphs, using the pipe factory as an illustration.

Cost Centers. A *cost center* is merely an accounting unit for which costs are accumulated. It may be an organizational unit, such as a department, but, as will be seen, there is no necessary connection between cost centers and identifiable organization units.

One type of cost center is a *product center;* that is, a center through which the product passes. Often a product center corresponds to a production department, but a group of similar machines, such as a bank of screw machines, may be a product center, and so may a single machine, such as each printing press in a printing job shop.

A *service center,* another type of cost center, is a department or other unit that incurs costs, but that does not work directly on products, for example, the maintenance department and the general factory offices. If each machine in one department is a product center, then there is also a departmental service center in which the departmental costs not directly traceable to machines are collected.

As shown in Illustration 13–2, our pipe factory has three product centers—the Bowl department, the Stem department, and the Assembly department—and two service centers—Occupancy and General. The Occupancy center is used to accumulate building depreciation, building maintenance, heat, light, and other occupancy costs. The General center is used to accumulate the costs of factory supervision and miscellaneous general costs not traceable directly to other cost centers.

Cost Accumulation by Cost Centers. The first step in the allocation of indirect costs is to estimate the amounts that will be spent directly in each of the product centers and service centers. This procedure involves estimating the elements of cost that are traceable to each. Note that in this step, each cost component is recorded in one, and only one, cost center, so that the sum of the costs for all the cost centers exactly equals total

Illustration 13–2

CALCULATION OF OVERHEAD RATE

Cost Element	Product Centers				Service Centers	
	Total	Bowl	Stem	As-sembly	Occu-pancy	General
Indirect labor...........	$ 9,700	$ 3,100	$ 2,700	$	$	$ 3,900
Indirect supplies.........	4,000	900	600	500	400	1,600
Other.................	12,000	3,900	1,200	700	4,300	1,900
Subtotals...........	$25,700	$ 7,900	$ 4,500	$1,200	$4,700	$ 7,400
Allocation of Service Centers						
Occupancy.............		1,900	1,400	900	(4,700)	500
General...............		3,600	2,600	1,700		$(7,900)
Total Cost........	$25,700	$13,400	$ 8,500	$3,800	....	....
Direct labor cost........		$15,800	$10,600	$4,200		
Overhead rate per direct labor dollar..........		$0.85	$0.80	$0.90		

indirect costs. These estimates appear in the upper section of Illustration 13–2. Ordinarily, these estimates are based on past experience, adjusted for changes in wage rates, prices, or other factors that may be anticipated for the ensuing year.

Transfer of Service Center Costs. The second step is to transfer all service center costs to product centers, for this is the way in which they become a part of product costs. There are two general ways of doing this: (1) by a direct charge and (2) by allocation.

Some service center costs are charged directly to the product centers. Maintenance department costs may be charged to operating departments on the basis of the maintenance service actually performed, for example. The same possibility exists for other service activities, although beyond a certain point the rationale becomes so tenuous as not to be practicable. Theoretically, but not practically, the president's time could be charged directly to each of the cost centers he deals with.

Other service center costs are *allocated* to product centers on some basis that seems to have a reasonable relationship to "benefits received," or to a "fair share." The dozens of possible bases of allocations that are used in practice can be grouped into the following principal categories:

1. *Labor related.* Fringe benefits, personnel department costs, and other costs associated with employees may be allocated on the basis of the number of employees or total direct labor costs. Alternatively, as mentioned above, some or all of these costs may enter into the calculation of direct labor costs and hence not appear as overhead costs at all. If indirect costs are ultimately charged to products by means of a direct labor rate, the ultimate effect of collecting these labor-related costs in overhead is the same as that of charging them as part of direct labor costs.

2. *Material related.* This category, also discussed above, may be allocated on the basis of the volume or cost of material used in the product center, or, alternatively, it may be excluded from overhead and charged to products as part of direct material cost.

3. *Space related.* These are costs associated with the space that the cost center occupies, and are charged to cost centers on the basis of the relative areas or cubic content of the centers. Occupancy cost in Illustration 13–2 is an example. Assuming that the Bowl center has 40 percent of the total floor space, the Stem center 30 percent, the Assembly center 20 percent, and the General center 10 percent, the total occupancy cost of $4,700 is allocated to the other centers according to these percentages.

4. *Activity related.* Some costs are roughly related to the overall volume of activity, or size of the cost center; or at least there is a presumption that the larger the cost center, the more costs are properly chargeable to it. Electrical costs and steam costs, if not directly chargeable by meters, fall into this category, and so do a variety of other service center costs which, although not demonstrably a function of activity, are more fairly apportioned in this way than in any other. The measure of activity may be closely related to the item, as, for example, allocating electrical costs on the basis of the total horsepower of motors installed; or it may be an overall measure, such as total labor cost, total direct costs, or sales value of products processed. The General service center in Illustration 13–2 falls in this category. The total cost of $7,900 is allocated to the product centers on the basis of the relative direct material and labor costs of these centers, here assumed to be 46 percent for Bowl, 33 percent for Stem, and 21 percent for Assembly.

Step-Down Order. Note that in Illustration 13–2, part of occupancy cost is charged to the General service center. It may be that part of General's cost should be charged to Occupancy. When there are a number of service centers, the interrelationships among them could theoretically lead to a long series of redistributions and re-redistributions, but in practice this is avoided by distributing the service center costs in a prescribed order, which is called the *step-down order*. In the illustration, the order is Occupancy first, and General second. No additional cost is allocated to a service center after its costs have been distributed. Since the step-down order is adhered to in all calculations, the results are always consistent.

Overhead Rates. Having brought all the costs to product centers, we now seek some equitable means of loading them onto the products passing through the center, step three in the process of allocating indirect costs.

Essentially, the calculation of an overhead rate requires an answer to the question: Why should one unit of product bear more overhead than another? Possible answers are the following: (1) because more work has been done on it; (2) because the product is worth more and therefore is able to bear more overhead; (3) because it requires more labor, and overhead is largely associated with labor; and so on. These answers suggest some quantitative bases of making the charge, respectively: (1) the number of direct labor hours or machine hours required for the product; (2) total direct costs of the product; (3) direct labor cost; and so on. Of these, the machine hours basis is common for cost centers that consist primarily of one machine (such as a paper machine) or a group of related machines. The direct labor cost basis is perhaps most frequently used in other situations, since it is readily available on the job cost card. Direct labor hours are also often used if the number of hours worked on each job is readily available.

In our pipe factory, let us assume that a direct labor cost basis will be used in each product center. (Actually, the same basis of measurement is not necessarily used in all product centers.) All that remains, therefore, is to estimate the total direct labor cost for each product center in the ensuing year and divide this into the total indirect cost of the center. The result is the amount of indirect cost that is to be charged to pipes for each dollar of direct labor incurred. In the Bowl center, for example, the overhead rate is $0.85 per dollar of direct labor.

Allocation of Indirect Costs. The fourth step in the total process of accumulation and allocation of indirect cost is to apply the rate calculated above to the products passing through the product center. If for a given lot of pipes the direct labor cost in the Bowl center is $100 and the overhead rate is $0.85 per dollar of direct labor, the indirect cost of this lot of pipes is $85.

Because of the nature of the methods used, two observations should be made about the indirect cost: (1) The total amount transferred in this way may not coincide exactly with the total actual incurred costs for the period under consideration. If there are differences, then indirect cost is under- or overabsorbed, and various accounting techniques are used for handling such amounts. (2) The whole process, being based on subjective judgments of what is a "fair" distribution, cannot result in an *accurate* cost. These points are discussed in the following sections.

Unabsorbed and Overabsorbed Overhead

In any accounting period, the overhead costs charged to pipes worked on in the Bowl cost center will equal the total indirect costs charged to the cost center if, but only if, total indirect costs are exactly 85 percent of total direct labor costs. This is not likely to happen. If more overhead is charged to products than is actually incurred, overhead is said to be *overabsorbed*, and if less, it is *underabsorbed* (or more commonly, *unabsorbed*). For management purposes, the amount of unabsorbed or overabsorbed overhead is useful information, as will be discussed in Chapter 17.

For financial accounting purposes, this amount can be handled in one of three ways: (1) charge or credit it entirely to the income of the period on the income statement (often as an adjustment to cost of goods sold); (2) divide it between inventory and period expense in the proportion that inventory is to cost of goods sold; or (3) do nothing, in the expectation that unabsorbed overhead in one period will be offset by overabsorption in a succeeding period. An argument for the first alternative is that the difference between estimated and actual costs may reflect events occurring in the period and therefore should affect income of the period. An argument for the second alternative is that the difference may reflect an inability to make accurate estimates, and that the estimated costs in inventory and cost of goods sold should be corrected accordingly. The third alternative is not a generally accepted accounting practice for annual financial statements, but it is often used for monthly or other interim internal statements both as a matter of convenience and to avoid having income affected by short-term fluctuations in indirect cost absorption.

In the interests of simplicity, no account for overabsorbed or unabsorbed overhead was shown in Illustration 7–1 or 13–1. Such an account could be fitted into the system in either of two places, depending on whether the overhead charged to the cost center was the amount absorbed in the period or the amount incurred. If the cost center was debited for the amount of overhead *absorbed*, then the over- or underabsorbed account would take up the difference between this amount and the total overhead costs incurred as shown in the various overhead cost accounts (i.e., the $2,000 in Illustration 13–1). If the cost center was debited for the overhead cost *incurred*, then the balance in the cost center account would later be adjusted to remove the difference between cost incurred and cost absorbed onto products.

If there are seasonal variations either in costs (as in heating costs) or in the level of activity, the amount of overhead cost charged to the cost center each month is often a *normalized* amount rather than the actual amount of cost incurred. This normalized amount is set in such a way that the unit costs do not vary from month to month because of volume changes or seasonal factors. The difference between the normalized amount and actual costs incurred is held in an overabsorbed or underabsorbed account, with the expectation that over the course of a year, overabsorptions will be washed out by underabsorptions.

Accuracy of Indirect Costs

By definition, indirect costs are not traced directly to products; therefore the indirect cost charged to a product cannot be the "actual" indirect cost incurred in making the product in any literal sense of this word. Through the collection and allocation mechanism described above, we have indeed succeeded in adding a portion of building depreciation, for example, onto the cost of each unit of product, but judgments as to what is fair and reasonable were involved in each step of this process: in deciding on the costs applicable to the *period* (what really is the depreciation expense of this period?), in deciding how much of this cost is applicable to each *cost center*, and in deciding how much of the cost center's cost is applicable to each *product*. Two equally capable accountants can arrive at quite different amounts of indirect cost per unit, and there is no way of proving that one is right and the other wrong, that is, that one indirect cost figure is accurate and the other is inaccurate.

Definition of Cost Center

The amount of indirect cost charged to a product can also be significantly influenced by judgment as to how a cost center is defined. In some companies each important machine is a cost center. At the other extreme, the entire plant is a single cost center (giving rise to a *plantwide* overhead rate). There are a number of choices between these two extremes. In general, the more narrow the definition of a cost center, the more equitable is the resulting indirect cost of the product.

EXAMPLE: Assume a plant with two product departments. Department A does machining with expensive machine tools requiring much floor space, power, and supplies; and Department B does bench work and assembly with only inexpensive hand tools. Overhead rates are determined as follows:

Department	Estimated Annual Hours	Estimated Overhead Cost	Overhead Rate per Hour
A	20,000	$200,000	$10.00
B	40,000	100,000	2.50
Total plant	60,000	$300,000	$ 5.00

Assume a job that requires 20 hours in Department A and 100 hours in Department B. If the company used separate overhead rates for each department, the overhead cost for this job would be:

> Dept. A...... 20 hours × $10.00 = $200
> Dept. B......100 hours × $ 2.50 = 250
> Total overhead cost...........$450

If the company used a plantwide overhead rate, the overhead cost of the same job would be:

> 120 hours × $5 = $600.

The overhead cost of $600 is less equitable than the $450 cost derived from the departmental rates because the plantwide rate costed each hour at $5, despite the fact that almost all the hours on this job were incurred in Department B, where the rate was only $2.50 per hour.

On the other hand, it is also true that the more narrow the definition of the cost centers, the more cost centers there will be, and therefore the more work involved in computing and applying separate overhead rates. The choice of cost centers in a particular situation depends on the balance between the increase in the equity of the overhead rates and the increased work involved. If all products spend approximately the same proportion of time in each department, the differences in indirect costs assigned by means of a series of rates for each department and indirect costs assigned by a plantwide rate will be small. In such a situation, little increase in equity is gained by using a number of rates.

A few companies compute what they call "actual" indirect costs by going through the process shown in Illustration 13–2 at the end of the period, rather than prior to the beginning of the period. At the end of the period the actual indirect cost and the actual level of activity are available, and these are used to calculate a rate that, when applied to products, will result in the exact absorption of indirect cost. Since under this procedure no jobs can be costed until the period has ended, it is rarely used. Furthermore, although this procedure does absorb indirect cost in total, it does not eliminate the judgment made with respect to the amount of costs applicable to the period, to the product center, or to the individual product, and hence the detailed indirect cost allocations cannot be said to be, literally, "actual" even under this procedure.

The following excerpts from publications of the National Association of Accountants are relevant:

A cost is joint when it is incurred for a group of segments as a unit and no portion of the cost can be traced exclusively to any of the individual segments. . . .[6]

---

[6] National Association of Accountants, *Concepts for Management Accounting*, 1966, p. 42.

To the extent that costs are joint, individual products in a combination have no objectively determinable separate costs.

Joint costs can be allocated, but all bases for allocation imply assumptions that cannot be objectively verified. . . . While a chosen basis can be rationalized, it cannot be proved more correct than another by any objective process. As a consequence, equally competent accountants may arrive at different costs for the same product.[7]

Product Line Reporting

Currently, there is considerable controversy over a proposal of the Securities and Exchange Commission to require disclosure of revenues and costs for each substantial product line or other segment of a conglomerate, that is, a company that operates in more than one industry. The controversy is symptomatic of the differences that exist among companies in their method of accounting for product costs. Opponents of the SEC proposal claim that these differences are so great that the reported figures would be meaningless to the reader of the financial statement, or to anyone not thoroughly familiar with the rules of product costing used in the company.

Selling and General Costs

Although, in accordance with generally accepted accounting principles, selling costs cannot be included in product costs for the purposes of measuring the amounts of inventory and cost of sales, a company may nevertheless assign selling costs to products for other purposes. The same approach is used as described above; that is, costs are classified as either direct (e.g., commissions on sales) or indirect, and products are charged with the direct selling costs and an equitable share of the indirect selling costs. Selling costs may also be collected by geographical regions or sales offices, or by channels of distribution.

Even though a company may decide to omit certain general and administrative costs from its inventory and cost-of-sales computations, it may decide to include these in its product costs for other purposes. If so, the approach is the same as that described above for manufacturing costs.

STANDARD COSTS

The basic objective of the system outlined above was to charge units of product with a fair share of the *actual* costs incurred in making these products. Many cost accounting systems, in contrast, are based wholly or

---

[7] National Association of Accountants, *Costing Joint Products* (Research Series No. 31), 1957, pp. 1 and 4.

in part on the principle that the costs charged to individual products are the costs that *should have been incurred* on those products rather than the costs that *actually were incurred*. Such a system is called a *standard cost system*.[8] The essential nature of standard costs, then, is that they represent costs that should have been incurred rather than costs that actually were incurred.

In a standard cost system, each unit of product has a standard material cost, a standard labor cost, and a standard overhead cost for each product cost center. The total standard cost for the month is obtained by multiplying these standard unit costs by the number of units flowing through the cost center in that month.

Illustration 13–3 shows the system for our pipe factory shifted to a standard cost basis. It is the same as the actual cost system shown in Illustration 7–2 except that three *variance accounts* have been added. Standard costs are usually different from the costs actually incurred, and variance accounts are a repository for these differences. For example, if actual labor costs for the month were $2,500, the credit to the liability account Wages Payable must be $2,500. If the standard labor costs of the operations performed totaled only $2,100, Goods in Process would be debited for $2,100, and the $400 difference would be debited to the Labor Variance account. Entries to variance accounts are debits if actual costs are greater than standard costs, and they are credits if actual costs are less than standard costs.

A standard cost system may have several advantages. First, it is often simpler and requires less work than an actual cost system. This is so because once the standard cost for a unit of product has been determined, this cost remains unchanged for relatively long periods, instead of being recalculated for each separate unit or job.

Second, a standard cost system produces the same costs for physically identical units of product, whereas an actual cost system may not. For example, in our pipe factory there may be two equally efficient men making identical sizes and shapes of pipe bowls. If one man, because of seniority or other reasons, has a higher wage rate than the other, under an actual job cost system the pipes that he makes will have a higher labor cost than the pipes the other man makes; yet realistically there is no difference in the finished pipes—no reason why one should be said to "cost" more than another. This fact also makes standard costs a better basis for estimating selling prices than are actual costs.

Third, a standard cost system provides the beginning of a mechanism for checking on the efficiency with which the work was done, in that the

---

[8] Some accountants limit the term "standard costs" to costs determined on the basis of engineering estimates and use the term "estimated costs" for costs determined on the basis of estimates made by persons who are not engineers. As a practical matter, the distinction is not of great significance.

Illustration 13-3

A STANDARD COST SYSTEM

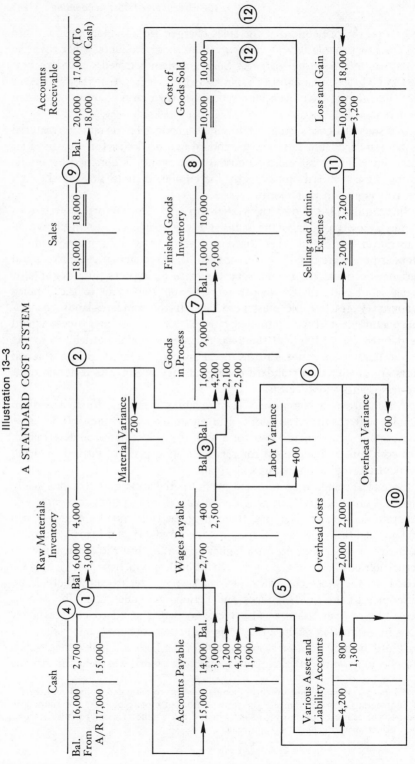

NOTE: Circled numbers refer to events described in Chapter 7.

Bal. = Net income before taxes.

balance in the variance account may be an indication of good or bad performance. The validity of this statement depends on the accuracy with which the standard cost actually measures what should have been incurred; this point is discussed in Chapter 17.

Companies which use standard costs do not necessarily use a *complete* standard cost system, that is, a system that treats all elements of cost on a standard basis. Some, for example, use standard direct labor and indirect costs but use actual material costs.

Standard costs may be inserted into the system at any one of several places. Thus, material may be taken up in Raw Materials Inventory at a standard price, with the difference between actual purchase price and the standard price being entered in a Raw Materials Price Variance account; in Illustration 13–3 this account would be placed to the left of the Raw Materials Inventory account. Another alternative is to charge all elements of cost into Goods in Process at actual; the conversion to a standard cost basis would then be made between Goods in Process and Finished Goods Inventory. In the latter system, the variance account would occur between Goods in Process and Finished Goods Inventory. The essential point is that one or more variance accounts are inserted in the system at whatever point the shift from actual to standard is made.

The variance accounts may or may not be closed at the end of the accounting period. The possibilities are the same as those already discussed with respect to under- or overabsorbed overhead, which is one type of variance account.

ILLUSTRATION: BLACK METER COMPANY

As an illustration of some of the procedural details of a cost accounting system, the system of the Black Meter Company (which is the disguised name for an actual company) is described below. This is a standard cost system, but many of the procedures are equally applicable to so-called actual cost systems.

Product

The Black Meter Company manufactures water meters in one standard design but in a wide range of sizes for industrial and residential applications. The water meters installed in the basements of most homes are an example of its product. The meters consist basically of a hard rubber piston that is put in motion by the flow of water past it, a gear train that reduces this motion and registers it on a dial, and two heavy bronze castings which are bolted together around the measuring device.

Production

The company is organized into several functional departments to manufacture almost all the parts for these meters. The casings and many interior parts are cast in the foundry and then are sent to one of the three machining departments, depending upon their size. The machining departments are equipped with most of the machines which are common to the metalworking industry. Many of the finished parts are sent to a subassembly department to be subassembled into gear trains. The other parts go directly to the meter assembly departments. There are also several departments that provide service to the producing departments.

The Standard Cost System

The controller has described the essentials of the system as follows:

The Black Meter Company uses a standard cost system to control costs and to obtain monthly operating statements. The basic difference between this standard cost system and an actual cost system lies in the way we value our inventories, from raw materials to finished goods. In an actual cost system the debits for the amounts of materials, direct labor, and manufacturing overhead added to the inventories are made at actual cost. In a standard cost system like ours, normal or standard costs are established for these elements, and every debit to the inventory account is made at standard cost. The fact that all the inventory items are valued at standard costs allows us to forget about the actual cost of every item, thereby greatly simplifying the accounting procedure.

During the month, actual costs are accumulating. Material is purchased, workers are paid, manufacturing overhead items, such as water or electricity, are purchased and paid for at actual cost. But the *values* of these items are debited into inventory at predetermined standard costs for each cost factor. Often the actual cost varies from the standard costs, and this fact causes variations that we journalize and post to variance accounts. At the end of a month we examine the variations between actual and standard; consequently, we are able to control costs by focusing our attention on these variances, or *exceptions*, rather than on the bulk of the cost data.

Setting Up Standard Costs

The first step in setting up standard costs in this company is to establish a standard cost for every type of material that is purchased. This is done by adjusting the current market price for any irregularities that are not expected to continue for the following year. For example, if copper at the end of a year costs 30 cents a pound and no change is predicted, the standard cost for copper for the next year wil be 30 cents a pound. The same procedure is followed for every purchased item.

Having established standard costs for all materials, the accountants next calculate standard rates for direct labor and manufacturing overhead. They do this on a departmental basis, and set up the rates to be applied according to the number of standard direct labor hours incurred in the processing of each product.

From each department they obtain data for the past few years on the actual direct labor payroll and the number of direct labor hours worked. On the basis of these data and from estimates of future conditions, the accountants select a figure for total labor cost and a figure for hours worked under normal conditions of activity in each department. By dividing this payroll figure by the normal number of hours, they obtain a standard direct labor rate per standard direct labor hour for each department.

The same type of calculation is made to determine standard manufacturing overhead rates for each department. The procedure is complicated by the necessity of allocating all service department costs to the producing departments. The first step is to calculate from past records the total cost of each of the service departments at normal volume. Then various methods are used to allocate the service department costs to the producing departments. For example, the total cost of the boiler room is allocated to the producing departments according to the number of square feet of floor space taken up by each. The maintenance department expense is allocated on the basis of the number of hours the maintenance men normally work for each producing department.

After the cost of the service departments has been allocated to the producing departments, it is necessary to calculate the manufacturing overhead costs that normally are incurred within each producing department. The sum of the allocated and the internal costs gives the total manufacturing overhead cost for each department under normal conditions. These totals are divided by the standard number of direct labor hours for each producing department, the same totals that were used in calculating the labor rate. In this way, a manufacturing overhead rate per standard direct labor hour is obtained for each department, as shown in Illustration 13–4.

The next step in setting up this standard cost system is to apply the standard rates to each of the items manufactured. This is accomplished on the manufacturing orders, examples of which can be seen in Illustrations 13–5 through 13–8. The part described is a ⅝ inch chamber ring that is manufactured for assembly into a ⅝ inch HF meter. The standard costs of most parts are calculated on the basis of 100 pieces.

The standard material cost is figured in the second line of the foundry order (Illustration 13–5). These parts are cast from government bronze

Illustration 13–4

STANDARD RATES EFFECTIVE JANUARY 1

Depart-ment No.	Department Name	Labor	Burden	Total Rate
103	Carpenter and pattern shop	$2.06	$1.07	$3.13/hour
104	Toolroom	2.35	1.26	3.61/hour
108	Pattern storage	--	--	0.02/pound
120A	Foundry -- molding	2.50	3.78	6.28/hour
120B	Foundry -- grinding and snagging	1.50	0.90	2.40/hour
122	Small parts manufacture	1.72	1.38	3.10/hour
123	Interior parts manufacture	1.68	1.73	3.41/hour
124	Case manufacture	1.98	4.02	6.00/hour
125	Plating -- rack	--	--	2.50/100 pcs.
130	Train, register, and interior assembly	1.70	1.97	3.67/hour
131	Small meter assembly	1.50	2.01	3.51/hour
132	Large meter assembly	1.90	3.98	5.88/hour
133	Meter testing	2.11	1.56	3.67/hour
134	Meter repair	1.50	1.66	3.16/hour

that has a standard cost of $0.3265 a pound. Since the standard weight of 100 pieces is 91 pounds, the standard material cost is $29.712 as shown in the deliveries-to-stores box. The $0.020 figure in the pattern cost box is a standard pattern cost per pound which results in a $1.82 standard pattern charge.

In order to apply the standard direct labor and manufacturing overhead rates to any part, it is necessary to calculate the standard time needed to perform the operations to make that part. This task is simplified for the Black Meter Company because all operations have been time-studied. Using the results of the time studies, the accountants fill in the first column of the foundry order. For example, the standard time to mold 100 chamber rings is 1.76 hours, to grind them 0.45 hours, and to snag them 0.68 hours. In the first column of figures on the right-hand side of the foundry order, the combined standard direct labor and manufacturing overhead (i.e., burden) rate per standard direct labor hour

Illustration 13–5

					FOUNDRY ORDER						
Drawing No. X-2408			Part 5/8" HF Chamber Rings				Deliveries to Stores		Order No.		
Material Gov't Bronze 100 Pieces 91.0# At 0.3265/#							$29.712				
									Quantity Ordered		
Weight			Plating			Econ. Lot	Pattern Cost 0.02		$1.82		
Rate Number	Std. Man Hrs.Per 100 Pcs.	Std. Basic Rate	Prod. Center	Opr. No.	Operation and Tools		Machine	Man No.	Std. Rate /Hr.	Man No.	Total Cost	Total
	1.76		120 A	1	Mold		Match Plate		6.28		11.053	
	.45		120 B	2	Grind		Wheel		2.40		1.08	
	.68		120 B	3	Snag		Bench		2.40		1.632	
											$45.297	

Illustration 13–6

RR-7					PARTS ORDER							
Drawing No. X-2408			Part	5/8" HF Chamber Rings			Deliveries to Stores $45.297			Order No.		
Plating H.T. & E.T.			Material	Gov't Bronze 100 Pieces 89#	W'gt per 100					Quantity Ordered		
Econ. Lot 2,000					L'gth per 100		Date Wanted					
Rate Number	Hours per 100 pc.		Set-up St'd	Prod. C't'r	Opr. No.	Operation and Tools		Machine	Man No.	Std. Rate /Hr.	Total	
	St'd	All'w'd										
	0.75			122	1	Broach out let #734		P.P.		3.10	2.325	
	0.55			123	2	Finish tap plate bore & face		Heald		3.41	1.876	
	0.93			123		Drill 6 holes		Drill		3.41	3.171	
	0.47			123	3	C-Sink 3 holes tap plate side		Drill		3.41	1.603	
	0.17			123		Tap 3 holes tap plate side		Heskins		3.41	0.560	
	5.00			123	4	Rough & finish inside & outside		Heald		3.41	17.050	
	0.20			123		C-Sink 3 holes on bottom		Drill		3.41	0.682	
	0.30			123	5	Tap 3 holes on bottom		Drill		3.41	1.023	
	0.47			123		Spline inside		Spliner		3.41	1.603	
	0.50			123	6	Spline outside		Miller		3.41	1.705	
	5.80			123		Dress		Bench		3.41	19.778	
					7						96.673	

is recorded for the department in which the operation takes place. For example, Illustration 13–4 shows the labor and burden rate for molding in Department 120A as $6.28 per standard man-hour. This amount appears on the foundry order for the molding operation, and multiplied by the standard time gives a standard cost of labor and burden of $11.053. The same procedure is followed for the three foundry operations, and the total standard foundry cost of 100 chamber rings is $45.297.

Illustration 13–6 traces these 100 chamber rings through the interior parts manufacture department. They enter the parts department at the

Illustration 13–7

ASSEMBLY ORDER

Drawing No. 2400			Assembly	5/8" Disc Interior					Sheet No. of			
Used on Assemblies of			5/8' HF & HD Meters						Order No.			
Parts of Assembly				Delivered	Parts of Assembly		Delivered		Quantity Ordered			
K-2408 Chamber Ring				96.673								
K-2414 Chamber Top Plate				43.550					Date Ordered			
K-2418 Chamber Bot. Plate				40.120								
X-2465 Disc Piston Assem.				79.010					Date Wanted			
K-2422 Disc Chbr. Diaphragm				3.660								
									Deliveries to Stores			
					K-4521 Chamber Screws (6)		7.000					
Rate Number	Std. Man Hrs. Per 100 Pcs.	Std. Basic Rate	Prod. Center	Oper. No.	Operation and Tools	Machine	Man No.	Std. Rate /Hr.	Man No.	Total Cost	Total	
2.6			130	1	Assemble Top Plate to Ring	Bench		3.67		9.542		
0.9			130	2	Fit Abutment for Interior	Bench		3.67		3.303		
1.1			130	3	Mill & Scrape Diaphragm for Interior	Bench		3.67		4.037		
3.9			130	4	File Diaphragm Slots in Piston	Bench		3.67		14.313		
										301.208		

Illustration 13–8

ASSEMBLY ORDER

Drawing No. 2735	Assembly	5/8" HF Meter ET FB		Sheet No. of	
Used on Assemblies of				Order No.	
Parts of Assembly	Delivered	Parts of Assembly	Delivered	Quantity Ordered	
2761 Top Case	170.60	K-5030 5/8 HF Dur. Bolt (6)	32.880		
K-2776 Casing Gasket	3.25	K-4630 5/8 HF ac Nut (6)	25.440		
X-2770 Bottom Case	50.14	K-5068 5/8 HF Washers (6)	10.140	Date Ordered	
2779 Casing Strainer	6.95	2782 Chamber Pin	1.966		
3209 5/8 Closed Train	200.01	6172 Misc. Train Conn.	7.120		
2400 5/8 HF Int. Assem.	301.208			Date Wanted	
2412 5/8 HF Sand Plate	5.00				
				Deliveries to Stores	

Rate Number	Std. Man Hrs. Per 100 Pcs.	Std. Basic Rate	Prod. Center	Oper. No.	Operation and Tools	Machine	Man No.	Std. Rate /Hr.	Man No.	Total Cost	Total
4.6			131	1	Assem. Train & Strainer to Case	Bench		3.51		16.146	
5.6			131	2	Assem. Int. & Bottom to Meter			3.51		19.656	
										850.506	

standard cost of $45.297—the same cost at which they left the foundry. After 11 operations have been performed on them, they become finished chamber rings with a standard cost of $96.673. As shown in Illustrations 13–7 and 13–8 these parts are assembled into ⅝ inch HF disc interiors, and finally, into the ⅝ inch meters. The total cost of the meters is $850.506.

In the same manner, standard costs have been calculated for all the meter sizes that the Black Meter Company manufactures. These standards are revised annually to recognize any significant changes in the costs of labor, materials, or overhead.

Accounting Entries

Once the standards have been established, all material, direct labor, and manufacturing overhead are charged into the Inventory account at standard costs that do not change. This means that actual costs need only be collected in total for the period, and the actual cost of each individual item in inventory is forgotten.

MATERIAL. When material is purchased, the standard cost of that material is penciled on the vendor's invoice. Each purchase is journalized in an invoice and check register containing columns in which to credit the actual cost of the material to Accounts Payable, to debit an inventory account for the standard cost, and to debit or credit the difference to a variance account called "Purchase Loss or Gain." The com-

Illustration 13–9

INCENTIVE JOB CARD

MACH. NO.	PROD. CENTER 130	QUANTITY ORDERED 3000 3000	ORDER NUMBER 2I - 86572 1I - 86572	334 CLOCK NO.
TOTAL FIN. 1250 3000	PART NAME	5/8 " Cl. Trains.		
PREV. QUAN. FIN. 0 1150	OPR. NO. 9	OPERATION NAME Finish Assem.		
QUAN. FINISHED 1250 1850	STD. HOURS PER 100 1 75	STD. HOURS 54 25	STD. RATE 1 70	STANDARD LABOR 92 23
QUAN. FINISHED 3,100	ALL'D HOURS PER 100 1 75	ALL'D HOURS 54 25	**INCENTIVE JOB CARD**	B. Hanig NAME
Sept. 20	STOP 40.0	ACTUAL HOURS 40 0	D.W. RATE 1 65	EARNINGS 89 51
Sept. 20	START 00.0		FOREMAN	GAIN OR LOSS 2 72

pany has a single inventory account in its general ledger which lumps together raw materials, work in process, and finished goods inventory; therefore no accounting entry is made when material is issued for use in production.

Labor. The basic document for controlling direct labor costs is the incentive job card. Each productive employee fills out a card for each order on which he works during the week. The card reproduced as

Illustration 13–10

CARBON COPY OF SALES INVOICE

Village of Vernon, Att. Village Clerk, Vernon, N.Y.	41740	9/11/--			
	NY 931	9/10/--			
Village of Vernon, Water Dept., Att: E. J. Blackburn, Mayor Vernon, N.Y.	7/31/--	Boston			
	8/13/--				
STIBBS	Prepaid				
10	5/8 x 3/4 Model HF Meters SG SH ET FB & 3/4" #3015331-340	Cons. 40%	21.80	218.00	
1	Charge Gear #46X -- shipped 8-10-		.25	130.80	
	Plus 10%		.03	.28	131.08
	Meters Parts			130.80 .28	85.05 .18
	Ship gear by P. Post				

Illustration 13–9 shows that Mr. Harris worked all week on one order so that he turned in only one card for that week. On the card he has recorded the quantity finished, the actual hours worked, and the allowed hours, which are usually the same as the standard hours. A payroll clerk enters each employee's daywork rate, the standard direct labor

Illustration 13–11

BLACK METER COMPANY

Income Statement
Six Months Ending June 30

Sales..		$3,148,234.13
Less: Cash discounts......................		3,030.13
Net sales..................................		$3,145,204.00
Standard cost..........................	$2,045,127.63	
Variances.............................	118,080.55*	2,163,208.18
Gross manufacturing profit....................		$ 981,995.82
Selling expense..............................		504,032.35
Operating profit.............................		$ 477,963.47
Administrative expense.......................		108,236.76
Adjusted operating profit....................		$ 369,726.71
Nonoperating profit.........................		6,415.93
Net Profit.................................		$ 376,142.64

*Variances

Deductions from gross profit:		
Direct labor variance.....................................	$	26,389.14
Factory burden unabsorbed..............................		48,137.61
Material price variance.................................		39,298.01
Unused space and equipment............................		210.00
Inventory adjustments..................................		12,875.30
Loss due to changes in manufacturing methods..............		10,146.50
Total Deductions.....................................	$	137,056.56
Additions to gross profit:		
Cash discounts taken.....................................	$	9,699.60
Gain from sale or salvage................................		9,276.41
Total Additions.......................................	$	18,976.01
Net Variances...	$	118,080.55

rate for that department, and extends the actual and standard direct labor cost of the work completed.

By totaling all the incentive job cards, the payroll clerk obtains the actual wages accrued for each employee in each department, and the standard labor cost of the work done in each department. He credits accrued wages for the actual amount to set up the liability and debits the Inventory account for the standard amount of direct labor. The variance is closed out to a Direct Labor variance account.

MANUFACTURING OVERHEAD. The method of handling manufacturing overhead is very similar in each department. A cost clerk multiplies the standard direct labor hours worked by the manufacturing overhead rate for that department (Illustration 13–4) to obtain the amount of manufacturing overhead to be absorbed by the department that month. He debits the Inventory account for the total amount of the absorbed manufacturing overhead. During the month actual manufacturing overhead expenses have been accumulating in the invoice and check register and in various adjusting entries. The difference between the sum of the actual expenses

Illustration 13–12

FLOW CHART

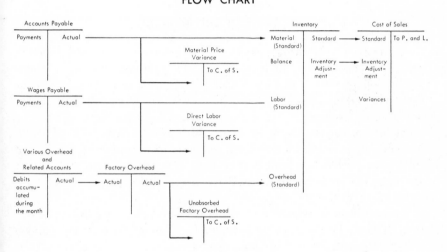

and the absorbed manufacturing overhead cost is the under- or over-absorbed manufacturing overhead variance, which is closed to the overhead variance accounts.

When these transactions have been recorded, all material, direct labor, and manufacturing overhead have been charged into the Inventory account at standard cost, and three variance accounts have been debited or credited for the difference between actual and standard.

A physical inventory is taken every six months, and is valued at standard cost. Any difference between this figure and the total value of the inventory as shown in the Inventory account is debited or credited to an Inventory Adjustment variance account.

COST OF SALES. Before monthly operating statements can be prepared, a cost clerk has to make an analysis of sales for the month. A duplicate copy of each invoice is sent to the cost office, where a clerk enters in pencil the standard cost of the items sold (see Illustration 13–10). At the end of the month the cost clerk simply totals the figures on these duplicate invoices to get figures for sales and the standard cost of those sales for the month. The standard cost of sales is a credit to the Inventory account and a debit to the Cost of Sales account. The total sales amount is a credit to Sales and a debit to Accounts Receivable. When this work has been completed, the cost department is in a position to obtain the monthly income statements (see Illustration 13–11) by closing the ledger.

The accounting entries are summarized on the flow chart shown in Illustration 13–12.

JOINT PRODUCTS AND BY-PRODUCTS

In some manufacturing plants, two or more dissimilar end products may be made from a single batch of raw material or from a single production process. The classic example of these *joint products* is the variety of end products—the hide, the many different cuts of meat, and so on—that are made from the single raw material, a steer. Beyond a certain point in the manufacturing process, which is called the *split-off point,* separate end products are identified, and costs are accumulated for each of them. The problem of joint costing is to find some reasonable basis for assigning to the joint products the material, labor, and indirect costs incurred up to the split-off point.

This problem is essentially the same as that of allocating indirect costs. In both cases, the objective is to assign a fair share of the joint or common costs to the separate end products, and in neither case can the results be scientifically accurate.

One common basis of allocating joint costs is in proportion to the *sales value* of the end products, adjusted for processing and marketing costs incurred beyond the split-off point. If the selling price depends on cost, this method involves a certain amount of circular reasoning, but there may be no better alternative. If gasoline sells for twice the price of kerosene, it is perhaps reasonable that gasoline should bear twice as much of the crude oil and joint refining costs. Another basis of allocation is weight; in the case of the steer, this would assume that the stew meat is as valuable as the tenderloin, which is unrealistic; but in other situations, this might be a reasonable assumption. In any event, the amount charged to each end product must be recognized as resulting from an allocation. If some scientifically correct method of assigning the cost were available, the product would not be a joint product, by definition.

By-products are a special kind of joint product. If management wishes to make Products A and B in some predetermined proportion, or if it wishes to make as much of each as possible from a given quantity of raw material, then they are ordinary joint products. If, on the other hand, management's objective is to make Product A, but some quantity of Product B inevitably emerges from the production process, then Product A is a main product and Product B is a by-product. The intention is to make from a given amount of joint material as much of the main product and as little of the by-product as possible. As management's intention changes, the classification changes. Kerosene was once the main product made from crude oil; subsequently, with the growth in consumption of gasoline, many petroleum companies considered kerosene a by-product; and currently it has become a main product again, because it is an important component of jet engine fuel. Certain tars and petrochemicals, once by-products, are now main products.

A number of alternative procedures are used in costing by-products. At one extreme, they may be assigned zero cost, with all costs being charged to the main products. At the other extreme, by-products may be assigned a cost equal to their sales value, with the result that no profit or loss is attributed to the by-product and the entire profit of the process is attributed to the main product.

DIRECT COSTING

Although not now a generally accepted financial accounting practice, mention should be made of the practice of *direct costing*, which is widely discussed and used by an increasing number of companies in their internal accounting systems.[9] "Direct costs," as used here, are costs that vary with changes in production volume; therefore they correspond to variable costs, and not to direct costs in the sense of traceable or separable costs as the term was used in the preceding section.[10]

In the conventional system, the basic concept is *full costing;* that is, products should bear a fair share of all the costs involved in making them. In the direct cost system, only the variable costs are charged to products and thus pass through inventory accounts; nonvariable costs are charged off as expenses in the period in which they are incurred. Consequently, nonvariable overhead costs affect net income more quickly in the direct cost system than in a full cost system. This effect can be seen in Illustra-

---

[9] Of 365 respondents to a 1959 Financial Executives Institute survey, 77, or 21 percent, reported a use of direct costing, and nearly half of these had started using the system within the previous five years.

[10] This confusion in terminology is another example of the differences in the definition of cost that cause trouble in practice unless they are recognized.

tion 13–13, in which it is assumed that one unit is manufactured each period, but that the unit manufactured in the first period is not sold until the second period. The sales price is $100 per unit, variable costs are $30 per *unit*, and nonvariable overhead is $50 per *period*. In the conventional full cost system, the entire manufacturing cost of $80 is held in inventory at the end of Period No. 1, and is released as cost of goods sold in Period No. 2, along with the cost of the unit made and sold in that period. In direct costing, only the $30 of variable cost is held in inventory at the end of Period No. 1, and the $50 of nonvariable overhead is charged as an expense of the period.

Illustration 13–13

COMPARISON OF FULL COSTING AND DIRECT COSTING

	Under Full Costing		*Under Direct Costing*	
	Period No. 1	*Period No. 2*	*Period No. 1*	*Period No. 2*
Activity:				
Units manufactured........	1	1	1	1
Units sold..............	0	2	0	2
Income Statement:				
Sales....................	$ 0	$200	$ 0	$200
Cost of goods sold........	0	160	0	60
Manufacturing overhead....	0	0	50	50
Selling and administrative...	10	10	10	10
Net Income or Loss..........	$(10)	$ 30	$(60)	$ 80
Ending Inventory (Balance Sheet)..................	$ 80	$ 0	$ 30	$ 0

The conventional system is also called *absorption costing* because all costs are absorbed by products, in contrast with direct costing, in which nonvariable overhead is not absorbed by products.

In direct costing, nonvariable manufacturing indirect costs are viewed as being essentially the same as administrative costs; that is, these are costs associated with being in business rather than costs associated with the specific units of product manufactured. Proponents of direct costing assert that management can be misled by the income reported in a period if these costs are hidden away in inventory. Direct costing is the extreme case of differences of opinion about which costs are product costs and which are period costs.

Since direct costing is not a generally accepted practice for financial accounting, companies that use it for internal purposes recompute their inventory valuation and cost of goods sold for their published financial statements. They do this by computing an overhead rate, usually on a plantwide basis, which they use solely for this purpose.

RELATION TO FINANCIAL ACCOUNTING

It should be emphasized that the product costing systems described above are an integral part of financial accounting, with the same rules of debit and credit. The accounting entries described in this chapter are made for the same purpose as those described in Chapter 7. The only substantive difference is that in Chapter 7 we assumed that the company did not have a way of directly obtaining the cost of items moving from Raw Materials, through Goods in Process, to Finished Goods, and out to Cost of Goods Sold; we therefore had to find these amounts by the process of deduction. In the present chapter, a method of finding the amounts directly has been described. The other differences, such as the classification of goods in process into cost centers, are merely differences in detail.

Cost information is sometimes collected outside the debit and credit structure. Such a system is called a *statistical* cost system, in contrast with a *tied-in* cost system. A statistical system is simpler to operate but does not permit the checks on accuracy that are possible in the tied-in system.

RESPONSIBILITY ACCOUNTING

Product costing is one of the two principal types of management accounting. The other is responsibility accounting. The objective of product costing is to assign an equitable share of costs to products; the objective of responsibility accounting is to assign to responsibility centers the costs incurred by them. Product costing and responsibility accounting, although here described separately, are actually two aspects of a single management accounting system. They do not involve two "sets of books," but only two ways of aggregating the same detailed bits of information. Indeed, we need to refer to only two important distinctions between the two types of information:

1. In responsibility accounting, costs are assigned to responsibility centers rather than to products.

2. In responsibility accounting, a clear distinction must be made between costs that are controllable by the head of the responsibility center and costs that are not controllable by him.

Responsibility Centers

A responsibility center is an organization unit headed by a responsible person, its manager. It is responsible for performing some function, which is its *output*. In performing this function, it uses resources, or *inputs*. The costs assigned to a responsibility center are intended to measure the inputs that it consumes in a specified period of time, such as a week or a month.

Within a business there is a whole hierarchy of responsibility centers. At the top, there is the president or chief executive officer, who is held responsible by the owners for the overall profitability of the enterprise. Beneath him, the several operating and staff departments are each responsibility centers, and at still lower levels, responsibility centers may consist of sections, subsections, or even individuals. The delineation of responsibility centers is in practice a difficult task, and the installation of a control system often uncovers instances of overlapping responsibility which need to be corrected. If the company's organization chart reflected the actual lines of responsibility, this difficulty would not exist, but for various reasons the chart may not do this.

In a given company, responsibility centers are often synonymous with cost centers. This is because production departments are often defined as cost centers, and these departments are also responsibility centers since the department foreman is a responsible supervisor. When individual machines or other segments of a department are used as cost centers, costs for the responsibility center can be obtained simply by adding up the relevant costs of these separate cost centers. At the other extreme, if the whole factory is a single cost center (as is the case when a plantwide overhead rate is used), separate accounts are set up to collect the costs for the individual responsibility centers in the plant. Likewise, if cost centers are departments and responsibility centers are individual work shifts or other departmental subdivisions, separate accounts for these subdivisions are required.

In short, costs are collected for the cost center or the responsibility center, whichever is the smaller unit, and costs for the other are obtained by addition. Thus, the fact that a cost center is not necessarily the same as a responsibility center raises no particular problem of cost collection.

Service centers headed by responsible supervisors, such as the maintenance department, the personnel department, the accounting department, and so on, are also responsibility centers. Service centers that are mere aggregates of cost without reference to personal responsibility are not. An example of the latter is the Occupancy service center described in a preceding section, which is not in itself a responsibility center, although its costs are part of the responsibility center of the plant manager. All costs in a company are assigned to some responsibility center.

Controllable Costs

The costs incurred in a responsibility center are those associated with accomplishing its function, whatever that function may be. Some of these costs are controllable by the head of the responsibility center, and others are not so controllable. Since responsibility center costs are used principally in the control process, it is important that the controllable costs be shown separately from the noncontrollable costs. The line between controllable and noncontrollable costs is difficult to draw; it is discussed in Chapter 14.

Some companies collect only controllable costs by responsibility centers. Others collect both controllable and noncontrollable costs. When a responsibility center is synonymous with a cost center, the latter practice is often more convenient because the same set of costs can then be used for both purposes—the controllable costs for control, and the sum of controllable and noncontrollable costs for product costing.

In product costing, we need only to know the total cost to be charged to products, but for management control, the total must be broken down in a way that facilitates the analysis of performance. Thus, in responsibility accounting, costs are classified according to *type* (also called "object," or "natural element," or "function"). Indirect labor, supplies, power, heat, overtime premiums, and spoilage are examples from the long list of cost types that might be useful in a given situation.

For analysis purposes, it may also be useful to separate *variable costs* (which are costs that change proportionately with changes in production volume or other measure of activity) from nonvariable costs, but such separation usually requires only that each cost type be designated either as variable or as nonvariable. Variable costs are discussed further in Chapter 14.

In summary, *responsibility accounting* requires that costs be classified: (1) by responsibility centers; (2) within each responsibility center, by whether controllable or noncontrollable; and (3) within the controllable classification, by cost types, or natural elements, in a way that provides a useful basis for analysis.

As mentioned above, product costing and responsibility accounting are part of a single system, in which detailed cost information is aggregated in two different ways in different purposes. The lowest common denominator of the system is called the *account building block*, which consists of a single type of cost (e.g., direct material, supplies, overtime) incurred in the *smaller* of either a cost center or a responsibility center. All summaries of cost information are obtained by combining these building blocks in one of two principal ways: (1) according to products, or (2) according to the hierarchy of responsibility centers.

SUMMARY

A management accounting system consists of two principal parts, called respectively product cost accounting and responsibility accounting. In some companies, there is a third part, in order to conform to the requirements of regulatory agencies.

In product costing, each product worked on is charged with what is believed to be a fair share of the total manufacturing costs incurred. Products in inventory are valued at this cost, and this is the cost used in figuring the cost of goods sold. Direct labor and direct material costs applicable to each product can usually be measured with reasonable accuracy; for these costs, the principal problem is the mechanical one of accumulating the various labor and material costs that belong to the product. The remaining cost elements, collectively called overhead or indirect cost, cannot be traced directly to products. These costs are accumulated by cost centers, and the total costs of the cost center are allocated to products going through the center on some reasonable basis. *Whenever allocated costs are involved, the resulting product cost cannot be said to be accurate.*

Also, when joint or common costs are involved there can be no scientifically correct way of splitting them up among time periods, among cost centers, or among products passing through cost centers. A pig is a pig; there is no way of knowing how much of its cost belongs to the hide and how much to the bacon. This is *not* merely difficult; it is impossible.

But the objective of product cost accounting is not to ascertain a scientifically correct cost; rather it is to charge products with a *fair share* of the total costs incurred in the manufacturing process. This it can do.

Since costs are also used for management control, the elementary building blocks of cost are arranged by type in responsibility centers, and by proper combination and summarization they can serve both purposes.

SUGGESTIONS FOR FURTHER READING

DEARDEN, JOHN. *Cost and Budget Analysis.* Englewood Cliffs, N.J.: Prentice-Hall, Inc., 1962.

DICKEY, ROBERT I. (ed.). *Accountants' Cost Handbook.* 2d ed.; New York: Ronald Press Co., 1960.

MATZ, ADOLPH; OTHEL J. CURRY; and GEORGE W. FRANK. *Cost Accounting.* 4th ed.; Cincinnati: South-Western Publishing Co., 1967.

MOORE, CARL L., and ROBERT K. JAEDICKE. *Managerial Accounting.* 2d ed.; Dallas, Texas: Southwestern, 1967.

NEUNER, JOHN J. W., and SAMUEL FRUMER. *Cost Accounting: Principles and Practice.* 7th ed.; Homewood, Ill.: Richard D. Irwin, Inc., 1967.

NICKERSON, CLARENCE B. *Managerial Cost Accounting and Analysis.* 2d ed.; New York: McGraw-Hill Book Co., Inc., 1962.

SHILLINGLAW, GORDON. *Cost Accounting: Analysis and Control.* Rev. ed.; Homewood, Ill.: Richard D. Irwin, Inc., 1967.

THOMAS, WILLIAM E. (ed.). *Readings in Cost Accounting, Budgeting and Control.* 3d ed.; Cincinnati: South-Western Publishing Co., 1967.

CHAPTER 14

THE MANAGEMENT CONTROL PROCESS

One of the uses of accounting information is in the process called management control. This chapter gives an overview of that process. Aspects of it are discussed in more detail in succeeding chapters.

MANAGEMENT CONTROL

Management control is *the process by which managers assure that resources are obtained and used effectively and efficiently in the accomplishment of an organization's objectives.*

As this statement suggests, management control takes place within an organization that already exists and that already has a set of objectives or goals. Every organization has objectives, that is, it exists for some purpose, and these objectives are taken as given. The control process is not concerned with whether these objectives are good or bad; the process occurs both in the Roman Catholic Church and in the Cosa Nostra. It occurs in governments and other nonprofit organizations as well as in profit-seeking corporations.

The control process is facilitated when the objectives of the organization are clear-cut, but in most organizations objectives are by no means clear. The statement that the objective of a business corporation is "to make a profit" is both too simple and too vague to be of much use. It is an oversimplification because corporations usually have more than one objective. "Survival" is usually listed as an objective that is at least as important as making a profit. Fulfilling the organization's responsibility to society and being a good place in which to work are other possible objectives that, although not easily measurable, are often also important. The profit objective is too vague because for effective control one needs to know the strategies that the top management in a particular company has chosen: the products it has decided to manufacture, the scale and location of manufacturing activities, the markets in which these products are to be sold, the method of reaching these markets, the organizational structure, the sources of financing, and so on. The process of deciding on these policies is called *strategic planning*. Strategic planning establishes a framework within which management control takes place.

Characteristics of Management Control Systems

Ordinarily, a management control system is a *total* system in the sense that it embraces all aspects of the company's operation. It needs to be a total system because an important management function is to assure that all parts of the operation are in balance with one another; and in order to examine balance, management needs information about each of the parts.

With rare exceptions, the management control system is *built around a financial structure;* that is, resources and outputs are expressed in monetary units. Money is the only common denominator by means of which the heterogeneous elements of output and resources (e.g., hours of labor, type of labor, quantity and quality of material, amount and kind of products produced) can be combined and compared. Although the financial structure is usually the central focus, nonmonetary measures such as minutes per operation, number of persons, and reject and spoilage rates are also important parts of the system.

The management control process tends to be *rhythmic;* it follows a definite pattern and timetable, month after month and year after year. In budgeting, which is an important part of the management control process, certain steps are taken in a prescribed sequence and at certain dates each year: dissemination of guidelines, preparation of original estimates, transmission of these estimates up through the several echelons in the organization, review of these estimates, final approval by top management, dissemination back through the organization, operation, reporting, and the appraisal of performance. The procedure to be followed at each step in this process, the dates when the steps are to be completed, and even the forms to be used can be, and often are, set forth in a manual.

A management control system is, or should be, a *coordinated, integrated system;* that is, although data collected for one purpose may differ from those collected for another purpose, these data should be reconcilable with one another. In a sense, the management control system is a *single* system, but it is perhaps more accurate to think of it as a set of interlocking subsystems. In many organizations, for example, three types of cost information are needed for management control: (1) costs by responsibility centers, used for planning and controlling the activities of responsible supervisors; (2) full program costs, used for pricing and other operating decisions in normal circumstances; (3) direct program costs, used for pricing and other operating decisions in special circumstances, such as when management wishes to utilize idle capacity. ("Program" is here used for any activity in which the organization engages. In industrial companies, programs consist of products or product lines, and "product costs" can be substituted in the above statements.)

Line managers are the focal points in management control. They are the persons whose judgments are incorporated in the approved plans, and they are the persons who must influence others and whose performance is measured. Staff people collect, summarize, and present information that is useful in the process, and they make calculations that translate management judgments into the format of the system. Such a staff may be large in numbers; indeed, the control department is often the largest staff department in a company. However, the significant decisions are made by the line managers, not by the staff.

MOTIVATION

Management control involves human beings, from those in the lowest responsibility center of the organizational hierarchy up to and including members of top management. The management control process in part consists of inducing these human beings to do certain things and to refrain from doing others. Although for some purposes an accumulation of the costs of manufacturing a product is useful, management literally cannot "control" a product, or the costs of making a product. What management does—or at least what it attempts to do—is control the actions of the people who are responsible for incurring these costs.

Principles of Motivation

Since management control involves the behavior of human beings, the relevant principles are those drawn from such disciplines as social psychology and organizational behavior, rather than from economics, mathematics, or any discipline that focuses on impersonal relationships rather than on human behavior. An adequate discussion of psychological principles is outside both the scope of this book and the competence of its author. Furthermore, social psychologists regard the currently accepted principles of the behavior of individuals in groups as extremely tentative, since the evidence from which they are derived is both inconclusive and often contradictory. There are, however, generalizations relevant to the design of a management control system on which many behavioral scientists agree. Some of these are as follows:[1]

1. An individual has a number of basic motives or needs. He joins an organization and contributes toward the accomplishment of its objectives because in this way he believes he can satisfy at least some of his needs. Among these needs are:

a) Physiological considerations, such as food, bodily comfort, and sex, which are basic in the sense that these needs ordinarily must be satisfied before consideration is given to "higher" needs.

b) Realistic recognition of his abilities and achievements by his colleagues and superiors (need for achievement).

c) Status and social acceptance as a member of a group (need for affiliation).

d) Self-esteem, a sense of personal worth.

e) Security, including an understanding of what is expected of him and a belief that his performance will be judged fairly.

f) Autonomy, the freedom to exercise discretion.

g) The desire to change other people's behavior, leadership (need for power).

2. Individuals are influenced either by the expectation of reward or the fear of punishment. *Reward* is the satisfaction of a need, and *punishment* is the deprivation of satisfaction. Individuals tend to be more strongly motivated by reward than by punishment.

3. Monetary compensation is an important means of satisfying certain needs, but beyond the subsistence level the amount of compensation is not necessarily so important as nonmonetary rewards. Nevertheless, pay is often important indirectly as an indication of how achievement and ability are regarded. (A man earning $50,000 a year may be unhappy if a colleague of perceived equal ability receives $51,000 a year.)

4. The effectiveness of reward or punishment diminishes rapidly as the time elapses between an action and the reward or punishment administered for it.

---

[1] For further reading on this subject, see:

J. W. Atkinson, *An Introduction to Motivation* (Princeton, N.J.: D. Van Nostrand Company, 1964).

Edwin J. Caplan, "Behavorial Assumptions of Management Accounting," *Accounting Review,* July 1966, p. 496–509.

R. M. Cyert and J. G. March, *A Behavorial Theory of the Firm* (Englewood Cliffs, N.J.: Prentice-Hall, Inc., 1963).

G. C. Homans, *Social Behavior: Its Elementary Forms* (New York: Harcourt, Brace & World, 1961).

P. R. Lawrence and J. W. Lorsch, *Organization and Environment: Managing Differentiation and Integration* (Boston: Division of Research, Harvard Business School, 1967).

D. C. McClelland, *The Achieving Society* (Princeton, N.J.: D. Van Nostrand Company, 1961).

5. Needs may be unconscious, or they may be expressed as aspirations or goals. Motivation is weakest when the individual perceives a goal as either unattainable or too easily attainable. Motivation is strong when the goal can be attained with some effort and when the individual regards its attainment as important.

6. An individual tends to accept evidence of his performance more willingly and to use it more constructively when it is presented in a manner that he regards as objective, that is, without personal bias.

7. Individuals are receptive to learning better ways of doing things only when they personally recognize the inadequacies of their present behavior.

8. Beyond a certain point, pressure for improved performance accomplishes nothing. This optimum point is far below the maximum amount of pressure that conceivably could be exerted. (When the coach says, "Don't press; don't try too hard," he is applying this principle.)

9. Individuals differ greatly in the importance they attach to various need satisfactions. Their attitudes also change with time and circumstances and are heavily influenced by the attitudes of their colleagues and superiors.

In view of the differences among individuals mentioned in the ninth point above, precise rules for designing control systems could not be constructed even if the above list of generalizations were fully substantiated by experiment. They nevertheless seem to be sufficiently valid so that useful concepts for control can be derived from them. Some of these are described in the next section.

Management Sponsorship

A control system will probably be ineffective unless the organization is convinced that management considers the system to be important. Some systems are installed with no more management backing than the directive, "Let's have a good control system," and with no subsequent interest or action by managements. Such a system, instead of being a part of the management process, becomes a paper shuffling routine whose principal virtue is that it provides employment for a great many clerks. In a talk describing the remarkable reorganization of Ford Motor Company, Mr. Ernest R. Breech gave an excellent illustration of the importance of this point:[2]

In the course of reorganizing Ford Motor Company, by 1948 we had set up

---

[2] Ernest R. Breech, "Planning the Basic Strategy of a Large Business," *Harvard Business School Bulletin*, Summer 1955, pp. 28, 29. Mr. Breech was at that time Chairman of the Board.

a modern cost control system and a supplemental compensation plan. Having done so, we were startled to find that nothing in particular happened. We had built, or so we thought, a log fire under the company. But we had not, up to that point, applied the torch of internal competition.

In the fall of 1948 we called together several hundred of our top management men. We analyzed and compared the profit performance of each key operation, and showed how performance was reflected in the supplemental compensation fund. It was quite a show, and each man went out of that meeting determined to put his own house in order. Each man in turn set up similar meetings of his own supervisors and the process continued on down the line. These meetings were held, and still are, at regular intervals. The results were almost unbelievable.

Our direct labor costs were reduced from an off-standard of 65% in July of 1948 to only 6% off-standard in 1951, and manufacturing overhead improved 48 percentage points during the same period. We never could have achieved that performance without a real incentive system and internal competition that reached deep into our management structure.

Action is a sure signal, probably the only effective signal, that management is interested in the control system. Basically, this action involves praise or other reward for good performance, criticism of or removal of the causes for poor performance, or questions leading to these actions. If, in contrast, reports on performance disappear into executive offices and are never heard from again, the organization has reason to assume that management is not paying attention to them. And if management does not pay attention to them, why should anyone else?

Participation and Understanding

Control is exercised in part by setting up standards of expected performance and comparing actual performance with these standards. Whatever standard of good performance is adopted, it is likely to be effective as a means of control only if the person being judged agrees that it is an equitable standard. If he does not agree, he is likely to pay no attention to comparisons between his performance and the standard; and he is likely to resent, and if possible reject, an attempt by anyone else to make such a comparison.

The best way to assure this agreement is to ask the person whose performance is to be measured to participate in the process of setting the standard. This was not the usual practice some years ago. The earliest budgets were "imposed budgets"; that is, they were edicts promulgated by management, which said, in effect, to the organization: "Thou shalt do such and such." The results obtained from these imposed budgets were frequently unsatisfactory because the organization tended to resent and disregard them. The more recent trend is in the direction of permitting the person who is being held responsible for performance to have a considerable voice in the preparation of the budget. This trend is a manifestation of the general tendency to decentralize decision making to lower echelons in the organization.

Although the responsible supervisor participates in the budgeting process, he is not solely responsible for deciding on the budget allowances. Rather, the supervisor and his superior discuss the matter until they *jointly* agree.

In order to participate intelligently, the supervisor needs to understand clearly what the control system is, what he is expected to do, what basis he is going to be judged on, and so on. As illustrated by the remarks of Mr. Breech quoted above, such an understanding probably cannot be achieved by written communication. Frequent meetings of supervisors for discussion and explanation are required.

The process of educating the individuals involved in the system is necessarily a continuous one. Not uncommonly, a system is introduced with a loud fanfare, works well for a time, and then gradually withers away in effectiveness as the initial stimulus disappears.

Incentives

Many management control systems rely for the strength of their motivation on the attitude and actions that management takes in response to reported performance. Some tie the supervisor's compensation to his performance. In view of the importance which people attach to monetary compensation, this is a strong motivation indeed. In some cases it may be too strong, for unless the standards are very carefully worked out, incessant arguments will go on about the justice and equity of the reported results. If the system is being used only for praise or blame, inequities in the figures can be allowed for in interpreting the results, but this is not possible when a bonus is computed mechanically on the basis of reported performance. Thus, a bonus plan is most successful when there is general agreement that the basis of measurement is fair.

Individual Differences

As pointed out above, individuals differ in their needs and in their reactions to rewards and punishments of various types. An important function of the manager, at each level, is to adapt the system to the personalities of the individuals whom he supervises. Thus, the impersonal system can never be a substitute for personal management; rather, the system is a framework that is adapted by management to fit individual situations.

Goal Congruence

It is reasonable to expect that a person will act according to what he perceives his own best interests to be. Essentially, therefore, the control system should be designed so that actions that it leads people to take in accordance with their perceived self-interest are actions that are also in the best interests of the company. In the language of social psychology, the system should encourage *goal congruence;* that is, it should be structured so that the goals of people in the organization are, so far as feasible, consistent with the goals of the organization as a whole.

Perfect congruence between individual goals and organizational goals does not exist, but as a minimum the system should not encourage the individual to act *against* the best interests of the company. For example, if the system signals that the emphasis should be only on reducing costs, and if the individual responds by reducing costs at the expense of adequate quality, or by reducing costs in his own department by measures that cause a more than offsetting increase in some other department, he has been motivated, but in the wrong direction. It is therefore important to ask two separate questions about a control technique: (1) What will it motivate people to do in their own selfish interests? and (2) Is this action in the best interests of the company?

An Example: Maintenance Costs

As an illustration of this point, let us consider the problem of the control of maintenance costs in a factory that has a separate maintenance department. The maintenance function is that of insuring that the buildings and equipment are in good operating condition. This is partly the responsibility of the maintenance department, which incurs costs when it makes repairs or does other maintenance work; and it is partly the responsibility of the operating department foreman, who can influence the amount of required maintenance work by how well he takes care of his equipment. In addition, some maintenance work, such as outside painting, is required simply because of the uncontrollable forces of nature.

There are at least a dozen ways in which the costs of the maintenance department can be charged to the several operating departments, and each gives a different "message" to the foremen as to how they should view their responsibility for maintenance. Here are a few of the possibilities and the implications that each is likely to convey:

Method No. 1: Do not charge any maintenance costs to the operating departments.

Message: The operating foreman has no responsibility for maintenance costs. He requests the maintenance department to do whatever work he thinks needs to be done, and the maintenance department has the responsibility for doing this work. (Note that this system does not motivate the foreman to curb unnecessary requests for maintenance work.)

Method No. 2: Prorate total maintenance costs to the operating departments on the basis of the volume of activity in the department.

Message: Maintenance costs in total are expected to vary proportionately with plant activity. However, the foreman of each department has no direct responsibility for maintenance work, and the maintenance department, as in the first method, has full responsibility. The operating foreman is told what is his "fair share" of total maintenance costs incurred, which may make him interested in the magnitude of such costs.

Method No. 3: Charge departments for each maintenance job at a prescribed cost for each type of job.

Message: The operating foreman is responsible for situations that create the need for maintenance work, such as machine breakdowns. The maintenance department is responsible for the cost of doing a given maintenance job. The foreman therefore need not be concerned with the efficiency with which maintenance men work, once he has requested that the job be done, since he will be charged a prescribed amount no matter how much is actually spent in doing the job.

Method No. 4: Charge each department for maintenance work at a prescribed hourly rate for each hour that a maintenance man works in the department.

Message: The operating foreman is responsible both for situations that create the need for maintenance work and for the time taken by the maintenance people to do the work. Presumably, he has some control over the work of the maintenance men. In some situations, he may even be authorized to hire outside maintenance people if he believes that they will do the work less expensively than the rates charged by the maintenance department.

None of the above methods is necessarily better than the others. Each of them tends to motivate the foreman differently. The best method is the one that motivates the foreman to act most nearly as management wants him to act. Depending on what top management wishes to accomplish, any one of these methods, or other methods not listed, or some combination of them, may be best for a given company.

THE MANAGEMENT CONTROL SYSTEM

Much of the management control process is informal; it occurs by means of memoranda, meetings, conversations, and even by such signals as facial expressions. Such control devices are not amenable to a systematic description. Many companies also have a formal system, consisting of some or all of the parts described briefly below and in more detail in succeeding chapters.

Information in a management control system can be classified as (1) planned and (2) actual data on (*a*) outputs and (*b*) inputs. Prior to actual operations, decisions and estimates are made as to what outputs and inputs are to be; during actual operations, records are maintained as to what outputs and inputs actually are; and subsequent to operations, reports are prepared that compare actual outputs and inputs to planned outputs and inputs. The principal steps in the formal process are:

1. Programming.
2. Budgeting.
3. Accounting.
4. Reporting and analysis.

As indicated in Illustration 14–1, each of these steps leads to the next. They recur in a regular cycle, and together they constitute a "closed loop."

Programming

In the programming phase, decisions are made with respect to the major programs in which the organization is to engage during the coming period. These decisions either are made within the context of the objectives and strategies that have previously been decided upon, or they represent changes in strategy. (If the latter, they are part of the strategic planning process, rather than the management control process; the two processes merge into one another in the programming phase.) A few companies state their programs in the form of a "long-range plan" which shows planned outputs and inputs for a number of years ahead—usually 5 years, but possibly as few as 3 or (in the case of certain public utilities) as many as 20. The majority of companies do not have such a formal mechanism for recording their overall future programs; they rely instead on reports or understandings as to specific, important facets of the program, particularly the amounts to be invested in capital assets and the means of financing these assets.

In an industrial company, the "Programs" are usually products or product lines, plus activities (such as research) that are not relatable to specific products. The plans have to do with the amount and character of resources (i.e., inputs) that are to be devoted to each program, and with the ways in which these resources are to be used. The accounting information used as a basis for such plans therefore tends to be program or cost accounting data, rather than responsibility accounting data.

Illustration 14–1

SEQUENCE OF MANAGEMENT CONTROL TECHNIQUES

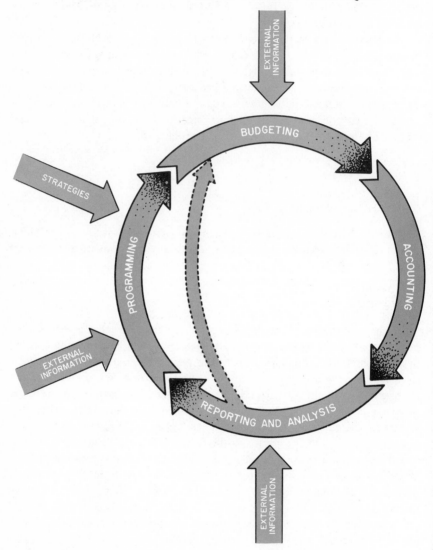

Budgeting

A budget is a plan expressed in quantitative, usually monetary, terms. It covers a specified period of time—usually a year, but in some companies six months or three months. In the budgeting process the program is translated into terms that correspond to the responsibility of those who are charged with executing it. Thus, although the plans are originally made in program terms, in the budgeting process they are translated into responsibility terms. The process of arriving at the budget is essentially one of negotiation between the managers of responsibility centers and their superiors. The end product of these negotiations is a statement of the outputs that are expected during the budget year and the resources that are to be used in achieving this output. The process is discussed more fully in Chapter 16.

Accounting

During the period of actual operations, records are kept of resources actually consumed and outputs actually achieved. As described in Chapter 13, the records of inputs (i.e., costs) are structured so that costs are collected both by product or programs and by responsibility centers. Costs in the former classification are used as a basis for future programming, and those in the latter are used to measure the performance of the heads of responsibility centers.

The degree to which outputs and inputs can be measured quantitatively varies greatly in different responsibility centers. In a department making a tangible homogeneous product (e.g., cement), the *quantity* of output often can be measured precisely; but when the products are heterogeneous (e.g., different styles and grades of shoes, parts produced by a machine shop), problems arise in summarizing the separate outputs into a meaningful measure of the total. Converting the disparate physical products to a monetary equivalent is one way of solving this problem. The *quality* of product also involves measurement problems, which often are solved by a "go, no-go" procedure: either the product is of satisfactory quality, or it is not.

When the outputs are services or other intangibles, the problem of measuring them becomes formidable. It is always difficult and often not feasible to measure, even approximately, the outputs of such staff units as the legal department or the research department of a company, or the outputs of hospitals, schools, government agencies, or churches. Nevertheless, these organizations *have* outputs; the difficulty of measurement does not alter this fact.

In addition to the products and services usually thought of as outputs, responsibility centers produce other intangible effects, some intentional and others unintentional. They may prepare employees for advancement; they may instill attitudes of loyalty and pride of accomplishment (or, alternatively, attitudes of disloyalty and indolence); and they may affect the image of the whole organization that is perceived by the outside world. Some of these outputs, such as better trained employees, are created in order to benefit operations in future periods; that is, they will become inputs at some future time. Such outputs are therefore "investments," since a business investment is a commitment of current resources in the expectation of deriving future benefits.

In the typical responsibility center, inputs are a heterogeneous mixture of resources: labor, materials, and services. Some common denominator must be found if these heterogeneous elements are to be aggregated into a measure of the total resources consumed by the responsibility center. Money is the most frequently used common denominator. The total resources consumed by a responsibility center, when measured in monetary terms, are the expenses of that responsibility center. Total recorded expenses are at best an approximation of the true inputs. Some inputs are not included as expenses, either because the effort required to translate them into monetary terms is not worthwhile (e.g., minor supplies and services, small amounts of borrowed labor) or because measurement is not possible (e.g., certain types of executive or staff assistance, training).

Reporting and Analysis

Accounting information, along with a variety of other information, is summarized, analyzed, and reported to those who are responsible for knowing what is happening in the company and for improving performance. As indicated above, these reports essentially compare planned outputs and inputs with actual outputs and inputs. Chapter 17 describes analyses that can be made of this information.

Need for Internal Consistency

It seems obvious that control is not possible unless actual performance and the standard against which it is being measured are comparable; yet instances of complete noncomparability do occur. This often happens when a management accounting system is separated from the financial accounting system, perhaps being operated by different staff organizations. An extreme case is that of the federal government, notably the Defense Department. For cost control purposes, an operating manager in the Defense Department should be judged on the basis of the costs *incurred* in doing his job. Nevertheless, until recently and despite the recommendations of two Hoover Commissions, the Congress attempted to exercise control through a limitation on obligations, which are essentially the cost of goods and services *purchased*. Since purchases are made by different persons from those who actually use the goods and services, and since they are made in different time periods from the time of consumption, this basis of control did not permit a matching of the control standard, the obligation, against the desired basis of control—costs incurred in responsibility centers. Although the practice is currently being corrected in the federal government, similar situations continue to exist in some businesses.

Inconsistencies between the standard desired by management and the standard as perceived by the organization also arise when aspects of performance are being measured in separate control systems. If a supervisor's performance as to quality is being measured in one system, his performance as to cost control in another, and his performance as to volume in a third, he may be uncertain as to the relative weights that he should attach to these three aspects of performance. He will tend to regard one of these aspects as more important than the others, but his choice may be different from what management actually intends.

RESPONSIBILITY CENTERS

In motivating and measuring performance, the control system is focused on the responsibility center, which is an organization unit headed by a responsible person. There are three types of responsibility centers: (1) expense centers, (2) profit centers (also called financial performance centers), and (3) investment centers.

Expense Centers

If the control system measures the expenses incurred by an organization unit, but does not measure the monetary value of its output, the unit is an expense center. Although every organization unit *has* outputs (i.e., it does something), in many cases it is neither feasible nor necessary to measure these outputs in monetary terms. It would be extremely difficult to measure the monetary value that the accounting department contributes to the whole business, for example, and although it would be relatively easy to measure the monetary value of the outputs of an individual production department, there is no reason for doing so if the responsibility of the factory foreman is simply to produce a stated *quantity* of output at the lowest feasible cost.

Thus most individual production departments and most staff units are expense centers. For these, the accounting system records expenses incurred, but not revenue earned.

Profit Centers

Revenue is a monetary measure of output, and expense is a monetary measure of inputs, or resources consumed. Profit is the difference between revenue and expense. Thus if performance in a responsibility center is measured in terms of both the revenue it earns and the cost it incurs, it is called a *profit center*.

Although in financial accounting, revenue is considered as being earned only when it is realized, in management accounting it is quite all right to define revenue as the value of the output of the center, whether realized or not. Thus, the factory may be a profit center, "selling" its production to the sales department; or service departments, such as the maintenance department, may "sell" their services to the departments receiving them.

Since the term "profit center" seems inappropriate in a nonprofit organization, the term "financial performance center" is used in such organizations for exactly the same concept.

The profit center concept is a powerful one. If properly operated, it has the effect of "putting the supervisor in business for himself," a business in which he can earn a profit. The development of this concept is one of the factors that has made possible the recent tendency for large companies to decentralize.

TRANSFER PRICE. A profit center is created by a conscious act of management. Usually, this requires that transfer prices be established. A transfer price is a price used to measure the exchange of products or services between responsibility centers within a company, as contrasted with a market price, which measures exchanges between a company and the outside world. Such internal exchanges result in revenue for the responsibility center furnishing the product or service and in cost for the responsibility center receiving the good or service. There are two general approaches to the construction of a transfer price: the market-based price, and the cost-based price.

If a market price for the product or service exists, such a price is usually preferable to a cost-based price. The "buying" responsibility center should not ordinarily be expected to pay more internally than it would have to pay if it purchased from the outside world, nor should the "selling" center ordinarily be entitled to more revenue than it could obtain by selling to the outside world. If the market price is abnormal, as for example when an outside vendor sets a low "distress" price in order to use temporarily idle capacity, then such temporary aberrations are ordinarily disregarded. The market price may be adjusted for cash discounts and for certain selling costs that are not involved in an internal exchange.

In a great many situations, there is no reliable market price that can be used as a basis for the transfer price, and in these situations, the transfer price is based on cost. Two general types of cost-based price are discussed in the literature: (1) marginal cost and (2) full cost plus profit. The marginal cost approach is consistent with the economic model of the firm that assumes that managers make decisions on the basis of complete knowledge of all factors affecting the firm, but it is not much used in practice.[3]

If the full cost approach is used, the method of computing cost and the amount of profit to be included is set by management in order to lessen

---

[3] For the argument for the marginal cost approach, see: Jack Hirshleifer, "On the Economics of Transfer Pricing," *Journal of Business* (July, 1956) pp. 172–84; and his "Economics of the Divisionalized Firm," *Journal of Business* (April, 1957) pp. 96–108.

arguments that would otherwise occur between the buying and the selling responsibility centers. If feasible, the cost should be a *standard* cost, for if it is an actual cost, the selling responsibility center can pass along its inefficiencies to the buying responsibility center; they will be included in the transfer price. The costs are not necessarily related to the costs actually incurred in the selling responsibility center; they may instead be built up from the costs that would be incurred by the most efficient producer, if these costs can be estimated. A transfer price based on such external costs may be a better measure of the output of the selling responsibility than a price based on the manufacturing practices and equipment actually being employed.

Whatever the approach to setting the transfer price, there is usually a mechanism for *negotiating* the price of actual transactions between the buying and the selling units. For example, the selling unit may be willing to reduce the normal market price in order to obtain the business, rather than having the buying unit take advantage of a temporarily low outside price, and the two parties negotiate such "deals." Unless the managers of responsibility centers have complete freedom to act, these negotiations will not always lead to an equitable result because the parties have unequal bargaining power; that is, the prospective buyer may not have the power of threatening to take his business elsewhere, and the prospective seller may not have the power to refuse to do the work. Thus, there usually needs to be an arbitration mechanism to settle disputes concerning transfer prices.

CRITERIA FOR PROFIT CENTERS. With some ingenuity, practically any expense center could conceivably be turned into a profit center, because some way of pricing its output can usually be found. Since the profit center concept is relatively new, its possibilities have by no means been fully exploited, and its use is growing rapidly. Its extension will be limited in accordance with criteria such as the following:

1. Extra record keeping is involved in a profit center to measure output, and in the receiving responsibility center to record costs. The gains in better information for decision making and in better motivation of managers must be important enough to offset these additional costs.

2. When top management *requires* responsibility centers to use a certain service (e.g., internal auditing), the service probably should be furnished at no charge, and the service unit therefore should not be a profit center.

3. If the manager of a responsibility center has little authority to decide on the quantity and quality of his outputs and on the relation of output to costs, then a profit center is usually of little value as a control device. This does not imply that the manager of a profit center must have complete control over outputs and inputs, for few if any managers have such authority.

4. If output is fairly homogeneous (e.g., cement), a nonmonetary measure of output (e.g., hundredweight of cement produced) may be adequate, and there may be no substantial gain in converting this to a monetary measure of revenue.

5. To the extent that a profit center puts a manager in business for himself, it promotes a spirit of competition. Up to a certain point, this is desirable, but beyond that point, the device may lead to too much friction between profit centers at the expense of the whole company's welfare, or too much interest in short-run "profits" to the detriment of long-run results (e.g., by undermaintaining his equipment). These difficulties are likely to arise when managers have an inadequate understanding of the management job, and they often can be overcome by education. If, however, they cannot be overcome, the profit center technique should be abandoned.

Investment Centers

An investment center is a responsibility center in which the manager is held responsible for the use of assets, as well as for revenues and expenses. It is therefore the ultimate extension of the responsibility idea. The manager is expected to earn a satisfactory return on *capital employed* in the responsibility center. Measurement of capital employed, or the *investment base*, poses many difficult problems, and the idea of the investment center is so new that there is considerable disagreement as to the best solution of these problems. For example, consider cash. The cash balance of the company is a safety valve, or shock absorber, protecting the company against short-run fluctuations in funds requirements. An investment center needs very little cash, however, since it can obtain funds on short notice from headquarters. Part of the headquarters cash balance therefore exists for the financial protection of the operating investment centers, and headquarters cash can therefore logically be allocated to the investment center as part of their capital employed. There are several ways of allocating this cash, just as there are several ways of allocating general overhead costs.

FIXED ASSETS. Perhaps the most controversial aspect of measuring capital employed has to do with fixed assets, both the machinery and other assets that are directly employed in the investment center, and an equitable share of the fixed assets that are allocated to the investment center (such as a building used by several investment centers). Assets may be valued at (1) replacement cost, which is usually measured by their insured value; (2) gross cost; or (3) net book value, which is gross cost less accumulated depreciation. Replacement cost, although conceptually sound, is rarely used because it cannot be substantiated by accounting records. Gross cost disregards differences in age, and hence in the accumulated depreciation; but it is widely used because the omission of depreciation may roughly counterbalance the omission of the effect of price inflation, which is not taken into account in the accounting records. Net book value has the advantage of being the figure that appears in the accounting records; but when this approach is used, an investment center with old, almost fully depreciated assets may show an extremely high rate of return solely for this reason.

DEPRECIATION METHODS. The method of depreciation affects not only the net book value of assets, but it also affects the amount of expense, and hence of profit, that is reported for the investment center. Various depreciation methods were discussed in Chapter 6. The annuity method, which was only briefly mentioned there because it is rarely used in financial accounting, appears to have merit in management accounting, although it is rarely used at present. The annuity method, coupled with profit calculated as a fixed percentage of the book value of assets, is the only method that provides a level charge each year, assuming no change in other costs, and it is a method that matches the method used to analyze proposed capital equipment acquisitions that will be described in Chapter 19.[4]

EFFECTIVENESS AND EFFICIENCY

The performance of the head of a responsibility center can be measured in terms of his "effectiveness" and his "efficiency." By effectiveness, we mean *how well* the manager does his job—that is (to quote the dictionary), "the extent to which he produces the intended or expected result." Efficiency is used in its engineering sense—that is, the amount of output per unit of input. An efficient machine generates a given quantity of outputs with a minimum consumption of inputs, or generates the largest possible outputs from a given quantity of inputs.

Effectiveness is always related to the organization's goals. Efficiency, per se, is not related to the goals. An efficient manager is one who does whatever he does with the lowest consumption of resources; but if what he does (i.e., his output) is an inadequate contribution to the accomplishment of the organization's goals, he is ineffective.

In many responsibility centers, a measure of efficiency can be developed that relates actual expenses to some standard—that is, to a number that expresses what expenses should be incurred for the amount of measured output. Such a measure can be a useful indication of efficiency, but it is never a perfect measure for at least two reasons: (1) recorded expenses are not a precisely accurate measure of resources consumed,

---

[4] For further discussion, see "Accounting for Capital Costs" in *Management Control Systems*, by Robert N. Anthony, John Dearden, and Richard F. Vancil (Homewood, Ill.: Richard D. Irwin, Inc., 1965), p. 343.

and (2) standards are, at best, only approximate measures of what resource consumption ideally should have been in the circumstances prevailing.

Effectiveness cannot be measured in financial terms in an expense center. Effectiveness is related to outputs, and in an expense center, by definition, outputs are not measured in financial terms. In some types of profit centers an approximate measure of effectiveness is possible. When one goal of the whole organization is to earn profits, then the contribution to this goal by a profit center is a measure of its effectiveness. This is so because in a profit center, by definition, the relationship between outputs and inputs is measured in monetary terms, and profit is a term describing such a relationship; that is, profit is the difference between revenue, which is a measure of output, and expense, which is a measure of input.

Actually, profit is influenced both by how effective a manager is and by how efficient he is; so profit measures both effectiveness and efficiency. When such an overall measure exists, it is unnecessary to determine the relative importance of effectiveness versus efficiency. When such an overall measure does not exist, it is feasible and useful to classify performance measures as relating either to effectiveness or to efficiency. In these situations, there is the problem of balancing the two types of measurements. For example, how do we compare the profligate perfectionist with the frugal manager who obtains less than the optimum output?

Profit is, at best, a crude measure of effectiveness and efficiency for several reasons: (1) monetary measures do not exactly measure either all aspects of outputs or all inputs, for reasons already given; (2) standards are not accurate; and (3) at best, profit is a measure of what has happened in the short run, whereas we are presumably also interested in the long-run consequences of decisions.

In view of the inadequacies of the profit measure, even under the best of circumstances, and in view of the absence of any profit measure in an expense center, many companies set other ways of measuring effectiveness. They may, for example, work out with the managers of responsibility centers a list of the objectives which are to be attained in the year—including such nonmonetary statements as, "Develop a new organization manual"; "Send three persons to management development programs"; "Reduce clerical errors by 50 percent"—and they then measure actual performance against these plans. This is called "management by objectives."

FUNCTION OF THE CONTROLLER

There is a tendency to regard the controller as the person who is primarily responsible for exercising control. Such an inference is natural because of the similarity between the two words, but it is erroneous. Generally, the controller is responsible for the design and operation of the *system* by means of which control information is collected and reported, but the *use* of this information in actual control is the responsibility of line management. The controller is something more than an accountant and something less than a chief executive. In addition to his responsibility for collecting figures, the controller may also be responsible for analyzing figures, for pointing out their significance to management, and for making recommendations as to what should be done. Moreover, he may police the adherence to limitations on spending laid down by the chief executive. He controls the integrity of the accounting system and is responsible for safeguarding assets from theft and fraud. In recent years the controller-ship function has become increasingly important in companies generally.

The controller does *not*, however (unless *de facto* he *is* the chief executive), make or enforce management decisions. The responsibility for control runs from the president down through the line organization, not through the controller, who is a staff officer.

Control of the Control System

Like a fruit tree, a management control system can become both unsightly and unproductive unless it is pruned periodically. What happens is that a new technique, usually in the form of a new report, is created to meet a particular problem, but once the problem has been solved, the report nevertheless continues. To avoid this result, companies either have a periodic overhaul of their control structure to eliminate such reports, or they have a person whose job is to ascertain that proposed new reports are likely to be worth the cost of preparing and using them and that existing reports continue to fill a real need. The work of keeping the system pruned is usually a function of the controller.

SUMMARY

Accounting information is useful in management control, a process that takes place after the objectives and strategies of an organization have been determined, and that is intended to assure managers that resources are used effectively and efficiently in the accomplishment of these objectives.

The scientific discipline most closely related to this process is social psychology, and its principles, rather than those of mathematics or economics, underlie the design of sound management control systems. Of these principles, the most important are those relating to motivation. The control system should be goal-congruent; that is, it should be designed so that when members of the organization are working in their own perceived self-interest they are also working toward the organization's objectives.

The control process involves the following sequential steps: (1) programming (which is also related to the process of strategic planning); (2) budgeting, which involves preparing and agreeing upon a plan for a specific time period, usually a year; (3) accounting, or the collection of information about what actually transpired during the period; and (4) reporting and analyzing performance, which essentially involves a comparison of actual outputs and inputs with planned outputs and inputs.

Management control focuses on responsibility centers. There are three types of responsibility centers: (1) expense centers, in which only inputs are measured in monetary terms; (2) profit centers (also called financial performance centers), in which both inputs and outputs are measured in monetary terms, the difference between them being profit—a recent development of great significance in control; and (3) investment centers, in which both profits and assets employed are measured in monetary terms—an even more recent and significant development.

In the measurement of performance, the focus is on effectiveness, which means how well the job was done, and on efficiency, which has to do with the amount of resources consumed in doing the job.

The control system is designed and operated by the controller, but he is not responsible for the acts of control; these are the responsibility of line management.

SUGGESTIONS FOR FURTHER READING

BARNARD, CHESTER I. *The Functions of the Executive.* Cambridge, Mass.: Harvard University Press, 1968.

BONINI, CHARLES P. et. al., eds. *Management Controls.* New York: McGraw-Hill Book Co., 1964.

JEROME, WILLIAM TRAVERS. *Executive Control; The Catalyst.* New York: John Wiley & Sons, Inc., 1961.

MARCH, JAMES G., and HERBERT A. SIMON. *Organizations.* New York: John Wiley & Sons, Inc., 1958.

TANNENBAUM, ARNOLD S. *Control in Organizations.* New York: McGraw-Hill Book Co., 1968.

CHAPTER **15**

CHARACTERISTICS OF COST

This chapter discusses some additional aspects of the nature and behavior of costs that are relevant in management accounting. A number of cost concepts have been described in previous chapters, viz, the distinction between:

—Capital costs and operating costs, i.e., between assets and expenses, in Chapter 6.
—Product costs and period costs, in Chapter 7.
—Historical costs and current costs, in Chapter 9.
—Direct, or traceable, costs and indirect (allocated, common, joint) costs, in Chapter 13.
—Actual costs and standard costs, in Chapter 13.
—Direct costs and full costs, in Chapter 13.
—Program, or product, costs and responsibility costs, in Chapter 13.

To this list, we add, in the current chapter, the distinction between:

—Variable and nonvariable costs.
—Controllable and noncontrollable costs.
—Engineered, discretionary, and committed costs.

Different Costs for Different Purposes

We emphasize again the point that the word "cost" is slippery. It is used indiscriminately with quite different meanings, and the reader or listener often has difficulty in deducing which meaning is intended. In particular, it is important to remember that there is no such thing as "the" cost of something in any situation in which joint or common costs are involved, and they are involved in most situations. When someone refers to "cost" under such circumstances, he may mean full costs, direct costs, variable costs, controllable costs, or whatever.

The appropriate definition depends on the purpose for which the cost is to be used. Consider the factory superintendent's salary. In costing a product for inventory purposes, some fraction of the superintendent's salary is usually included. For overall planning purposes, it is the whole amount of the salary, and not the fractions allocated to individual products, that needs to be studied. As the basis for certain specific decisions (such as whether to buy a new machine), the salary is completely excluded from the figures; for other types of decisions (such as whether to shut down the factory), the salary is an important consideration. In the evaluation of performance, only those costs for which the person being judged is responsible should be taken into account. Thus, in an appraisal of the performance of a departmental foreman, the superintendent's salary is not an element of cost, but in an appraisal of the performance of the whole company, it is. In summary, some of these purposes require the full amount of the actual salary, some require a fraction of that amount, some require an estimate of what the amount (full or fractional) will be in the future, and some require that the amount be completely omitted.

The fact that different purposes require different cost constructions is obvious, but failure to appreciate this fact is perhaps the most important cause both of the misuse of cost figures and of the common but unwarranted criticism that cost accountants can't be pinned down to a definite statement on what "the" cost is.

RELATION OF COSTS TO VOLUME

In general usage, the word "variable" means simply "changeable," but in accounting "variable" has a more restricted meaning. It refers not to changes that take place over time, or to changes associated with the seasons, but only to changes associated with the *level of activity*, that is, with volume. If a cost goes up as volume goes up, it is a variable cost; otherwise, it is not. More specifically, we can distinguish three types of cost patterns: variable, nonvariable, and semivariable (or partly variable).

Variable costs vary directly and proportionately with volume; that is, as volume increases by 10 percent, the cost also increases by 10 percent. Direct labor, direct material, lubricants, power costs, and supplies often are examples of variable costs.

Nonvariable costs do not vary at all with volume. Building depreciation, property taxes, supervisory salaries, and occupancy costs (heat and light) often behave in this fashion. These costs are incurred with the passage of time, and are independent of the level of activity within a time period. They are sometimes called "fixed" costs, but this term implies that they cannot be changed, which is not so.

Semivariable costs vary directly, but less than proportionately, with volume; that is, as volume increases by 10 percent, the cost increases, but by less than 10 percent. Examples may be indirect labor, maintenance, and clerical costs.

Illustration 15–1

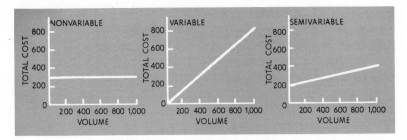

A generalized picture of the behavior of these types of cost is shown in Illustration 15–1. The nonvariable cost is $300 regardless of the level of activity; the variable cost is $0.80 per unit of volume; and the semivariable cost starts at $200 and increases at a rate of $0.20 per unit of volume. Note that the semivariable cost can be decomposed into two elements, a nonvariable element of $200 and a variable element of $0.20 per unit.

Cost-Volume Diagrams

A characteristic of the cost-volume diagrams shown in Illustration 15–1 should be noted, since it is common to all diagrams showing the relationship between cost and volume: cost is always plotted on the vertical, or *y*, axis, and volume is plotted on the horizontal, or *x*, axis. A conventional rule in geometry is that the "dependent variable" is plotted on the *y* axis and the "independent variable" is plotted on the *x* axis. In the above diagrams, therefore, cost is implicitly assumed to be the "dependent variable" and volume the "independent variable." In these diagrams, the measure of volume is not defined; various possibilities will be described in a subsequent section.

Behavior of Total Costs

If the separate cost elements behave according to one of the three patterns shown above, then the total cost, which is the sum of these separate elements, must vary with volume, as shown in Illustration 15–2, which was constructed simply by merging the separate elements shown in Illustration 15–1.

Since the semivariable item can be split into nonvariable and variable components, the *behavior of total costs can be described in terms of only two components—a total amount, and an amount per unit of volume.* In Illustration 15–2, the nonvariable amount is $500 and the variable amount is $1 per unit of volume. There is therefore no need to consider semivariable costs as a separate category; from this point on, we shall consider only the nonvariable and variable components.

Illustration 15–2

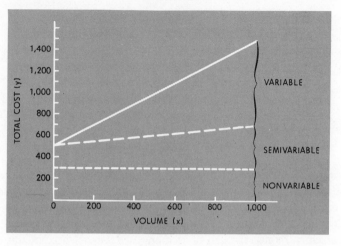

Cost Assumptions

Illustration 15–2 is based on several implicit assumptions as to the behavior of costs, two of which are discussed below. The first is usually a reasonable one, but the second is actually quite unrealistic.

THE LINEAR ASSUMPTION. One cost behavior assumption is that all costs behave according to one of the three patterns described above. Actually, some costs may vary in steps, as in Illustration 15–3. This happens when the cost occurs in discrete "chunks," as when one indirect worker is added for every 160 additional hours of direct labor per week. Others may vary along a curve rather than a straight line, and others, such as maintenance of idle machines, may actually decrease as volume increases.

In most situations, however, the effect of these discontinuities and nonlinear cost functions on total costs is minor, and the assumption that

Illustration 15–3

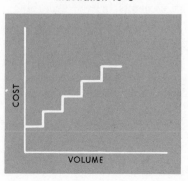

total costs vary in a linear relationship with volume is a satisfactory working approximation. This is a most fortunate fact. Many theoretical treatises discuss cost functions with various types of complicated curves. The formulas for these functions are difficult to understand and to work with. Such complicated curves are rarely used in practice, for it is usually found that the simple straight line, although perhaps not a perfect representation of cost-volume relationships, is close enough for practical purposes.

FULL-RANGE ASSUMPTION. A second cost behavior assumption implicit in Illustration 15–2 is that costs move along a straight line throughout *the whole range* of volume. This is unrealistic. At zero volume, for example, when the factory is shut down, a special set of conditions operate, and these may make costs considerably higher or considerably lower than the $500 shown in the diagram. When production gets so high that a second shift is required, costs may behave quite differently from the way in which they behave under one-shift operations. Even within the limits of a single shift, it is to be expected that costs will behave differently when the factory is busy, from the way they do when it is operating at low volume levels. In short, a single straight line gives a good approximation of the behavior of costs *only within a certain range of volume*. We can indicate this fact by using a straight line for the range within which the relationship is valid, and using a dotted line simply to indicate where an extension of the line crosses the *y* axis, as shown in Illustration 15–4.

Illustration 15–4 shows the same cost pattern as Illustration 15–2, but the solid line representing total costs now extends only over a selected range of volume, here 600 units to 1,200 units. The dotted line extending back to zero does not imply that costs will behave in this fashion at low

Illustration 15–4

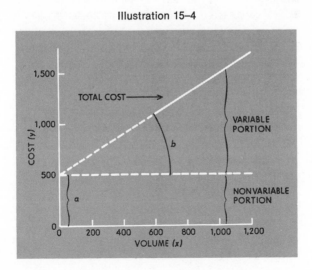

volumes; rather it is drawn on the diagram solely as a means of finding the nonvariable component of total costs.

Formula for the Cost Line

As already pointed out, cost at any volume is the sum of the nonvariable component ($500) and the variable component ($1 per unit). For example, at a volume of 1,000 units, cost is $500 + ($1 per unit times 1,000 units) = $1,500. Designating cost as y, volume as x, the nonvariable component as a, and the variable component as b, the cost at any volume can be found from the formula, $y = a + bx$; this is simply the general formula for a straight line.[1] For example, $1,500 = $500 + ($1) (1,000).

If the values of a and b for a given line are not known, they can be deduced provided total costs are known for any two points or volume levels on the line. One method of doing this is as follows:

1. Subtract total cost at the lower volume from total cost at the higher volume, and subtract lower volume from higher volume.
2. Divide the difference in cost by the difference in volume, which gives b, the amount by which cost changes with a change of one unit of volume.
3. Multiply either of the volumes, x, by b and subtract the result from the total cost at that volume, thus removing the variable component and leaving the nonvariable component, a.

Unit Costs

It should be emphasized that the line we are studying shows *total* costs at various volumes. This line should not be confused with a line showing *unit* costs. If total costs have a linear relationship with volume, then unit costs will be a curve, showing how unit costs decrease as volume increases. Illustration 15–5, is a unit cost curve derived from Illustration 15–4.

Estimating Cost-Volume Relationship

In many practical situations costs are expected to vary with volume in the straight-line relationship shown in Illustration 15–4. The formula for this line of expected costs can be estimated by any of the following methods:

1. Estimate the cost at any two volumes in order to establish two points on the line. Find the values of a and b by the method described above. (This is sometimes called the "high-low" method because one of

---

[1] In many geometry texts, the notation used is: $y = mx + b$. In such a notation, m represents the slope, or cost per unit, and b represents the nonvariable component.

Illustration 15–5

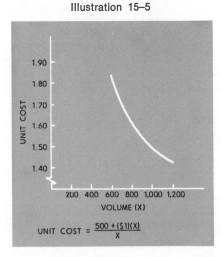

the volumes selected is likely to be high, and the other is likely to be low.)

2. Estimate the cost at one volume, and estimate how cost will change with a given change in volume. This gives *b* directly, and *a* can be found by subtraction, as described above.

3. Build up separate estimates of the behavior of each of the elements that make up total cost.

4. Make a "scatter diagram" in which actual costs recorded in past periods are plotted against the volume levels in those periods, and draw a line that best fits these observations. Such a diagram is shown in Illustration 15–6. A statistical technique, called the "method of least squares" may be used to find the line of best fit (see Appendix), but in many cases a line drawn by visual inspection is just as good as, and in some cases it is better than, a mathematically fitted line.

Illustration 15–6

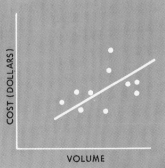

PROBLEMS WITH SCATTER DIAGRAMS.   Estimating cost-volume relationships by means of a scatter diagram is a common practice, but the results
can be misleading. In the first place, this technique shows, at best, what
the relationship was in the past, whereas we are interested in what it is
now or what it will be in the future. The past is not necessarily a mirror
of the present or the future. Also, the relationship we seek is that
obtaining under a *single set of conditions*, whereas each point on a scatter
diagram may represent changes in factors other than the two being
studied, namely, cost and volume.

Illustration 15–7 shows a common source of difficulty. In this scatter
diagram, volume is represented by sales revenue, as is often the case. Each

Illustration 15–7

SCATTER DIAGRAM, ILLUSTRATING DRIFT

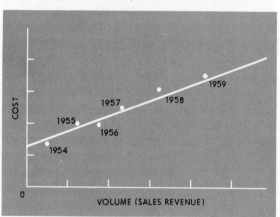

dot is located by plotting the cost for one year on the *y* axis and the sales
revenue for that year on the *x* axis. The dots lie along a well-defined path,
which is indicated by the straight line, but this line may *not* indicate the
present relationship between cost and volume. It may, instead, indicate
nothing more than the tendency for both revenue and cost to increase
over the past six years because of inflationary factors. If this is the case,
then the line shows the trend, or *drift*, of costs *through time*, not the
probable relationship between cost and volume *at a given time*. Any
scatter diagram covering a period of years in which sales were generally
increasing each year, or generally decreasing each year, is likely to have
this characteristic, and the longer the period covered, the more unreliable
the diagram becomes.

If, in order to avoid this difficulty, the figures for only the most recent
years are plotted on the diagram, there may not be enough difference in

the volumes of the several periods to indicate a reliable line of relationship. The choice of a series of observations that are recent enough so that they do not reflect an obsolete set of conditions, yet which cover a wide enough volume range to permit the drawing of a satisfactory line, is a difficult matter.

Sometimes, statistical techniques are used to adjust, or "deflate," historical observations so as to allow for changes in price and other factors. As a minimum, the historical relationship should be adjusted for anticipated changes in the underlying conditions.

Whatever the method used for estimating the relationship, the result is a line, described by the formula $y = a + bx$, which shows how costs are expected to vary with volume.

We have described the line as referring to total costs. The same technique can be used to study various parts of the total. In fact, it is common to restrict analyses of this type to overhead costs, since direct material and direct labor are presumed to be purely variable.

Measures of Volume

Thus far, "volume" has been used as an abstract concept. In a real situation, it must be measured in some concrete fashion. The best measuring stick of volume is one that most closely reflects the conditions that cause costs to change. Two basic questions must be answered: (1) Should the measuring stick be based on input or should it be based on output? and (2) Should the measuring stick be expressed in monetary terms or should it be expressed in physical quantities? Within each general category, there are many specific possibilities. The following discussion is limited to indirect costs, for it is here that the choice of the best measure of volume is especially important.

Input measures relate to the resources being used in the cost center; examples are the number of actual direct labor hours worked, actual machine-hours operated, or the pounds of raw material used. *Output measures* relate to the amount of product coming out of the center; examples are units of product completed or the standard direct labor costs absorbed by products worked on. Since indirect cost is itself an element of input, in many situations it tends to vary more closely with other input factors than with output. For example, it is reasonable to expect that indirect cost items associated with direct labor, such as fringe benefits, social security taxes, and payroll accounting, tend to vary more closely with the actual quantity of direct labor used than with the standard labor content of products produced. In general, an input measure is likely to be more accurate than an output measure. Some overhead costs, such as inspection costs and plant transportation, however, might vary more closely with the quantity of products produced.

A measuring stick expressed in physical quantities, such as direct labor hours, is often better than one expressed in dollars, such as direct labor cost, because the former is unaffected by changes in prices. A wage increase would cause direct labor costs to increase, even if there were no actual increase in the volume of activity. On the other hand, if price changes are likely to affect both labor and overhead to the same degree, the use of a monetary measuring stick may be a means of allowing implicitly for the effect of these price changes.

These theoretical considerations must be tempered by practicality. Total direct labor costs are often available in the cost system without extra calculation, whereas the computation of total direct labor hours, or machine-hours, may require considerable additional work. Also, since the measuring stick of volume for control purposes is often (but not always) the same as that used in allocating overhead costs to products for the purpose of financial accounting, the appropriateness of the measure for the latter purpose must also be taken into account.

The Overhead Rate and Standard Volume

It will be recalled from Chapter 13 that the overhead rate for product costing purposes is found by dividing total overhead costs by a measure of activity. When the same measure of activity is used in a cost-volume diagram, such as that in Illustration 15–4, this total overhead cost is one point on the cost line. This point is the total cost expected at *standard volume* (or *normal volume*).

Standard volume is defined in one of three ways. In some companies, it is the volume anticipated for the next year or other short period of time; in other companies, it is the average volume expected over a number of years in the future, and in still other companies it is the volume at capacity operations. Overhead costs *per unit* (i.e., the overhead rate) decrease as volume increases because the same amount of nonvariable cost is spread over a larger number of units. Therefore, the overhead rates resulting from the application of one of these three concepts of standard volume can differ substantially from one another.

When the standard volume is taken as the volume expected next year, total overhead costs incurred in the year will be approximately absorbed onto products if the estimates are made with reasonable accuracy. This method therefore meets the objective of financial accounting. It may, however, cause difficulty if the costs are being used as a basis for pricing, for unit costs will tend to be high in a year of low volume. If the low volume implies a business recession, the high unit cost may lead to an increase in selling prices at the very time when it is probably most unwise to attempt such an increase.

A standard volume based on an average of several years is used by automobile manufacturers and by a number of other leading companies. It avoids the pricing paradox mentioned above, but does result in a large variance in a year of abnormally high or abnormally low volume.

A measure based on capacity is not widely used, except by companies that expect to operate at capacity, and in these situations it is the same as the first method. "Capacity" means, not the theoretical maximum amount of product that can be produced if everything goes perfectly, but rather "practical capacity," which is a reasonably attainable amount. It may mean the capacity of 40 hours a week, or 168 hours a week, or anywhere in between.

THE PROFITGRAPH

The cost/volume diagram in Illustration 15–4 can be turned into a useful device called the *profitgraph* (or "Profit-Volume graph," or "P/V graph") simply by the addition of a revenue line to it, for a profitgraph is a diagram showing the expected relationship between cost and revenue at various volumes.[2] On a profitgraph, the measure of volume may be the number of units produced and sold, or it may be sales revenue. We have already stated the formula for the cost line: $y = a + bx$.

Revenue is plotted on the assumption of a constant selling price per unit. Assuming that volume is to be measured as units of product, and designating the unit selling price as p, total revenue (y) at any volume (x) equals the unit selling price (p) times the number of units of volume (x); or, for revenue $y = px$. For example, if the unit selling price is $2, the total revenue from 1,000 units will be $2,000.

A profitgraph of these relationships is shown in Illustration 15–8. Note that as on Illustration 15–4, the lines are dotted at very low volumes to emphasize the fact that the relationships are expected to hold only within a limited volume range (in practice, the lines are usually drawn solid throughout, and it therefore is easy to overlook the fact that the relationship is not valid outside the normal range).

At the *break-even volume*, cost equals revenue. (This is simply a geometric fact; the break-even point is of little practical interest in a profitable company, since attention is focused on the profit area considerably above it.) At lower volumes, a loss is expected; and at higher volumes, a profit is expected. The amount of loss or profit expected at any volume is the difference between points on the cost and revenue lines at that volume. The break-even volume is not the same as the "normal" volume used as a basis for determining the overhead rate. In a profitable business, normal volume is considerably higher than the break-even volume.

---

[2] This device is also called a "break-even chart," but such a label has the unfortunate implication that the objective of a business is merely to break even.

Illustration 15–8

A PROFITGRAPH

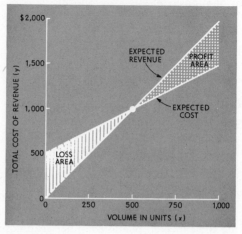

Construction of a Profitgraph

If volume (the x axis) is expressed in terms of sales revenue, the revenue line on a profitgraph is simply the straight line $y = x$. If volume is expressed as number of units sold, revenue at any volume is found from the formula $y = px$, as described above. Sometimes several revenue lines are drawn on a profitgraph, each one showing what revenue would be at that selling price. This procedure helps to show how a change in selling price affects the profit at any given volume.

Interpretation of the Profitgraph

The profitgraph is a useful device for analysis of the overall profit characteristics of a business. To illustrate such an analysis, assume the following situation, which is the same as that shown in previous diagrams:

Nonvariable costs...............................$500
Variable costs...................................$1 per unit
Normal volume..................................1,000 units
Selling price....................................$2 per unit

In this situation, total costs at normal volume will be $500 (nonvariable) plus $1,000 (variable), or $1,500. The cost of the product as shown on the accounting records will therefore be $1,500 ÷ 1,000 units, or $1.50 per unit. At a selling price of $2 per unit, the normal profit will be $0.50 per unit.

COMPUTATION OF BREAK-EVEN VOLUME. Recall that the break-even volume is the volume at which cost equals revenue.

Since revenue (y) at any volume (x) is $\hspace{4cm}$ $y = px$
And cost (y) at any volume (x) is $\hspace{4.3cm}$ $y = a + bx$
And since at the break-even volume, cost = revenue:
Therefore the break-even volume is the volume at which $\hspace{1cm}$ $px = a + bx$

If we let x equal the break-even volume, then for the above situation, we have

$$\$2x = \$500 + \$1x$$
$$x = 500 \text{ units.}$$

At the break-even volume of 500 units, revenue equals 500 units × $2 per unit, which is $1,000, and cost equals $500 + (500 units × $1 per unit), which is also $1,000.

MARGINAL INCOME. From the relationships of cost and revenue at various volumes, an important conclusion can be drawn: although the normal profit is $0.50 per unit, this unit profit will be earned *only* at the normal volume. At lower volumes the profit will be less than $0.50 per unit, and at higher volumes it will be more than $0.50 per unit. The relationship between cost, revenue, and volume can be summed up by the statement that for each change of one unit in volume, profit will change by $1. This $1 is the *marginal income*, the difference between selling price and *variable cost* per unit. Below the break-even point, losses will be incurred at the rate of $1 for each unit decrease in volume.

The break-even volume can also be determined by the relationship between nonvariable costs and marginal income. In the illustrative situation where the marginal income is $1 per unit and nonvariable costs are $500, 500 units must be sold before enough revenue will be earned to cover nonvariable costs. After that, a profit of $1 per unit will be earned.

Improving Profit Performance

These revenue-cost-volume relationships suggest that a useful way of studying the profit factors of a business is to consider, not the profit per unit (which is different at every volume), but rather the nonvariable costs and the marginal income, which is the difference between selling price and marginal cost. In these terms, there are four, and only four, ways in which the profit of a business can be increased:

1. Increase selling prices per unit.
2. Decrease variable costs per unit.
3. Decrease nonvariable costs.
4. Increase volume.

The separate effects of each of these possibilities are shown in the following calculations and in Illustration 15–9. Each starts from the current situation, assumed to be "normal" (selling price, $2; variable costs,

Illustration 15–9

EFFECT OF 10 PERCENT CHANGE IN PROFIT FACTORS

A. Increase Selling Price   B. Decrease Variable Cost

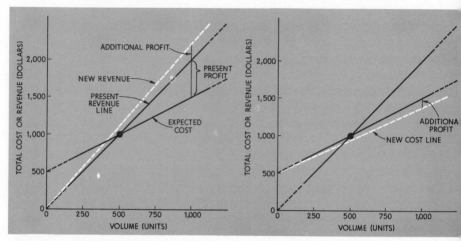

C. Decrease Nonvariable Cost   D. Increase Volume

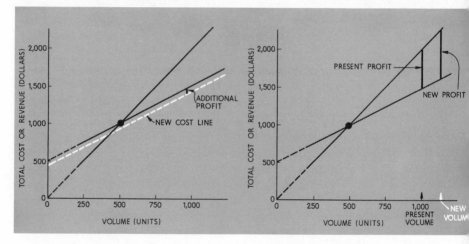

$1 per unit; nonvariable costs, $500; and volume, 1,000 units). The effect of a 10 percent change in each factor is calculated:

A. A 10 percent increase in selling price would add $200 to revenue and would therefore increase the current profit of $500 by 40 percent.

B. A 10 percent decrease in variable cost would reduce variable costs by $100 and would therefore increase profit by 20 percent.

C. A 10 percent decrease in nonvariable cost would amount to $50, and would result in an increase in profit of 10 percent.

D. A 10 percent increase in volume would increase profit by the marginal income of $1 per unit times an additional 100 units, or $100, an increase of 20 percent.

If we look at some of the interrelationships, we can calculate, for example, that a 20 percent (i.e., $100) increase in nonvariable costs could be offset by a 5 percent increase in selling price, a 10 percent increase in volume, or a 10 percent decrease in variable costs.

Another calculation made from a profitgraph is the *margin of safety*. This is the amount or ratio by which the current volume exceeds the break-even volume. Assuming current volume is 1,000 units, the margin of safety in our illustrative situation is 500 units, or 50 percent, of current volume. Sales volume can decrease by 50 percent before a loss is incurred, other factors remaining equal.

Limitations on Profitgraph Analysis

The foregoing calculations assume that each of the factors is independent of the others, a situation that is rarely the case in the real world. An increase in selling price often is accompanied by a decrease in volume, for example. Changes in the factors must therefore usually be studied simultaneously rather than separately as was done above.

Also, the diagram assumes that the company, in effect, sells only one product. If several products with different marginal incomes are sold, the profitgraph for the whole company shows the average marginal income for all products, and is affected by changes in the mix of products. Under these circumstances, profitgraphs for each product, or for each group of approximately homogeneous products, are more useful for analysis than is the single overall diagram.

The profitgraph analysis also implicitly assumes that changes in the four factors are not accompanied by changes in the amount of capital employed. If a decrease in variable cost arises because of the purchase of a new machine, for example, the effect on the return on investment is not given by the profitgraph. In part, the effect shows up as an increase in the nonvariable depreciation cost, but one cannot tell from this alone what the effect is on the overall rate of return.

MARGINAL INCOME ANALYSIS STATEMENT

The marginal income idea suggests a way of recasting the conventional income statement so as to provide more useful information to management. Illustration 15–10 shows such a recasting for a dry cleaning and laundry business. The top section is the conventional income statement. The lower section shows the same basic information in the form of a "Marginal Income Analysis Report."

Illustration 15–10

MARGINAL INCOME ANALYSIS STATEMENT

A. Conventional Income Statement for June

Sales...		$3,540
Salaries...	$1,640	
Supplies..	900	
Heat, light, power...................................	210	
Employer's payroll tax...............................	89	
Advertising..	88	
Telephone..	66	
Rent...	100	
Depreciation...	483	
Amortization of leasehold improvements...............	140	
Insurance..	95	
Total expenses.......................................		3,811
Net Loss...		$(271)

B. Same Data Recast in Format of a Marginal
Income Analysis Report

		Dry Cleaning		Laundry
Sales......................................		$2,800		$740
Variable costs:				
Salaries.................................	$ 790		$200	
Supplies.................................	760		140	
Heat, light, power.......................	150		25	
Employer's payroll tax...................	43	1,743	10	375
Contribution to nonvariable costs..........		$1,057		$365
Less: Depreciation on equipment...........		200		100
Contribution to unassigned nonvariable costs.......	$1,122	$ 857		$265
Unassigned nonvariable costs:				
Salaries...........................	$650			
Advertising........................	88			
Telephone..........................	66			
Heat, light, power.................	35			
Employer's payroll tax.............	36			
Rent...............................	100			
Depreciation.......................	183			
Amortization.......................	140			
Insurance..........................	95	1,393		
Net Loss for the Period.............		$ 271		

SOURCE: Adapted from material collected by Professor W. W. Haynes, University of Kentucky, and Professor J. L. Gibson, Arlington State College, for the Small Business Administration.

To construct this report, the cost elements are first segregated into variable and nonvariable categories. For some items (e.g., heat, light, and power in the illustration), part of the cost is variable and part is nonvariable. For each activity, the variable costs relating to the activity are subtracted from revenue, giving the marginal income, or, as labeled here, "contribution to nonvariable costs." In the illustration, nonvariable costs assignable to each activity (i.e., depreciation on equipment) are also shown, although this is not always done. Then the other nonvariable costs are listed, but they are not allocated among activities.

The message given by the conventional statement is quite different from that given by the marginal statement. In the conventional statement, the message is that the business as a whole was operated at a loss; a breakdown into its two elements, dry cleaning and laundry, would show that on a full-cost basis, each of them was operating at a loss, and the argument could easily be made that one or the other of these elements should be discontinued in order to reduce losses. The marginal statement shows that each of the elements made a contribution to nonvariable costs, and that losses would therefore not be reduced by discontinuing either of them. Indeed, other things being equal, the loss would be $1,057 greater if the dry cleaning segment were discontinued and $365 greater if the laundry segment were discontinued.

In the illustration, the revenue and variable costs are broken down by revenue-earning activities. Marginal income analysis statements are also prepared in which the breakdown is by products or product groups.

LEARNING CURVES

Cost-volume diagrams and profitgraphs are two-dimensional; they show only what happens to cost when volume changes. Actually, costs change for a variety of other reasons, such as (1) changes in price levels (e.g., inflation), as already noted; (2) changes in efficiency (e.g., Parkinson's first law: "Costs tend to increase, regardless of the work done"); and (3) productivity. Many studies have shown that the change in cost associated with a change in productivity has, in many situations, a characteristic curve that can be estimated with reasonable accuracy. This is called the *learning curve*, or the *experience curve*.

The phenomenon was first observed in the aircraft industry, where it was found that certain costs tend to decrease, per unit, in a predictable pattern as the workers and their supervisors become more familiar with the work; as the flow of work, tooling, and methods improve; as less scrap and rework result; as fewer skilled workers need to be used; and so on. The decreasing costs are a function of the learning process, which results in fewer and fewer man-hours being necessary to produce a unit of product as more units of the same product are completed. It should be noted, however, that not all costs decrease; for instance, material costs are not usually subject to the learning process, although they may decrease to the extent to which waste is eliminated. Packaging and trucking costs are other examples of costs that usually are not subject to the learning process.

The research done in the aircraft industry indicates that there is probably an average learning curve rate that can be applied to the increase in production efficiency, insofar as costs subject to the learning function are concerned. This rate approximates an "80 percent curve," which means that when quantities of production are doubled on an item, cumulative average man-hours per unit should be reduced 20 percent. As an illustration of this concept, assume that a company has purchased 250 machined castings at $50 each from XYZ Company. To simplify this case, assume further that material costs are insignificant and that the elements of labor, overhead, selling, and administration expense and profit, which make up the $50 per unit price, all vary in relation to the man-hours

Illustration 15–11

EIGHTY PERCENT LEARNING CURVE—MACHINED CASTINGS

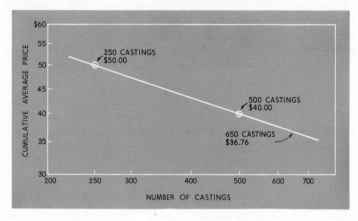

required to produce one machined casting; that is to say, all the elements of the $50 price are subject to the learning curve. Before production of the 250 castings has been completed, another 400 castings of the same type are ordered from the XYZ Company. What should the additional 400 castings cost?

Assuming that an "80 percent curve" can be applied in this situation, the $50 price is plotted at the 250-unit quantity level on log-log graph paper (see Illustration 15–11). The second point on the graph is established at double the quantity and 80 percent of the price of the first order. A straight line is drawn through and extended past these two points. (Log-log graph paper shows the 80 percent curve as a straight line, whereas arithmetic graph paper shows the 80 percent curve as a complex curve that is difficult to plot.) The point on this line that locates the sum of the quantities of the old and new orders (250 plus 400 units) indicates also the cumulative average unit price for the total units, or $36.76.

Multiplying the total quantity of 650 units by the new cumulative average price of $36.76 gives the *total cost* for *both* orders, $23,894. Because the first order of 250 castings cost $12,500 in total, this is subtracted from the total price of both orders. The remaining $11,394 is divided by the number of units to be purchased in the new order (400) to give the estimated unit cost of $28.48 for the new castings.

This characteristic decline in unit costs as an increasing number of units are produced does not come about automatically; rather, it depends on management efforts to force costs down. It is important that the existence of the learning phenomenon be recognized and exploited; otherwise, management may be satisfied with cost performance as indicated on a cost-volume graph, whereas such costs may be significantly too high.

CONTROLLABLE COSTS

An element of cost is controllable if the amount of cost incurred in (or charged to) a responsibility center is significantly influenced by the actions of the manager of that responsibility center. Otherwise, it is noncontrollable. There are two important implications of this definition: (1) it refers to a specific responsibility center, and (2) it suggests that controllability results from *some* influence, rather than *complete* influence.

The word "controllable" must be used in the context of a specific responsibility center, rather than as an innate characteristic of a given cost element; because when the organization is viewed as a complete entity, all costs are controllable. For any element of cost, there is someone, somewhere in the company, who can take actions that influence it. In the extreme case, costs for any segment of the business can be reduced to zero by closing down that segment; costs incurred in manufacturing a component can be changed by purchasing that component, and so on. Thus, the important question is not what costs are controllable in general, but rather what costs are controllable in a given responsibility center, for it is these costs on which the management control system must focus.

Degree of Influence

The definition refers to a "significant" influence rather than to "complete" influence because only in rare cases does one individual have complete control over *all* the factors that influence a given cost element. The influence of the foreman of a manufacturing department over labor costs may actually be quite limited, since wage rates may be established by the personnel department or by union negotiations; the amount of labor required for a unit of product may be largely determined by the engineers who designed the product and who specified how it was to be manufactured; and the number of units produced, and hence total labor costs, may be influenced by the output of some other department, by the ability of the purchasing department to obtain materials, or by a variety of other factors. Nevertheless, the foreman usually has a significant influence on the amount of direct labor cost incurred. He has some control over the amount of idle time in his department, the speed and efficiency with which work is done, and other factors which to some extent affect labor costs.

The use of a *standard cost* is one way of distinguishing between those parts of a cost element for which a person is responsible and those for which he is not. A standard labor cost, for example, presumably states what the cost should be, considering the influence of wage rates, product design, and other factors over which the foreman has no control. Ideally, the difference between standard cost and actual cost incurred represents the effect of actions by the foreman, and it is this difference for which the foreman is held responsible. As explained in Chapter 17, there are many reasons why this concept does not work out precisely in practice, but it nevertheless may work well enough to provide an acceptable basis for control.

Direct material and direct labor costs are usually controllable. With respect to the overhead costs in a cost center, some are controllable and others are not. Indirect labor, supplies, and electricity are usually controllable. So are charges from service centers based on services actually rendered by the service center. By definition, *an allocated cost is not controllable;* the amount of the charge varies in accordance with the formula used for allocation, not with the actions of the supervisor. This is so unless the cost is actually a direct cost that is allocated only for convenience, as in the case of social security taxes on direct labor that are as controllable as other elements of the direct labor cost.

CONTRAST WITH DIRECT COSTS.   Controllable costs are not synonymous with direct costs. All controllable costs are direct since by definition an allocated cost is not controllable, but not all direct costs are controllable. For example, depreciation on departmental equipment is a direct cost of the department, but the depreciation charge is often noncontrollable by the departmental supervisor since he may have no authority to acquire or dispose of equipment. The rental charge for rented premises is another example of a direct but noncontrollable cost.

CONTRAST WITH VARIABLE COSTS.   Neither are controllable costs necessarily the same as *variable costs.* Variable costs vary with volume. Some costs, such as indirect labor, heat, light, and magazine subscriptions, may be unaffected by volume, but they are nevertheless controllable. Conversely, some variable costs are noncontrollable. Raw material and parts, whose consumption varies directly with volume, may be entirely outside the influence of the departmental supervisor. For example, in an automobile assembly department, the fact is that the car requires an engine, a body, five wheels, and so on, and there is nothing the supervisor can do about it. He is responsible for waste and spoilage of material, but not for the main flow of material itself.

Similarly, direct labor, which is usually thought of as the prime example of a controllable cost, may be noncontrollable in certain types of responsibility centers. If, for example, an assembly line has 20 work stations and cannot be operated unless it is manned by 20 persons of specified skills and hence specified wage rates, direct labor cost on that assembly line may be noncontrollable. Situations of this type must be examined very carefully, however, in order to insure that the noncontrollability is real. Supervisors tend to argue that more costs are noncontrollable than actually is the case, in order to avoid being held responsible for them.

Converting Noncontrollable Costs to Controllable Costs

A noncontrollable element of cost can be converted to a controllable element of cost in two related ways: (1) by changing the management control system; and/or (2) by changing the locus of responsibility for decisions.

CONVERTING ALLOCATED COSTS TO DIRECT COSTS. By definition, allocated costs are noncontrollable. Many elements of costs that are allocated to responsibility centers could be made into controllable costs simply by devising a method of charging the cost that reflects actions taken by the head of the responsibility center. To take the simplest situation, if all electricity coming into a plant is measured by a single meter, there is no way of measuring the actual electrical consumption of each department in the plant, and the electrical cost is therefore necessarily allocated for each department and is noncontrollable. This cost element can be changed to a controllable cost for the several departments in the plant simply by installing electrical meters in each department.

Similarly, services that a responsibility center receives from service units can be converted to controllable costs by charging these costs to the responsibility center on some basis that measures the services actually rendered.

EXAMPLE: As described in Chapter 14, if maintenance costs are charged to responsibility centers as a part of an overhead rate, they are noncontrollable; but if responsibility centers are charged on the basis of an hourly rate for each hour that a maintenance man works there and if the head of the responsibility center can influence the requests for maintenance work, then maintenance is a controllable element of cost.

As pointed out in Chapter 13, practically any element of overhead cost could conceivably be converted to a direct cost, but for some (such as charging the president's salary on the basis of the time he spends on the problems of various parts of the business), the effort involved in doing so clearly is more than the benefit that would be derived. There are nevertheless a great many unexploited opportunities in most companies.

The same principle applies to costs actually incurred in a responsibility center but which are not charged to the responsibility center at all, even on an allocated basis. Under these circumstances, the material or services are "free" insofar as the head of the responsibility center is concerned, and since he does not have to "pay" for them (as part of the costs for which he is held responsible), there is little reason to expect him to be concerned about careful use of the resources that these costs represent.

DECENTRALIZATION. The most important decisions affecting costs are made at or near the top of an organization, both because people at the top presumably have more ability and because they have a broader viewpoint. On the other hand, the farther removed these decisions are from the "firing line," the place where resources are actually used, the less responsive they can be to conditions currently existing at the point of spending. Although there is no way of drawing a precise line, an organization in which a relatively high proportion of decisions are made at the top is said to be *centralized,* and one in which lower level managers can make relatively more decisions is said to be *decentralized.*

In the context of our present discussion, a decentralized organization is one in which a relatively large fraction of costs are controllable in the lower levels of responsibility centers. Many companies have found that, given a good system for controlling performance, they can safely delegate responsibility for many decisions affecting cost and thus take advantage of the knowledge of the man who is on the spot where spending actually occurs. Perhaps the most dramatic example of a shift from centralized to decentralized management is the change that has taken place in Communist countries. Beginning with Yugoslavia in the 1950's, and later extending to the U.S.S.R., there has been a recognition that the highly centralized planning and control process envisioned by Lenin simply does not work well in practice; consequently, individual plant managers have been given much more authority to make decisions affecting the costs of their plants.

Recording Noncontrollable Costs

In control reports, it is obviously essential that controllable costs be distinguished from noncontrollable costs. Some people argue that the *separation* of controllable from noncontrollable costs is not enough; they insist that noncontrollable costs should not even be recorded in a management accounting system. Actually, there may be good reasons for charging all, or certain types of, noncontrollable costs to responsibility centers.

One reason is that management may want the supervisor to be concerned about such costs, the expectation being that his concern may indirectly lead to better cost control. For example, an operating unit may be charged with part of the costs of the personnel department, even though the foreman of the unit has no direct responsibility for that department. Such a charge can be justified either on the ground that the foreman will be careful about making unnecessary requests of the personnel department if he is made to feel some responsibility for personnel department costs, or on the ground that the foreman may in various ways influence the head of the personnel department to exercise good cost control in his own department.

Another reason for charging all costs is that the collection of all costs in responsibility centers may facilitate the calculation of selling prices, a topic to be discussed in Chapter 18. A third reason is that if the supervisor is made aware of the total amount of costs that are incurred in the operation of his unit, he may have a better understanding of how much the company contributes to the operation. Such a practice may boomerang, however, for the supervisor may conclude that his controllable costs are so small, relative to the costs that he cannot control, that they are not worth worrying about.

ENGINEERED, DISCRETIONARY, AND COMMITTED COSTS

The final classification of costs to be discussed in this chapter is that between (1) engineered, (2) discretionary, and (3) committed costs. Although both engineered and discretionary costs are controllable, the approach to the control of one is quite different from that of the other. Committed costs are not controllable in the short run, but they are in the long run.

Engineered Costs

These are elements of cost for which the *right* or *proper* amount of costs that should be incurred can be estimated. Direct labor is an example. Given the specifications for a product, engineers can determine the necessary operations to be performed and can estimate, within reasonably close limits, the time that should be spent on each operation. The total amount of direct labor costs that should be incurred can then be estimated by translation of these times into money by means of a wage rate and multiplication by the number of units of product produced. Since production engineering is not an exact science, these amounts are not necessarily the exact amount that should be spent, but the estimates can usually be made close enough so that there is relatively little ground for disagreement as to what the cost should be. In particular, there can be no reasonable ground for denying that there is a direct relationship between volume and costs; two units require more direct labor than does one unit.

Discretionary Costs

These costs are also called "programmed" or "managed" costs. They can be whatever management wants them to be, within wide limits. There is no scientific way of deciding what the "right" amount should be, or at least there is no scientific basis that the management of the particular company is willing to rely on. How much should we spend for research and development? for public relations? for employees' parties and outings? for donations? for the accounting department? No one knows. In most companies, the discretionary cost category includes all general and administrative functions, all order-getting costs, and a great many items of factory overhead cost.

In the absence of an engineering standard, the amount to be spent must be a matter of judgment. Usually, this judgment is arrived at by joint agreement between the supervisor concerned and his superior, as part of the budgeting process. Indeed most of the discussion in the budgeting process occurs with respect to the permitted level of discretionary costs.

Although there is no "right" level for the total amount of a discretionary cost item, there may be usable standards for controlling some of the detail within it. Although no one knows the right amount to spend for accounting, it is nevertheless possible to measure the performance of individual clerks in the accounting department in terms of number of postings or number of invoices typed per hour. And although we cannot know the "right" amount of total travel expense, we can set standards for the amount that should be spent per day or per mile.

Furthermore, new developments in management accounting result in a gradual shift of items from the discretionary cost to the engineered cost categories. Several companies have recently started to use what they believe to be valid techniques for determining the "right" amount that they should spend on advertising in order to achieve their sales objectives, or the "right" number of salesmen.

ANALYSIS OF PERFORMANCE. With respect to engineered costs, the general rule is "the lower they are, the better." The objective is to spend as little as possible, consistent with quality standards, safety standards, and so on. The supervisor who reduces his engineered costs usually should be congratulated.

With respect to discretionary costs, the situation is quite different and much more complicated. Often, optimum performance consists of *spending the amount agreed on,* for spending too little may be as bad as, or worse than, spending too much. A factory supervisor can easily reduce his costs by skimping on maintenance or on training; a marketing manager can reduce his advertising or sales promotion expenditures; top management may eliminate research. None of these actions may be in the overall best interest of the company, although all of them result in lower costs on the current income statement.

Committed Costs

Committed costs are those that are the inevitable consequences of commitments previously made. Depreciation is an example; once a company has purchased a building or a piece of equipment, there is an inevitable depreciation charge so long as the building continues to be owned.

In the short run, committed costs are noncontrollable. They can be changed only by changing the commitment, for example, by disposing of the building or equipment whose depreciation is being recorded.

Spurious Relationships

The decision on how much to spend for a discretionary cost item may take several forms, such as "spend the same amount as we spent last year," or "spend b. percent of sales," or "spend b. dollars plus a percent of sales." These decision rules result in historical patterns which, when plotted against volume, have the same superficial appearance as the patterns of engineered cost. The first rule gives a nonvariable cost line, the second a variable cost line, and the third a semivariable cost line.

These relationships are fundamentally different from those observed for engineered costs, however. For engineered costs, the pattern is inevitable; as volume increases, the direct labor cost *must* increase. For discretionary costs, the relationship exists only because of the management decision, and it can be changed simply by changing the management decision. For example, a company may decide that research and development cost should be 3 percent of sales. There can be no scientific reason for such a decision, for no one knows the optimum amount that should be spent for research; in all probability, such a rule exists primarily because management thinks that this is what the company can afford to spend. In such a situation there will be a linear relationship between sales volume and research/development costs. There is, however, little significance to such a relationship, and no reason to believe that research/development costs in the future should follow the same pattern.

ORDER-GETTING COSTS. Order-getting costs are those incurred in order to make sales. They include the costs of the selling organization, advertising, sales promotion, and so on. These costs may vary with sales volume, but the relationship is the reverse of that for factory costs: order-getting cost is the independent variable, and sales volume is the dependent variable. Order-getting costs vary not in response to sales volume but rather *in anticipation of* sales volume, according to decisions made by management.[3] They are therefore discretionary costs.

If management has a policy of spending more for order-getting activities when sales volume is high, then a scatter diagram of the relationship between selling costs and sales volume will have the same appearance as the diagram for production costs and production volume, Illustration 15–6. The two diagrams should be interpreted quite differently, however. The production cost diagram indicates that cost *necessarily* increases as volume increases, while the selling cost diagram shows that cost has been *permitted* to increase with increases in volume; there is no necessary relationship in the latter case. Further, subject to some qualifications, it may be said that for total factory overhead costs, the lower they are the better; but lower selling costs may reflect inadequate selling effort. The "right" level of selling costs is a judgment made by management.

Nor is there always a direct relationship between order-getting cost and sales volume. Take advertising as an example. Management may decide either (1) to increase advertising expenditures when sales *increase,* on the theory that the company can afford to spend more when revenue is high; (2) to spend the same amount for advertising, regardless of sales volume; or (3) to increase advertising expenditures when sales *decrease,* in the belief that additional effort is necessary to regain lost volume. Each of these policies gives a different line of relationship, and the pattern is further obscured by the fact that sales volume is influenced not only by advertising, or indeed sales effort in total, but also by general business conditions and other factors outside the company's control.

SUMMARY

The word "cost" has many meanings, and care must always be taken to make sure that the context applying to a given situation is understood.

Variable costs are those that vary with volume. Although some costs are semivariable, they usually can be decomposed into variable and non-variable components. The relationship between costs and volume is usually linear within a normal range of volume.

When a revenue line is added to a diagram showing the cost-volume relationship, the diagram is called a profitgraph, an important tool in analysis of the factors that affect profit. Marginal income, which is the difference between revenue and variable cost, is a significant concept in such an analysis.

Controllable costs in a responsibility center are those that can be

---

[3] Exceptions are salesmen's commissions and other payments related to sales in that sales is the basis of figuring the cost. These of course vary directly with sales.

significantly influenced by the head of the responsibility center. This does not mean that the head of the responsibility center has complete responsibility, because few cost elements are the complete responsibility of any single person in an organization. Noncontrollable costs often can, and should, be converted to controllable costs by changing either the control system or the amount of authority delegated to lower responsibility centers, or both.

Controllable costs may be further classified as either engineered costs or discretionary costs. Methods of estimating and analyzing the former are basically different from those applicable to the latter.

APPENDIX

Fitting a Straight Line by Least Squares

If the variable measured on the vertical axis is designated y and that on the horizontal axis x, then *any* straight line is described by the general formula, $y = a + bx$. In order to describe a *specific* straight line, we must assign specific numerical values to the two constants (or "parameters"), a and b.

EXAMPLE: Illustration 15–12 shows the line $y = 2 + \frac{1}{2}x$. Notice that the line cuts the y axis at a value of 2, and that for each unit increase in x, y increases $\frac{1}{2}$ unit.

The technique of fitting a straight line by the method of least squares makes use of this formula for a straight line. We assume here that the distances from the point to the line are measured *vertically*, that is, parallel to the y axis. We write down in two adjacent columns every value of x and beside each value of x the corresponding actual value of y.

Illustration 15–12

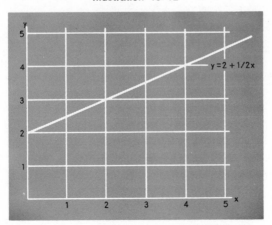

In a third column we put the square of each value of x, and in the fourth, the product of each x times the corresponding y. We total each column and use the symbol Σx^2 to denote the total of the squares of the x values, Σxy to denote the total of the products of x times the corresponding y, etc. (Notice that Σx^2 does *not* denote the square of the sum of the x's, nor does Σxy denote the total of the x's times the total of y's.) We then determine the constants a and b in the equation for a straight line by solving the two simultaneous "normal equations":

$$Na + b(\Sigma x) = \Sigma y$$
$$a(\Sigma x) + b(\Sigma x^2) = \Sigma xy$$

N is the number of items, that is, the number of x, y pairs.

Suppose we have the following data (simplified for the purpose of illustration):

Visits	Sales
0	10
1	12
2	13
3	15

We write the figures:

(1) x	(2) y	(3) x^2	(4) xy
0	10	0	0
1	12	1	12
2	13	4	26
3	15	9	45
6	50	14	83

Therefore,

$$\Sigma x = 6,\ \Sigma y = 50,\ \Sigma x^2 = 14,\ \Sigma xy = 83,\ N = 4;$$

and the normal equations given above become

$$50 = 4a + 6b$$
$$83 = 6a + 14b.$$

To solve for a and b, multiply the first equation by 3 and the second equation by 2 and get—

$$150 = 12a + 18b$$
$$166 = 12a + 28b.$$

Subtract the first equation from the second and get—

$$16 = 10b$$
$$b = 1.6.$$

Therefore, $50 = 4a + 9.6$ (from the first normal equation with 9.6 written in place of $6b$):

$$4a = 40.4$$
$$a = 10.1.$$

Therefore, the equation of the least-squares regression line is:

$$y = 10.1 + 1.6x.$$

SUGGESTIONS FOR FURTHER READING

ANTHONY, ROBERT N. *Planning and Control Systems: A Framework for Analysis.* Boston: Harvard Graduate School of Business Administration, 1965.

ANTHONY, ROBERT N., JOHN DEARDEN, and RICHARD F. VANCIL. *Management Control Systems: Cases and Readings.* Homewood, Ill.: Richard D. Irwin, Inc., 1965.

BEYER, ROBERT. *Profitability Accounting for Planning and Control.* New York: Ronald Press, Co., 1963.

CYERT, RICHARD M., and JAMES G. MARCH. *A Behavioral Theory of the Firm.* Englewood Cliffs, N.J.: Prentice-Hall, Inc., 1963.

LEWIS, RALPH F. *Management Uses of Accounting.* New York: Harper & Bros., 1961.

SOLOMONS, DAVID. *Divisional Performance: Measurement and Control.* New York: Financial Executives Institute, 1965.

CHAPTER 16

BUDGETING

All managements make plans. One cannot conceive of an organization of any kind whose leaders were not giving some thought to what the organization's objectives should be and to the best way of reaching those objectives. A group of people not operating under some sort of plan is merely an incoherent, directionless mob, not an organization.

Although all managements plan, there are considerable differences in the way in which they plan. Some people do their planning entirely in their heads, others make notes and rough estimates on the backs of old envelopes, and still others express their plans in quantitative terms and commit these to paper in some orderly, systematic fashion. The process engaged in by the latter group is called "budgeting," for a *budget* is merely a plan expressed in quantitative terms. We are here primarily concerned with budgets that are expressed in monetary terms, although some budgets are expressed in units of product, number of employees, units of time, or other nonmonetary quantities. In addition to its use in planning, the budget is also used for control and for coordination.

Types of Budgets

There is a considerable diversity of practice in budgeting, much greater than the diversity in accounting practice. Most companies except the smallest have some sort of budget, but a great many do not have a truly comprehensive budgeting system. Such a system consists of three types of budgets: an *operating* budget, showing planned operations for the forthcoming period; a *cash* budget, showing the anticipated sources and uses of cash; and a *capital* budget, showing planned changes in fixed assets.

These types of budgets, the relationships between them, and the principal segments of which they are composed, are shown in Illustration 16–1.

The illustration shows only one of the large number of ways in which budgets are structured in various companies.

Illustration 16–1

TYPES OF BUDGETS

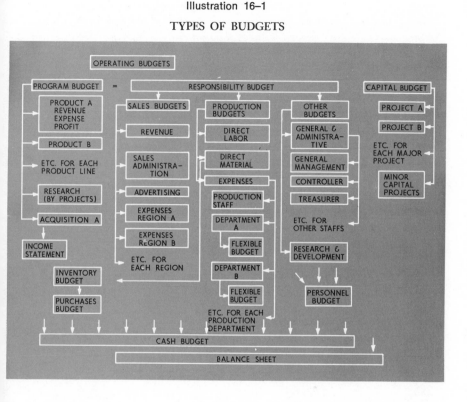

THE OPERATING BUDGET

An operating budget usually consists of two parts, a "program" budget and a "responsibility" budget. These represent two ways of depicting the overall operating plan for the business, two different methods of slicing the pie; therefore, both arrive at the same figure for projected net income and return on investment.

The *program budget* describes the major programs the company plans to undertake. Such a budget might be arranged, for example, by products lines and show the anticipated revenue and costs associated with each product. This type of budget is useful to an executive examining the overall balance among the various programs of the business. It helps to answer such questions as these: Is the profit margin on each product line satisfactory? Is production capacity in balance with the size and capability of the sales organization? Can we afford to spend so much for research?

Are adequate funds available? And so on. A negative answer to any of these questions indicates the necessity for revising the plan.

The *responsibility budget* sets forth plans in terms of the persons responsible for carrying them out. It is therefore primarily a control device, since it is a statement of expected or standard performance against which actual performance can later be compared. In the factory, for example, there may be a responsibility budget for each department, showing the costs that are controllable by the foreman of the department. There may also be a program budget showing costs for each product, including both direct costs and allocated costs. The figures on both sets of budgets add up to total factory costs, but the product-cost budget would not be useful for control purposes, since the costs shown on it could not ordinarily be related to the responsibility of specific individuals.

If the costs in a responsibility center are expected to vary with volume, as is the case with most production departments, the responsibility budget may be in the form of a *variable budget* or *flexible budget*. Such a budget shows the expected behavior of costs at various volume levels. The variable budget may be expressed in terms of the cost-volume equation described in Chapter 15, that is, a nonvariable amount and a variable amount per unit of volume, or $y = a + bx$. It may also be expressed as the costs that are expected at discrete levels of volume; that is, there may be a column for the costs expected at 60 percent of normal volume, another at 70, 80, 90, 100, 110, 120, 130, and 140 percent. In the latter case, a comparison of actual costs with budgeted costs requires an interpolation when actual volume is between two of the specified levels.

In addition to the responsibility budgets for costs, there also may be budgets showing planned inventory levels of finished products and raw materials; a budget of the planned purchases of materials; personnel budgets showing planned manpower levels, and plans for promotions, participation in training programs, and retirements; and budgets for a variety of other special purposes.

Relationships among the Budgets

The budget should constitute a coherent whole; therefore, the pieces should be consistent with one another. The costs in the individual production centers in the responsibility budget should add up to the same amount as the total product costs in the program budget, for example. If variable budgets are used, then one point on the cost-volume line must be selected as the volume at which product costs are to be calculated. This point is the expected volume for the year, and the costs at this volume are used in preparing the estimated income statement.

The program budget ordinarily cannot be used for control purposes, since the costs shown on it cannot ordinarily be related to the responsibilities of specific individuals. The costs of a product, for example, include a fraction of the costs of all the production departments through which the product passes during the manufacturing process. In some situations, however, individual responsibility can be related to specific programs, and in these situations, the program budget serves as a means of control. The producer of a motion picture or a television "special," for example, has a budget for his particular program, and control is exercised in terms of that budget. This is also the case in the construction of major capital assets: buildings, dams, roads, bridges, ships, weapons systems, and the like. Within such a program, the budget may be subdivided according to the organizational units responsible for various aspects of it, and these units are responsibility centers.

The Budget Process

The preparation of a budget can be studied both as an accounting process and as a management process. From an accounting standpoint, the procedures are essentially the same as those described in Part I, and the end result of the recording and summarizing operations is a set of financial statements—a balance sheet and an income statement—identical in format with those resulting from the process of recording historical events. The only difference is that the budget figures are estimates of what will happen in the future rather than historical data on what has happened in the past.

From a management standpoint, the budgeting process is so closely associated with the operation of the business that a complete description of the factors and considerations involved would take us far beyond the scope of this book. Rather than attempt such a description, we shall merely indicate some of the important general considerations in the budget process.

Choice of Time Periods

The majority of companies prepare budgets once a year. For control purposes, the annual totals may simply be divided by 12 to obtain monthly budgets, but if seasonal influences are important, separate budget estimates are made for each month or each quarter. In many companies data are shown by months only for the next three months or the next six months, with the balance of the year being shown by quarters.

Some companies follow the practice of preparing a new budget every quarter, but for a full year ahead. Every three months the estimates for the quarter just completed are dropped, the figures for the succeeding three quarters are revised if necessary, and estimates for the fourth succeeding quarter are added. This is called a *rolling budget*.

Organization for Preparation of Budgets

A *budget committee,* consisting of several members of the top management group, may oversee the work of preparing the budget. This committee will set the general guidelines that the organization is to follow, coordinate the separate budgets prepared by the various organizational units, resolve differences among them, and submit the final budget to the president and to the board of directors for approval. In a small company, this work is done by the president himself, or by his immediate line subordinate. Instructions go down through the regular chain of command, and the budget comes back up for successive reviews and approvals through the same channels. The essential point is that decisions about the budget are made by the line organization, and the final approval is given by the head of that organization, the president or the board.

The line organization usually is assisted in its preparation of the budget by a staff unit headed by the *budget director,* preferably reporting to the controller. If he reports to the president, as is sometimes the case, he is likely to be performing the functions described above for the budget committee and therefore acting in a line, rather than a staff, capacity.

As a staff man, the budget director's functions are to disseminate instructions about the mechanics of budget preparation (the forms and how to fill them out), to provide data on past performance that are useful in preparation of the budget, to make computations on the basis of decisions reached by the line organization, to assemble the budget figures, and to see that everyone submits his figures on time. Thus, the budget organization may do a very large fraction of the budget work. It is not the crucial part, however, for the significant decisions are always made by the line organization. Once the members of the line organization have reached an agreement on labor productivity and wage rates, for example, the budget man can calculate all the detailed figures for labor costs by products and by responsibility centers; this is a considerable job of computation, but it is entirely based on the judgments of the line supervisors.

The budget organization is like a telephone company, operating an important communication system; it is responsible for the speed, accuracy, and clarity with which messages flow through the system, but not for the content of the messages themselves.

The Budget Timetable

As indicated in Illustration 16–1, "the" budget for a typical company consists of several parts: the sales budget, the sales expense budget, the inventory and purchases budget, the production budget, the administrative budget, the research and development budget, the budgeted income statement and balance sheet, and the cash budget, among others. Some of these pieces are affected by decisions or estimates made in constructing other pieces. Most of them are affected by the estimate of sales volume. The factory budget is affected by estimated sales volume and decisions as to inventory levels. The purchases budget is affected by estimated production volume and decisions as to material inventory levels, and so on. Thus, there has to be a carefully worked out timetable specifying the order in which the several parts of the budget are to be prepared and the time when each must be completed. In general, the steps covered by this timetable are as follows:

1. Setting guidelines.
2. Making the sales estimate.
3. Initial preparation of the other parts of the budget.
4. Negotiation of agreed estimates.
5. Coordination and review.
6. Final approval.

In a company of average complexity, the elapsed time for the whole process is approximately three months, with the most hectic part (steps 4, 5, and 6 above) requiring approximately one month. In highly complex organizations, the elapsed time may be six months, or occasionally even longer. At the other extreme, a small business may go through the whole process in one afternoon.

Setting Guidelines

Ideally, the budget process is *not* the mechanism by which major policy decisions are made, but rather a means of implementing these decisions. These major decisions are made whenever the need or the opportunity arises. (In practice, there are exceptions to this statement, because the act of preparing the budget may uncover a need to make new major decisions.)

In any event, when budget preparation begins, a great many decisions affecting the budget year already have been made, some of which are irrevocable and some of which are subject to modifications. The maximum scale of manufacturing operations is set by the available facilities, for example, and if an expansion is to take place during the budget year, the decision would ordinarily have to have been made a year or more previously because of the time required to build buildings and to acquire and install machinery. If a new product is to go into volume production, considerable time would have already been spent prior to the budget year on product development, design, testing, and initial promotional work. Thus, the budget is not a *de novo* creation; it is built within the context of the ongoing business.

LONG-RANGE PLANNING. The decisions described above are part of the *programming* process. In a small, but growing, number of companies programming decisions are incorporated in a formal long-range plan. Such a plan shows the estimated revenues and expenses (and possibly asset acquisitions and other information) over each of the next several (i.e., three, four, or five) years that are implied in policy decisions that have already been taken. When such a plan exists, the revenue and expense estimates for the budget year column of the long-range plan provide a starting point in preparing the budget. They do not by any means provide the budget automatically, for they must be refined and be brought up to date; the other steps in the process must be followed even when a long-range plan exists.

The long-range plan, if one exists, is a guideline that governs the preparation of the budget. Alternatively, or in addition, top management may describe in more general terms the policies that are to govern budget preparation. These guidelines vary greatly in detail. At one extreme, there may be only a brief general statement, such as, "Assume that volume will be 5 percent greater than the current year." More commonly, detailed information and guidance is given on such matters as projected general economic conditions, allowance to be made for price increases and wage increases, changes in the product line, changes in the scale of operations, allowable personnel promotions, anticipated productivity gains, and a variety of other topics. In addition, detailed instructions will be issued as to what information is required for the budget, and how this information is to be recorded on the budget documents.

These guidelines are of great interest to competitors, so they are circulated only to those who need to know them. If it is particularly important that a new strategy be concealed, it may be omitted from the statement, with necessary adjustments in the budget being made subsequently at the headquarters level. In the absence of statements to the contrary, the organization customarily assumes that the budget year will be similar to the current year.

An example of a guideline statement is given below. It was prepared by a large bank, and is relatively general and brief:

It is customary for the committee to summarize for your general guidance current thinking regarding deposits, loans, and loan rates. The expectations outlined below are for the overall bank. Therefore, it is important that the head of each earning unit analyze the impact of expected general economic trends on the conditions peculiar to his own area of activity in order to project specific goals which he may reasonably expect to attain.

DEPOSITS

There is every indication that money market conditions will be such that demand deposit levels in our area will expand. In our judgment, we anticipate at least a 5 percent growth in demand deposits for all banks. Our overall goal, however, should be set somewhat higher to reflect an improvement in our relative position. Savings deposits will continue to climb moderately. Current rates for time and savings deposits should be used to project interest costs.

LOANS AND LOAN RATES

In all probability loan demand will slacken seasonally in the early months of next year; in fact, many economists believe that the decline may continue through the second quarter of the year. We firmly believe that sometime between the March tax date and early in the third quarter, loan demand should strengthen.

For the most part, the recent decline in the prime rate is reflected in the loan rate structure at this time. Accordingly, except where necessary rate adjustments are still anticipated, the existing rate structure should prevail.

EXPENSES

Before preparing the budget, it is imperative that each supervisor closely evaluate every controllable expense in his area and consider all means of economizing and reducing costs, particularly in such areas as personnel staffing, overtime, entertainment, stationery, etc. The salary administration policies explained on pages 19 and 20 in the Budget Instructions[1] should be strictly followed.

In order to complete the budget for the entire bank by year-end, your full cooperation is necessary in meeting the deadlines which appear in the attached General Instructions.

BUDGET COMMITTEE

---

[1] The policies referred to are as follows:

Your current appraisal of each employee's performance as E (excellent), AA (above average), A (average), or P (poor) is to be shown immediately following the individual's name on schedule 4A, as a guide for your own budgeting and for the subsequent review by the budget committee.

Salary administration policies, as expressed in Bulletin III of the Personnel Policies Manual are not expected to change. Our salary rates are competitive, and as in recent years, any projected increases should be based solely on merit or, where plans are sufficiently advanced, on anticipated bona fide promotions.

In general, the budget committee anticipates that we will be able to maintain our competitive position with total bankwide increases to deserving employees, averaging no more than 5 percent of their salaries. In order to achieve this purpose, all departments must cooperate in observing the following guides:

a) In all cases, *merit* and not length of service is to be the basis for the forecasting of increases.

b) Individual merit increases should be roughly 5 to 5½ percent of the range midpoint with no increase less than $156 nor more than 10 percent of the range midpoint, ($500 maximum), and in multiples of $1.00 weekly.

c) Individual increases exceeding the guidelines in (*b*) above should be thoroughly documented both in budget submittal and in subsequent actual review for salary purposes.

d) An employee rated average should not receive appreciably more than the midpoint of his salary range. The top half of the range is reserved for those employees who demonstrate above-average performance.

e) In case of promotion, the increase or increases to be scheduled should normally bring the salary within a reasonable period to the minimum for the new job.

The Sales Estimate

In almost all companies, the most difficult estimate to make is that of sales revenue. There are in general two ways of proceeding: to make a *statistical* forecast on the basis of an analysis of general business conditions, market conditions, product growth curves, and the like; or to make an *internal* forecast, by collecting the opinions of executives and salesmen. In some companies salesmen are asked to estimate the sales of each product made to each of their customers; in others, they estimate total sales in their territory; in still others, salesmen do not participate in the estimating process. There are advantages and weaknesses in both the statistical and the internal methods; both are often used together, but neither can be guaranteed to yield an even reasonably close estimate in view of the inevitable uncertainties of the future.

The sales budget is more than a sales *forecast*. A forecast is merely passive, while a budget should reflect the positive actions that management plans to take in order to influence future events. For example, this may be the sales forecast: "With the present amount of sales effort, we expect sales to run at about the same level as currently." By contrast, the sales *budget* may show a substantial planned increase in sales, reflecting management's intention to add salesmen, increase advertising and sales promotion, or redesign the product.

The sales estimate may or may not be disseminated as part of the budget guidelines. It is a piece of information in which competitors are greatly interested, particularly as it relates to new products, so its distribution may be restricted for that reason. Instead of disseminating the detailed estimate, some companies send only summaries of it, with enough information to permit necessary planning of material purchases, additional personnel, and other needed resources.

Initial Budget Preparation

The budget guidelines prepared by top management are sent down through the successive levels in the organization, and the management at each level may add other, more detailed, information for the guidance of its subordinates.

When the guidelines arrive at the lowest responsibility centers, the heads of these responsibility centers make the budget estimates, working within the guidance and restraints specified in the guidelines. The respective roles of the line supervisor and the staff budget man in this process are as described above; that is, the accounting and budget staff assist the line supervisor by making detailed calculations, by providing historical data, and by summarizing and recording the estimates, but the line supervisor, not the accountant, is responsible for the estimates themselves.

For each expense center, the supervisor makes an estimate of each significant element of controllable expense. If noncontrollable expenses are reported, these estimates are usually added subsequently by the budget staff.

Whenever feasible, estimates for quantities and for unit prices should be shown separately in order to facilitate the subsequent analysis of performance. Material cost is preferably shown as number of pounds times cents per pound, labor costs as number of hours times the hourly wage rate, and so on. The basic reason for doing this is that different factors, and often different people, are responsible for changes in the quantity component and the price component, respectively. The purchasing officer is responsible for the cost per pound of material, but the factory foreman is responsible for the quantity used, for example. For similar reasons, the estimates are broken down by product lines, by significant items of cost, and in other ways that will facilitate subsequent analysis of actual performance.

Usually, the current level of expenses is used as a starting point in making these estimates. The guidelines may provide specific instructions as to the permitted changes that can be made from current expenses, such as, "Assume a 3 percent increase for purchased materials and services." In addition to following these instructions, the person who prepares the budget, i.e., the budgetee, expresses his judgment as to the behavior of costs not covered by the instructions.

Negotiation

Now comes the crucial stage in the process from a control standpoint, the negotiation between the budgetee and his superior. The value of the budget as an estimate of what is going to happen, as a motivating device, and as a standard against which actual performance will be measured, depends largely on how skillfully this negotiation is conducted.

Several recent studies have shown that the budget is most effective as a motivating device when it represents a tight, but attainable, goal. If it is too tight, it leads to frustration; if it is too loose, it leads to complacency. The budgetee's superior therefore seeks to arrive at this desirable middle ground.[2]

As did the budgetee, the superior usually must take the current level of expense as a starting point. There simply is not enough time during the budget review to reexamine each of the elements of expense and insure

---

[2] The policy of some companies is to set the responsibility budget slightly tighter than the performance that reasonably can be expected. Under these circumstances, the responsibility budgets will not jibe with the program budget unless a specific allowance is subsequently added for the difference between the budget goals and expected performance.

that the current level is optimum. It is a fact, however, that the operation of Parkinson's first law ("Costs tend to increase regardless of the work done") strongly suggests that costs do drift out of line over a period of time, and that the current level of spending is therefore probably too high. One way of addressing this problem is to make an arbitrary cut, say 5 percent, in the budget estimates, but this is not satisfactory simply because of its arbitrariness; it affects the efficient and the inefficient alike. Furthermore, if the budgetees know that such a cut is going to be made, they can counter it by inflating the original estimates by a corresponding amount.

ZERO-BASE REVIEW.   Another approach to this problem is the zero-base review, a periodic study of the responsibility center made by a staff group, or by outside experts. Such a study builds up the costs from zero, rather than starting with the current level of costs. These studies are especially important when costs are of the discretionary cost type. Basic questions are raised, such as: (1) Should the function be performed at all? (2) What should the quality level be? Are we doing too much? (3) Should it be performed in this way? (4) How much should it cost?

One way of examining costs is to make a comparison with similar functions in other parts of the company, or with information obtained from trade associations and similar sources about the cost of performing similar functions in other companies. Although there are problems of comparability; although, by definition, there is no way of finding a "correct" relationship between cost and output in a discretionary cost situation; although there is a danger in taking an outside average as a standard; and although many other criticisms can be raised about such comparisons, they nevertheless can be useful. For example, they often lead to the following interesting question: If other companies can get the job done for $X, why can't we?

The zero-base review is time consuming, and it is also likely to be a traumatic experience for the heads of responsibility centers. It therefore cannot be made every year, but rather is scheduled so that all responsibility centers are covered once in four or five years. This review establishes a new base for the budget, and the annual budget review attempts to keep costs reasonably in line with this base for the intervening four or five years.

The superior has various tactics for doing this. He asks for a full justification of any proposed cost increases. He seeks reasons why costs may be expected to decrease, such as a decrease in the work load of the responsibility center, an increase in productivity, or the operation of the learning phenomenon described in Chapter 15, recognizing that these prospective decreases may not willingly be disclosed by the budgetee. (Some managements, knowing that overall productivity in America increases by approximately 3 percent per year, expect similar productivity gains within their companies. As a rough rule of thumb, some companies expect productivity gains to offset inflationary price increases, and so expect total expenses to show a net change of zero from one year to the next.)

For his part, the budgetee defends his estimates. He justifies proposed cost increases by additional work that he is expected to do, by the effect of inflation, by the need for better quality output, and so on.

THE COMMITMENT. The end product of this negotiation[3] is an agreement which represents an implicit commitment by each party. By agreeing to the budget estimates, the budgetee says to his superior, in effect: "I can and will operate my department in accordance with the plan described in the budget." By approving the budget estimates, the superior says to the budgetee, in effect: "If you operate your department in accordance with this plan, you will do what we consider to be a good job." Both of these statements contain the implicit qualification of "adjusted for changes in circumstances" since both parties recognize that actual events, such as price levels and general business conditions, may not correspond to those assumed when the budget was prepared and that these changes will inevitably affect the plans set forth in the budget. In judging whether the commitment is in fact being carried out as the year progresses, management must take these changes into account.

The nature of the commitment, both as to individual elements of expense and as to the total expense of the responsibility center, may be one of three types: (*a*) It may represent a *ceiling* (e.g., "Not more than $X should be spent for books and periodicals"); (*b*) it may represent a *floor* (e.g., "At least $Y should be spent for employee training"); or (*c*) it may represent a *guide* (e.g., "Approximately $Z should be spent for overtime"). Often, the individual items are not explicitly identified as to which of these categories they belong in, but it is obviously important that the two parties have a clear understanding as to which item belongs in which category.

Coordination and Review

The negotiation process is repeated at successively higher levels of responsibility centers in the organizational hierarchy. The subsequent negotiations may, of course, result in changes in the detailed budgets that have been agreed to at lower levels, and if these changes are significant, the budget may have to be recycled back down the organizational chain. If, however, the guidelines are carefully described, and if the budget process is well understood and conducted by those who participate in it, such recycling is not ordinarily necessary. In the successive stages of

---

[3] In a perceptive study, D. H. Hofstede describes this process as a "game"; see *The Game of Budget Control* (Assen, The Netherlands: Van Gorcum & Co., N.V., 1967). A negotiation is a game, in the formal sense.

negotiation, the person who has the role of supervisor at one level becomes the budgetee at the next higher level. Since he is well aware of this fact, he is strongly motivated to negotiate budgets with his budgetees that he can defend successfully with his superiors. If his superior demonstrates that the proposed budget is loose, this is a reflection on the budgetee's ability as a manager.

As the individual budgets move up the organizational hierarchy, they are also examined in relationship to one another, and this examination may reveal aspects of the plan that are out of balance. If so, certain of the underlying budgets may need to be changed. Major unresolved problems are submitted to the budget committee for resolution. The individual responsibility budgets may also reveal the need to change estimates in the program budget, and these changes may in turn disclose parts of the program that appear to be out of balance. Various summary documents, especially the budgeted income statement and the budgeted balance sheet, are also prepared at this time.

Final Approval

Just prior to the beginning of the budget year, the proposed budget is submitted to top management—usually to the board of directors—for approval. If the guidelines have been properly set and adhered to, the proposed budget should contain no great surprises to top management, and approval should therefore be forthcoming after a relatively brief discussion. This approval is by no means perfunctory, however, for it signifies the official agreement of top management to the proposed plans for the year. The approved budget is then transmitted down through the organization.

Variations in Practice

The preceding is a "textbook" description of the budget process. Not all companies have a budget for each responsibility center, and some of those that do have complete budgets treat the process more casually than is implied in the above description. Some companies formulate their budgets in a process that is the reverse of that described; that is, instead of having budget estimates originate at the lowest responsibility centers, the budget is prepared by a high-level staff, blessed by top management, and then transmitted down to the organization. This *imposed* budget is an unsatisfactory motivating device, and it is becoming less common.

Revisions

The budget is formulated in accordance with certain assumptions as to conditions that will be prevailing during the budget year. Actual conditions will never be exactly the same as those assumed, and the differences may be significant. The question then arises as to whether or not the budget should be revised to reflect what is now known about current conditions. There is considerable difference of opinion on this question.

Those who favor revising the budget point out that the budget is supposed to reflect the plan in accordance with which the company is operating, and that when the plan has to be changed because of changing conditions, the budget should reflect these changes. If the budget is not revised, it is no longer a statement of plans.

The opponents of revising the budget argue that the process of revision not only is time consuming, but also may obscure the goals that the company originally intended to achieve and the reasons for departures from these goals, especially since a revision may reflect the budgetee's skill in negotiating a change that hides his inefficiency, rather than one that reflects an actual change in the underlying assumed conditions. They refer disparagingly to a frequently revised budget as a "rubber standard." Many companies therefore do not revise their budgets during the year, and take account of changes in conditions when they analyze the difference between actual and budgeted performance.

Other companies solve this problem by having two budgets, a *baseline* budget set at the beginning of the year, and a *current* budget, reflecting the best current estimate of revenue and expenses. A comparison of actual performance with the baseline performance shows the extent of deviation from the original goals, and a comparison of the current budget with the baseline budget shows how much of this deviation has been attributed to changes in current conditions from those originally assumed.

Some managers use current budgets in lieu of reports of actual performance. Such a manager says: "I am not interested in actual costs because I literally can't do anything to control them; they have already happened. What I am interested in is a comparison of how we now think we are going to come out, compared with how we originally planned to come out, as expressed in the baseline budget. If this comparison is not satisfactory, I can at least investigate what can be done to bring the situation back into line." As Charles F. Kettering said, "We should all be concerned about the future because we will have to spend the rest of our lives there."

Such an approach is particularly useful in the case of a program budget for the construction of a building or other capital equipment. Presumably the program was undertaken because the originally foreseen relationship between its costs and the benefits to be achieved was deemed to be satisfactory. If current estimates indicate that this relationship has been significantly changed with the passage of time—for example, that it is now estimated that the program will cost significantly more than originally contemplated—then the whole program needs to be reexamined, and possibly redirected or even discontinued.

Uses of the Budget

From the above description, it should be apparent that the budget is useful: (1) as a device for making and coordinating plans, (2) for communicating these plans to those who are responsible for carrying them out, (3) in motivating managers at all levels, and (4) as a standard with which actual performance subsequently can be compared.

Although basic planning decisions are usually made prior to the beginning of the budget cycle, the process of formulating the budget leads to a refinement of these plans, and, when it discloses inbalances or unsatisfactory overall results, may lead to a change in plans.

As a communication device, it should be recognized that management's plans will not be carried out (except by accident) unless the organization understands what the plans are. Adequate understanding includes not only a knowledge of programs and objectives (e.g., how many units are to be manufactured, what methods and machines are to be used, how much material is to be purchased, what selling prices are to be) but also a knowledge about policies and restrictions to which the organization is expected to adhere. Examples of these kinds of information follow: the maximum amounts that may be spent for such items as advertising, maintenance, administrative costs; wage rates and hours of work; desired quality levels; and so on. A most useful device for communicating quantitative information concerning these objectives and limitations is the approved budget.

If the atmosphere is right, the budget process can be a powerful force in motivating managers to work toward the goals of the overall organization. Such an atmosphere is created when heads of responsibility centers understand that top management regards the process as important, and when they participate in the formulation of their own budgets in the manner described above.

A carefully prepared budget is the best possible standard against which to measure actual performance, and it is increasingly being used for this purpose. Until fairly recently, the general practice was to compare current results with results for last month or with results for the same period a year ago; and this is still the basic means of comparison in many companies. Such a historical standard has the fundamental weakness that it does not take account either of changes in the underlying forces at work or of the planned program for the current year.

> EXAMPLE: In a favorable market situation, a certain company increased its volume and its selling prices and hence increased its net income in 1968 by 25 percent over the net income of 1967. If 1968's results are compared with 1967's, there is an apparent cause for rejoicing. However, the company had *planned* to increase profits by 35 percent, and performance when measured against the plan was not so

good. The company quite properly took steps to find out, and if possible to correct, the factors accounting for the difference between actual and budgeted results.

In general, it is more significant to answer the question, "Why didn't we do what we planned to do?" than the question, "Why is this year different from last year?" Presumably, the principal factors accounting for the difference between this year and last year were taken into consideration in the preparation of the budget.

The foregoing discussion presupposes a carefully prepared budget. If management does not trust the budget, then there is good reason to use last year's performance as a benchmark, for it at least has the merit of being a definite, objective figure.

THE CASH BUDGET

The operating budget is usually prepared in terms of revenues and expenses. For financial planning purposes, it must be translated into terms of cash receipts and cash disbursements. This translation results in the *cash budget*. The financial people use the cash budget to make plans to insure that the company has enough, but not too much, cash on hand during the year ahead.

There are two approaches to the preparation of a cash budget:

1. Start with the budgeted balance sheet and income statements and adjust the figures thereon to reveal the sources and uses of cash. This procedure is exactly the same as that described for the cash flow statement in Chapter 12, except that the data are estimates of the future rather than historical. It therefore is not described again here.

2. Project directly each of the items that results in cash receipts or cash disbursements. A cash budget prepared by this means is shown in Illustration 16–2. Some useful points in connection with this technique are mentioned below.

Collections of accounts receivable is estimated by applying a "lag" factor to estimated sales or shipments. This factor may be based simply on the assumption that the cash from this month's sales will be collected next month; or there may be a more elaborate assumption, for example, that 10 percent of this month's sales will be collected this month, 60 percent next month, 20 percent in the second month, 9 percent in the third month, and the remaining 1 percent will never be collected.

The estimated amount and timing of *raw materials purchases* is obtained from the purchases budget, and is translated into cash disbursements by applying a lag factor for the time interval that ordinarily elapses between the receipt of the material and the payment of the invoice.

Illustration 16–2

CASH FORECAST, 1969
(in thousands)

	January	February	March	April	May	June	July	Totals for Year
Gross shipments	1,200	1,987	2,063	1,387	2,363	2,325	1,575	21,000
Cash balance beginning of month	375	396	222	150	257	160	192	375
Add: Cash receipts:								
Collections of accounts receivable	1,380	1,350	1,605	1,635	1,680	2,055	2,205	19,305
Miscellaneous receipts	66	81	70	105	105	97	97	1,050
Total receipts	1,446	1,431	1,675	1,740	1,785	2,152	2,302	20,355
Total cash available	1,821	1,827	1,897	1,890	2,042	2,312	2,494	20,730
Less: Cash disbursements:								
Operating expenses	810	915	1,035	885	975	1,020	960	10,730
Raw materials purchases	503	570	1,050	600	607	555	345	7,140
Taxes		60	412	13		395	3	1,310
Equipment purchases					100			100
Dividends	112			135			135	517
Pension contribution		210						247
Total disbursements	1,425	1,755	2,497	1,633	1,682	1,970	1,443	20,044
Cash balance or (deficiency) end of month before bank loans or (repayments)	396	72	(600)	257	360	342	1,051	686
Bank loans or (repayments)		150	750	(200)	(150)	(450)	0
Cash Balance End of Month	396	222	150	257	160	192	601	686

Other *operating expenses* are often taken directly from the expense budget, since the timing of cash disbursements is likely to correspond closely to the incurrence of the expense. Depreciation and other noncash expenses are excluded from this item.

The bottom of the cash forecast in Illustration 16–2 shows how cash plans are made. In February, for example, cash on hand would drop to $72,000, which is considered to be too low for safety; so the company plans to borrow $150,000 to provide a better safety margin. It plans to borrow $750,000 more in March and to start repaying these bank loans in May, when cash receipts exceed cash disbursements.

A monthly cash forecast, as in Illustration 16–2, is especially useful in planning for short-term, seasonal needs of cash. In order to estimate needs for more permanent capital, such as that obtained from the issuance of stock or bonds, the same general procedure would be followed, but with longer time intervals.

It should be noted that the figures in Illustration 16–2 are rounded. This procedure is customary in budgets. The amounts could be shown to the last penny, but the users of the report do not need such precise estimates. Furthermore, such figures tend to give a spurious impression of accuracy. Two or three significant digits are usually adequate.

THE CAPITAL BUDGET

The capital budget is essentially a list of what management believes to be worthwhile projects for the acquisition of new capital assets together with the estimated cost of each project. Proposals for such projects may originate anywhere in the organization. The capital budget is usually prepared separately from the operating budget, and in many companies it is prepared at a different time and cleared through a capital appropriations committee that is separate from the budget committee.

Each proposal, except those for minor amounts, is accompanied by a justification. For some projects, the expected return on investment can be estimated by methods to be described in Chapter 19. For others, such as the construction of a new office building or remodeling of employee recreation rooms, no estimate of return is possible, and these are justified on the basis of improved morale, safety, appearance, convenience, or other subjective grounds. A lump sum usually is included in the capital budget for projects that are not large enough to warrant individual consideration by top management.

In the capital budget, projects are often classified under headings such as the following:

1. Cost reduction and replacement.
2. Expansion of existing product lines.

3. New products.
4. Health and safety.
5. Other.

The first three categories usually are susceptible to an economic analysis in which the return on investment can be estimated.

As proposals come up through the organization, they are screened at various levels, and only the sufficiently attractive ones flow up to the top and appear in the final capital budget. On this document, they are often arranged in what is believed to be the order of desirability, and the estimated expenditures are broken down by years, or by quarters, so that the funds required in each time period are shown. At the final review meeting, which is usually at the board-of-director level, not only are the individual projects discussed but also the total amount requested on the budget is compared with total funds available. Many apparently worthwhile projects may not be approved, simply because the funds are not available.

Approval of the capital budget usually means approval of the projects *in principle*, but does not constitute final authority to proceed with them. For this authority, a specific authorization request is prepared for the project, spelling out the proposal in more detail, perhaps with firm bids or price quotations on the new assets. These authorization requests are approved at various levels in the organization, depending on their size and character. For example, each foreman may be authorized to buy production tools or similar items costing not more than $100 each, provided the total for the year does not exceed $1,000; and at the other extreme, all projects costing more than $500,000 and all projects for new products, whatever their cost, may require approval of the board of directors. In between, there is a scale of amounts that various echelons in the organization may authorize without the approval of their superiors.

An increasing number of companies are instituting procedures to follow up on capital expenditures. These include both checks on the spending itself and also an appraisal, perhaps a year or more after the project is completed, as to how well the estimates of cost and earnings actually turned out.

SUMMARY

Budgets are used as a device for making and coordinating plans, for communicating these plans to those who are responsible for carrying them out, for motivating managers at all levels, and as a standard with which actual performance subsequently can be compared. In a fully developed budget system, there is a package of interrelated budgets, including the program operating budget, the responsibility operating budget (and its subcategory, the variable budget), the cash budget, and the capital budget.

The operating budget is prepared within the context of basic policies and plans that have already been decided upon. The principal steps are as follows: (1) the dissemination of guidelines stating the overall plans and policies and other assumptions and constraints that are to be observed in the preparation of budget estimates; (2) the preparation of a sales estimate; (3) the preparation of other estimates by the heads of responsibility centers, assisted by, but not dominated by, staff budget men and accountants; (4) the negotiation of an agreed budget between the budgetee and his superior, which gives rise to a bilateral commitment by these parties; (5) coordination and review as these initial estimates move up the organizational chain of command; and (6) approval by top management and dissemination of the approved budget back down through the organization.

The *cash budget* translates revenues and expenses into receipts and disbursements and thus facilitates financial planning.

The *capital budget* is a priced list of presumably worthwhile projects for the acquisition of new capital assets. Often it is prepared separately from the operating budget. Approval of the capital budget constitutes only approval in principle, and a subsequent specific authorization is usually required before work on the project can begin.

SUGGESTIONS FOR FURTHER READING

CHAMBERLAIN, NEIL W. *The Firm: Micro-Economic Planning and Action.* New York: McGraw-Hill Book Co., Inc., 1962.

HEISER, HERMAN C. *Budgeting, Principles and Practices.* New York: Ronald Press Co., 1959.

HOFSTEDE, D. H. *The Game of Budget Control.* Assen, The Netherlands: Van Gorcum & Co., N.V., 1967.

STEINER, GEORGE A. (ed). *Top Management Planning.* New York: The Macmillan Co., 1969.

WELSCH, GLENN A. *Budgeting: Profit Planning and Control.* 2d ed.; New York: Prentice-Hall, Inc., 1963.

CHAPTER 17

THE ANALYSIS
OF PERFORMANCE

This chapter describes some of the concepts and techniques that are useful in analyzing the performance of a responsibility center. Essentially, such an analysis involves comparing actual performance with what performance should have been under the circumstances prevailing, in such a way that reasons for the difference between actual and expected performance are identified, and, if feasible, quantified.

The appraisal of performance involves a paradox. A man's performance can be measured only *after* he has performed; but at that time the work has already been done, and nothing management does later can change what was done. Of what value, therefore, are techniques for judging performance?

There seem to be two valid answers to this question. First, if a person knows in advance that his performance is going to be judged, he tends to act differently from the way he will if he believes no one is going to check up on him. (Anyone who has received grades in school should appreciate the importance of this point.)

The second reason why the appraisal of performance is valuable is that even though it is literally impossible to change an event that has already happened, an analysis of how well a person has performed in the past may indicate, both to the person and to his superior, ways of obtaining better performance in the future. Corrective action taken by the person himself is of prime importance; the system should "help the man to help himself." Action by the superior is also necessary. Such action may range in severity from giving criticism or praise or suggesting specific means of improving future performance, to the extremes either of firing or of promoting the person.

376

STRUCTURE OF ANALYSIS

Inputs and Outputs

For the purpose of this analysis, it is useful to visualize the work of a responsibility center as in Illustration 17–1. The responsibility center uses resources, which are its *inputs*. These resources can be classified as material, labor, and services, and their consumption is measured in terms of cost. In the operation of the responsibility center, these resources are used to produce *outputs*. These outputs are supposed to help achieve the objectives of the organization of which the responsibility center is a part. Information on outputs can be divided into: (1) quantity, that is, how much was done, and (2) quality, that is, how well it was done. For a customer invoicing unit, for example, the *quantity* of output may be measured by the number of invoices processed, and the *quality* of output

Illustration 17–1

WORK OF A RESPONSIBILITY CENTER

by the percentage of invoices that have no errors. Usually, it is easier to measure quantity than to measure quality; for example, it is easier to count the number of invoices processed than to detect and count those that contain errors.

As described in Chapter 13, performance can be measured along two dimensions: (1) *effectiveness*, which is how well the responsibility center does its job, and which is therefore related to its outputs; and (2) *efficiency*, which is the ratio of outputs to inputs.

This structure suggests that three key questions need to be considered: (1) How much was accomplished? (2) How well was the work done? and (3) How much did it cost? In some situations, the analysis can be simplified by answering the second question on a "go, no go" basis; that is, quality was either satisfactory or it was not satisfactory. When this simplification is feasible, the analysis is reduced to a problem of comparing quantity of output with costs.

In still other situations, the analysis can be limited to only one of these questions. For example, if the manager of a production department has no control over the volume of production and if the quality of work is indicated by the amount of rework costs, his performance may be judged primarily on the basis of cost alone.

In the typical situation, however, all three questions need to be considered together, and mistakes are made when one facet of performance is given undue emphasis as compared with the others. For example, until recently the Soviet management control system emphasized the quantity of output, with substantial bonuses being paid to managers for exceeding volume quotas. This emphasis on volume led to inadequate attention being paid to quality and cost, and the system was consequently redesigned to give a more balanced emphasis to these factors.

The Search for a Standard

As described in Chapter 11, the task of analyzing performance is, essentially, to compare what a person *actually did* with what he *should have done* under the circumstances. In many cases, actual performance can be ascertained without difficulty. The trick is to find a *standard*, or basis of comparison, that states what performance should have been under the conditions existing at the time.

The task of judging performance in business is complicated because results are affected by a complex set of factors, and the net influence of all these factors is never identical at two different times or on two different jobs done at the same time. A man who runs the mile in 4:04 minutes has done an excellent job, but what can we say about a foreman who spent $404 on supplies? First of all, we are not even sure of the *direction* that represents good performance. Offhand, one might conclude that spending $404 is "better" than spending $504, but there are many situations in which such a conclusion would be incorrect. If the foreman had spent another $100, for example, the department might have been able to turn out a much larger quantity of products, or the quality of the products might have been better, or safety conditions might have been improved, or other results worth more than $100 might have been achieved. Secondly, the actual spending of $404 may have been occasioned by any of a large number of factors over which the foreman has no control—company policies, an accident, orders from a superior, and a long list of others. Unless we recognize these factors and measure their impact, we cannot obtain a good measurement of the phenomenon we are trying to measure: the performance of the foreman himself.

Despite these difficulties, judgments about performance must be made, and some kind of standard, imperfect though it may be, is used as a guide in making such judgments. The four possible types of standards have been described in Chapter 11 in connection with the specific problem of analyzing financial statements, and are repeated in more general terms below. They can be used either separately or jointly.

1. STANDARDS BASED ON EXPERIENCE. Although the techniques to be described in this chapter will generally focus on formal standards expressed in quantitative terms, the importance of intuitive, informal standards derived from a person's experience and expressing his feel for what is "right" in a given situation should not be minimized. Such standards may well be more valid than those derived from any of the other sources listed below, and they are not described more fully here simply because of the difficulty of fitting them into the context of a formal framework.

2. PREDETERMINED STANDARDS OR BUDGETS. These are statements of expected performance under an assumed set of circumstances. Although actual events will never exactly match the assumed conditions, the standard may nevertheless be an adequate approximation to what should have been done.

3. PERFORMANCE OF OTHERS IN COMPARABLE JOBS. Department A may be compared with Department B, and if conditions in the two departments are reasonably similar, the comparison may provide a useful basis for judging performance.

4. PERFORMANCE IN THE PAST. Results this month may be compared with results last month, or with results in the same month a year ago. In addition to the need to allow for circumstances that may have changed between the two periods, this comparison has the weakness that when a man is measured against his own record, there may be no way of knowing whether the prior period's performance was acceptable to start with. A foreman whose spoilage cost is $100 a week, week after week, is consistent, but we do not know, without other evidence, whether he is consistently good or consistently poor.

DIFFICULTIES IN PERFORMANCE MEASUREMENT

It is unfortunately true that the more relevant a piece of information is, the more difficult it is to measure. An estimate of future performance is more difficult to make than a record of past performance, but it is more useful. A timely report, that is, one furnished shortly after the events reported on, is more difficult to compile than a report submitted long after the period has ended, but it is more useful. A measurement requiring judgment is more useful than one obtained by reading meters or other objective information, but it is more difficult. Thus, in designing a performance measurement system, a balance must be drawn between what management would like to have and what it is feasible to furnish.

Difficulty in Measuring Outputs

In a responsibility center that produces a physical product, the quantity of output can often be measured in physical terms: so many pairs of shoes, hundredweights of cement, and so on. When the outputs are so heterogeneous that they cannot be summarized by any physical measure, as in a job shop making many different types of products, output can be expressed by a monetary measure, such as the total standard cost of all products produced. In a profit center, the revenue of the center is a measure of its output.

For a great many responsibility centers, however, there is no reliable way of expressing the quantity of output, much less the quality of output, by any numerical measure. This is the case with most staff departments of a company, such as the research and development department, the personnel department, the controller department, the treasurer's office, and the general administrative offices. It is also the case generally with nonprofit organizations, that is, organizations whose objective is to perform some service rather than to earn a profit. Such organizations include government bodies of all types, schools, hospitals, foundations, churches, and social welfare organizations.

If output cannot be measured, there is obviously no way of making a formal appraisal of effectiveness or of comparing outputs with inputs, and the formal analysis must be restricted to an analysis of inputs, i.e., costs. Such an analysis is often better than not attempting any analysis at all, but its validity is necessarily narrower than the analysis that can be made of a responsibility center for which there is a reliable measure of outputs. When the analysis is thus restricted to imputs, there is a temptation to overlook or minimize the importance of the elements that have not been reduced to numbers. Every responsibility center has outputs, even though they cannot be measured, and performance appraisal must always take appropriate account of the effectiveness of these outputs, even if this has to be done in an entirely subjective manner.

It should also be recognized that most measures of output do not encompass all the outputs of a responsibility center. Even in the case of a production department, its total output—its contribution to the objectives of the company of which it is a part—is only partially measured by the quantity and quality of the products it produces, for its outputs may also include training personnel for advancement, employee morale, contribution to the community, and other elements that are either unmeasurable or at best measurable as rough approximations.

Conversely, in responsibility centers for which there is no overall measure of the dominant element of output, there may be ways of measuring certain aspects of output. The number of patient days is a crude measure of output for a hospital, even though it takes no account of the quality of service rendered or of the variations in the complexity of care required for different patients. Such a crude measure is often useful, provided its limitations are recognized.

Long-Run versus Current Performance

Management control systems tend to measure current performance, rather than long-run performance; that is, they measure the profit earned this year, rather than the effect on future profits of actions taken this year.

EXAMPLE: The manager of a profit center can improve his current profits by reducing the amounts spent on research and development, advertising, training, or maintenance. Any of these actions may have an adverse effect on future profits. Since the company's goal is presumably to earn satisfactory profits over the long run, such actions may be dysfunctional. Reports of current profits may therefore be misleading.

It is important that this limitation of the management control system be kept in mind both in analyzing performance and in deciding on the amount of emphasis that should be given to current performance measures. If too much emphasis is given to current performance, as may happen when there is a sizable bonus based on current profits, managers may take actions that are detrimental in the long run in order to make current performance look good.

The Special Problem of Investment Centers

Investment centers (i.e. centers in which both profit and investment are measured) pose a special problem that is not present in profit centers or expense centers. This is the problem of measuring the assets employed. The problem relates to all assets, but it is most difficult with respect to depreciable assets, such as buildings and equipment. For reasons that are given elsewhere,[1] the most conceptually sound basis of measurement seems to be that based on the annuity method of depreciation although this method is rarely used in practice.

PERFORMANCE REPORTS

Control reports vary widely in format, and only a few general comments are in order. They should be *objective;* that is, they should report what actually happened without bias. They should be *timely;* if they are to be the basis of action, they must be received before the time for effective action has passed. They should be *clear and easily understood,*

---

[1] "Accounting for Capital Costs" in *Management Control Systems: Cases and Readings,* by Anthony, Dearden, and Vancil (Homewood, Ill.: Richard D. Irwin, Inc., 1965), p. 343. See also articles by John Dearden in the *Harvard Business Review* of May–June, 1960, May–June, 1961, and July–August, 1962.

although clarity should not be achieved by oversimplifying an inherently complicated situation. They should indicate, if possible, the *reasons why*, not only the facts about performance itself.

Control reports, in the literal sense, are intended as a basis for action. Copies of the same reports together with other data on performance may be used for *information*, even though the person receiving them is not expected to take action.

The Time Interval of Control

The proper control period is the shortest period of time in which management can usefully intervene and in which significant changes in performance are likely. The period is different for different responsibility centers and for different items within responsibility centers. Spoilage rates in a production operation may be measured hourly, or oftener. Other key cost elements of the center may be measured daily. Reports on overall performance, particularly those going to top levels of management, are often on a monthly basis, and sometimes for quarterly or longer intervals, since top management does not have either the time or the inclination to explore local, temporary problems.

Performance for a short period of time is influenced by random factors that tend to average out over longer periods; a system with a short time interval costs more to operate and consumes more time of the participants at all levels than a system with longer intervals; and frequent reports may be associated with unduly restrictive supervision. These considerations may be offset, of course, by the necessity for detecting serious trouble quickly: a change in the behavior of a continuous chemical processing operation must be known as soon as it occurs, or there may be an explosion.

Content of Reports

Costs should be collected and measured only to the extent that they are *significant*. Reporting a long list of cost elements, many of which have only minor amounts, tends to obscure the few really significant ones. This can happen when the report is a standard form containing a long list of cost items that are reported uniformly for each responsibility center. Preferably, the control system is tailor-made to the situation in each responsibility center, having in mind also the probable uses of the information for purposes other than control.

The significance of an item is not necessarily proportional to its size. Management may be interested in a cost item of relatively small amount if this cost is one which is largely discretionary and therefore warrants close attention (such as travel expense, professional dues, books and periodicals), or if costs incurred for the item may be symptomatic of a larger problem (such as spoilage and rework costs, which may indicate problems of quality control.)

Management by Exception

A management control system operated on the exception principle is one in which management's attention is focused on the relatively small number of items in which actual performance is significantly different from the standard; when this is done, little or no attention need be given to the relatively large number of situations where performance is satisfactory.

No control system makes a perfect distinction between the situations that warrant management attention and those that do not. For example, it is the usual practice to "red flag" those items for which actual spending significantly *exceeds* the budgeted amount, but an investigation of these items may reveal that a difference between actual and budgeted spending was entirely warranted. On the other hand, even though actual spending for an item exactly matches the budget allowance, an unsatisfactory situation may exist. The exception principle is thus tricky to apply in practice. It is nevertheless a useful starting point for indicating the significance of what would otherwise be a bewildering mass of data, provided that the need for some examination of the superficially unexceptional situations is not overlooked. Conforming precisely to the budget is not necessarily good, and departing from the budget is not necessarily bad.

The distinction between significant and insignificant results is usually a matter of judgment. Attempts are being made to define "significant" in statistical terms, and these new techniques will probably have applications to business problems in the future.

Feedback

In engineering, when information about what has actually happened is used to change the performance of a machine, the process is called *feedback*. If the temperature of a room drops below a prescribed level, the thermostat activates the furnace. Control reports are, in a sense, feedback devices, for they contain information that is used by management to alter future actions of the organization.

Although the analogy with thermostats is useful, an important difference between thermostats and control reports must be recognized. In the former, the action is automatic; in the latter, it is far from automatic. In an organization, action occurs only when management has recognized the need for action and when it has persuaded the person responsible to take the action desired.

FORMAL ANALYTICAL TECHNIQUES

All analyses of performance involve comparisons. We make judgments about current performance, not by using some abstract or absolute criterion, but rather by comparing data on current performance with some other data.

We shall refer to the data we are analyzing as the *actual* data, and to the data used as a basis for comparison as the *standard* data. As used here, therefore, the word "standard" has a broader connotation than in the phrase "standard cost"; it includes *any* figure with which actual performance is compared.

In cost accounting, the difference between actual and standard is called a *variance*.[2] We shall use the words "variance" and "difference" interchangeably. It is of little use to know only the amount by which actual profit differs from standard profit. In order to take effective action, we need to know what factors accounted for the difference. In this section techniques for decomposing a total difference into the elements that account for it are described.

In a given company the techniques actually used will depend on management's estimate of the value to be derived from them. Some companies use no formal techniques, others use only a few of those described here, and still others use even more complicated techniques. There is no prescribed pattern beyond the general rule that any technique should be worth more than the costs involved in using it.

Validity of the Standard

Presumably, we choose a certain standard because it is the best measure we can find of the job that should have been done; yet a standard is rarely, if ever, perfect. Thus, although it is often convenient to refer to "favorable" and "unfavorable" variances, these words imply value judgments that are valid only to the extent that the standard is a valid measure of what should have been done. Some of the limitations of various types of standards have been discussed in Chapter 11.

Even a standard cost may not be an accurate estimate of what costs "should have been under the circumstances." This situation can arise for either or both of two reasons: (*a*) the standard was not set properly, or (*b*) although set properly in the light of conditions existing at the time, those conditions have changed so that the standard has become obsolete.

An essential first step in analysis of a variance, therefore, is an examina-

---

[2] Note that this word has quite a different meaning in statistics.

tion of the validity of the standard. Judgments made on the basis of the variance must be tempered by the results of this examination. The importance of this first step cannot be overemphasized, but we must assume for the purpose of describing other analytical techniques that the standard has been properly set.

It should also be recognized that for the whole category of discretionary costs, the standard or budgeted amount represents not what should have been done, in any cause-and-effect sense, but rather what has been agreed to as the permitted level of spending. For discretionary costs, a variance between standard and actual indicates only that the manager spent more or less than the agreed upon amount. In particular, actual spending that is less than standard does not imply "good" performance. Presumably, good performance is spending approximately the amount budgeted, neither more nor less.

Even though the standard is valid, a variance may not reflect the performance of a responsible supervisor since it may result from a combination of causes, some of which he can control and some of which he cannot control. Analytical techniques make it possible to separate out, at least approximately, the controllable portion. These techniques are strictly mechanical, and at best provide a starting point for solution of the problem of performance evaluation.

FACTORS TO BE CONSIDERED

The operations of a business can be examined in terms of its outputs and its inputs. Outputs are measured in terms of revenue, and inputs in terms of cost or expense; profit is the difference between them. The difference between actual and standard profit is explainable principally by the existence of some or all of the following factors:

1. Noncomparable data.
2. Price per unit of input.
3. Quantity of inputs.
4. Mix of inputs.
5. Quality of outputs.
6. Price per unit of output.
7. Volume.
8. The measuring stick.
9. Assets employed in investment centers. (This factor will not be discussed further here.)

These factors explain the profit variance for a whole company. Some or all of them also explain the variance for any department or other responsibility center within the company.

Noncomparable Data

For many reasons, the data used as the standard may not be strictly comparable with the actual data. Possible differences in the accounting rules used and in the definition of terms have been discussed at length in previous chapters. It is also possible that simple arithmetic errors have crept into one or the other set of data. Before proceeding with the detailed analysis, therefore, it is important that one examine the data carefully, and adjust them to remove such sources of noncomparability whenever possible.

Price and Quantity of Inputs

In order to decompose variances in input factors into price and quantity elements, we must have available, for both standard and actual, the number of units and the price per unit. The procedure will be discussed first in terms of direct labor and then in terms of direct material.

DIRECT LABOR. The standard labor cost of a unit of product is constructed essentially by multiplying the standard time (e.g., number of hours) required to produce that unit by a standard rate per unit of time (e.g., standard wage rate per hour). Total standard labor cost for an accounting period is found by multiplying the standard labor cost per unit by the number of units of product produced. When employees are paid on an hourly basis, actual labor cost for the period is the product of actual hours worked times the actual labor rate per hour. These relationships suggest that it is possible to break the variance between actual and standard labor costs into two components: (1) the variance caused by the fact that actual *time* differed from standard time, and (2) the variance caused by the fact that actual *rates* differed from standard rates. The former is the input quantity variance, and the latter is the input price variance.

A commonly used pair of rules for isolating the effects of these components follows:

1. The *time* variance is the difference between standard hours and actual hours, priced at the standard rate per hour. (This variance is also known as a "usage," "spending," or "efficiency" variance, although the latter two terms connote too strong an inference as to the meaning of the results.)
2. The *rate* (or "price") variance is the difference between the standard rate per hour and the actual rate per hour, multiplied by the actual numbers of hours.

The *net* variance (or *total* variance) in labor costs is the algebraic sum of the time and rate variances. It follows that having found one variance, the other can be found by subtracting this variance from the net variance.

The net variance is also the difference between actual cost and standard cost.

The application of these rules is illustrated in Illustration 17–2 which is a diagram of this situation:

	Actual	*Standard*
Hours to produce one unit.....................	6	8
Wage rate per hour.........................	$ 3	$ 2
Cost of one unit (rate times hours).............	$18	$16

Illustration 17–2

ILLUSTRATION OF COMPUTATION OF TIME
AND RATE VARIANCES

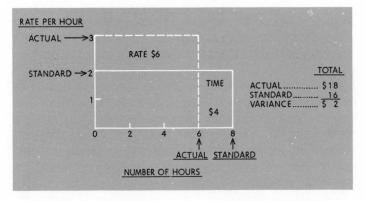

In the diagram, the solid rectangle indicates the standard cost (8 hours × $2 per hour = $16), and the dotted rectangle indicates actual cost (6 hours × $3 per hour = $18). The variances are the areas where the two rectangles do not coincide. The *time* variance is 2 hours times $2 per hour or $4; it is favorable because actual time is less than standard time. The *rate* variance is $1 per hour times 6 hours, or $6; it is unfavorable because the actual wage rate exceeds the standard rate. The net variance is the algebraic sum of these two variances, or $2, unfavorable; this is also the difference between actual cost and standard cost.

The calculations are repeated in terms of the rules given above:

1. (Std. Hours − Actual Hours) × Std. Rate = Time Variance
   (8 − 6) × $2 = $4
2. (Std. Rate − Actual Rate) × Actual Hours = Rate Variance
   ($2 − $3) × 6 = −$6
3. Std. Cost − Actual Cost = Net Variance
   $16 − $18 = −$2

These equations are set up in such a way that a plus answer means a favorable variance and a minus answer means an unfavorable variance, but it often is easier to find by inspection whether the variance is favorable or unfavorable than to remember this fact.

The Gray Area. When both the time and rate variances are favorable, or when both are unfavorable, the above rules do not give so clear-cut a result. The difficulty is demonstrated in Illustration 17–3, which shows the following situation:

	Actual	Standard
Hours to produce one unit	10	8
Wage rate per hour	$ 3	$ 2
Cost of one unit	$30	$16

In this situation, the unfavorable net variance of $14 is partly the result of the high wage rate and partly the result of the longer time required.

Illustration 17–3

COMPUTATION OF TIME AND RATE VARIANCES

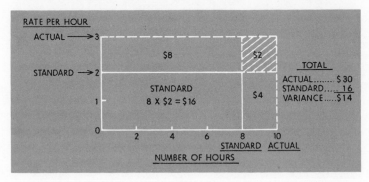

Clearly, at least $8 of the variance is a rate variance resulting because the work was done at a rate that was $1 per hour higher than standard, and at least $4 results because actual hours exceeded standard hours. But the remaining $2 is a *gray area;* it is an inextricable combination of the influence both of the high rate and the long time. The above rules have the effect of assigning the entire $2 as *rate variance.* Other possibilities would be just as logical, but in practice the rules given are usually used. The calculation is:

1. (Std. Hours — Actual Hours) × Std. Rate   = Time Variance
   (8   —   10   ) × $2   =   −$4
2. (Std. Rate — Actual Rate) × Actual Hours = Rate Variance
   ($2   — $3   ) ×   10   =   −$10

Interpretation of the Labor Variance. The reason for attempting to break down the total labor variance as described above is that the rate variance is often evaluated differently from the time variance. The rate variance may arise because of a change in wage rates for which the foreman cannot be held responsible, whereas the foreman may be held entirely responsible for the time variance, because he should control the time spent on a given job.

This distinction cannot be made in all cases, for there are many situations in which the two factors are interdependent. For example, the foreman may find it possible to complete the work in less than the standard time by using men who earn a higher than standard rate, and he may be perfectly justified in doing so. Even so, the use of the technique described above may lead to a better understanding of what actually happened.

The technique described provides only a partial explanation of the cause of the labor variance. It does not isolate any of a great number of other factors that may cause a difference between actual and standard labor costs. An incomplete list of such factors follows:

1. A standard labor cost per unit is valid only if labor costs vary proportionately with the number of units produced. Labor costs, in fact, may not vary proportionately with volume at all levels of production.
2. The measure of volume (e.g., number of units, pounds of product, etc.) may not be an accurate indication of the amount of direct labor required. For example, a standard labor cost of $1 a pound implies that each pound of product requires the same amount of labor, which, in fact, may not be the case.
3. The volume figure used to compute total standard costs may not correspond exactly to the volume figure that generated the actual labor costs, because of the nature of the system.
4. The elements included in standard cost (e.g., overtime, fringe benefits, shift premium) may differ from the elements included in actual costs.
5. Spoilage may not have been allowed for properly (see below).
6. Quality may have suffered or improved.
7. Labor performance may have affected, or may have been affected by, factors that are reflected in material or overhead costs.
8. There may have been changes in morale that have not affected current costs but which may have an important effect on future costs.
9. The total actual costs and total standard costs for a period may be influenced by offsetting forces for individual products or individual responsibility centers. The totals conceal these underlying forces.

Since the objective is to isolate that portion of the variance that is the result of efficiency or inefficiency and to hold the supervisor responsible for this portion, factors of the type mentioned above must be considered.

MATERIAL COST VARIANCES. The variance between actual and standard direct material costs can be broken down into what are commonly called *material usage variance* and *material price variance* by the same technique as that described above for direct labor. The diagram in Illustration 17–2 is made applicable to material costs simply by changing the names:

	Actual	*Standard*
Quantity (pounds) used to produce one unit.	6	8
Price per pound. . . . .$ 3		$ 2
Material cost for one unit. $18		$16

The *usage* variance, or *yield* variance, is 2 pounds times $2 a pound, or $4; and the *price* variance is $1 a pound times 6 pounds, or $6.

In some companies, the cost accounting system is constructed so that the price variance is removed as a part of the regular accounting entries; if such a system is used, there may be no need to separate out the price variance by the method described above. For example, if a company takes raw material into inventory at a standard price, the price variance is set up at the time the purchase is recorded. Raw Materials Inventory is debited at standard cost, Accounts Payable (or Cash) is credited at actual cost, and the difference is debited or credited to Material Price Variance. Even in such a case, a kind of price variance may later appear if material of a different *quality* from standard (hence, with a different standard cost) is used in the production process.

SPOILAGE AND REWORK. The material usage variance shows the difference between the actual and standard quantities of material *put into* the manufacturing process. If the product itself does not pass inspection at the end of the process or at some intermediate stage, it must either be discarded or sent back to have the defect corrected. If discarded, the labor, material, and overhead costs accumulated on it up to that point constitute *spoilage*. If sent back for correction, the extra *rework* cost is also a cost associated with substandard products.

There are several ways of accounting for spoilage and rework costs, only one of which is described here. A budgeted amount of spoilage is agreed on for each responsibility center. The actual cost of spoilage charged to the responsibility center is the cost of the defective products for which the responsibility center is responsible. This cost includes the material, labor, and overhead costs that have been accumulated on the defective product up to the point where the defect is discovered; thus, it may be the total cost of the product if the defect is not discovered until final inspection, or it may be a lesser amount if the defect is discovered during the manufacturing process. The costs of reworking products are charged to the responsibility center that caused the defect. Note that both spoilage costs and rework costs are charged to the responsibility center that *caused* the spoilage or rework, which is not necessarily the same as the responsibility center in which the defect was discovered or the responsibility center in which the rework was actually done.

The difference between the budgeted amount of spoilage and rework and the spoilage and rework costs charged to the responsibility center is the amount of variance attributable to the fact that actual spoilage and rework differed from the amount assumed in the budget.

Mix of Inputs

When the process uses several different materials, or several grades of the same material, that are supposed to be combined in a standard proportion, it is possible to compute a *mix variance* that shows the effect on cost of variations from the standard proportion. The mix variance for each item of material is the difference between the actual quantity of material used and the standard proportion (i.e., the quantity that would have been used if the standard proportions were adhered to), priced at the standard price. If a mix variance is calculated, the price variance is also calculated for each item of material separately.

To illustrate the calculation of the mix variance, we shall use a situation similar to that described in Illustration 17–2. We shall shift the situation from labor costs to material costs, simply to highlight the fact that the technique applies equally well to either type of cost; and instead of a single quantity and a single unit price, we shall assume that there are three items of material, each with its own quantity and unit price. The total amounts for the three items correspond to the totals shown in Illustration 17–2, signifying that the mix variance is a further decomposition of the differences analyzed there.

The calculation of the mix variance is shown in Illustration 17–4. As shown in the top block of the Illustration, a standard unit of product consists of Materials A, B, and C in the proportions $\frac{4}{8}$, $\frac{2}{8}$, and $\frac{2}{8}$, respectively. In the next block, these fractions are applied to the *actual* total quantity, 6 pounds, to give the standard mix of the three materials in such a quantity: namely, 3 pounds of A, 1.5 pounds of B, and 1.5 pounds of C. The difference between the actual quantity of each material and its standard mix, priced at its standard price and totaled, is the mix variance.

The price variance on each material is computed according to the rule already given: the difference between standard price and actual price, times the actual quantity. Note that the *sum* of the mix variances and price variances computed in this manner equals the price variance computed from the total quantity and average price given above, that is $(-\$4) + (-\$2) = -\$6$. The usage variance and the net variance are not affected.

Computation of the mix variance and price variance in this manner, although a little complicated, reveals information that might otherwise be concealed. It shows the effect of changes in the price of each material, which is hidden if averages are used. It also shows the effect of varying the mix of materials. These two may be interrelated; for example, it is

Illustration 17–4

MIX, PRICE, AND USAGE VARIANCES

A. Assumed Situation

	Standard			Actual		
	Quantity (Lbs.)	Unit Price	Total	Quantity (Lbs.)	Unit Price	Total
Material A............4	$1.00	$ 4.00		2	$3.50	$ 7.00
Material B............2	2.00	4.00		1	2.00	2.00
Material C............2	4.00	8.00		3	3.00	9.00
Total..............8	$2.00	$16.00		6	$3.00	$18.00

B. Computation of Mix Variance

	$\frac{Standard^*}{Mix}$ −	Actual Quantity =	Differ- ence	×	Std. Price =	Mix Variance
Material A...............3		2	+1		$1.00	$1.00
Material B...............1.5		1	+0.5		2.00	1.00
Material C...............1.5		3	−1.5		4.00	− 6.00
Total.................6		6				−$4.00

* This is the standard proportions ⅜, ⅜, and ⅜ applied to the actual total quantity.

C. Computation of Price Variance

	Std. Price	−	Actual Price =	Differ- ence	×	Actual Quality =	Price Variance
Material A................$1.00			$3.50	−$2.50		2	−$5.00
Material B................ 2.00			2.00	. . .		1	. . .
Material C................ 4.00			3.00	+ 1.00		3	+ 3.00
Price Variance...........							−$2.00

D. Computation of Usage Variance

$$\text{(Standard Quantity} - \text{Actual Quantity)} \times \text{Standard Price} = \text{Usage Variance}$$
$$(\quad 8 \quad - \quad 6 \quad) \times \quad \$2 \quad = \quad \$4$$

quite possible that a higher than standard proportion of one material was used in an attempt to offset the effect of an increased price of another material. The mix variance may also be related to the quality of the product, although this does not appear in the calculation; if one material is a low grade and another is a high grade, then the increase in the proportion of the lower grade material may have had an adverse effect on quality.

GENERAL USE OF THE MIX CONCEPT. The mix phenomenon arises whenever a cost or revenue item is analyzed by components, rather than in total. The price and quantity variances obtained from an analysis of each of the components will not add up to the price and quantity variance of the whole item if the actual proportions of the components differ from the standard proportions. Thus, if labor cost is being analyzed by employee skill classifications, if revenue is analyzed by individual products, or by individual geographic regions, a mix variance inevitably arises. Failure to appreciate this fact can lead to great frustration in trying to make the figures add up properly.

Quality of Output

In many situations, there is no numerical way of measuring the differences in quality or other characteristics between the standard and the actual output, the significance of this factor must therefore be judged intuitively. In some cases, it can be brought into the analysis explicitly. For example, if we are analyzing the differences between two bids to build a house, the fact that one contractor includes certain features that the other omits is an obvious factor to be taken into account.

Output Price and Volume

The sales revenue variance can be decomposed into a price factor and a quantity or volume factor. The *price variance* is the difference between the standard price per unit and the actual price per unit multiplied by the actual quantity sold. The *quantity variance* is the difference between standard quantity and actual quantity sold priced at the standard price per unit. Note the similarity between these rules and the rules for deriving the labor time and rate variances; whenever a total variance is to be broken down into a quantity element and a price element, the same general approach is used.

If revenue is analyzed by individual products or product lines, a mix variance will emerge, as described in the preceding section.

In many situations, it is more informative to analyze output in terms of gross margin, rather than in terms of sales revenue. The procedure is the same, except that gross margin per unit is used instead of selling price per unit. Such an analysis implies that the output of the sales organization is more usefully viewed as dollars of gross margin, rather than as dollars of sales revenue.

Volume and Overhead Costs

Direct labor and direct material costs usually vary directly and proportionately with volume. Consequently, *unit* direct labor and direct material costs are the same at all volume levels within the normal range; they are unaffected by volume. By contrast, overhead costs vary with volume but less than proportionately, as we saw in the diagrams presented in Chapter 15. This being so, *unit* overhead costs are inevitably higher at low volumes than they are at high volumes.

EXAMPLE: If the formula for the overhead cost line is $500 plus $1 per unit, overhead costs at various volumes are expected to be as follows:

Volume (in Units)	Total Overhead Cost	Unit Overhead Cost
800	$1,300	$1.62
900	1,400	1.56
1,000	1,500	1.50
1,100	1,600	1.45
1,200	1,700	1.42

Since the unit selling price presumably does not fluctuate with volume, whereas unit costs change with volume as seen above, unit profits are different at different volumes. Thus, if actual volume is different from standard volume, a volume variance results.

In order to measure this variance, we shall make use of the cost-volume relationship developed in Chapter 15. In Illustration 17–5, the line marked "budgeted" cost shows this direct, but less than proportional, relationship between costs and volume. Costs at any volume are expected to be the nonvariable amount, *a*, plus the variable rate, *b*, times the number of units of volume.

Recall that the overhead rate was set by choosing one level of volume, the *normal volume*, and dividing total costs at that volume by the number of units of volume. Thus, if the formula for the budgeted cost line is

Illustration 17–5

BUDGETED, ABSORBED, AND ACTUAL COSTS

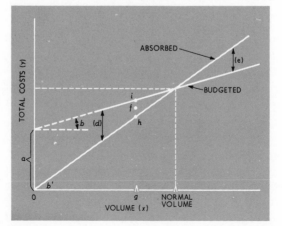

$500 + $1 per unit, and if normal volume is 1,000 units, total budgeted costs at 1,000 units are $1,500, and the overhead rate is $1.50 per unit.

At any volume, overhead costs would be *absorbed* into products at the rate of $1.50 per unit. The line of "absorbed" cost on the diagram shows the total costs that would be absorbed at any volume. At normal volume, budgeted costs equal absorbed costs, but at any other volume budgeted costs are different from absorbed costs, as indicated by the spread between the two lines. At lower volumes, costs are expected to be *underabsorbed*, as indicated by the amount *d*, and at higher volumes they are expected to be *overabsorbed*, as indicated by the amount *e*. They are underabsorbed or overabsorbed *because* actual volume differs from normal volume; hence, this amount is the volume variance. The volume variance results solely from the fact that actual volume in a given period differed from the normal volume that was used, *prior to the beginning of the year*, in setting the overhead rate.

If everything went as expected during an accounting period, actual costs incurred would coincide with budgeted costs at the level of activity prevailing in the period. For a variety of reasons, actual costs will probably be different from budgeted costs; the difference is called the *spending variance*. For control purposes, the spending variance is of particular interest as a starting point in appraising the supervisor's performance. It is only a starting point, since the variance may be the result of any of a number of uncontrollable factors, such as changes in prices, the method of overhead allocation, the rate and direction of change in volume, and changes in methods.

The overhead variance, as shown in the accounting records, is the algebraic sum of the volume variance and the spending variance. It is therefore useful to break down this *net variance* into its two components. The method for doing this is shown in Illustration 17–5 in a period when actual costs are at the point marked *f* and actual volume is *g*. Absorbed cost at this volume is the amount *h*, and budgeted cost the amount, *i*. Note that budgeted cost is the amount of cost budgeted for the volume level actually attained in the period. The following relationships will hold:

The *net variance* is the difference between absorbed cost, *h*, and actual cost, *f*. In the example, cost is underabsorbed.

As is stated above, this variance is also the algebraic sum of the volume variance and the spending variance. (The "favorable" and "unfavorable" variances can be designated by plus or minus signs, but it is usually easier to insert the proper signs from a consideration of the relationships than by memorizing the algebraic formulas.)

The *volume variance* is the difference between absorbed cost, *h*, and budgeted cost, *i*. In the example, this variance is unfavorable.

The *spending variance* is the difference between budgeted cost, *i*, and actual cost, *f*. In the example, this variance is favorable.

EXAMPLE: Assume that—
Actual volume in an accounting period is 900 units.
Actual cost is $1,380.
The budget formula is $500 plus $1 per unit.
The overhead rate is $1.50 per unit.
Then:

Budgeted cost at the actual volume	=	$1,400
Absorbed cost at the actual volume	=	1,350
Net variance (underabsorbed)	=	1,350 − $1,380 = −$30
Volume variance (unfavorable)	=	1,350 − 1,400 = − 50
Spending variance (favorable)	=	1,400 − 1,380 = 20

INTERPRETATION OF THE VARIANCES. Presumably, the supervisor is responsible for the spending variance that arises in his responsibility center. Because the budgeted cost line cannot take account of all the noncontrollable factors that affect cost, there may be a reasonable explanation for the spending variance. The existence of an unfavorable variance is therefore not, by itself, grounds for criticizing performance. Rather, it is a signal that investigation and explanation are required.

In some situations the supervisor may also be responsible for the volume variance. Failure to obtain standard volume may result from his inability to keep products moving through his department, for example. The volume variance is more likely to be someone else's responsibility, however. It may result because the sales department was unable to obtain the planned volume of orders, or because some earlier department in the manufacturing process failed to deliver materials as they were needed.

In appraising spending performance, the analyst will go behind the total spending variance and examine the individual overhead items of which it consists. The total budgeted cost is the sum of the allowances for each of the separate items. A spending variance can be developed for each item, as the difference between actual cost incurred and the budget allowance for the item; attention is focused on significant spending variances for individual items.

In terms of the structure established at the beginning of this section, the spending variance is a composite of input price and input quantity factors. After it has been separated from the volume variance, it could conceivably be broken down into its price and quantity elements, as was done for direct labor, but in practice the analysis is usually not carried this far.

It should be emphasized that the volume variance arises only from differences in the *level* of volume. The *speed* of change in volume from one level to another also can have an effect on costs. So can the *direction* of change, for actual costs often tend to be below the line of budgeted costs when volume is increasing and above the line when volume is decreasing. This phenomenon, which is called *lag* or *hysteresis*, shows up in the spending variance, not the volume variance.

Measuring Stick Variance

If the measure of volume is an input factor, such as actual direct labor hours, rather than an output factor, such as units of products produced or the standard direct labor hours in these products, then an additional complication arises. To illustrate it, let us assume that the unit of volume in Illustration 17–5 was *actual* direct labor hours, but that overhead costs were absorbed into products on the basis of $1.50 per *standard* labor hour in these products.

Assume further that actual direct labor in a month totaled 900 hours and that standard direct labor totaled only 860 hours, other conditions remaining as in the above illustration. The amount of overhead costs absorbed will then be 860 hours times $1.50 per hour, or $1,290. If standard hours had totaled 900, then $1,350 ($= 900 \times \$1.50$) would have been absorbed. The difference of $60 between this $1,350 and the $1,290 actually absorbed arises because the direct labor force worked at less than standard efficiency. This variance is therefore called the *efficiency variance*, although it can be seen that the word "efficiency" relates to the ultilization of direct labor, and not to overhead itself. It is the difference between actual hours and standard hours, priced at the standard rate per hour.

EXAMPLE: The complete analysis of this new situation is as follows:
Actual overhead cost incurred   = $1,380.
Budgeted cost at actual volume   = 1,400.
Absorbed cost, 860 standard hours $\times$ $1.50 = 1,290.
Net variance (underabsorbed)   = $1,290 - \$1,380 = -90.$
Volume variance (unfavorable)   = 1,350 - 1,400 = -50.
Spending variance (favorable)   = 1,400 - 1,380 =   20.
Efficiency variance (unfavorable) = $(860 - 900) \times \$1.50 = -60.$

The efficiency variance is not present in many situations, but only in those in which there is a difference in the way volume is measured for control and the way costs are absorbed for product costing.

AN ILLUSTRATIVE ANALYSIS

As a way of summarizing the techniques described above, the complete analysis of a simple hypothetical situation is shown in Illustration 17–6. Although the company in this example manufactures three products, we have simplified the calculation of manufacturing variances by making standard unit manufacturing cost the same for all products; this is simply for the purpose of avoiding numerous computations of mix variance. For further simplification of the arithmetic, we have assumed that only one kind of material and one class of labor are used. In the examination of revenue variances, we have carried through the three-product analysis in order to illustrate the calculation of a mix variance.

The income statement (Section A) shows a variance between actual and standard profit of $55. The question is: What accounts for this variance? The answer to this question is given in Section B, which decomposes the total variance into elements. The remainder of the illustration shows how these elements were found.

Illustration 17–6

COMPUTATION OF VARIANCES

A. Income Statements

	Standard	Actual	Variance
Sales.....................................	$540	$555	
Less: Standard cost of sales...............	440	418	
Gross margin at standard cost...............	$100	$137	$ 37
Less: Manufacturing variances.............	0	82	(82)
Gross margin............................	$100	$ 55	$(45)
General and admin. expense.................	40	50	(10)
Operating Profit before Taxes...............	$ 60	$ 5	$(55)

B. Summary of Variances

Sales volume............................	$(5)
Sales mix...............................	3
Sales price.............................	39
Net marketing...........................	$ 37
Material price...........................	$(16)
Material usage...........................	4
Labor time..............................	(24)
Labor price.............................	(8)
Overhead volume........................	(15)
Overhead spending.......................	(23)
Net manufacturing.......................	$(82)
General and admin.......................	$(10)
Net Profit Variance......................	$(55)

( ) = unfavorable

C. Underlying Data, Marketing Area

	Standard			Actual		
	Quan-tity	Unit Price	Total	Quan-tity	Unit Price	Total
Product A..................	100	$2.60	$260	80	$2.50	$200
Product B..................	60	2.80	168	60	3.00	180
Product C..................	40	2.80	112	50	3.50	175
Total..................	200	$2.70	$540	190		$555

Illustration 17–6 (Continued)

D. Computation of Marketing Variances

(1) Volume Variance

Actual Vol.	—	Std. Vol.	=	Diff.	×	Std. Gross Margin		
190	—	200	=	−10	×	$0.50	=	−$5.00

(2) Mix Variance

Actual Quantity	—	Std. Quantity*	=	Diff.	×	Std. Gross Margin	=	Variance
80	—	95	=	−15	×	$0.40	=	−$6.00
60	—	57	=	+ 3	×	0.60	=	+ 1.80
50	—	38	=	+12	×	0.60	=	+ 7.20
Total 190		190				Mix Variance =		+$3.00

* Based on standard proportions of $\frac{100}{200}$, $\frac{60}{200}$, $\frac{40}{200}$.

(3) Selling Price Variance

Actual Selling Price	—	Std. Selling Price	=	Diff.	×	Actual Quantity	=	Variance
$2.50	—	$2.60	=	−0.10	×	80	=	−$ 8.00
3.00	—	2.80	=	+0.20	×	60	=	+ 12.00
3.50	—	2.80	=	+0.70	×	50	=	+ 35.00
						Price Variance =		+$39.00

E. Underlying Data, Manufacturing Area

Item	Standard	Actual
Volume.................	200 units	170 units
Direct material...........	2 lbs./unit at $0.20/lb.	320 lbs. at $0.25 = $ 80
Direct labor..............	0.4 hrs./unit at $2.00/hr.	80 hrs. at $2.10 = 168
Overhead................	$100 + $0.50 per unit	$208

F. Computation of Manufacturing Variances

(1) Material Price Variance

Std. Price	—	Actual Price	=	Diff.	×	Actual Quantity	=	Material Price Variance
$0.20	—	$0.25	=	−$0.05	×	320	=	−$16

(2) Material Usage Variance

Std. Quantity	—	Actual Quantity	=	Diff.	×	Std. Price	=	Material Usage Variance
340	—	320	=	20	×	$0.20	=	+$4

Illustration 17–6 (Continued)

(3) Labor Time Variance

Std. *Hours*		*Actual* *Hours*	=	*Diff.*	×	*Std.* *Rate*	=	*Labor* *Time* *Variance*
68	−	80	=	−12	×	$2.00	=	−$24

(4) Labor Price Variance

Std. *Rate*		*Actual* *Rate*	=	*Diff.*	×	*Actual* *Hours*	=	*Labor* *Price* *Variance*
$2.00	−	$2.10	=	−$0.10	×	80	=	−$8

(5) Overhead Variances

Net Variance   = $170–$208 = −$38
Volume Variance   = $170–$185 = − 15
Spending Variance = $185–$208 = − 23

Marketing Variance

The first step in the computation is to make a breakdown of the variance for which the marketing department is held accountable. The basic data required for this part of the analysis are shown in Section C, and the computations are made in Section D. Mix, volume, and price variances are calculated, their algebraic sum totaling the $37 shown as a revenue variance on the income statement. In calculating marketing variances, notice that gross margin, not selling price or total revenues, is used. This is because the contribution of the marketing department is best measured by the gross margin it generates, rather than by sales revenue. Gross margin is found by subtracting *standard* cost of sales (which is $2.20 per unit) from selling prices. Using the *standard* cost of sales figure means that the marketing department is not held accountable for any manufacturing expense variances; rather, these are the responsibility of the manufacturing organization.

The volume variance is the loss or gain in gross margin that results from a difference between actual and standard sales volume. The mix variance is figured by multiplying the standard gross margin for each product by the difference between the actual and standard quantity. The selling price variance is determined by multiplying the actual sales quantities for each product by the difference between actual and standard selling price.

Note that revenue variances are favorable when actual is greater than standard, which is of course the opposite situation from expense variances.

EXAMPLE: In Illustration 17–6, the $37 excess of actual gross margin over standard gross margin is favorable, but the $82 excess of actual manufacturing variances over standard manufacturing variances is unfavorable.

It is advisable to use parenthesis (or red ink or asterisks) for unfavorable variances, i.e., those that decrease net profit, rather than to use them for excesses of actual over standard. This provides a clearer signal to the reader, for if the latter practice is followed, increases in cost, which are unfavorable, will have the same appearance as increases in revenue, which are favorable.

Manufacturing Variances

Next we turn to an analysis of the manufacturing expense variances. Note that, as shown in Section E, actual production volume is less than actual sales volume, the difference being made up out of inventory which is carried at standard cost. Carrying the inventory at standard cost means that expense variances are treated as period costs and charged directly to cost of sales during the period in which they occur and not put into inventory.

The labor, material, and overhead variances described earlier in the chapter are calculated in Section F. Their algebraic sum equals the $82 unfavorable variance noted on the income statement. This is charged directly to cost of sales.

An examination of the $10 unfavorable variance in general and administrative expenses completes the analysis of the net profit variance. This is not shown; it would consist of an analysis by class of expense of the amount of and reasons for differences between the budgeted expense and the actual expense.

ATTACKING AN APPRAISAL PROBLEM

Some or all of the techniques described above may be useful if the necessary data are available. The unfortunate fact is, however, that one rarely has all the data he would like to have in order to reach a sound judgment on performance. Under these circumstances, the analyst simply does the best he can with what he has. Everyone would agree that both the Union and Confederate leaders made mistakes at the battle of Gettysburg; but despite volumes of analysis by military experts and historians, there is not unanimous agreement, even today, as to what these mistakes were or who was responsible for them. Nevertheless, the field commanders at the time, without the benefit of any historical research, had to make judgments on the performance of those participating in this battle and take action on the basis of these judgments.

In view of the inevitable incompleteness of the data, the following guides may suggest a useful way of attacking a problem that involves the appraisal of performance:

1. From the information available or obtainable, decide on the best possible standard or basis of comparison.

2. Define the factors that are not included in the standard; attempt to estimate the importance of these factors; and either modify the standard to take them into account or reduce the degree of certainty attached to the comparison of actual against standard.

3. Find, and attempt to estimate the importance of, nonquanitative considerations that cannot be included in a standard (e.g., morale, quality, intangible future benefits).

4. Make a judgment and be prepared to act on it. (One possible judgment is that no action should be taken until more information is available. This judgment should be made only if one is reasonably confident that it is both feasible and necessary to obtain additional facts.)

SUMMARY

Conceptually, the performance of a responsibility center is judged by measuring the effectiveness of its outputs and the efficiency of its inputs. Effectiveness can be divided into quality and quantity, suggesting two key questions: (1) How much was accomplished? and (2) How well was the work done? Efficiency is measured by the ratio of outputs to inputs, that is, by the ratio of work done to resources used in doing the work.

In making judgments on effectiveness and efficiency, actual outputs and inputs are compared with standard outputs and inputs. These standards presumably represent what should have happened under the circumstances prevailing. They are derived from experience, from past performance of the responsibility center, from the performance of similar responsibility centers, or from predetermined standards or budgets.

Even the best standard is unlikely to be a perfectly valid measure of what should have happened. In many situations there is no way of expressing in numbers what output actually was, let alone what it should have been. Moreover, the analysis tends to focus on current performance, whereas the impact of current decisions on future performance may be as important, or even more important.

Formal techniques are available for decomposing the difference between actual performance and standard performance and showing the magnitude of the difference attributable to each factor. These techniques provide clues as to the reason for the variance, but they never provide a complete answer to the question, "Why did the variance occur?" At best, they show the areas in which further investigation should be concentrated in order to find the answer to this vital question.

PART IV

Accounting in Business Decisions

CHAPTER 18

DECIDING AMONG ALTERNATIVE COURSES OF ACTION

Businessmen are many times called upon to make decisions by choosing what they believe to be the best one of several possible alternative courses of action. Problems in this area are therefore called "alternative choice problems."

In a great many business problems, the decision is made intuitively; that is, there is no systematic attempt to define, measure, and weigh the advantages and disadvantages of each alternative. A person who makes an intuitive decision may do so simply because he is not aware of any other way of making up his mind, or he may do so, and with good reason, because the problem is one in which a systematic attempt to weigh alternatives is not useful, too difficult, too expensive, or simply not possible.

No mathematical formula will aid in solving a problem in which the attitudes or emotions of the individuals involved are the dominant factors, nor is there any point in attempting to make calculations if the available information is so sketchy or so inaccurate that the results are completely unreliable.

In many other situations, however, it is useful to reduce at least some of the anticipated consequences of the alternatives to a quantitative basis and to weigh these consequences in a more or less systematic manner. Usually, this process involves a consideration of accounting data, with particular attention to cost data. Some of the problems which managers are likely to face in using cost data as an aid in making these business decisions are discussed in this chapter.

APPROACH TO ALTERNATIVE CHOICE PROBLEMS

Criteria

In earlier chapters, we assumed that, insofar as it is measured quantitatively, the dominant objective of a business is to earn a satisfactory return on its investment. We now expand this concept by adding the commonsense idea that if two alternative courses of action are being considered, the management will select the one that is likely to lead to the higher return on investment, or if no investment is involved, the one with the higher profit.[1]

The fact that this criterion is limited to measurable objectives should again be emphasized. In many practical problems, personal satisfaction, friendship, patriotism, self-esteem, or other considerations may be much more important than return on investment. Or, the company may have other measurable objectives, such as maintenance of its market position, stabilization of employment, or avoidance of undue risk. When these considerations are important or dominant, the solution to the problem cannot be reached by the techniques discussed here. The most these techniques can do is show the effect on return on investment of seeking some other objective. The problem then becomes one of deciding whether the attainment of the other objective is worth the cost.

Outline of Approach

Return on investment may be expressed as the ratio:

$$\frac{\text{Revenue} - \text{Costs}}{\text{Investment}}.$$

Although the general approach to all alternative choice problems is similar, it is useful to discuss three types separately. First, there are problems that involve only the cost element of the ratio. Since revenue and investment are unaffected, the best alternative is the one with the lowest cost. Problems of this type are discussed in the next section. Second, there are problems in which both revenue and costs are involved. These are discussed in the latter part of this chapter. Third, there are problems that involve both the numerator and the denominator of the ratio. These are discussed in Chapter 19.

---

[1] "Profit" in this context is usually defined as in the ordinary accounting sense, but there are exceptions, because profit does not always measure the "well-offness" of a business, particularly in the short run. A more accurate, but also more vague, criterion is that the management will select the alternative that makes the business the "best off."

STEPS IN ANALYSIS. Before a separate discussion of these types is given, some general comments about approaching alternative choice problems are in order. Following is a list of steps that are useful for most problems:

1. Define the problem.
2. Define the most likely alternative solutions.
3. Measure and weigh those consequences of each alternative that can be expressed in quantitative terms.
4. Evaluate those consequences that cannot be expressed in quantitative terms and weigh them against each other and against the measured consequences.
5. Reach a decision.

The discussion in this chapter has to do primarily with costs, which are the best means of measuring those consequences that can be expressed in quantitative terms. Thus, we focus primarily on step 3. Brief mention will be made of the other steps, but in no sense is this a comprehensive discussion of the art of decision making.

Definition of the Problem and of Alternative Solutions

Unless the problem is clearly and precisely defined, quantitative figures that are relevant to it cannot be computed. In many situations, the definition of the problem, or even the recognition that a problem exists, may be the most difficult part of the whole process.

Quite often, the possible alternative solutions to the problem are by no means clear at the outset. For example, suppose that a factory manager is considering a machinery salesman's proposal that a certain machine should be used to perform an operation now done by hand methods. At first glance, there may appear to be two alternatives: (*a*) continue to perform the operation by hand or (*b*) buy the new machine. Actually, however, several additional alternatives should perhaps be considered, such as these: (*c*) buy a machine other than the one recommended by the salesman, (*d*) improve the present method of making the part, or even (*e*) eliminate the manufacturing operation altogether and buy the part from an outside source. Some thought should be given to these other possibilities before attention is focused too closely on the original proposal.

On the other hand, the more alternatives that are considered, the more complex the analysis becomes. For this reason, having thought about all the possible alternatives, the analyst should eliminate without more ado those that are clearly unattractive, leaving only a few for detailed analysis. In the simplest situation, only two alternatives are examined closely. These can be described in general terms as follows: (*a*) the continuation of what is now being done, or (*b*) the adoption of a proposed change—a new machine, a new process, a new selling price, and so on. Note that there must always be at least two alternatives. If only one course of action is open, the company literally has "no choice," and hence no analytical problem. In most problems one of the alternatives is to keep on doing what is now being done. This "no-change" alternative is often used as a bench mark against which other alternatives are compared.

Weighing and Measuring the Quantitative Factors

There are usually a number of advantages and a number of disadvantages associated with each of the alternative solutions of a problem. The task of the analyst is to evaluate each of the relevant factors and to decide, on balance, which alternative has the largest *net* advantage.

If the factors are stated solely in words, such an evaluation is an exceedingly difficult task. For example, consider the statement that a proposed manufacturing process will save labor but that it will result in increased power consumption and require additional insurance protection. Such a statement provides no way of weighing the relative importance of the saving in labor against the increased power and insurance costs. If, by contrast, the statement is made that the process will save $1,000 in labor, that increased power will cost $200, and that increased insurance will cost $100, the net effect of these three factors can easily be estimated; that is, $1,000 − $200 − $100 is a net advantage of $700 for the proposed process.

The reason why we try to express as many factors as possible in quantitative terms is made clear in the above illustration: once we have done this, it becomes easy to find the net effect of these factors by the simple arithmetic operations of addition and subtraction.

Evaluating and Weighing the Unmeasured Factors

For most problems there are important factors that are not measurable; yet the final decision must take into account *all* differences between the alternatives being considered, both those that are measured and those not measured. The process of weighing the relative importance of these unmeasured factors, both as compared with one another and as compared with the net advantage or disadvantage of the measured factors, is solely a judgment process.

It is easy to underestimate the importance of these unmeasured factors. The numerical calculations for the measured factors often require hard work, and they result in a figure that has the appearance of being definite and precise; yet all the factors that influence the final number may be collectively less important than a single factor that has not been measured. For example, there are many persons who could meet their transportation needs less expensively by using public conveyances rather than by operating an automobile, but who nevertheless own an automobile for reasons of prestige, convenience, or other unmeasured factors.

As another example, an analysis of trucking costs and freight movements indicated that a company could save $14,260 a year by operating its own truck instead of using common carriers. Nevertheless, the decision was made to continue using common carriers, and the reasons given were as follows:[2]

1. The difference in the densities of the products carried would complicate the truck loading.

2. The problem of scheduling the routing of the truck to insure maximum utilization would be difficult.

3. The length of the round trip would result in the truck's visiting some locations after working hours, thus missing the pickup or delivery.

4. Our company is not unionized. The question of unionization of the truck driver would be troublesome.

5. It may be possible to have the suppliers absorb the freight, thus eliminating the transportation cost entirely.

6. Who will administer the operation of the truck? The traffic manager has only one clerk.

7. How are the common carriers going to treat the company on the remainder of the items that cannot be carried on the company truck?

8. Freight rates and truck operating costs are subject to change.

9. The supply points may change.

10. Since there is only one truck and one driver, the risk of truck breakdown and illness of the driver would be too great.

Note that this list includes both factors that probably were unmeasurable (e.g., the consequences of unionization) and factors that could have been measured, but in fact were not (e.g., the cost of administering the operation of the truck).

Cost calculations make it possible to express as a single figure the net effect of many factors bearing on the decision. They therefore reduce the number of factors that must be considered separately in the final judgment process that leads to the decision; or, as is often said, they narrow the area within which judgment must be exercised. Rarely, if ever, do they eliminate the necessity for this crucial judgment process.

Reaching a Decision

Having gone through the above process, the analyst has only two choices: to seek additional information or to reach a decision and act on it. Most decisions could be improved by making the former choice; in a

---

[2] From "Norwalk Screw Company," a case prepared by Professor Harold Bierman, Jr.

complicated business situation, it is usually possible to obtain more information than is available when the analysis begins. However, obtaining this information always involves effort and, what is more important, it involves time. There comes a point, therefore, when the analyst concludes that he is better off to act than to defer a decision until more data have been collected.

PROBLEMS INVOLVING COSTS

In the first class of problems we shall discuss, the difficult part of the quantitative analysis involves costs; that is, revenue is either unaffected by the alternative or is affected in such an obvious way that no analytical problems are involved. Illustrative of these problems are the following questions: Will a proposed new method of doing something cost less than the present method? Which of several proposed methods is the best? Should we manufacture a certain part or buy it from an outside vendor? Shall we discontinue a department that is apparently losing money? Shall we produce on one shift or two shifts? Shall we shut down the plant temporarily? Problems of this type are often called *trade-off problems:* we wish to find out whether one alternative has an acceptable trade-off compared with another in terms of its costs and the advantages that we hope to obtain from adopting it.

The types of cost that are relevant in problems of this kind can be summed up in two brief statements: (1) they are *future* costs and (2) they are *differential* costs.

Future Costs

No decision made by man can change what has already happened. The past is history; decisions made now can affect only what *will* happen in the future. It follows that the only relevant cost figures are estimates of what costs will be in the future.

The difficulty in applying this obvious statement arises from the fact that in many instances our best information about future costs is derived from an analysis of historical costs. One can easily lose sight of the fact that historical costs per se are irrelevant. These historical costs, often obtained from the accounting records, may be a useful guide as to what costs are likely to be in the future, but using them as a guide is basically different from using them as if they were statements of what the future costs are in fact *going* to be.

Except where future costs are determined by long-term contractual arrangements, such costs are necessarily estimates, and they usually cannot be close estimates. An estimated labor saving of $1,000 a year for five years, for example, implies assumptions as to future wage rates, future fringe benefits, future labor efficiency, future production volume, and other factors that cannot be known with certainty at the time the estimate is prepared. Consequently, there is ordinarily no point in carrying computations of cost estimates to several decimal places; in fact, there is a considerable danger of being misled by the illusion of precision that such meticulous calculations give.

BOOK VALUE OF FIXED ASSETS. An historical cost that seems to cause considerable difficulty is the book value of fixed assets. Suppose that a new production process is proposed as a substitute for operations now performed on a certain machine. The machine was purchased six years previously for $10,000, and depreciation on it has been charged at $1,000 a year, a total of $6,000 to date. The machine therefore has a book value of $4,000. Assume that it has no market value, that is, the cost of removing it just equals its value as scrap metal, and assume that it would be of no further use to the company. If the new process requires additional labor and related costs of $600 a year, one could argue that in spite of this increase, adoption of the process would save a net of $400 a year, since the depreciation charge of $1,000 a year would no longer be a cost. The fact is, however, that the remaining book value must be written off the books; and this amount, of course, exactly offsets the total depreciation charge over the remaining life of the machine. Thus the depreciation charge is *not* relevant to the problem. It is a *sunk cost*, arising from actions taken in the past, and unaffected by any subsequent decision. Adoption of the proposed process would in fact result in a *loss* of $600 a year.

The cost of an asset is supposed to be written off over its useful life. In the above example, we know, by hindsight, that this was not done, for if it had been done, the book value of the machine would be zero at the time it became obsolete. This was an error, but it was an error made in the past, and no current decision can change it.

The irrelevance of sunk costs can be demonstrated by comparison of two income statements for the complete time periods of the remaining life of the machine, one showing the results of operations if the new process is adopted and the machine is scrapped, and the other showing the results if the process is continued on the present equipment, as in Illustration 18–1. This illustration demonstrates that there would be a loss of $2,400 over a four-year period if the new process were adopted.

If the machine had a *market value*, this fact would be a relevant consideration, since its disposal would then bring in additional cash. If the *tax effect* of writing off the loss on disposal were different from the tax effect of writing off depreciation over the four-year period, which is often the case, the effect on taxes is relevant. The book value of the machine itself is not relevant. Ultimately, the book value is going to be charged against income, but whether this is done through the annual depreciation charge or through a lump-sum write-off makes no ultimate

Illustration 18–1

COMPARATIVE INCOME STATEMENTS ILLUSTRATING
IRRELEVANCE OF SUNK COSTS

(For Four Years)

	A. If New Process Is Adopted		B. If New Process Is Not Adopted	
Sales...............................		$1,000,000		$1,000,000
Cost and expenses:				
Costs unaffected by the decision.......$700,000			$700,000	
Additional labor, etc................	2,400		0	
Depreciation on machine.............	0		4,000	
Book loss on disposal of machine......	4,000		0	
Total costs and expenses...........		706,400		704,000
Profit before income taxes..............		$ 293,600		$ 296,000
				−293,600
Loss if New Process Is Adopted.........				$ 2,400

difference. The facts given indicate that the new process should not be adopted.

Differential Costs

A great many cost items will be unaffected by the alternatives under consideration, and these may be disregarded. Attention is focused on items whose costs will be *different* under one alternative from what they will be under the others. Suppose, for example, that a company is considering the possibility of buying Part No. 101 from an outside supplier instead of manufacturing the part as it is now doing. In this case the alternatives are either: (*a*) to continue manufacturing Part No. 101, or (*b*) to purchase Part No. 101 from the outside supplier. All revenue items, all selling and administrative expenses, and all production costs other than those directly associated with the manufacture of Part No. 101 will probably be unaffected by the decision. If so, there is no need to consider them.

In some calculations, a listing of some or all of these unaffected costs may be useful, so as to insure that all relevant cost items have been considered. This was done, in Illustration 18–1, and there is no harm in doing so, provided the unaffected costs are treated exactly the same way under each of the alternatives. The *net difference* between the costs of the two alternatives, which is the figure we seek, is not changed by adding equal amounts to the cost of each alternative.

Costs from a Cost Accounting System.   In considering "costs that make a difference," figures drawn from a cost accounting system may be misleading, since differences in such figures may not reflect actual differences in cost arising because of the alternative under consideration. For example, for cost accounting purposes, the "cost" of Part No. 101 may include charges for rent, heat, light, and other occupancy costs that are prorated to this product on the basis of the number of square feet of floor space occupied by the department in which it is manufactured. If Part No. 101 were purchased from an outside vendor, the floor space formerly used in its manufacture would be saved. It does not necessarily follow, however, that the *costs* prorated to Part No. 101 on the basis of floor space used would actually be saved. The costs for rent, heat, light, and so on might not be changed at all by the decision not to manufacture the part. Unless there is some real saving in cash outlays (or their equivalent) or some real additional revenue possibilities resulting from the use of the freed floor space (e.g., renting it, or manufacturing some revenue-producing item in it), the "cost" of floor space should be ignored.

In general, when estimating differential costs, *allocated or prorated accounting charges should be viewed with skepticism*. In a cost accounting system, each unit of product manufactured is charged with its fair share of all manufacturing costs, including costs that are not directly caused by or traceable to the product. Such cost figures are not intended to show, and in fact do not show, the differential costs that are relevant in most alternative choice problems. A company may allocate overhead as 100 percent of direct labor; but this does *not* mean that if direct labor cost is decreased $575 by purchasing Part No. 101, there will be a corresponding decrease of $575 in overhead costs. Overhead costs may not decrease at all; they may decrease, but by an amount less than $575; or they may even increase, as a result of an increased procurement and inspection work load resulting from the purchase of Part No. 101. In order to estimate what will happen to overhead costs, we must go behind the overhead rate and analyze what will actually happen to the various elements of overhead under each of the alternatives being considered.

FRINGE BENEFITS. Labor costs are one of the important considerations in many business decisions. In many problems an allowance for fringe benefits should be added to the actual amount of wages earned for the work done. Fringe benefits include such items as taxes for old-age and unemployment compensation; insurance, medical, and pension plans; vacation and holiday pay; and the like. For business in general, these benefits average about 25 percent of wages earned, although there is so wide a variation among different companies that an overall average is unlikely to be reliable in a specific situation. To the extent that the cost of these fringe benefits varies directly with wages paid, they are relevant when costing an alternative that involves a change in labor costs.

OPPORTUNITY COSTS. Most, but not all, relevant cost figures are represented by actual cash outlays. In some cases, however, the concept of cost should be broadened to include sacrifices that are not immediately reflected in the cash account. Such amounts are called *imputed* costs or *opportunity* costs. Opportunity cost is measured by the sacrifice involved in accepting the alternative under consideration rather than the next best opportunity. The floor space item mentioned above provides an example. If the floor space required to make Part No. 101 can be used for some other revenue-producing purpose, then the sacrifice involved in using it for Part No. 101 is a cost of making that part. Note that this cost is measured by the income sacrificed if the floor space is used for Part No. 101; this is not necessarily the same as the allocated cost per square foot of floor space as developed in the cost accounting system.

In general, if accepting an alternative requires that facilities or other resources must be devoted to that alternative that otherwise could be used for some other purpose, there is an opportunity cost, and it is measured by the profit that would have been earned had the resources been devoted to the other purpose.

VARIABLE COSTS. The term "differential costs" does not have quite the same meaning as the term "variable costs." Variable costs are those that vary directly with, and roughly proportionately to, changes in the *volume of output;* that is, if output increases 50 percent, variable costs will increase approximately 50 percent. Differential costs are related to the specific alternatives that are being analyzed. If, in a specific problem, one of the alternatives involves a change in output, then differential costs may be the same as variable costs. Depending on the problem, however, the differential costs may include nonvariable items. A proposal to change the number of plant watchmen and their duties, for example, involves no elements of variable cost.

MARGINAL AND INCREMENTAL COSTS. The terms "marginal" and "incremental" cost are usually used in a sense that makes them synonymous with differential cost. A semantic problem can arise when these terms are used as general labels for cost elements, rather than with reference to the specific set of alternatives being analyzed, and caution is necessary before accepting such general statements as, "This cost is incremental." The proper question is, "Is it incremental in the specific problem being analyzed?"

IMPORTANCE OF THE TIME SPAN. The question of what costs are relevant depends to a considerable extent on the time span of the problem. If the proposal is to make only one unit of Part No. 101, only the direct material costs may be relevant; the work could conceivably be done without any differential labor costs if, for example, workers were paid on a daily basis and had some idle time. At the other extreme, if the proposal involves a commitment to make Part No. 101 over the foreseeable future, practically all the elements of manufacturing costs may be affected. In general, *the longer the time span of the proposal, the more items of cost are differential.* In the very long run, all costs are differential. Thus, in very long-run problems, differential costs include the same elements as the conventional accounting "full costs," for in the long run one must consider even the replacement of buildings and equipment, which are sunk costs in the short run. (Although the *elements* are the same, the amounts are different, since alternative choice problems involve future costs, not historical costs.) In the short run, relatively few cost elements may be subject to change by a management decision.

GENERAL CHARACTERISTICS OF DIFFERENTIAL COSTS. Few specific suggestions can be made as to what costs should be included in an alternative choice calculation. In general, we are looking for costs that *would* be incurred if the alternative were adopted but that *would not* be incurred if the alternative were not adopted. Labor costs are relevant in many problems; but if in a specific situation people are going to be employed regardless of which alternative is adopted, labor costs may not be relevant. For example, it can be demonstrated that a given quantity of material can be typed in less time with an electric typewriter than with a nonelectric typewriter, but an actual saving in labor costs will result from the purchase of an electric typewriter only if the time thus freed is used productively for some other purpose.

Mechanics of the Calculation

Any of several devices can be used for combining the various cost elements that are relevant to each alternative. Costs may, for example, be listed separately under each alternative, viz:

	If Part No. 101 Is Manufactured	*If Part No. 101 Is Purchased*
Purchased material	$ 572	$1,700
Labor	600	25*
Power	98	0
Other costs	150	0
Total	$1,420	$1,725
		1,420
Difference (Disadvantage of Purchasing)		$ 305

* Estimated handling cost.

Or, exactly the same result can be obtained by figuring the net differences between the alternatives, viz:

		If Part No. 101 Is Purchased
Purchase price of Part No. 101		$1,700
Costs saved by not manufacturing Part No. 101:		
Raw material	$572	
Labor	575	
Power	98	
Other costs	150	
Total costs saved		1,395
Net Disadvantage in Purchasing		$ 305

The same result also can be obtained by preparing a complete income statement for each alternative for the total time period involved in the proposal, as was done in Illustration 18–1. This requires more work than either of the other two types of calculations shown above, but it provides assurance that some cost or revenue elements have not been overlooked, and it may also provide a useful format for explaining the calculations to someone else.

The Margin of Error

Cost figures used in alternative choice problems are estimates, and in many cases they are very rough estimates. In some calculations, an attempt is made to express the margin of error in these estimates by making two sets of calculations, one in which costs are estimated on the high side and the other in which they are estimated on the low side. Even though the range between these two estimates is wide, the rough estimates may be more useful than none at all, since they set boundaries on the net influence of the factors that are contained in them.

Sometimes the high and low estimates are combined into a single "compromise" figure by averaging them. This is often a useful device, but it should be recognized that the compromise is not necessarily a more correct estimate than either the high or the low figure. The reliability of the estimate depends on the uncertainties involved, and there may be no way of eliminating or minimizing these uncertainties.

Example: Operating an Automobile

As an example of the fact that the cost elements that are relevant in an alternative choice problem vary with the nature of the problem, let us consider the costs that are relevant for various decisions that may be made about owning and operating an automobile. A study made by Runzheimer and Company and published by the American Automobile Association gives the national average cost in 1969 of operating a 1969 eight-cylinder Chevrolet Impala four-door hardtop (equipped with standard accessories —radio, automatic transmission, and power steering) as follows:

Variable Costs:	*Average per Mile*
Gasoline and oil	2.76 cents
Maintenance	0.68
Tires	0.51
Total	3.95 cents

Nonvariable Costs:	*Annual*
Fire and theft insurance	$ 44
Other insurance	256
License and registration	24
Depreciation	729
Total	$1,053

What costs are relevant? In answering this question, we shall assume that the car in question is comparable with that for which the averages were computed; that gasoline prices, insurance rates, and the like are "average" in the locality in which the automobile is to be operated; that the AAA figures are reliable; that the classification of certain costs as variable and others as nonvariable is valid; and that costs during the period in which the automobile will be operated will be the same as they were in 1969. Unless each of these assumptions is reasonable, the figures given above cannot be used. Accepting these assumptions, we can make the following statements about relevant costs:

1. When a person owns an automobile, already has it registered, and is deciding whether it is worthwhile to make a proposed trip, the relevant costs are 3.95 cents a mile times the estimated mileage of the trip. The nonvariable costs are not relevant since they will continue whether or not the trip is made. (Costs are shown here exactly as reported in the AAA table above; actually, you would undoubtedly round off the numbers rather than showing them to hundredths of a cent.)

2. When a person owns an automobile and is deciding whether to (*a*) register it for a year or (*b*) leave it idle and use some other form of transportation, the relevant costs are the insurance and fees of $324 plus 3.95 cents a mile times the number of miles he expects to travel by automobile during the year. The $324 has become a cost because it is affected by the decision as to registration.

3. When a person is deciding whether to (*a*) buy an automobile or (*b*) use some other means of transportation, the relevant costs are $1,053 a year plus 3.95 cents a mile times the number of miles he expects to travel. (Actually, in this case one probably would have a closer estimate for depreciation for the specific automobile under consideration than the average figure of $729.)

Other statements can be made for the costs relevant to other contemplated uses of the automobile. These illustrations may help to clarify the basic point that the relevant costs for a given decision are the costs affected by that decision; other costs can be ignored.

Example: Economic Lot Size

When manufacture of a product involves setup costs that are incurred once for each lot manufactured, the question arises of how many units should be made in one lot. If the demand is predictable and if sales are reasonably steady throughout the year, the optimum quantity to manufacture at one time, called the *economic lot size* or *economic order quantity*, is arrived at by considering two offsetting influences—setup costs and inventory costs. Consider an item with annual sales of 1,200 units. If the whole 1,200 were manufactured in one lot, only one setup a year would be necessary, but inventory costs would be high, since the inventory would start with 1,200 units and would average 600 units over the year.[3] By contrast, manufacture of 12 lots of 100 units each (i.e., one lot a month) would involve 12 setups but a low inventory carrying cost, since there would be an average of 50 units in inventory at any one time, that is, $\frac{1}{2}(100 + 0) = 50$.

Given this set of relationships, the mathematician can easily construct a formula from which the economic lot size can be found. His reasoning is as follows. Let:

Q = Economic lot size (number of units in one lot).
S = Setup costs, for one setup.
R = Annual requirements in units.
K = Inventory carrying charge, expressed as a percentage of average inventory value.
C = Factory cost per unit.

Then:

Number of lots made in one year $= \dfrac{R}{Q}$.

Annual setup cost = setup cost for one lot times number of lots made per year

$$= S\left(\frac{R}{Q}\right) = \frac{SR}{Q}.$$

Average number of units in inventory $= \dfrac{Q}{2}$.

Average value of inventory = average units in inventory times unit cost

$$= \left(\frac{Q}{2}\right)C = \frac{QC}{2}.$$

Annual carrying cost = K times average inventory value

$$= \left(\frac{QC}{2}\right)K = \frac{QCK}{2}.$$

Total cost will be at a minimum when the increase in carrying cost resulting from adding one more unit to a lot is equal to the corresponding

---

[3] Inventory is 1,200 units immediately after the lot has been manufactured and declines to zero a year later. Assuming that the decline is at a roughly even rate throughout the year, the average inventory for the year is one half the sum of the beginning plus ending inventories; thus: $\frac{1}{2}(1,200 + 0) = 600$.

decrease in setup costs. Using calculus, we can show that this minimum occurs when annual setup cost equals annual carrying cost,[4] or when:

$$\frac{SR}{Q} = \frac{QCK}{2}.$$

Solving for Q gives the desired formula:

$$Q = \sqrt{\frac{2SR}{CK}}.$$

At this point, the mathematician loses interest. As far as he is concerned, the problem has been solved, and all that remains is to insert the relevant numbers in the formula and do the arithmetic. But the important practical question is: what numbers? What are the setup costs that are relevant to this problem? Clearly, they include the differential labor costs involved in making the setup, they include fringe benefits on this labor, they include any differential overhead costs, and they also include such costs as moving the products to inventory if these are a function of the number of lots manufactured, even though these are not labeled as setup costs. Deciding which costs vary with the number of lots produced and are therefore differential setup costs is a difficult matter. Similarly, the unit cost used in valuing the inventory involves problems. Essentially, we need to know how much money will be tied up in inventory, and for this purpose it may be necessary to adjust the cost-accounting unit cost of the products to eliminate elements such as depreciation that do not represent current outlays of funds. Finally, the calculation of the inventory carrying charge includes an estimate of interest costs, and of the costs associated with the occupancy of warehouse space.

The point is that in this and many other types of business problems involving costs, the general approach to the problem may be quite simple and definite, but estimating the relevant cost figures may be exceedingly difficult.

PRICING

The second class of problems involves revenue considerations as well as cost considerations. The discussion here will focus on the pricing problem; that is, how much should we charge for our products? This is the most common problem in this category.

---

[4] It is not *generally* true that when it is desired to find a minimum total cost point for two costs, one of which is increasing and the other decreasing, the minimum will be found at the point where the two totals are equal. It happens to be true for the specific cost functions being considered here.

Theoretical Considerations

Some economics texts state that the selling price of a product should be set so as to maximize the difference between revenue and costs. In order to do this, one needs to be able to estimate (1) the demand schedule, which is the number of units that would be sold at each possible selling price; and (2) *marginal* costs. Marginal costs, which in this context are the same as differential costs, can be estimated by techniques already discussed, but estimating the demand schedule is a much more difficult matter. Who can estimate what quantity of product will be sold at one price, let alone at all possible prices? Indeed, the difficulty is so great that few companies ever attempt to estimate a demand schedule, and few managers have ever even seen one. Without a demand schedule, the elaborate diagrams and equations that economists have built up cannot be used to solve real-world pricing problems (although they are useful for classroom analysis).

Not only is the maximization approach to pricing unworkable, but also it leads to "gouging," "profiteering," "charging all the traffic will bear," and other unethical practices. A discussion of pricing that is built on the maximization foundation would therefore be both impractical and ethically indefensible.

This fact is one of the reasons why this book is not based on the profit maximization concept. (A second reason has to do with the cost-of-capital approach to investment decisions, discussed in Chapter 19.) But if we do not use profit maximization as an underlying premise, we must have an alternative concept. Some have advocated "long-run profit maximization," but this is too vague to serve as a basis for the solution of practical problems.

The concept that probably underlies the actions of most responsible businessmen is that of *satisfactory profit*, or satisfactory return on investment; that is, they have a notion of a fair or reasonable profit that should be earned in their business, and they strive to earn such a profit. This is the concept we shall use.

The satisfactory profit concept leads to what is called *full-cost pricing* as the normal approach to pricing problems, and to *contribution pricing* in certain unusual situations.

Full-Cost Pricing

Many companies have no pricing problem. A market price exists, customers will not pay more than this price, and there is no reason why the product should be sold for a lower price. Wheat and other products traded on commodity markets are the classic examples, but the situation also exists for companies in many other industries, such as small companies in industries where one or a few large companies exercise price leadership. Under such circumstances, a company makes no pricing calculations; it simply charges the market price.

If a company does have the problem of determining its selling prices, the usual practice is to compute the full cost of the product and add to this a profit margin, figured either as a percentage of cost or preferably as a percentage return on the investment involved in making the product. Note that the relevant costs are *full costs,* which are the direct costs plus a fair share of allocated costs; they are not the differential costs discussed in the preceding section.

The result of this calculation is a *first approximation* to the price; it is modified to take into account the strength of competition, the necessity of fitting the price into customary price lines (such as $9.98 dresses), and many other marketing considerations. Consequently, actual prices and hence actual profit margins on specific products may differ widely from this first approximation. The company plans, however, that overall it will obtain the desired profit, with extra profits on high-margin products offsetting thin profits on low-margin products. It will achieve this goal if a fair share of total costs is allocated to each product, and if it obtains a satisfactory profit margin above this cost, on the average, for the products it actually sells.

Adjustments to this first approximation may take the form of changing costs as well as changing profit margins. If it is thought that the computed price is too high, then the product may be redesigned to bring its costs down so that a satisfactory profit can be made at the attainable price. In this process, it is full costs rather than differential costs that are considered.

PROFIT MARGIN. In many companies, the profit margin is expressed as a percentage of cost. Increasingly, however, companies are figuring the profit margin as a return on the assets employed in manufacturing and selling the product. This newer practice relates prices to the overall objective of earning a satisfactory return on investment.

Assume, for example, that a company manufactures two products, A and B, the manufacturing cost of each being $6 per unit. At a mark-on of 50 percent of cost (33 percent of selling price), the normal selling price of each product would be $9, and if 100,000 units of each are sold, the total margin would be $600,000. Under return-on-investment pricing, the company would first estimate the total assets employed for the two products. Assume that this works out to $3 million, or $30 per unit, for Product A and $1 million, or $10 per unit, for Product B. If the company desires 15 percent return on its investment, the normal margin would be $4.50 for Product A and $1.50 for Product B, making the normal selling prices $10.50 and $7.50 respectively. These prices produce the same total margin, $600,000, as the alternative prices calculated as a 50 percent mark-on on cost. Product A's higher price reflects the fact that more assets are required to make a unit of Product A than a unit of Product B.

ADDING OR DROPPING PRODUCTS.   In making decisions about whether or not to add a new product and whether or not to discontinue an existing product, similar considerations normally govern. A new product is normally added to the line only if it is expected to produce a satisfactory return on the investment. If an existing product has a low margin, and if the situation cannot be corrected by increasing prices or reducing costs, then the product normally is replaced with a more profitable one. Again, marketing considerations may dictate departures from the normal procedure. Many low-margin products are retained so that the company may offer its customers a full line; equipment may be sold at a low margin in order to induce the sale of high-margin accessories and supplies;[5] no replacement product with an adequate margin may be known; and so on.

PRICE REGULATIONS.   A further reason for basing price on full costs rather than on differential costs is the fact that the Robinson-Patman Act prohibits differentials in the prices charged competing customers unless these differentials "make due allowance for differences in the cost of manufacture, sale, or delivery resulting from the differing methods or quantities in which commodities are to such purchasers sold or delivered." The Federal Trade Commission and the courts have interpreted these "due allowances" as related to full costs, and they have rejected defenses that are based on differential cost calculations. Many states prohibit the sale of certain products or services below cost, with "cost" either specified as, or interpreted as meaning, the full cost.

TIME AND MATERIAL PRICES.   One of the commonly used pricing formulas based on full costs is the *time and material* price. This price consists of a charge for material plus a charge per labor hour. Profit may be included as part of the material element, or the labor element, or both of them. The usual price for repairing an automobile consists of the material priced at cost plus a profit margin, plus labor priced at an hourly rate. The hourly rate includes the direct labor cost, a fair share of overhead, and profit. Most other service work (television repair, plumbing, carpentry, electrical work, etc.) is priced on this basis. In job shops, where each job is done according to the customer's specifications, this is a common basis for pricing.

Contribution Pricing

Although the full cost is the normal basis for pricing, and although a company must recover its full cost or eventually go out of business, there

---

[5] A company cannot *compel* its customers to buy its own accessories and supplies. Such "tie-in" agreements are illegal.

are many situations where differential (i.e., marginal, or incremental) costs are appropriately used. In general, these may be described as *crisis* situations. In normal times, a company may refuse to take orders at prices that will not yield a satisfactory profit, but if times are bad, such orders may be accepted if the differential revenue obtained from them exceeds the differential costs involved. The company is better off to receive some revenue above its outlays than to receive nothing at all. Such orders make some contribution to profit,[6] and the selling price is therefore called a *contribution price*, to distinguish it from a normal price. Here, differential costs are the same as those discussed in the preceding section; that is, the costs that will be incurred if the order is accepted and that will not be incurred if it is not accepted.

Dumping, which is the practice of selling surplus quantities of a product in a selected marketing area at a low price, is another version of the contribution idea. However, dumping may violate the Robinson-Patman Act in domestic markets, and may be prohibited or unwise for other reasons in foreign markets.

In times of crisis a product may be retained in the line if it makes some contribution to profits, even though it has such a low profit margin that in normal times it would be dropped.

It is difficult to generalize on the circumstances that determine whether full costs or differential costs are appropriate. Even in normal times, an opportunity may be accepted to make some contribution to profit by using temporarily idle facilities. Conversely, in crisis times the contribution concept may be rejected on the grounds that the low price may "spoil the market," or that orders can in fact be obtained at normal margins if the sales organization works hard enough. Finally, it must be recognized that some companies do not price on the basis of full costs simply because they do not know what their full costs are. Dun & Bradstreet's annual analysis of bankruptcies invariably lists inadequate knowledge of costs as one of the principal factors responsible for business failure.

ADVANCED TECHNIQUES

The foregoing is an introductory description of approaches to the analysis of alternative choice problems. In recent years, a number of techniques have been developed for increasing the power of such an analysis. They are described in the books listed at the end of this chapter, but a brief description of some of these techniques is given here as an indication of the possibilities.

---

[6] Some prefer to regard this as a contribution to *overhead*, which is merely another way of looking at it.

Probability Theory

All the figures used in making business decisions are estimates of what will happen in the future. In the foregoing, we have assumed that these estimates were "single valued," that is, that each of them was a single number representing someone's best guess as to the future situation. Some companies are experimenting with estimates made in the form of probability distributions. For example, instead of stating, "I think sales of Item X will be $100,000 next year," the estimator states a range of possibilities, together with his estimate of the probability that each will occur. The sum of these separate possibilities, weighted by the probability that each will occur, is called the *expected value* of the probability distribution. It is computed as in the following example:

Possible Sales (a)	Estimated Probability (b)	Weighted Amount (a × b)
$ 60,000	0.1	$ 6,000
80,000	0.1	8,000
100,000	0.4	40,000
120,000	0.2	24,000
140,000	0.2	28,000
	Expected Value....	$106,000

The probability 0.1 means that there is 1 chance in 10 that sales will be about $60,000. The sum of the probabilities always adds to 1.

Businessmen do not find it easy to state their estimates in the form of probability distributions; but if they can do so, the usefulness of the estimates can be greatly increased. For one thing, probability distributions tend to fall into a limited number of patterns. Many of them are the familiar "normal," or bell-shaped, curves. These patterns are described by mathematical equations, and important characteristics of the distributions may be inferred from them. Historical data can often be fitted into the same patterns, and used more powerfully than hitherto to improve the accuracy of the estimates.

Mathematical Models

A mathematical model is a set of equations or other expressions that states what are believed to be the significant factors in a situation and the relationships among them. A balance sheet is a mathematical model, with the relationships among the balance sheet items being governed by the principles of financial accounting. A budget is also a model, and probably a more useful one than a balance sheet.

In the budget, individual revenue and expense items are combined by the arithmetic operations of addition and subtraction to give anticipated net income. The newer models attempt to describe or *simulate* the basic forces at work in the business (or, rather, as many as can be reduced to quantitative terms) and the interrelationships among them in much more elaborate manner. For example, whereas the variable budget may state that a $10,000 increase in sales will result in a $4,000 increase in labor costs, the more sophisticated model may relate labor costs not solely to sales volume but also to the desired level of inventory, the cost of hiring and training an additional worker, other costs associated with changing the level of production, and so on. Furthermore, the model may take into account the delay, or lag, that occurs between the receipt of a sales order and the actual incurrence of labor costs to fill the order.

As these models become more accurate simulations of the real situation, they can provide an effective way of testing the effect on profits of proposed alternatives, because the model incorporates interrelationships and secondary consequences of proposed actions which are often otherwise overlooked. This type of model serves the same function as a pilot plant; it permits inexpensive experimentation with various proposals so that mistakes in full-scale operation can be avoided. Since a single experiment often involves many millions of separate calculations, these models require the use of a computer.

A model is necessarily a simplification of the real situation because the real situation is too complex to be handled on even the largest computers, but if it is *over*simplified, it is useless. Very few companies have, up to the present, devised a model of their overall situation that is both sufficiently simple to be manipulated and also sufficiently realistic so that they trust it as an aid for making decisions. Many companies are working on this problem however.

Model building will become increasingly important to business. As Dr. Oskar Morgenstern has said: "The penetration of mathematics into new fields has, without exception, brought about profound changes. Whenever mathematics has entered, it has never again been pushed out by other developments."

Linear Programming

One of the models developed in recent years is the *linear programming* model. It is useful when the alternatives under consideration interact with one another.

EXAMPLE: A company makes two products, each of which has to go through two departments, the daily capacity of each department being as follows if only one of the products is made in it:

	Capacity in Units	
	Dept. 1	Dept. 2
Product A	200	120
Product B	100	200

Any amount of Product A can be sold, but a maximum of 90 units of Product B can be sold per day. The contribution margin (i.e., difference between revenue and variable costs) of Product A is $2 per unit, and for Product B it is $2.50 per unit. How many units of each product should be produced?

A "commonsense" solution to the above problem would be to make the maximum 90 units of Product B, since it has the higher contribution margin, and to use the remaining capacity for Product A. By the use of linear programming, however, it can be demonstrated that a higher profit will result with a combination of 86 units of Product A and 57 units of Product B.[7]

Linear programming involves a great deal of arithmetic, but a standard program for doing this arithmetic is available on most computers. The analyst need only know enough about these programs to permit him to plug in the proper numbers; he does not need to know the equations themselves.

NONPROFIT ORGANIZATIONS

Since the criterion underlying the analysis described in this chapter was profit, there may be a tendency to conclude that the techniques are not applicable in organizations that do not have a profit objective, such as government agencies, universities, hospitals, and the like. Indeed, these techniques are not used in some nonprofit organizations. This is a mistake.

Many alternative choice problems involve a choice between two ways of reaching the same objective. Neglecting nonquantitative considerations, the one with the lower cost is the better alternative. It is better in a profit-seeking company because it leads to higher profits, and it is better in a nonprofit organization because it means that the objective of the organization, whatever it may be, can be accomplished with fewer resources. Thus, the techniques described in this chapter can be applied to problems of this type in nonprofit organizations.

Cost-Benefit Analysis

For problems involving both outputs and inputs, however, the problem of quantifying the factors is usually quite difficult in a nonprofit organization. In a profit-seeking company, outputs are measured by revenue, and the best alternative is the one with the greatest difference between differential revenue and differential costs, that is, the one that adds the most to profit. In a nonprofit organization, there often is no feasible way of

---

[7] For the solution, see Charles T. Horngren, *Cost Accounting: A Managerial Emphasis* (Englewood Cliffs, N.J., Prentice-Hall, Inc., 1967) pp. 828–33.

measuring output in monetary terms, and hence no way of using the above criterion.

Nevertheless, formal analytical techniques can be used in many such alternative choice problems in nonprofit organizations. Two general approaches are coming into common use, and both are described as techniques of *cost-benefit analysis.*

In one approach, the outputs, or benefits, anticipated under each alternative are expressed in some quantitative way, and a cost per unit of benefit is then computed. Neglecting nonquantitative considerations, the alternative with the lowest cost per unit is the best alternative. For example, the Department of Defense evaluates various strategic postures by estimating the "cost per delivered megaton of destruction"; the Department of Transportation evaluates alternative highway safety measures by the "cost per reduced fatality"; the amount of research funds to be allocated to various diseases can be roughly studied in terms of cost related to reduction in mortality; alternative ways of providing new recreational facilities are gauged by the cost per person benefited; and so on.

In the other approach, no attempt is made to quantify the benefits. A careful estimate of the cost is made, and the decision maker arrives at a judgment by asking: "Are the benefits worth *at least* the cost?" Or, if two alternatives are being considered, the differential costs of one over the other are estimated, and the question then becomes: "Are the incremental benefits likely to be worth the differential costs?"

These calculations rarely, if ever, provide the solution to the problem by themselves, because they do not include the effect of all the relevant considerations. But, as has been emphasized throughout this chapter, this is characteristic of all such calculations. If they help to reduce significantly the area within which judgment must be exercised, then they are worthwhile.

SOME PRACTICAL POINTERS

The following points may be helpful in attacking specific problems:

1. Use imagination in choosing the possible alternatives to be considered, but don't select so many alternatives that you bog down before you begin. There is only a fine line between the alternative that is a "stroke of genius" and the alternative that is a "harebrained idea," but it is a crucial one.

2. Don't yield to the natural temptation to give too much weight to the factors that can be reduced to figures, even though the figures have the appearance of being definite and precise.

3. On the other hand, don't slight the figures because they are "merely" approximations. A reasonable approximation is much better than nothing at all.

4. Often, it is easier to work with total costs rather than with unit costs. Unit cost is a fraction in which total cost is the numerator and number of units the denominator, that is,

$$\frac{\text{Total Cost}}{\text{Number of Units}} = \text{Unit Cost}.$$

Changes in either the numerator or the denominator result in changes in unit costs. An error is made if one of these changes is taken into account and the other is overlooked.

5. There is a tendency to underestimate the cost of doing something new because all the consequences often are not foreseen.

6. The *number* of arguments is irrelevant in an alternative choice problem. A dozen reasons may be, and often are, advanced against trying out something new, but all these reasons put together may not be so strong as a single argument in favor of the proposal.

7. Be realistic about the margin of error in any calculation involving the future. Fancy figures cannot be made out of rough estimates, nor is an answer necessarily precise or valid just because you spent a long time calculating it.

8. Despite uncertainties, a decision should be made if as much information is available as you can obtain at reasonable cost and within a reasonable time. Postponing action is the same as deciding to perpetuate the existing situation, which may be the worst possible decision.

9. Show clearly the assumptions you made and the effect of these on ·your estimates so that someone going over your analysis can substitute his own judgments if he wishes.

10. Do not expect that everyone will agree with your conclusion simply because it is supported with carefully worked-out figures. Think about how you can sell your conclusion to those who must act on it.

SUMMARY

Differential costs are the costs that are incurred if a project is undertaken but that would not be incurred if it is not undertaken. When an alternative choice problem involves changes in costs but not changes in revenue or investment, the best solution is the one with the lowest differential costs, insofar as cost information bears on the solution.

When the problem involves both cost and revenue considerations, full costs are often a useful first approximation in normal times, but differential costs are used in times of crisis. Managements differ as to their opinion of the circumstances under which each is appropriate.

Cost calculations alone rarely provide the answer to any business problem, but they facilitate comparisons and narrow the area within which judgment must be applied.

SUGGESTIONS FOR FURTHER READING

BIERMAN, H.; C. P. BONINI; L. E. FOURAKER; and R. JAEDICKE. *Quantitative Analysis for Business Decisions.* Rev. ed.; Homewood, Ill.: Richard D. Irwin, Inc., 1965.

RAIFFA, HOWARD. *Decision Analysis.* Reading, Mass.: Addison-Wesley, 1968.

SIMON, HERBERT A. *The New Science of Management Decision.* New York: Harper and Row, 1960.

CHAPTER 19

PLANNING CAPITAL
ACQUISITIONS

Of the several types of alternative choice problems, those involving proposed investments in new assets, i.e., *capital budgeting* problems, are both the most important and the most difficult. These problems are important not only because they involve large sums of money but also because the decision may influence the whole conduct of the business for years to come. A decision to build a new plant, for example, tends to commit a company to a certain locality and to a certain character and scale of manufacturing activity for the life of the plant. Investment problems are difficult because they require that estimates be made of conditions several years in the future, and also because allowances must be made for differences in timing of the relevant inflows and outflows of funds.

Any investment involves the commitment of funds *now* with the expectation of earning a satisfactory return on these funds over a period of time in the future. The word "investment" immediately calls to mind the commitment of funds to stocks or bonds. The commitment of funds to land, building, equipment, inventory, and other types of assets has the same essential characteristic as these financial investments: namely, that the commitment is made with the expectation of earning a satisfactory return on the investment in the future.

Illustrative of these capital budgeting problems are the following:

1. *Expansion.* Shall we build or otherwise acquire a new plant? (The expected earnings on this investment are the profits from the products produced in the new plant.)
2. *Replacement.* Shall we replace existing equipment with more efficient equipment? (The expected earnings on this investment are the savings

resulting from lower operating costs, or the profit from additional volume produced by the new equipment, or both.)

3. *Cost Reduction.* Shall we buy equipment to perform an operation now done manually, i.e., shall we spend money in order to save money? (The expected earnings on this investment are the savings resulting from lower operating costs.)

4. *Choice of Equipment.* Which of several proposed items of equipment shall we purchase for a given purpose? (The choice often turns on which item is expected to give the largest return on the investment made in it.)

5. *Buy or Lease.* Having decided to acquire a building or a piece of equipment, should we lease it or should we buy it? (The choice turns on whether or not the investment required to purchase the asset will earn an adequate return as compared with leasing.)

Investment problems fall into two broad categories; they are either screening problems or preference problems. In a *screening* problem, the issue is whether or not a proposed investment is likely to earn a satisfactory return; that is, the problem is to screen out the satisfactory proposals from all the investment proposals that are made. In a *preference* problem, also referred to as a *ranking* or *rationing* problem, the task is to decide which of several proposals is the best, which is the next best, and so on. The screening problem is conceptually simpler, and the first part of this chapter will be restricted to a discussion of this problem. The preference problem will be discussed in the last section of the chapter.

The comments in Chapter 18 about the types of costs and revenues that should be used in alternative choice problems are equally relevant in capital budgeting problems. As also noted in that chapter, the techniques are applicable only to those problems or parts of problems for which quantitative information is available and important. In nearly every problem, there are important unmeasured considerations that must be weighed in order to make a final decision, and in many problems these considerations are so important that calculations of the type described here are not worth making. Decisions regarding investments in employee recreational facilities, or in research equipment, or in office furniture, ordinarily are not based on an estimate of the return on investment.

FRAMEWORK OF ANALYSIS

Essentials of a Business Investment

If the company purchases a machine, the funds so invested are initially tied up, or frozen, and they are gradually liquidated through the profitable operation of the machine. Any investment involves a risk, and even if the money to finance the purchase is borrowed, it is the owner of the machine who incurs the risk. A businessman will ordinarily not risk funds in an investment unless he believes that he will obtain a satisfactory return on these funds.

Since the purchase of proposed equipment will presumably result in additional earnings, the issue to be resolved in an investment problem is *whether the proposed investment is justified by the earnings it will create over its life.* The techniques to be described are methods for comparing these essentially unlike elements: (1) a single lump-sum investment made now, and (2) a stream of future earnings.

Concept of Return on Investment

When a bank lends $1,000 and receives interest payments of $80 at the end of each year for five years, with the $1,000 loan being repaid at the end of the fifth year, the bank is said to earn a return of 8 percent on its investment of $1,000. Note that the percentage is always expressed on an

Illustration 19–1

DEMONSTRATION OF MEANING OF RETURN ON INVESTMENT

Year	Total Earnings (a)	Return at 8% of Investment Outstanding (b)	Balance, to Apply against Investment c = (a − b)	Investment Outstanding End of Year (d)
0...........	$...	$..	$...	$1,000
1...........	250	80	170	830
2...........	250	66	184	646
3...........	250	52	198	448
4...........	250	36	214	234
5...........	250	19	231	3

annual basis and that it is found by dividing the annual return by the amount of the investment outstanding during the year.

If a bank lends $1,000 and is repaid $250 at the end of each year for five years, the problem of finding the return becomes more complicated. In this situation, only part of the $250 annual payment represents interest, and the remainder is a repayment of the principal. By a method to be described below, it turns out that this loan also has a return of 8 percent, in the same sense as the loan described in the preceding paragraph: namely, the $250 annual payments will repay the loan itself and in addition will provide a return of 8 percent of the *amount still outstanding each year.* The fact that the return is 8 percent is proved in Illustration 19–1. Of the $250 earned in the first year, $80, or 8 percent of the $1,000 then outstanding, is the return, and the remainder, or $170, goes to reduce the investment, making it $830. In the second year, $66 is a return of 8 percent on the $830 then outstanding, and the remainder, $184, reduces the investment to $646. And so on. (The residual of $3 at the end of the fifth year arises because the true return is not exactly 8.000 percent.)

Thus, when an investment involves annual interest payments with the full amount of the investment being repaid at its termination date, the computation of the return is simple and direct; but when the annual payments combine both principal and interest, the computation is more complicated. Some business problems are of the simple type. If a business buys land for $1,000, for example, and rents it for $80 a year for five years, selling the land for $1,000 at the end of five years, the return is 8 percent. Many business investment decisions, on the other hand, relate to depreciable assets, whose characteristic is that they have no, or very little, resale value at the end of their useful life. The earnings on these investments must therefore be large enough for the investor both to recoup the investment itself during its life and to earn a satisfactory return on the amount not yet recouped, just as in the situation shown in Illustration 19–1.

Concept of Present Value

A businessman will not invest $1 today unless he expects to get back somewhat more than $1 later on; that is, he expects to earn a return on the investments he makes. By the same token, if a certain proposal will produce earnings of $1 at the end of one year, the businessman will be willing to invest only somewhat less than $1 in it today. The expectation of receiving $1 one year hence therefore has a *present value*, a value today, of somewhat less than $1. How much less depends on how much the businessman expects to earn on money he invests. If he expects to earn 10 percent, for example, the expectation of receiving $1 a year from now has a present value of $0.909, since if he invested $0.909 today for one year at a rate of 10 percent, he would earn $0.091 on the investment and have $1 at the end of the year.

The present value for a payment of $1 to be received n years hence at any rate of return (i) can be found with the formula:

$$\frac{1}{(1 + i)^n} .$$

The formula itself need not be used, however, since present values computed from it are given in Table A (p. 477). It is important that the meaning of the numbers in this table be clearly understood. Note, for example, that the first figure in the 10 percent column is the same $0.909 used in the preceding paragraph. It means that, at a rate of 10 percent, the expectation of receiving $1 a year from today has a present value of $0.909.

The next figure in the 10 percent column, $0.826, means that the expectation of receiving $1 *two* years from today has a present value of $0.826. This can be checked, as follows: if $0.826 is invested today, at 10 percent, $0.0826 would be earned during the first year, and the total amount would therefore increase to $0.9086; during the second year, 10 percent of the $0.9086, or $0.09086, would be earned, so that by the end of the second year, the total would have increased to $0.99946, or practically $1.[1] Tracing through any other figure in Table A will produce the same result; namely, the final figure will be practically $1.

Table A shows the present value of $1. The present value of any amount other than $1 can be found simply by multiplying that amount by the appropriate figure in the table. Thus the present value of $1,000 to be received two years hence at a rate of 10 percent is $826.

Present Value Method

The foregoing concepts can be used to construct methods for making decisions about investment proposals, always keeping in mind the fact that these methods are necessarily limited to those aspects of the proposal that can be reduced to money amounts. One such method is called the *present value* method. The rule here is: *Neglecting nonmonetary considerations, an investment proposal should be accepted if the present value of its earnings equals or exceeds the amount of the investment required.* Earnings are *cash flow* earnings; that is, they are the cash or cash equivalent amounts which are relevant in alternative choice problems, as explained in Chapter 18. To find the present value of these earnings, they are *discounted* at a specified rate of return, using the numbers in Table A. This rate will henceforth be referred to as the *required earnings rate.*

EXAMPLE 1. Should a proposed investment of $1,000 with expected earnings of $1,080 one year hence be accepted if the required earnings rate is 8 percent? In Table A, we find that the present value of $1 to be received one year hence at 8 percent is $0.926. The present value of $1,080 is therefore $1,080 × $0.926 = $1,000. The proposal should be accepted.

EXAMPLE 2. Should a proposed investment of $1,000 with expected earnings of $250 a year for five years be accepted if the required earnings rate is 8 percent? The present value of the earnings is found as follows:[2]

---

[1] The difference of $0.00054 arises from rounding.

[2] Calculations in all examples are rounded to emphasize the fact that the numbers are only estimates. In real problems, results that came so close as those in these two examples would certainly be decided on other grounds than the results of the arithmetic calculations, because of the inevitable margin of error in the estimates.

Year	Earnings (a)	Present Value of $1 at 8% (b)	Total Present Value (a × b)
First..........	$250	0.926	$230
Second........	250	0.857	214
Third..........	250	0.794	198
Fourth..........	250	0.735	184
Fifth..........	250	0.681	172
		Total Present Value..	$998

The present value being slightly less than $1,000, the proposal is not acceptable, neglecting nonquantitative considerations.

Present Value of a Stream of Payments

Table B (p. 478) has, for many problems, a more convenient set of present value figures than those in Table A. It shows the present value of $1 to be received annually for *each* of the next *n* years. Each figure on Table B was obtained simply by cumulating, that is, adding together, the figures for the corresponding year and all preceding years in the same column on Table A. Table B can be used directly to find the present value of a stream of equal payments received annually for any given number of years, and therefore reduces considerably the arithmetic required in problems of the type worked in Example 2 above.

EXAMPLE: Same question as in Example 2 above. The present value of $1 *a year* for five years at 8 percent, as shown in Table B, is $3.993; therefore the present value of $250 a year for five years is 250 × $3.993 = $998, which is the same result as in Example 2.

Although the values in Table B are cumulative from year 1, they can be used to find the present value of a stream of earnings between any two points in time. The procedure is to subtract the value for the year *preceding* the first year of the flow from the value for the last year of the flow.

EXAMPLE: What is the present value of $1,000 a year to be received in years 6 through 10, if the discount rate is 8 percent? Solution:

Present value of $1 a year for 10 years at 8 percent....$6.710
Less: Present value of $1 for years 1–5 at 8 percent....−3.993
Difference (equals present value years 6-10)..........$2.717
$1,000 × $2.717 = $2,717

Other Present Value Tables

Tables A and B are calculated on the assumption that earnings are received once a year and on the last day of the year. For many problems this is not a realistic assumption because earnings in the form of increased revenues and lower costs are likely to be incurred throughout the year. Nevertheless, annual tables are customarily used in business investment problems, on the grounds that they are easier to understand than tables constructed on other assumptions, and that they are good enough considering the inevitable margin of error in the basic estimates.

Annual tables *understate* the present value of earnings if earnings are in fact received throughout the year rather than entirely on the last day of the year. The amount of the understatement can be seen in Illustration 19–2. Tables are available showing the present values of earnings flows

Illustration 19–2

EFFECT OF RAPID RECEIPTS

Approximate Ratio of Present Value of Faster Receipts to Present Value of Annual Receipts at Various Discount Rates

Frequency of Receipt	Discount Rates			
	6%	*10%*	*15%*	*25%*
Semiannually............1.01	1.03	1.04	1.06
Monthly................1.03	1.05	1.07	1.11
Continuously............1.03	1.05	1.08	1.12

that occur quarterly, monthly, or even continuously, but they are not commonly used. Close results often can be obtained from a table that is based on the assumption that the amount is received at the *middle* of the year rather than at the *end* of the year.

The calculations in this chapter will use only the annual tables: Table A for a single amount to be received n years from now, and Table B for a stream of uniform amounts to be received for each of the next n years. The two are often used in combination, as illustrated in the next example, which also relates the mechanism discussed here to the basic meaning of return on investment discussed at the beginning of this section.

EXAMPLE: Should a proposed investment of $1,000 with annual earnings of $80 a year for the next five years with the $1,000 to be repaid at the end of five years be accepted if the required earnings rate is 8 percent? Solution: As shown by the following calculation, the earnings have a present value of $1,000, so the proposal is acceptable:

Year	Payment	8% Discount Factor	Present Value
1–5..............$80/year	3.993 (Table B)	$ 319
End of 5.........$1,000	0.681 (Table A)	681
		Total Present Value...$1,000

Unadjusted Return on Investment

Since the depreciation mechanism provides, in a sense, for the recovery of the cost of a depreciable asset, one might suppose that the return on an investment could be found by relating the investment to its income after depreciation, but such is *not* the case.[3] In our illustrative situation, if a depreciation allowance of $200 a year is subtracted from the gross annual earnings of $250, and the net amount of $50 is divided by the investment of $1,000, the indicated return is 5 percent. Note that this is substantially less than the 8 percent that we now know to be the true return. The return of 5 percent, calculated as above, is called the "accounting" return or the "unadjusted" return. It is unadjusted in the sense that it makes no allowance for the differences in present values of the earnings of the various years; that is, it treats each year's earnings as if they were as valuable as those of every other year, whereas actually the prospect of earning $250 next year is more attractive than the prospect of earning $250 two years from now, and *that* $250 is more attractive than the prospect of earning $250 three years from now, and so on.

The unadjusted return method, computed as above, will always understate the true return. The shorter the time period involved, the more serious is the understatement. For investments involving very long time periods, the understatement is insignificant. An unadjusted return can be computed in other ways, such as using one half the investment as the divisor. All these variations have the same conceptual error, although some of them yield a close approximation to the true return under certain conditions.

ESTIMATING THE VARIABLES

In order to make the calculation described above, four types of estimates must be made: (1) the required earnings rate; (2) the amount of earnings in each year; (3) the economic life, which is the number of years for which earnings are anticipated; and (4) the amount of investment. Each is discussed below. The examples will be limited to the *equipment replacement* problem, although the same considerations apply to problems of all types. Essentially, the alternatives in this problem are (*a*) to continue to use the present equipment, or (*b*) to replace it, with the expectation that savings in operating costs or other factors will be sufficient to recoup the investment and earn a satisfactory return on the funds that have been frozen in the new equipment.

---

[3] Unless depreciation is calculated on the annuity method, which is rare in practice.

Required Earnings Rate

The selection of the appropriate earnings rate is a crucial matter of top-management judgment. The problem can usefully be subdivided into two parts: (1) selection of the average rate required on the average investment and (2) consideration of factors that make a specific proposed investment different from the average.

AVERAGE EARNINGS RATE. In many companies, the choice of an average required earnings rate is largely subjective. Management decides that a sufficient number of investment opportunities can be found that will earn 10 percent, 15 percent, or some other number, and this percentage becomes the prescribed minimum below which the company refuses to make investments of average risk and uncertainty.

COST OF CAPITAL. Some people argue that the required earnings rate should be equal to the company's *cost of capital*, which is the aftertax cost of debt capital plus the cost of equity capital, weighted by the relative amount of each in the normal capital structure (the aftertax cost of debt is used because interest on debt is a tax deductible expense); thus:

Type	Cost	Weight	Weighted Total
Debt (bonds).............	3%	0.4	1.2%
Equity (stock)............	15	0.6	9.0
Total..................		1.0	10.2%

The indicated cost of capital is 10.2 percent or, rounded, 10 percent. The trouble with the cost-of-capital approach is that the cost of equity capital is extraordinarily difficult to estimate.[4] One starts with the market price of the stock, and then tries to estimate what fraction of the market price is attributable to the market's judgment of profits on the present equity, and what fraction is attributable to the market's judgment of future profits that will be earned on retained earnings. Few people have much confidence in the results of such estimates. The discussion here has been cursory for this reason.

PRO FORMA APPROACH. A less exact but more feasible approach is to construct a *pro forma* (i.e. hypothetical) balance sheet and income statement for a "satisfactory" future situation. The balance sheet will show the real values of the assets (as distinguished from their book value), perhaps using half the current cost of fixed assets as an indication of their average future value. It will show a proportion of fixed debt to equity capital that

---

[4] See Hunt, Williams, and Donaldson, *Basic Business Finance: Text and Cases* (3d ed.; Homewood, Ill.; Richard D. Irwin, Inc., 1966). The economists' profit maximization model requires that a cost-of-capital figure be estimated. This is the second reason why this book is not based on the profit maximization assumption. The other reason was discussed on page 420.

management considers satisfactory. The income statement will show the income that management considers as being an acceptable and attainable level of earnings for such assets. The required earnings rate is calculated as follows:

1. Find the aftertax interest cost. This is the actual interest cost of long-term debt multiplied by one minus the income tax rate; it is approximately one half the actual interest cost.
2. Add this to the net income after taxes.
3. Divide the amount obtained in step 2 by the sum of long-term debt plus owners' equity.

The procedure is shown in Illustration 19–3.

Illustration 19–3

ESTIMATING THE REQUIRED EARNINGS RATE

A. "Satisfactory" Balance Sheet
(in thousands)

ASSETS			EQUITIES	
Working capital....		$ 2,000	Long-term debt (6%).......	$ 3,000
Fixed assets, gross..	$16,000		Owners' equity............	7,000
Less: Average depreciation.	8,000	8,000		
Total Assets...		$10,000	Total Equities.........	$10,000

B. "Satisfactory" Income Statement

Revenue...	$11,000
Less: All costs except interest and taxes.................	9,000
Income before interest and taxes.........................	$ 2,000
Interest..	180
Income before taxes....................................	$ 1,820
Income taxes (50%)....................................	910
Net Income..	$ 910

C. Calculation of Required Earnings Rate

$$\frac{\text{Aftertax Interest} + \text{Net Income}}{\text{Debt} + \text{Equity}} = \frac{90 + 910}{4,000 + 6,000} = 10 \text{ Percent}$$

OTHER APPROACHES. Many companies arrive at the average required earnings rate by a process that is essentially trial and error. If a given rate results in the rejection of projects that management intuitively feels are desirable, there is an indication that the rate is too high, and it is lowered. An average required rate of 10 percent after taxes is found in many industrial companies and government agencies, with lower rates in public utilities (say, 8 percent) and higher rates (15 or 20 percent) in companies in industries where profit opportunities are unusually good or risks are unusually high.

Sometimes income taxes are ignored, in which case the rate is a pretax rate, which is higher than the aftertax rate in the same company.

INTEREST RATE. Whatever the rate selected, it is almost certain to be considerably higher than an *interest* rate, that is, the rate for borrowing money (say, 5 to 8 percent before taxes). The required earnings rate includes interest, but it also includes an additional allowance for risks that are borne by the business rather than by the lender of money, and for which the business expects compensation.

ADJUSTMENT OF THE AVERAGE RATE. The required earnings rate for the whole business reflects the average risk of investments in various classes of assets. This average results from a composite of many different types of risks, ranging from investments in government bonds, where the risk is very low, to investments that may be almost pure gambles, such as those in untried new products. The earnings rate required on the particular investment under consideration should reflect, if feasible, the relative risk of this investment compared to the average.

It may also reflect the uncertainty that the estimated savings will actually be realized. The figures on costs, savings, and economic life are *estimates* of what will happen in the future. Often, a higher than average earnings rate is used when these uncertainties are believed to be great. (Uncertainty can also be allowed for by arbitrarily shortening the estimate of economic life. Care should be taken not to *overallow* for uncertainty by using both a short life and a high required earnings rate.)[5]

Finally, the required earnings rate is sometimes adjusted to compensate for the "administrative bother" that may be entailed in going into the venture—the unmeasured, but sometimes significant, cost of the additional management headaches and worry that may be a consequence of making the proposed investment.

PROFIT CENTER RATES. If the company has several profit centers or divisions it may or may not use the same required earnings rate for all profit centers. If it uses different required earnings rates in different profit centers, the rates chosen will tend to influence the flow of corporate funds to the various profit centers; for the higher the required rate, the fewer proposed investments will be accepted. It is erroneous to derive these profit center rates from the actual earnings of the profit centers; for example, it is erroneous to assign a low rate to a division that currently has

---

[5] Uncertainty can also be taken into account by mathematical techniques. These include (a) *sensitivity analysis*, that shows the change in the present value of earnings that results from systematically varying each of the main elements of the earnings calculations, and (b) calculation of a large number of earnings estimates, each based on different estimates of the main elements of the earnings calculation, and study of the resulting frequency distribution. These techniques are not difficult if a computer is available.

a low return on its investment. Such a practice would tend to perpetuate, or even enlarge, mature divisions whose profit potential is low, at the expense of young divisions that have a high profit potential and need large investments to exploit that potential.

FINANCIAL PROBLEMS. In some problems, the issue is not whether to acquire an asset, but rather the manner in which to finance it; in other problems, a certain method of financing may be an integral part of the proposal. In these situations, the relevant required earnings rate must be tailored to the facts of the problem. If a company has already decided to acquire a building, and the issue is whether to buy it with borrowed funds or to acquire it through a long-term noncancelable lease, the required earnings rate is close to the cost of borrowing funds rather than the overall earnings rate for the whole company.

Unless the method of financing is closely related to the proposition itself, it is usually better to consider the means of obtaining the funds as a separate problem. Ordinarily, the question as to whether the proposed investment is or is not desirable is an operating matter, decided by operating people; the question of how to finance it is a financial matter, decided by financial people.

Earnings

The earnings from an investment are essentially the additional cash that the company estimates it will earn from the investment as compared with what the company's earnings would be if it did not make the investment. The *differential* concept emphasized in Chapter 18 is therefore equally applicable here. Consider, for example, a proposal to replace an existing machine with an even better machine. We note first that the existing machine must still be usable, for if it can no longer perform its function, there is no analytical problem; it *must* be replaced. The existing machine has a certain set of labor, material, power, repair, maintenance, and other costs associated with its future operation. If the alternative machine is proposed as a means of reducing costs, there will be a different, lower set of costs associated with its use. The difference between these two sets of cost is the *earnings* anticipated if the new machine is acquired. These earnings are figured on an annual basis.

If the proposed machine increases the company's productive capacity, and if the increased output can be sold, the incremental profit on this increased volume is the earnings anticipated from acquisition of the proposed machine. Incremental profit is the difference between added sales revenue and incremental costs, which usually include direct material, direct labor, direct selling costs, and any other costs that will not be incurred if the increased volume is not manufactured and sold.

Depreciation on the proposed equipment is not a relevant cost item; the present value tables automatically provide for recouping the investment itself, and to include a depreciation charge would be counting this recoupment twice. Depreciation on the existing equipment is likewise not relevant because, as explained in Chapter 18, this represents a sunk cost that is unaffected by the present decision.

The earnings stream in a capital budgeting problem usually must be estimated for a considerable period of time in the future. Such estimates are fraught with uncertainty and must be treated accordingly. A particularly troublesome aspect of these estimates is what assumption to make about changes in price levels. If the analyst believes, as many people do, that labor rates and material prices will generally tend to move upward, it may be desirable to incorporate in the calculation of earnings an explicit assumption about inflation.

In general, the earnings are cash flows. As explained in Chapter 18, changes in prorated or allocated costs are not relevant unless they actually represent differential costs.

INCOME TAXES. Presumably, the purpose of making an investment is to increase the owners' equity. Owners' equity will not be increased by the full amount of the cost savings or additional income resulting from the investment, however, since a substantial fraction of these savings or income usually will be paid to the government in the form of additional income taxes. Owners' equity will be increased only by the amount remaining after these additional taxes have been deducted.

If "earnings," as defined above, were the same as "additional profit subject to income tax," then profit after taxes could be found simply by multiplying the profit by the complement of the estimated future tax rate (i.e., one minus the tax rate). Thus, if 50 percent is accepted as a reasonable estimate of future applicable tax rates, the profit after taxes would be one half the profit before taxes.

In estimating earnings, however, depreciation was intentionally omitted from the calculations. Since depreciation is an allowable expense for tax purposes, "additional profit subject to income tax" will not correspond to earnings in any problem where depreciation is a significant factor. In effect, the depreciation on the equipment being purchased provides a "tax shield"; it shields earnings from the full impact of income taxes.

EXAMPLE: A proposed machine costing $1,000 is expected to result in cash savings of $320 a year for five years. Assuming a required earnings rate of 10 percent, is this a good investment?

The additional income subject to taxes will be, not the whole $320, but rather $320 less the depreciation charge. If straight-line depreciation is used, this will be $200 a year ($1,000 ÷ 5 years). The additional income subject to tax will be $320 − $200 = $120. At a tax rate of 50 percent, income taxes will be increased half of this, or $60, so the net savings will be $320 − $60 = $260. Savings of $260 a year for 5 years at 10 per-

cent has a present value of 260 × $3.791 = $986. Since this is less than the
$1,000 investment, the machine is not a good investment.

ACCELERATED DEPRECIATION. In the preceding example we assumed
that depreciation would be calculated on a straight-line basis for tax
purposes. Many companies use one of the accelerated bases of depreciation, however (see Chapter 6 for description). Assuming the sum-of-
years' digit basis is used, the tax deductible depreciation and the earnings
after taxes for the proposal described in the preceding example would be
as follows:

Year	Cash Earnings (a)	Depreciation (b)	Earnings Subject to Tax (c = a − b)	Tax at 50% (d)	Cash Earnings after Tax (e = a − d)
1............	$ 320	$ 333	$ −13	$ −6	$ 326
2............	320	267	53	26	294
3............	320	200	120	60	260
4............	320	133	187	94	226
5............	320	67	253	126	194
Total.....	$1,600	$1,000	$600	$300	$1,300

We could then find the present value of the earnings by discounting each
of the five after-tax cash earnings amounts in the last column, as follows:

Year	Earnings after Tax	Discount at 10%	Present Value
1..................	$ 326	0.909	$ 297
2..................	294	0.826	243
3..................	260	0.751	195
4..................	226	0.683	154
5..................	194	0.621	121
Total............	$1,300		$1,010

TABLE C. There is a way of greatly simplifying the above calculation.
It involves the use of Table C, page 479, which shows the present value of
a stream of depreciation charges figured by the sum-of-years' digit
method. (Double declining balance, which is the other commonly used
accelerated method, gives practically the same results.) Using this table,
the total present value of the depreciation tax shield can be figured easily
in a single computation, and this amount can then be added to the present
value of the aftertax cash earnings to give the total present value of the
earnings.

The procedure is as follows:

1. Multiply the annual cash earnings, neglecting depreciation, by the complement of the tax rate to find the aftertax cash earnings.

2. Multiply the aftertax cash earnings by the appropriate discount amount from Table B, to find their present value.

3. Multiply the depreciable investment by the appropriate amount from Table C to find the present value of the stream of depreciation charges.

4. Multiply this present value by the tax rate to find the present value of the depreciation tax shield.

5. Add the amounts in steps 2 and 4 to find the aftertax present value of earnings.

> EXAMPLE: Same problem as above, but using Table C.
>
> The cash earnings after taxes, but *neglecting depreciation*, are 50 percent of $320, or $160 a year. The present value of $1 a year for five years at 10 percent is $3.791; therefore the present value of the cash earnings is 160 × $3.791   = $ 607
>
> The present value of depreciation of $1 of investment spread over five years is, from Table C, $0.806. For an investment of $1,000, it is therefore 1,000 × $0.806 = $806. The present value of the depreciation tax shield is $806 times the tax rate, 50 percent,   =   403
>
> The total present value therefore equals $1,010

Note that the result in the above example is exactly the same as in the year-by-year calculation given above. Note also how the use of accelerated depreciation increases the attractiveness of the investment; its present value rises from $986 under straight-line depreciation to $1,010, and the proposal now meets the criterion that the present value of its earnings exceeds the investment. This result occurs because a larger fraction of the depreciation tax shield occurs in the early years, where present values are relatively high; it is the reason why accelerated depreciation has become so popular for tax purposes.

If the proposed machine is to replace a machine that has not been fully depreciated for tax purposes, then the tax shield is only the differential depreciation, that is, the difference between depreciation on the present machine and that on the new machine, because if the new machine is purchased, the old machine will presumably be disposed of, so its depreciation will no longer provide a tax shield. In this case, the present value of the tax shield of the remaining depreciation on the old machine must be calculated (usually year by year), and this amount must be subtracted from the present value of the depreciation tax shield on the proposed machine.

OMISSION OF TAX CALCULATION.   In many types of alternative choice problems, the question of income taxes may be omitted entirely, since the alternative that produces the most profit *before* taxes will also produce the most profit *after* taxes. This is the case with pricing problems and many make-or-buy problems. In problems involving depreciable assets, however, there is unlikely to be a simple relationship between savings before taxes and savings after taxes, and the above calculation is therefore necessary.

TAX EFFECT OF INTEREST. Interest actually paid (as distinguished from imputed interest) is an allowable expense for income tax purposes; therefore, if interest costs will be increased as a result of the investment, it could be argued that interest provides a tax shield similar to depreciation and that its impact should be estimated by the same method as that shown for depreciation, above. Customarily, however, interest is *not* included anywhere in the calculations either of earnings or of taxes. This is because we usually seek the overall rate of return on the investment, without regard for whether the funds required for the investment are borrowed (which involves interest) or whether they come from the shareholders (which does not involve interest).

In problems where the method of financing is an important part of the proposal, the tax shield provided by interest may appropriately be considered. In these problems, the rate of return that results from the calculation is a return on that part of the investment which was financed by the shareholders' equity, not a return on the total funds committed to the investment.

> EXAMPLE: Suppose a company is considering an investment in a parcel of real estate, and intends to finance perhaps 70 percent of the investment by a mortgage loan on the property. It may wish to focus attention on the return on its own funds, namely, the remaining 30 percent. It would be appropriate to include in the calculation of such a return both the interest on the mortgage loan and the effect of this interest on taxable income.

Economic Life

The cash flow analysis is carried out for the time period corresponding to the life of the proposed project, the period over which benefits can be estimated. The end of this period is called the *horizon* for the project, the word suggesting that beyond this point earnings are not visible. When the proposed project involves the purchase of equipment, this time period corresponds to the economic life of the equipment.

There are at least three ways of defining the "life" of equipment:

1. Its physical life.
2. Its technological life.
3. Its product-market life.

The economic life is the *shortest* of these three types of life. Economic life can rarely be estimated exactly; nevertheless, making the best possible judgment of the economic life is extremely important.

PHYSICAL LIFE.   There is a tendency, when thinking about the life of a machine, to consider primarily its physical life; that is, the number of years the machine will probably be of use to the company in performing the technical job for which it was acquired. This concept of life is sometimes used in calculating depreciation for accounting purposes and for income tax purposes. It is of little use in investment decisions.

TECHNOLOGICAL LIFE.   This refers to the period of time that elapses before a new machine comes out that makes the present machine obsolete. It is this life that, for most companies, corresponds to the economic life. Improvements will almost certainly be made sometime in all machines now in existence, but the question of *which* machines will be improved and *how soon* the improved machines will be on the market is a most difficult one to answer. Unless special information is available, the answer can be little more than a guess. Yet it is a guess that must be made, for the investment in a machine will cease to earn a return when and if this machine is replaced by an even better machine.

PRODUCT-MARKET LIFE.   Although the machine may be in excellent physical condition, and although there may be no better machine available, its economic life has ended, as far as the owner is concerned, as soon as the company ceases to market the product made on the machine. The "product-market" life of the machine may end because the particular operation performed by the machine is made unnecessary by a change in style or a change in process, or because the market for the product itself has vanished. A machine for making buggy whips may last physically for 100 years, and there may be no possibility of making technological improvements in it; yet such a machine cannot earn a return on its investment if the buggy whips produced on it cannot be sold.

The product-market life of a machine also ends if the company goes out of business. Most managements quite properly operate on the premise that the company will be in business for a long time to come. There are instances, however, when a businessman foresees an end to his business, or to a particular part of it, in the relatively near future. In such a case, the economic life of a machine *to him* is limited to the period during which he believes his business is going to operate.

UNEVEN LIVES.   For many types of equipment, it is reasonable to assume that the present machine can be used, physically, for a period of time at least as long as the economic life of the proposed machine. In situations in which this assumption is not valid, however, earnings on a proposed machine purchased now will not in fact occur each year of the period being considered, for a new machine must be purchased anyway when the physical life of the present machine ends. Thereafter, there may be no difference in the annual cost of the two alternatives (buy now versus don't buy now), since the same machine will be involved in both of them.

If the expected physical life of the present machine is significantly shorter than the expected economic life of the proposed machine, some way must be found of making an equivalence between the time periods covered by the two alternatives. For example, if the proposed machine has an economic life of 10 years but the present machine has a remaining physical life of only 6 years, the relevant earnings will occur for only 6 years. This fact raises the difficult question of treating the situation that will exist at the end of the sixth year.

Since the purchase now of a new machine eliminates the need of purchasing another one six years from now, this future purchase price will have been saved and its present value can therefore be counted as a cash inflow in the sixth year. However, the machine purchased now presumably will have to be replaced at the end of 10 years; whereas if a machine is not purchased until 6 years from now, it will last until 16 years from now. So, if the proposal is accepted, there will be an additional cash outflow at the end of the 10th year. This intricate reasoning can be extended indefinitely through later replacement cycles. Estimates of these distant values are tenuous, and this whole procedure is based on the assumption that there will be no further changes in technology or price levels; but the roughness of the estimates is somewhat mitigated by the fact that the present values become less significant as the time span increases, so that the calculations need not be carried out indefinitely.

Another approach is to estimate the remaining value of the new machine at the end of the sixth year of its life. The analysis would then cover only the six-year period, with this remaining value being treated as a residual value, or implicit cash inflow at the end of the period. Such an estimate is extremely difficult to make, however.

The problem of uneven lives does not arise often, and this is fortunate, because the timing and consequences of the future replacements under each alternative are difficult to visualize.

Investment

The amount of the investment is the amount that the company risks if it accepts the proposal. The relevant investment costs are the differential or incremental costs. These are the outlays that will be made if the project is undertaken and that will not be made if it is not undertaken. The cost of the machine itself, its shipping costs, cost of installation, and the cost of training operators are examples. These outlays are part of the investment, even though some of them are not capitalized in the accounting records.

INVESTMENT CREDIT. At present (mid 1969) a company may receive an "investment credit" of up to 7 percent of the cost of a new machine as a reduction in its income taxes. The amount of company funds involved may therefore be only 93 percent of the invoice cost of the machine.

EXISTING EQUIPMENT. If the purchase of new equipment makes possible the sale of existing equipment, the proceeds from the sale may reduce the amount of incremental investment. In other words, the investment represents the total amount of *additional* funds that must be committed to the operation. To subtract this resale value from the gross investment, however, is to assume implicitly that (*a*) if the proposed machine is not purchased, the present machine will continue to be used, and its resale value will decrease to zero through its continued use; and (*b*) if the proposed machine is purchased, the present machine will in fact be sold or converted to some other productive use. If either of these assumptions is not valid, and if the amount involved is significant, the resale value of the present machine should be treated separately as a cash inflow in some future year, not netted against the gross investment in the proposed machine.

TAX EFFECTS. The disposition of the present machine may involve a write-off of undepreciated book values or a sale at a price above book value. In either of these cases, special tax considerations may apply, since the write-off may give rise to a capital loss and the sale to a capital gain. The capital gains rate is, in effect, 25 percent. Nevertheless, under most circumstances, gains and losses on the disposition of machinery and equipment (not buildings) are taxed at the regular rate of approximately 50 percent. No tax gain or loss arises if the new machine replaces one of "like kind." Expert tax advice is needed on problems involving gains and losses on the sale of depreciable assets, for the line between the assets giving rise to capital gains or losses and other assets is difficult to define. In any event, when existing assets are disposed of, the relevant amount by which the net investment is reduced is the proceeds of the sale, adjusted for taxes.

RESIDUAL VALUE. A machine may have a salvage or resale value at the end of its useful life. In a great many cases, the estimated residual value is so small and occurs so far in the future that it has no significant effect on the decision. Moreover, any salvage value that is realized may be almost, or completely, offset by removal and dismantling costs.

In situations where residual value is significant, the net residual value (after removal costs) is a cash inflow in the year of disposal, and is included with the other cash inflows. Other assets, such as repair parts or inventory, may also be released at the end of the project, and these are treated in the same fashion.

SUNK COSTS. As emphasized in Chapter 18, sunk costs are irrelevant. If $100,000 has been sunk in research leading to a new product, and if the new product will require an additional investment in new facilities of $10,000 and is expected to generate profits of $5,000 a year for five years, the relevant investment figure is $10,000, not $110,000. The $100,000 may be regretted, but it cannot be recouped.

INVESTMENTS IN WORKING CAPITAL. An investment is the commitment, or locking up, of funds in any type of asset. Although a machine has here been used as an example, land and buildings also are investments, and so are commitments of funds to additional inventory and other current assets. In particular, if the new equipment is to produce a new product, additional funds will probably be tied up in inventories, accounts receivable, and increased cash needs. Part of this increased working capital will be supplied from increased accounts payable and accrued expenses. The net increase in working capital is as much an investment as the equipment itself, although in a more liquid state.

Often it is reasonable to assume that the residual value of investments in working capital items is approximately the same as the amount of the investment; that is, that at the end of the project, they can be liquidated at their cost. Under these circumstances, the amount of working capital is treated as a cash inflow in the last year of the project, and its present value is found by discounting at the required earnings rate.

SEVERAL ALTERNATIVES. Some proposals involve a choice among several alternatives, each involving a different amount of investment. A useful way of approaching such problems is to start with the alternative that requires the smallest investment and to analyze the next most expensive alternative in terms of its *incremental* investment and its *incremental* earnings above those of the least expensive alternative. This question is asked: Is the *additional* investment in the second alternative justified by the *additional* earnings that are expected from it, over and above the earnings expected from the least expensive alternative? If it is not, the proposal with the smaller investment should be accepted.

DEFERRED INVESTMENTS. Many projects involve a single commitment of funds at one moment of time, which we have called "the present." For some projects, on the other hand, the commitments are spread over a considerable period of time. The construction of a new plant may require disbursements over several years, or it may involve the construction of one unit now and a second unit five years later. In order to make the return-on-investment calculations, these investments must be brought to a common point in time, and this is done by the application of discount rates to the amounts involved. In general, the appropriate rate depends on the uncertainty that the investment will be made; the lower the uncertainty, the lower the rate. Thus, if the commitment is an extremely definite one, the discount rate may be equivalent to the interest rate on bonds (which also represents a definite commitment) whereas if the future investments will be made only if earnings materialize, then the rate can be the required earnings rate. In effect, in the latter case, the future investment is treated as a cash outflow.

Summary of the Process

Following is a summary of the steps involved in using the present value method:

1. Select a required earnings rate. Presumably, once selected, this rate will be used for all proposals in the same risk category.

2. Estimate the differential cash inflows, or "earnings," for each year or sequence of years including:

   a) The cash earnings, neglecting depreciation, after taxes, for each year of the economic life.

   b) The depreciation tax shield, using Table C.

   c) Residual values at the end of the economic life, consisting of disposal value of equipment plus working capital that is to be released.

3. Estimate the cash outflows other than the investment itself, if there are any, for the year in which they occur.

4. Find the net present value of all future inflows and outflows by discounting them at the required earnings rate, using Table A or Table B.

5. Find the net investment, which includes the additional outlays made at "the present time," less the proceeds from disposal of existing equipment (adjusted for tax consequences), plus the present value of investment outlays made at some time other than the present. Use a low discount rate if these future outlays are quite certain to be made.

6. If the present value of the cash flows exceeds the amount of the net investment, decide that the proposal is acceptable, insofar as the monetary factors are concerned. This comparison is often made by treating the net investment as a cash outflow in year 0; i.e., with a present value of 1.000. When this is done, adding the numbers algebraically gives the result directly. A positive sum indicates an acceptable proposal; a negative sum, an unfavorable one.

7. Taking into account the nonmonetary factors, reach a final decision. (This part of the process is at least as important as all the other parts put together, but there is no way of generalizing about it, other than to offer the list of suggestions given in Chapter 18.)

As an aid to visualizing the relationship, it is often useful to make a rough diagram of the flows such as that shown in Illustration 19–4.

The diagram is for the same situation given in the example on page 442, with the addition of an estimated residual value of $200; namely, a machine costing $1,000, and estimated cash earnings (say, from savings in labor costs) of $320 a year for five years. As an illustration of the whole process, the analysis of this proposal will be described, arranged according to the steps given above.

1. The required earnings rate is 10 percent. (The company has arrived at this rate by one of the methods described above.)
2. The differential cash inflows are:
   a) The cash earnings of $320 a year, which, after adjustment for an estimated income tax of 50 percent, becomes $160 a year for five years.
   b) The depreciation tax shield, which, assuming the whole investment of $1,000 is subject to depreciation for tax purposes, has a present value of $403, as calculated in the preceding example.
   c) The residual value at the end of the fifth year, which is $200. (Note that this differs from the assumption of zero residual value made for tax purposes.)

Illustration 19–4

CASH FLOW DIAGRAM

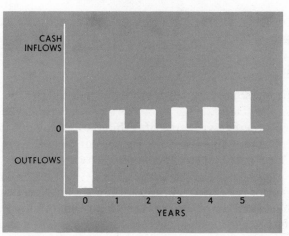

3. There are no noninvestment cash outflows in this problem.
4. The net present value of the cash flows, other than the investment are the sum of (*a*) the aftertax cash earnings of $160 a year for five years, which has a present value, already calculated, of $607; plus (*b*) the present value of the depreciation tax shield of $403; plus (*c*) the present value of the residual value of $200, which, discounted at 0.621 (from Table A), amounts to $124. These amounts total $1,134.
5. The net investment is the gross investment of $1,000, less the investment credit, here assumed to be 2 percent, a net of $980. (The investment credit is not always 7 percent; the amount varies, depending principally on the estimated life of the asset.)
6. Since the present value of the inflows, $1,134, exceeds the net investment, $980, the indication is that the proposal is acceptable insofar as the monetary factors are concerned.

7. The final decision would also take into account nonmonetary factors which, although not discussed here, may be as important as or more important than the monetary factors.

OTHER METHODS

Time-Adjusted Return

With the present value method, the required earnings rate must be selected in advance. There exists an alternative method, which finds the earnings rate at which the present value of the earnings equals the amount of the investment. This rate is called the *time-adjusted return*, or *internal rate of return*, or *project rate of return*. The method is called by one of the above names and also by the terms "discounted cash flow method" and "investor's method." We shall refer to it as the time-adjusted return method.

LEVEL EARNINGS. If the earnings are level—that is, the same amount each year—the process is simple. It will be illustrated by a proposed investment of $1,000 with estimated earnings of $250 a year for five years. The procedure is as follows:

1. Divide the investment, $1,000, by the annual earnings, $250. The result, 4, is called the "factor."
2. Look across the five-year row of Table B. The column in which the figure closest to 4 appears shows the rate of return. Since the closest figure is 3.993 in the 8 percent column, the return is slightly less than 8 percent.
3. If management is satisfied with a return of slightly less than 8 percent, then it should accept this project (neglecting nonquantitative considerations); if it requires a higher return, then it should reject the project.

The factor 4 is simply the ratio of the investment to the annual earnings. Each figure on Table B shows the ratio of the present value of a stream of earnings to an investment of $1 made today, for various combinations of discount rates and numbers of years. The number 4 opposite any combination of years and discount rates means that the present value of a stream of earnings of $1 a year for that number of years discounted at that rate is $4. The present value of a stream of earnings of $250 a year is in the same ratio; therefore it is $250 times 4, or $1,000.

In this procedure, it is usually necessary to interpolate, that is, to estimate the location of a number that lies between two figures appearing in the table. There is no need to be precise about these interpolations because the final result can be no better than the basic data, and the basic data are ordinarily only rough estimates. A quick interpolation, made visually, is usually as good as the accuracy of the data warrants. Computations of fractions of a percent are rarely, if ever, warranted.

COMPUTING SEVERAL RETURNS. Since the most uncertain estimate of all is often the number of years during which there will be earnings, it is often useful to locate several combinations of years and rates that have the specified factor. For example, an investment of $20,000 and annual earnings of $4,000 give a factor of 5. Some of the combinations found on Table B for a factor of 5 are as follows:

If the Life Is:	Then the Rate of Return Is about:		If the Required Rate of Return Is:	Then the Life Must Be at Least:
6 years	6%	Or figured another way:	6%	6 + years
8 years	12%		10%	7 + years
10 years	15%		15%	10 years
12 years	17%		18%	14 years

If the proposed investment is expected to have a longer life, *and* if the required earnings rate is lower than any one of the combinations selected, the investment is attractive; otherwise, it is not attractive.

PAYBACK. The figure referred to above as the "factor" is also called the "payback" because it is the number of years over which the investment outlay will be recovered or paid back from earnings *if* the estimates turn out to be correct; that is, the project will "pay for itself" in this number of years. The payback figure is often used as a quick but crude method of appraising investments. If the payback period is equal to or only slightly less than the estimated life of the project, then the proposal is obviously a poor one. If the payback period is considerably less than the estimated life, then the project begins to look attractive.[6]

If several investment proposals have the same general characteristics, then the payback period can be used as a valid way of screening out the acceptable proposals. For example, if a company finds that production equipment ordinarily has a life of 10 years, and if it requires a return of at least 15 percent, then the company may specify that new equipment will be considered for purchase only if it has a payback period of 5 years or less; Table B shows that this payback period is equivalent to a return of approximately 15 percent if the life is 10 years. Stating the criterion in this fashion avoids the necessity of explaining the present value concept to the members of the operating organization.

The danger of using the payback figure is that it gives no consideration to differences in the lives of various projects. There may be a tendency to conclude that the shorter the payback period, the better the project;

---

[6] Professor Myron Gordon has shown that the reciprocal of the payback (i.e., 1/payback period) is a close approximation of the time-adjusted return IF the estimated life of the project is somewhat more than twice the payback period and IF earnings are level. The return found by this simple method slightly overstates the true return (*Journal of Business,* October 1955, p. 253).

whereas the project with the longer payback may actually be better if it will produce satisfactory earnings for a longer period of time.

UNEVEN EARNINGS.   If earnings are not the same in each year, the time-adjusted return must be found by trial and error; that is, the earnings for each year and the residual values are listed, and various discount rates are applied to these amounts until a rate is found that makes their total present value equal to the amount of the investment. This rate is the time-adjusted return.

This method is illustrated by a problem in which it is assumed that the net investment is $1,000 and that earnings are estimated to be $300 a year for the first 5 years but only $100 a year for the 6th through the 10th year.

As a first trial, the present value of these earnings will be computed at an earnings rate of 18 percent. From Table B, we find that the present value of $1 a year for the next five years at 18 percent is $3.127. Table B does not tell us directly the present value of an amount to be received from the 6th through the 10th year, but, as already explained, this can easily be found by subtraction. The amount for 10 years is $4.494, and the amount for the first 5 of these years is $3.127; therefore, the amount for the 6th through the 10th years must be the difference between these figures, or $1.367. The present value of the estimated earnings can be computed by use of these factors, as follows:

Time Period	Earnings	Factor at 18%	Present Value
Years 1– 5............	$300/year	3.127	$ 938
6–10............	100/year	1.367	137
		Total......	$1,075
		Investment..	1,000
		Difference..+$	75

When the present value exceeds the net investment, a higher earnings rate is used on the next trial; when the present value is less than the net investment, a lower rate is used.

In this case, therefore, a higher rate must be used, and 20 percent is selected. Another trial is made, as follows:

Time Period	Earnings	Factor at 20%	Present Value
Years 1– 5............	$300/year	2.991	$ 897
6–10............	100/year	1.201	120
		Total......	$1,017
		Investment..	1,000
		Difference..+$	17

This calculation gives a present value slightly above the net investment, which indicates that the time-adjusted return is slightly more than 20 percent.

In a similar fashion, all the elements involved in an investment can be compared with all the elements involved on the earnings side of the equation, with the difference in the timing of the money flows being recognized by the application of a trial discount rate. Eventually a rate will be found that makes the present value of the outflows approximately equal to the present value of the inflows. Usually, a satisfactory approximation to this rate can be found in two or three trials.

MAPI Method

Dr. George Terborgh of the Machinery and Allied Products Institute (MAPI) has developed a method that is specifically intended to help decide whether a machine should be replaced now or whether replacement should be deferred until some future time. Special forms and charts make this method quite easy to use. The charts are constructed in accordance with certain assumptions, the most important of which is that earnings will decline each year as the machine ages, in accordance with a prescribed pattern. Doctor Terborgh asserts that this is the typical situation with respect to replacement equipment, both because equipment becomes less efficient and requires higher maintenance costs with the passage of time and because the probability of obsolescence increases as time goes on.

If this and the other assumptions built into the method fit facts of the situation being analyzed, then the "urgency rating," which is the end product of the MAPI method, is a close approximation to the time-adjusted return. This method is fully described in a reference at the end of this chapter.

Comparison of Methods

Given the same set of raw data, the time-adjusted return method will produce the same results at the present value method in the class of problems we have called screening problems; that is, if one method signals that a proposal is acceptable, so will the other. Under most circumstances, the MAPI method will also give the same signal if the special assumptions built into this method are used in the other methods. As will be seen, this similarity of results does not hold true in the other class of problems, called preference problems.

PREFERENCE PROBLEMS

So far, the discussion has been limited to *screening* or "go, no go" problems, where this is the question: Is the proposal acceptable, or isn't it? We turn now to the more difficult *preference* problem, where we must decide which of two competing proposals is preferable, or where we must rank a series of proposals in order of their attractiveness. Both the time-adjusted return and the present value methods are used for this purpose.

If the time-adjusted return method is used, the preference rule is as follows: the higher the return, the better the project. A project with a return of 20 percent is said to be preferable to a project with a return of 19 percent.

Profitability Index

If the present value method is used, the present value of the earnings of one project cannot be compared directly with the present value of the earnings of another unless the investments are of the same size. Most people would agree that a $1,000 investment that produces earnings with a present value of $2,000 is better than a $1,000,000 investment that produces earnings with a present value of $1,001,000. In order to compare two proposals, we must relate the size of the earnings to the amount of money that is risked. This is done simply by dividing the present value earnings by the amount of investment, to give a ratio that is called the *profitability index*. The preference rule is as follows: the higher the index number, the better the project.

Comparison of Preference Rules

Conceptually, the profitability index is superior to the time-adjusted return as a preference device, for the time-adjusted return method will not always give the correct preference as between two projects with different lives or with different patterns of earnings.

As an example, consider two proposals. Proposal A involves an investment of $1,000 and earnings of $1,200 received at the end of one year; its time-adjusted return is 20 percent. Proposal B involves an investment of $1,000 and earnings of $300 a year for five years; its time-adjusted return is only 15 percent. But Proposal A is *not* necessarily preferable to Proposal B. It is preferable only if the company can expect to earn a high return during the following four years on some other project in which the funds released at the end of the first year are reinvested. Otherwise, Proposal B, which earns 15 percent over the whole five-year period, is preferable.[7]

The error illustrated above is not present in the profitability index

---

[7] Note that this problem arises when a choice must be made between two competing proposals, only one of which can be adopted. If the proposals are noncompeting and the required earnings rate is less than 15 percent, then *both* of them are acceptable.

method. Assuming a required earnings rate of 10 percent, the two proposals described above would be analyzed as follows:

Proposal (a)	Earnings (b)	Discount Factor (c)	Present Value $(d = b \times c)$	Investment (e)	Index $(f = d \div e)$
A.........$1,200—1 yr.		0.909	$1,091	$1,000	1.09
B.........$ 300—5 yrs.		3.791	1,137	1,000	1.14

The index signals that Proposal B is better than Proposal A, which is in fact the case if the company can expect to reinvest the money released from Proposal A so as to earn only 10 percent on it.

Although the profitability index method is conceptually superior to the time-adjusted return method, and although the former is also easier to calculate since there is no trial-and-error computation, the time-adjusted return method is widely used in practice. There seem to be two reasons for this. First, the profitability index requires that the earnings rate be established before the calculations are made, whereas many analysts prefer to work from the other direction; that is, to find the return and then see how it compares with their idea of the earnings rate that is appropriate in view of the risks involved. Second, the index is an abstract number that is difficult to explain; whereas the time-adjusted return is similar to interest rates and earnings rates with which every businessman is familiar.

Concluding Comment

Not every businessman uses a discounting technique in analyzing investment proposals. In some cases, this is because the businessman is not familiar with the techniques. But there is a much better reason than this in many instances. Some businessmen, having studied the approach carefully, have concluded that it is like trying to make a silk purse out of a sow's ear; that is, in their opinion the underlying estimates are so rough that the refinement of discounting them is more work than it is worth. They therefore use a payback method or some alternative that does not involve discounting.

Those who do use one of the discounting methods argue that the extra work involved is small, and that the results, although admittedly rough, are nevertheless better than not even attempting to allow for the time element.

SUMMARY

The capital investment problem is essentially that of determining whether the anticipated earnings from a proposed project are sufficiently attractive to warrant risking the investment of funds in the project. The investment is typically made at one moment of time, whereas earnings flow in over a period of time in the future. The analysis technique must take this difference in timing into account.

For screening purposes, that is, for deciding whether a proposal is or is not attractive, two techniques are available. In the present value method, the *present value* of the earnings is found by discounting earnings at a required rate. If this present value equals or exceeds the amount of the investment, the proposal is acceptable. In the *time-adjusted return* technique, a discount rate is found that makes the present value of the earnings equal to the investment. If this rate equals or exceeds the required earnings rate, the proposal is acceptable.

Similar techniques may be used to establish preferences. The *profitability index* derived from the present value method is conceptually superior to the time-adjusted return method in signaling preferences, but both methods are widely used in practice.

These techniques can be used only to the extent that the facts of a proposal can be reduced to dollar amounts for investment and earnings. For many proposals, nonquantitative considerations are dominant, and the techniques are not applicable. In nearly every problem there are some nonquantitative considerations, and these must be used to temper the numerical result.

SUGGESTIONS FOR FURTHER READING[8]

GRANT, EUGENE L., and WILLIAM G. IRESON. *Principles of Engineering Economy*. 4th ed.; New York: Ronald Press Co., 1960.

SOLOMON, EZRA (ed.). *The Management of Corporate Capital*. Glencoe, Ill.: Free Press, 1959.

TERBORGH, GEORGE. *Business Investment Policy*. Washington, D.C.: Machinery and Allied Products Institute, 1958.

WESTON, J. FRED and DONALD H. WOODS. *Basic Financial Management: Selected Readings*. Belmont, Calif.: Wadsworth Publishing Co., 1967.

---

[8] See also "Suggestions for Further Reading" for Chapter 18.

CHAPTER 20

AUTOMATED DATA PROCESSING

Automated data processing is, as the name suggests, the processing of data without human intervention. It was made possible by the development of electronic computers. Although the first computer for business purposes began operation as recently as 1951, growth has been extremely rapid, and computers now have a significant impact on management accounting. The purpose of this chapter is to describe what automated data processing is, what its impact is currently, and what its impact is likely to be in the future.

For this purpose a detailed understanding of what goes on inside the computer is not required, any more than one needs a detailed knowledge of what goes on under the hood in order to understand how to use an automobile.

DESCRIPTION OF ELECTRONIC COMPUTERS[1]

A general purpose, digital computer (hereafter, simply "computer") performs these operations:

1. It stores data.
2. It performs arithmetic operations on data.
3. It compares two pieces of data and determines whether or not they are equal.
4. It rearranges stored data.
5. It prepares reports or otherwise displays all or any desired part of the data stored within it.

---

[1] This description is limited to general purpose, digital computers, thereby omitting (a) special purpose and (b) analog computers. Neither special purpose nor analog computers are now, nor are they likely to be, of major consequence in the field of management accounting. *Special purpose* computers are designed to perform a single task, such as calculating the course of an aircraft or missile. *Analog* computers work with approximations rather than with cardinal numbers; a slide rule is a manually operated analog computer.

The components of a computer are shown schematically in Illustration 20–1. They are: input, storage, processing, and output. Each is described below.

Illustration 20–1

SCHEMATIC OF AN ELECTRONIC COMPUTER

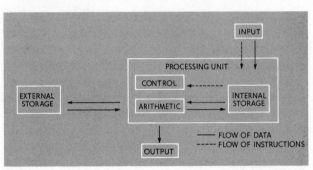

Input

COMPUTER CODES. In the computer each numerical digit, alphabetical letter, or other symbol (e.g. $, %, #, *) is represented by a combination of electrical impulses. Each such combination is called a *character*. Illustration 20–2 shows part of this code for one computer system (not all

Illustration 20–2

COMPUTER CODES

Code	Represents
0●0●0000●	1
0●0●000●0	2
0●0●00●●	3
0●0●●00●	9
●0●0000●	A
●0●0000●0	B
●0●0000●●	C

SOURCE: American Standard Code for Information Exchange, as used in the IBM 360 computers.

computers use exactly the same code). On the printed page, the code is represented by a combination of black and white dots. Inside the computer, it is represented by a combination of electrical states, such as the presence or absence of an electrical charge (e.g., "on" or "off"). These electrical states can be manipulated almost with the speed of electricity (which is the speed of light), and this is the basic reason that the computer operates so rapidly. A computer works on one character at a time, so the usual way of describing the capacity of a computer is in terms of the number of characters it can store, and the usual way of describing its speed is in terms of the number of characters it can process in a second or other unit of time.[2]

INPUT DEVICES. In the input operation, data are fed into the computer and translated electrically into the code that the computer will use in all subsequent operations. Instructions which tell the computer what to do with these data, called the *program*, are also fed in. In the earliest computers, this step involved preparing a punched card for each item of data, and these cards were then fed into the computer. This is still the most common input method, but the preparation of punched cards is relatively expensive; in the typical business data processing situation, it is many times more expensive than all the succeeding operations combined. Punched-card input is also relatively slow, the maximum speed being approximately 1300 characters per second.[3] The usual practice therefore is to convert the original data to computer code in a preliminary operation, often with an inexpensive computer, and to hold it temporarily on magnetic tape. The magnetic tape is used subsequently as input to the main computer. A 2,400-foot reel of magnetic tape can hold 40 million characters, and these can be inputted to the computer at a maximum rate of 300,000 characters per second.

MACHINE-READABLE INPUT. Not only is the preparation of punched cards expensive and slow, but it also is an operation that is susceptible to errors, since the cards are prepared by human beings. Much work has therefore been done to develop input mechanisms that eliminate most of this manual process. The first such machine-readable input to come into widespread use is magnetic ink character recognition (MICR), which is now used on most bank checks and deposit slips. On such documents, a number identifying the depositor and his bank appears in a form that can be read by humans, viz:

⑆0511⑈00031⑆ 07⑈05141149⑈

The printing ink contains a metallic substance which permits these characters to be read automatically by the computer. The computer does this by comparing the characteristics of each MICR character with a file

---

[2] Another unit of measurement is called the *byte*. In some computers, one byte equals one character. In other computers, two numerical characters are included in a single byte.

[3] All computer characteristics given in this chapter are rough approximations. There is considerable variation between computers, and speed also varies with the nature of the work being done.

of characteristics contained in its memory. When it obtains a match, it creates the corresponding computer code for the character.

Some success has also been achieved with optical devices that will permit the computer to read characters that are printed with ordinary ink. Currently, most of these devices work only with characters that conform to a fairly rigid format and are positioned in a prescribed area of the document, but a few computer input devices are able to read ordinary typewritten material, and these devices will soon be widely used.

DIRECT INPUT. Another solution to the input problem is to have input information created automatically by a machine that is located at the point where the transaction originates; this information is then transmitted by wire directly to the computer. For example, in a job shop, there may be input devices in each department or section. When an employee begins a job, he inserts in the device one card containing his own employee number and another card containing the number of the operation he is about to perform. He does the same thing when the job is completed. The input device notes the beginning and ending time from a clock and sends all this information by wire to the computer.

Storage

The processing unit of the computer works on only one or a few characters at one time. It is therefore necessary that a means of storing data be provided. Since the data are represented by combinations of electrical states, the storage medium can be anything in which there are two states and which can be changed from one state to the other electrically. The earliest computers used vacuum tubes, which are either on or off, or switches, which are either open or closed. In more recent developments, the two-state characteristic is obtained by coatings which can be either magnetized or not magnetized, or by cores or metallic film, in which the two states are represented by the clockwise or counterclockwise direction of a magnetic field.

The storage medium consists of cells, each containing the code for one or a few characters, much like letter boxes in a post office contain the mail of one box holder. There must be a means of identifying the cell in which a given character is stored. This is called the *address*. Since the stored data are in the form of electrical impulses, they are invisible. When a new piece of data is entered into a storage cell, any data previously in the cell are automatically erased. Thus, unlike an accounting ledger page, which is also a means of storing information, computer storage can be reused indefinitely.

There are two general categories of storage, internal and external, and several types within each category. They essentially represent different trade-offs between cost and access time. *Access time* is the time required to locate a character in storage and transfer it to the place where it will be used.

INTERNAL STORAGE. Internal storage or *memory* is used in the computing process, to be described next. Since hundreds of thousands of computations are made each second, and since, for each computation, data must be moved out of memory, worked on, and then returned to memory, it is essential that access time of internal storage be very short in order not to slow down the computations any more than is absolutely necessary.

Storage devices with fast access time are much more expensive per character stored than storage devices with slow access time. Because of the high cost, internal storage is relatively small, with a capacity on the order of 50,000 to one million characters, which is about the amount of input data that can be received in a second or so.

EXTERNAL STORAGE. Until shortly before they are needed in a computation, data are stored in external storage devices. Various combinations of these devices may be used in a given computer. At one extreme, there are fast-access but expensive devices similar to those used for internal storage. In the middle are the magnetic tapes already described. In a moderately large computer at least four *tape drives*, each of which handles one reel of tape, will be connected to the computer, and in large computers the number can be ten tape drives or more. Large quantities of information can also be stored on magnetic disks, which resemble phonograph records in appearance. Typical disk devices have a storage capacity of from 3 million to 100 million characters.

When magnetic tape is used, the tape must be used sequentially, which makes the process of searching for a desired piece of information very slow—as long as several minutes, if its general location on the tape is not known. In magnetic disks, the search process can be random, and much faster—from $\frac{1}{20}$ to $\frac{1}{2}$ second (i.e., 50 to 500 milliseconds) to locate one character. At the other extreme are mass storage devices which hold tremendous quantities of information, but which have a relatively long access time. An IBM "Data Cell," for example, weighs about five pounds; it contains 200 strips of magnetic tape, on which 400 million characters can be stored. About 200 of these data cells can be used in a medium-sized computer system.

Processing

The processing section consists of (1) an *arithmetic unit*, which performs the computations, and (2) a *control unit*, which contains the program and which directs the movement of characters out of and back to storage and the manipulation of these characters in the arithmetic unit. The arithmetic unit does only two things: (1) it computes, that is, performs the arithmetic operations of addition, subtraction, multiplication and division; and (2) it compares two characters and determines whether or not they are equal; in some computers, if the characters are unequal, the computer determines which one is larger. If a computer only computed, it would be nothing more than a very fast, accurate calculating machine (up to three million additions per second.) It is the second operation, that of comparison, that gives the computer its extraordinary power. In order to understand why this is so, a description of the programming process is necessary.

PROGRAMMING. A program is a set of instructions specifying each operation that the computer is to perform. If the computer is to add two numbers, a and b, stored in addresses x and y, the control unit must give the following instructions:

1. Transfer the contents of address x from storage to the arithmetic unit.
2. Transfer the contents of address y from storage to the arithmetic unit.
3. Add.
4. Transfer the sum to address z.

Most data processing procedures consist not of a single operation, such as adding two numbers together, but rather of a series of operations performed one after the other, and the rules for performing each of these operations may vary with the circumstances. For example, in computing an employee's pay, a certain percentage must be deducted for social security taxes if, *but only if*, the total of such deductions for the year to date has not exceeded a certain amount (in 1969, $374.40). Thus, for a given employee, the social security deduction may or may not be made, depending on the circumstances. The instructions to the computer will provide for these circumstances by something like the following (which is condensed by eliminating the details of moving data to and from storage):

1. Are this employee's social security deductions to date less than $374.40?
2a. If no, do not make a social security deduction; go to the next operation.
2b. If yes, multiply his gross pay by 0.048, record this as his social security deduction for this week, and add it to his accumulated social security deduction for the year.
3. Does the total deduction now exceed $374.40?
4a. If yes, subtract the difference and to go the next operation.
4b. If no, go to the next operation.

The first and third of these instructions illustrates the comparison feature. It is this feature that permits the computer to handle any conceivable set of circumstances, *providing* these circumstances have been foreseen and instructions for handling them have been incorporated in the program. This is a large proviso, for one of the great difficulties that the programmer must contend with is to visualize in advance every contingency that might arise in the procedure that he is programming.

As an indication of the possibilities opened up by this comparison feature, a greatly simplified portion of an order processing program is given in Illustration 20–3. The illustration is in the form of a *block*

Illustration 20–3

BLOCK DIAGRAM OF ORDER
PROCESSING PROCEDURE

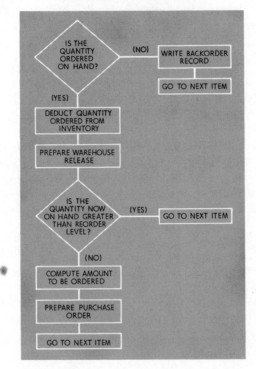

diagram and shows, not the detailed instructions, but rather the main steps in the procedure, for each of which there will be a detailed set of instructions. Note that at various points the program *branches* into either of two directions, depending on the conditions found to exist at that point.

The comparison or logic feature also enables the computer to sort records into numerical, alphabetical, or any desired order; to merge two or more sets of records together; to update a set of records, and indeed to manipulate the data in any conceivable way that can be reduced to a written instruction. "Data" as used here means letters as well as numbers. Some computer programs operate on straight textual material; for example, the U.S. Code and all the laws of many states are now available on magnetic tape so that references to specific topics can be located quickly.

COMPUTER LANGUAGES.   In the earliest computers, the programmer had to write down each step that the computer was to take, in as much detail as that given for the addition operation above. This is no longer necessary in most cases. Instead, the programmer uses a computer language, such as BASIC, COBOL, or FORTRAN. He writes his instructions in the vocabulary and grammar of that language, which closely resembles ordinary English and the symbols of algebra. The simplest of these languages, BASIC, can be learned by high school students in a few hours. The program written in this language is inputted to the computer, and the computer, using a special compiler program, translates this program into the detailed instructions that it requires.

> EXAMPLE: In Chapter 19, the formula for finding the present value of a future payment of $1 was given as $P = 1 \div (1 + r)^n$. With CAL, which is a widely used computer language, the user would simply input the following instruction:
>
> TYPE 1/ (1 + R) ⏏ N FOR R = .1 FOR N = 1 TO 50.
>
> The computer would then compute the 10 percent column of the present value Table A (p. 477), the whole operation requiring less than a minute. (Actually, only a fraction of a second of this is computation time; most of the time is required to get data into and out of the computer.)

The users of a computer language also have access to standardized instructions for many procedures, such as "sort in alphabetical order," "raise to the nth power," and also whole routines, such as those for linear programming, payroll, and order processing. Some of these routines they can use "as is"; others require modification to fit the needs of a particular company. All these developments simplify and speed up the task of preparing programs for computers.

Output

The results of the computations are stored initially in computer code. If the results are to be printed on a form or a report, they are often first transferred to magnetic tape, and this tape actuates a separate machine that does the printing. Since printing is slow relative to computation speed, this procedure avoids tying up the computer's processing unit during the printing operation. The program instructs the computer how to "format" these reports, that is, the program will cause the computer to arrange the data in rows and columns in any desired format. Some computers will print the results in the form of dots at prescribed locations on the page, thus producing graphs automatically. The output can also be displayed on a cathode-ray tube (a television screen is a cathode-ray tube). The computer can even be connected to a tape file containing a spoken sound for each number and for certain common words, and this permits its output to be communicated audibly over an ordinary telephone.

Processing Modes

Computers operate basically in one of two modes, on-line or off-line.

In the *on-line* mode, the computer is kept loaded with a program and related data file. The user is connected directly to the computer with an input-output device. He inputs his specific problem or question, and the computer solves this problem or answers the question and communicates the output to the user in a few seconds. The first extensive application of on-line processing was for airline seat reservations. The computer storage contains the number of seats still available on each flight for the next month or so. A ticket agent at any ticket counter in the country who wishes to inquire whether space is available on a certain flight simply pushes a few buttons or writes his query on an electric typewriter. This query is transmitted to the computer over ordinary telephone wire, and the computer, in a second or so, responds with information on whether the space is available on the desired flight or on alternative flights. If the ticket agent then sells the space, he makes another input, and the computer automatically adjusts its record of seats available. Similarly, many banks are doing deposit accounting on an on-line basis; that is, each teller has an input-output device that he uses both to find the balance in a customer's account and to record deposits and withdrawals at the instant they are made.

In the *off-line* mode, users are not connected directly to the computer. They submit their problems to the computer center, which processes these, together with routine, recurring programs, on a predetermined schedule. This method of operation is called *batch processing*. Instructions and data in internal storage are removed from the computer after each job has been completed, and the computer therefore starts fresh with each new job. Thus, the payroll computation might be run weekly; order processing work, once a day; financial statements, monthly; and so on. The off-line mode is much less expensive than the on-line mode, so it is used for those data processing jobs where an immediate response is unnecessary. For example, individuals are paid once a week or once a month, so payroll programs are run off-line.

TIME SHARING. Large computers are constructed so that the processing unit can work on several problems practically simultaneously. Many users can enter their problems into the computer, where they are held in storage until time on the processing unit becomes available. This usually happens within a few seconds, because the processing unit makes several hundred thousand computations a second. The computer then processes the problem and transmits the output back to the user. The airline reservation and bank deposit applications mentioned above are examples of one type of time sharing, using the on-line mode.

With time sharing, a user with an input-output console in his office can, at relatively small cost, have access to the largest computer at the same time that any of a hundred or more other users are connected to it.

SUMMARY OF CAPABILITIES. It is difficult for anyone to comprehend the power of the computer compared with alternative ways of processing data. One example must suffice: In February 1968, enemy rockets demolished a warehouse at Da Nang Air Base in South Vietnam and destroyed its contents, which consisted of 16,000 items of spare parts for F-4 aircraft. The attack occurred at midnight. By 8 o'clock the next morning, the computer had located the records of each of the 16,000 items stored in that warehouse (out of the several hundred thousand items stored on the whole base), had corrected these records, had computed the quantity to be reordered in accordance with its economic order quantity rules, and had prepared 10,000 requisitions for these amounts.

COMPUTER ECONOMICS

Some conclusions about the type of work for which the computer is suitable can be deduced from the above description and from the following facts:

1. Computers can compute faster and more accurately than human beings.

2. The computer itself, the "hardware," is expensive. A large computer with its associated input, output, and external storage equipment costs several million dollars. A medium-sized computer costs several hundred thousand dollars.

3. The preparation of programs, or "software," for business data processing is also expensive. Companies typically spend at least half as much on software as they spend on the hardware.

4. If input data must be prepared manually, this is a relatively expensive operation; as automatic inputs become increasingly available, input costs will decrease.

5. The incremental cost of processing data once it is in machine-readable form is trivial.

6. Rapid-access storage is much more expensive than slower storage.

7. The cost per calculation is much less for large computers than for small computers, assuming each is used at capacity.

8. Developments in technology are reducing both storage costs and processing costs rapidly. The cost per calculation for computers intro-

duced in the early 1960's was roughly one tenth that of those in use in 1955, and the cost in the late 1960's is roughly one tenth of that in the early 1960's. Developments anticipated in the relatively near future will reduce storage costs still further.

9. Development of better program languages and the increased availability of standard programs or sections of programs will reduce software costs.

Conclusions

These facts would seem to lead to the following conclusions:

1. Because of the high investment cost, both in hardware and in software, and the low operating cost, it is desirable to operate computers, especially large computers, close to capacity. Most large computers operate around the clock, except for necessary maintenance work and a safety margin for unexpected jobs and breakdowns.

2. Time sharing permits users with relatively small requirements to obtain the benefits of large computers. It should grow rapidly.

3. Most business data processing involves rather simple arithmetical calculations. Because of the relatively high programming cost, the computer is most advantageous when used in repetitive, high-volume work. (In scientific problems, by contrast, the calculations are typically long, so the computer pays for itself in reducing calculating costs, even for nonrepetitive problems.) However, as new technological developments lead to still lower processing and storage costs, and as programming becomes even simpler, there will be a corresponding increase in the number of tasks that can be performed less expensively by the computer than by humans.

4. As machine-readable input supersedes punched-card input in more and more applications, the number of economical uses of computers will increase. The high payoff from such developments is a strong incentive for manufacturers to bring them to fruition quickly.

5. Since the processing of data is very inexpensive once it has been converted to computer code, businesses will seek additional ways to use the same raw data.

6. A program is expensive to prepare, and it is also expensive to revise. There may therefore be a tendency for an undesirable rigidity in programs, a reluctance to change them as conditions change.

SOME IMPLICATIONS FOR MANAGEMENT ACCOUNTING

In 1961, ten years after the first business computer was delivered, total industry revenue from the sale or lease of general-purpose digital computers was approximately $600 million. In 1967, six years later, revenue was more than $3 billion.[4]

This $3 billion is equal to 5 percent of the total purchases of new plant and equipment in that year. The number of business computers in use rose from 1 in 1951, to 1,000 in 1956, to 31,000 in 1966. This growth will undoubtedly continue. Clearly, computers have already had a significant effect on business data processing, and they are likely to have an increasing effect in the future. Some of these implications are discussed below, arranged roughly in the order in which topics were presented in the preceding chapters.

First, as an overall observation, it seems clear that almost all companies will make some use of computers. The individual physician's office, with perhaps a nurse and a secretary, is a small business entity, but an increasing number of physicians have their billing and accounts receivable done at computer service centers.

Although most companies will use computers, it is by no means clear that most companies will have their own computers. Because of the great advantage that large computers have over small computers in terms of cost per calculation, it is quite possible that all but the large companies will use time on computers owned by someone else. A few such "computer utilities" are already in existence.

Financial Accounting

One of the criteria used in arriving at accounting principles is feasibility, and with the widespread use of computers it can no longer be argued that a proposed principle should not be adopted because the computations that it requires are too complicated to be feasible. This consideration is dominant in only a few situations, however. The possibility of calculating depreciation on individual items of fixed assets, rather than on a group or composite basis, is one example, but there are not many others. With this exception, it seems unlikely that the widespread use of computers will have much effect on accounting *principles*.

Financial accounting *procedures*, by contrast, are changing rapidly. The journal and the ledger, in the form described in Chapter 4, are disappearing, although the basic concepts are unchanged: the journal concept is now computer input, the ledger concept is computer storage. The work sheets and other devices described in Chapter 4 as mechanical aids to bookkeeping are replaced by computer programs. Indeed, of all the topics discussed in Part 1, the only significant changes are likely to be those relating to the material of Chapter 4 on bookkeeping.

One interesting development is the tendency to record more data than

---

[4] These estimates appear in the suit filed by the U.S. Justice Department against International Business Machines Corporation, January 17, 1969. Other experts put 1967 revenue as high as $6 billion.

was feasible under manual methods. Thus, in a manual accounts receivable record, it is customary to record the name and address of the customer company, its credit rating, and the dollar amount of each sale and cash receipt. It is now feasible to record a variety of additional information about the customer company, including information about its product line, its sales potential, and the details of individual sales transactions. Such information is useful in market analysis, statistics on sales of individual items, and so on.

Financial Analyses

As mentioned in Chapter 11, the computer is already a powerful tool in the analysis of financial statements. Voluminous financial data are available in machine-readable form; they can be purchased for a fee and used for comparative analyses. Furthermore, all sorts of ratios can now be computed as a matter of routine, at trivial cost. These computations provide better information on which to base judgments about financial performance, but they do not lessen the need for sound judgment.

Cost Accounting

If there are advantages in more sophisticated allocations of cost to cost centers and to products, such allocations can now be made automatically and at low cost. Shortcuts in the calculation of direct material and direct labor costs that may have been used on the ground that more exact methods were too costly, are no longer necessary.

Management Control

The mechanics of programming, budgeting, and measurement of performance are facilitated by the use of computers. Computers help to insure that the calculations are accurate. More importantly, they shorten the time required to compile and disseminate information and thus speed up corrective action if it is required. Computers also make it feasible to take into account many more variables in analyzing the difference between planned and actual performance, and to use more sophisticated analytical techniques in this process. The management control process is, however, fundamentally a behavioral process, and the computer does not eliminate the manager nor alter the basic fact that managers obtain results by working with other human beings.

Alternative Choice Problems

The fact that computers can be programmed to perform a long sequence of operations rapidly, inexpensively, and without human intervention, means that it is now feasible to use quantitative techniques for many types of problems for which their use has not hitherto been practical; and the fact that the computer can be programmed to make choices means that machines can now make certain types of decisions formerly made by humans. For example, the computer can be programmed to decide when a purchase order should be placed to replenish a routine item carried in inventory, the quantity that should be ordered, and the date when the new stock should arrive; and it can even write the purchase order without human intervention, although humans are necessary to supervise the operation and to make certain that the transaction is actually "routine." The computer can do this job better than people can do it; "better" in the sense that if its program truly expresses what management intends to be done, the computer will carry out these intentions more accurately and more consistently than the humans normally employed for these routine operations.

Companies have developed computer programs that handle, as a routine matter, make-or-buy problems, buy-or-lease problems, production scheduling, product pricing strategies, capital budgeting analyses, and other problems of the types discussed in Chapters 18 and 19. These practically eliminate the drudgery of the calculations required for such problems, and make obsolete the argument that a certain procedure should not be used because it is too complicated.

Fortunately for us humans, the computer is limited to operations that can be precisely described. It does not eliminate the need for judgment in defining the problem and specifying and evaluating the factors that have not been quantified, nor can these calculations produce results that are more accurate than the validity of the data fed into them. Thus, the computer provides great assistance to managers and analysts, but it replaces only the computational part of their work; it does not replace the people themselves.

Integrated Data Processing

The dream of every system builder is a system in which every relevant piece of raw data is recorded once, and only once, and is then combined, summarized, and analyzed automatically in a variety of ways to produce all the reports and other output documents that the business needs. Such a system can easily be described in general terms, but to develop it in practice is a far more complicated task than any group of mortals has so far been able to accomplish. It now appears that the computer may make feasible such an integrated data processing system, if not for all the data in a business, at least for substantial chunks of it. Such a system will not be developed overnight, but it is a goal that is not now completely fanciful.

Integrated data processing implies a blurring of the distinction that hitherto has existed among different categories of data, and this is a development that is indeed occurring. There is no longer a sharp distinction between the system for financial accounting data and that for management accounting data, or between input data and output data, or between accounting data and nonmonetary data, or even between numbers and words. The computer processes them all. Thus it may soon be undesirable to define management accounting as being restricted to monetary information; it may be more useful to view it as encompassing all recurring information that is of use to management.

There is a temptation to be too enthusiastic about the future of the computer. The fact is that at present computers tend to spew out too much information, and this tends to hinder rather than help the management process. But this is almost certainly a temporary condition, symptomatic of the haste with which computer programs have been developed, and the necessity for learning how best to use the computer's power. As time goes on, it is reasonable to expect that outputs will be better organized and more relevant to management's needs.

SUMMARY

A computer basically does only a few things: it stores data, makes computations, makes comparisons, rearranges data, and produces reports; but it does these things a million times faster than a human being can do them, it can perform a long and involved sequence of such operations without human intervention, and it does its work with virtually perfect accuracy. Thus computers are rapidly taking over the routine data processing work of business. It seems likely that they will take over such work in all businesses except the smallest, and those without a number of recurring transactions.

Computers also provide a powerful way of analyzing the data relevant to management problems of all types. They thus improve the quality of such analyses, although the results can be no better than the quality of the raw data, nor can the computer substitute for management judgment.

SUGGESTIONS FOR FURTHER READING

BLUMENTHAL, SHERMAN. *Management Information Systems.* Englewood Cliffs, N.J.: Prentice-Hall, 1969.

DEARDEN, JOHN and F. WARREN MCFARLAN. *Management Information Systems.* Homewood: Richard D. Irwin, Inc., 1966.

MEIER, ROBERT C., W. NEWELL, and H. POZER. *Simulation in Business and Economics.* Englewood Cliffs, N.J.: Prentice-Hall, 1969.

Appendix Tables

Table A

PRESENT VALUE OF $1

Years Hence	1%	2%	4%	6%	8%	10%	12%	14%	15%	16%	18%	20%	22%	24%	25%	26%	28%	30%	35%	40%	45%	50%
1	0.990	0.980	0.962	0.943	0.926	0.909	0.893	0.877	0.870	0.862	0.847	0.833	0.820	0.806	0.800	0.794	0.781	0.769	0.741	0.714	0.690	0.667
2	0.980	0.961	0.925	0.890	0.857	0.826	0.797	0.769	0.756	0.743	0.718	0.694	0.672	0.650	0.640	0.630	0.610	0.592	0.549	0.510	0.476	0.444
3	0.971	0.942	0.889	0.840	0.794	0.751	0.712	0.675	0.658	0.641	0.609	0.579	0.551	0.524	0.512	0.500	0.477	0.455	0.406	0.364	0.328	0.296
4	0.961	0.924	0.855	0.792	0.735	0.683	0.636	0.592	0.572	0.552	0.516	0.482	0.451	0.423	0.410	0.397	0.373	0.350	0.301	0.260	0.226	0.198
5	0.951	0.906	0.822	0.747	0.681	0.621	0.567	0.519	0.497	0.476	0.437	0.402	0.370	0.341	0.328	0.315	0.291	0.269	0.223	0.186	0.156	0.132
6	0.942	0.888	0.790	0.705	0.630	0.564	0.507	0.456	0.432	0.410	0.370	0.335	0.303	0.275	0.262	0.250	0.227	0.207	0.165	0.133	0.108	0.088
7	0.933	0.871	0.760	0.665	0.583	0.513	0.452	0.400	0.376	0.354	0.314	0.279	0.249	0.222	0.210	0.198	0.178	0.159	0.122	0.095	0.074	0.059
8	0.923	0.853	0.731	0.627	0.540	0.467	0.404	0.351	0.327	0.305	0.266	0.233	0.204	0.179	0.168	0.157	0.139	0.123	0.091	0.068	0.051	0.039
9	0.914	0.837	0.703	0.592	0.500	0.424	0.361	0.308	0.284	0.263	0.225	0.194	0.167	0.144	0.134	0.125	0.108	0.094	0.067	0.048	0.035	0.026
10	0.905	0.820	0.676	0.558	0.463	0.386	0.322	0.270	0.247	0.227	0.191	0.162	0.137	0.116	0.107	0.099	0.085	0.073	0.050	0.035	0.024	0.017
11	0.896	0.804	0.650	0.527	0.429	0.350	0.287	0.237	0.215	0.195	0.162	0.135	0.112	0.094	0.086	0.079	0.066	0.056	0.037	0.025	0.017	0.012
12	0.887	0.788	0.625	0.497	0.397	0.319	0.257	0.208	0.187	0.168	0.137	0.112	0.092	0.076	0.069	0.062	0.052	0.043	0.027	0.018	0.012	0.008
13	0.879	0.773	0.601	0.469	0.368	0.290	0.229	0.182	0.163	0.145	0.116	0.093	0.075	0.061	0.055	0.050	0.040	0.033	0.020	0.013	0.008	0.005
14	0.870	0.758	0.577	0.442	0.340	0.263	0.205	0.160	0.141	0.125	0.099	0.078	0.062	0.049	0.044	0.039	0.032	0.025	0.015	0.009	0.006	0.003
15	0.861	0.743	0.555	0.417	0.315	0.239	0.183	0.140	0.123	0.108	0.084	0.065	0.051	0.040	0.035	0.031	0.025	0.020	0.011	0.006	0.004	0.002
16	0.853	0.728	0.534	0.394	0.292	0.218	0.163	0.123	0.107	0.093	0.071	0.054	0.042	0.032	0.028	0.025	0.019	0.015	0.008	0.005	0.003	0.002
17	0.844	0.714	0.513	0.371	0.270	0.198	0.146	0.108	0.093	0.080	0.060	0.045	0.034	0.026	0.023	0.020	0.015	0.012	0.006	0.003	0.002	0.001
18	0.836	0.700	0.494	0.350	0.250	0.180	0.130	0.095	0.081	0.069	0.051	0.038	0.028	0.021	0.018	0.016	0.012	0.009	0.005	0.002	0.001	0.001
19	0.828	0.686	0.475	0.331	0.232	0.164	0.116	0.083	0.070	0.060	0.043	0.031	0.023	0.017	0.014	0.012	0.009	0.007	0.003	0.002	0.001	
20	0.820	0.673	0.456	0.312	0.215	0.149	0.104	0.073	0.061	0.051	0.037	0.026	0.019	0.014	0.012	0.010	0.007	0.005	0.002	0.001	0.001	
21	0.811	0.660	0.439	0.294	0.199	0.135	0.093	0.064	0.053	0.044	0.031	0.022	0.015	0.011	0.009	0.008	0.006	0.004	0.002	0.001		
22	0.803	0.647	0.422	0.278	0.184	0.123	0.083	0.056	0.046	0.038	0.026	0.018	0.013	0.009	0.007	0.006	0.004	0.003	0.001	0.001		
23	0.795	0.634	0.406	0.262	0.170	0.112	0.074	0.049	0.040	0.033	0.022	0.015	0.010	0.007	0.006	0.005	0.003	0.002	0.001			
24	0.788	0.622	0.390	0.247	0.158	0.102	0.066	0.043	0.035	0.028	0.019	0.013	0.008	0.006	0.005	0.004	0.003	0.002	0.001			
25	0.780	0.610	0.375	0.233	0.146	0.092	0.059	0.038	0.030	0.024	0.016	0.010	0.007	0.005	0.004	0.003	0.002	0.001				
26	0.772	0.598	0.361	0.220	0.135	0.084	0.053	0.033	0.026	0.021	0.014	0.009	0.006	0.004	0.003	0.002	0.002	0.001				
27	0.764	0.586	0.347	0.207	0.125	0.076	0.047	0.029	0.023	0.018	0.011	0.007	0.005	0.003	0.002	0.002	0.001	0.001				
28	0.757	0.574	0.333	0.196	0.116	0.069	0.042	0.026	0.020	0.016	0.010	0.006	0.004	0.002	0.002	0.002	0.001	0.001				
29	0.749	0.563	0.321	0.185	0.107	0.063	0.037	0.022	0.017	0.014	0.008	0.005	0.003	0.002	0.002	0.001	0.001	0.001				
30	0.742	0.552	0.308	0.174	0.099	0.057	0.033	0.020	0.015	0.012	0.007	0.004	0.003	0.002	0.001	0.001	0.001					
40	0.672	0.453	0.208	0.097	0.046	0.022	0.011	0.005	0.004	0.003	0.001	0.001										
50	0.608	0.372	0.141	0.054	0.021	0.009	0.003	0.001	0.001	0.001												

Table B

PRESENT VALUE OF $1 RECEIVED ANNUALLY FOR *N* YEARS

Years (N)	1%	2%	4%	6%	8%	10%	12%	14%	15%	16%	18%	20%	22%	24%	25%	26%	28%	30%	35%	40%	45%	50%
1	0.990	0.980	0.962	0.943	0.926	0.909	0.893	0.877	0.870	0.862	0.847	0.833	0.820	0.806	0.800	0.794	0.781	0.769	0.741	0.714	0.690	0.667
2	1.970	1.942	1.886	1.833	1.783	1.736	1.690	1.647	1.626	1.605	1.566	1.528	1.492	1.457	1.440	1.424	1.392	1.361	1.289	1.224	1.165	1.111
3	2.941	2.884	2.775	2.673	2.577	2.487	2.402	2.322	2.283	2.246	2.174	2.106	2.042	1.981	1.952	1.923	1.868	1.816	1.696	1.589	1.493	1.407
4	3.902	3.808	3.630	3.465	3.312	3.170	3.037	2.914	2.855	2.798	2.690	2.589	2.494	2.404	2.362	2.320	2.241	2.166	1.997	1.849	1.720	1.605
5	4.853	4.713	4.452	4.212	3.993	3.791	3.605	3.433	3.352	3.274	3.127	2.991	2.864	2.745	2.689	2.635	2.532	2.436	2.220	2.035	1.876	1.737
6	5.795	5.601	5.242	4.917	4.623	4.355	4.111	3.889	3.784	3.685	3.498	3.326	3.167	3.020	2.951	2.885	2.759	2.643	2.385	2.168	1.983	1.824
7	6.728	6.472	6.002	5.582	5.206	4.868	4.564	4.288	4.160	4.039	3.812	3.605	3.416	3.242	3.161	3.083	2.937	2.802	2.508	2.263	2.057	1.883
8	7.652	7.325	6.733	6.210	5.747	5.335	4.968	4.639	4.487	4.344	4.078	3.887	3.619	3.421	3.329	3.241	3.076	2.925	2.598	2.331	2.108	1.922
9	8.566	8.162	7.435	6.802	6.247	5.759	5.328	4.946	4.772	4.607	4.303	4.031	3.786	3.566	3.463	3.366	3.184	3.019	2.665	2.379	2.144	1.948
10	9.471	8.983	8.111	7.360	6.710	6.145	5.650	5.216	5.019	4.833	4.494	4.192	3.923	3.682	3.571	3.465	3.269	3.092	2.715	2.414	2.168	1.965
11	10.368	9.787	8.760	7.887	7.139	6.495	5.937	5.453	5.234	5.029	4.656	4.327	4.035	3.776	3.656	3.544	3.335	3.147	2.752	2.438	2.185	1.977
12	11.255	10.575	9.385	8.384	7.536	6.814	6.194	5.660	5.421	5.197	4.793	4.439	4.127	3.851	3.725	3.606	3.387	3.190	2.779	2.456	2.196	1.985
13	12.134	11.343	9.986	8.853	7.904	7.103	6.424	5.842	5.583	5.342	4.910	4.533	4.203	3.912	3.780	3.656	3.427	3.223	2.799	2.468	2.204	1.990
14	13.004	12.106	10.563	9.295	8.244	7.367	6.628	6.002	5.724	5.468	5.008	4.611	4.265	3.962	3.824	3.695	3.459	3.249	2.814	2.477	2.210	1.993
15	13.865	12.849	11.118	9.712	8.559	7.606	6.811	6.142	5.847	5.575	5.092	4.675	4.315	4.001	3.859	3.726	3.483	3.268	2.825	2.484	2.214	1.995
16	14.718	13.578	11.652	10.106	8.851	7.824	6.974	6.265	5.954	5.669	5.162	4.730	4.357	4.033	3.887	3.751	3.503	3.283	2.834	2.489	2.216	1.997
17	15.562	14.292	12.166	10.477	9.122	8.022	7.120	6.373	6.047	5.749	5.222	4.775	4.391	4.059	3.910	3.771	3.518	3.295	2.840	2.492	2.218	1.998
18	16.398	14.992	12.659	10.828	9.372	8.201	7.250	6.467	6.128	5.818	5.273	4.812	4.419	4.080	3.928	3.786	3.529	3.304	2.844	2.494	2.219	1.999
19	17.226	15.678	13.134	11.158	9.604	8.365	7.366	6.550	6.198	5.877	5.316	4.844	4.442	4.097	3.942	3.799	3.539	3.311	2.848	2.496	2.220	1.999
20	18.046	16.351	13.590	11.470	9.818	8.514	7.469	6.623	6.259	5.929	5.353	4.870	4.460	4.110	3.954	3.808	3.546	3.316	2.850	2.497	2.221	1.999
21	18.857	17.011	14.029	11.764	10.017	8.649	7.562	6.687	6.312	5.973	5.384	4.891	4.476	4.121	3.963	3.816	3.551	3.320	2.852	2.498	2.221	2.000
22	19.660	17.658	14.451	12.042	10.201	8.772	7.645	6.743	6.359	6.011	5.410	4.909	4.488	4.130	3.970	3.822	3.556	3.323	2.853	2.498	2.222	2.000
23	20.456	18.292	14.857	12.303	10.371	8.883	7.718	6.792	6.399	6.044	5.432	4.925	4.499	4.137	3.976	3.827	3.559	3.325	2.854	2.499	2.222	2.000
24	21.243	18.914	15.247	12.550	10.529	8.985	7.784	6.835	6.434	6.073	5.451	4.937	4.507	4.143	3.981	3.831	3.562	3.327	2.855	2.499	2.222	2.000
25	22.023	19.523	15.622	12.783	10.675	9.077	7.843	6.873	6.464	6.097	5.467	4.948	4.514	4.147	3.985	3.834	3.564	3.329	2.856	2.499	2.222	2.000
26	22.795	20.121	15.983	13.003	10.810	9.161	7.896	6.906	6.491	6.118	5.480	4.956	4.520	4.151	3.988	3.837	3.566	3.330	2.856	2.500	2.222	2.000
27	23.560	20.707	16.330	13.211	10.935	9.237	7.943	6.935	6.514	6.136	5.492	4.964	4.524	4.154	3.990	3.839	3.567	3.331	2.856	2.500	2.222	2.000
28	24.316	21.281	16.663	13.406	11.051	9.307	7.984	6.961	6.534	6.152	5.502	4.970	4.528	4.157	3.992	3.840	3.568	3.331	2.857	2.500	2.222	2.000
29	25.066	21.844	16.984	13.591	11.158	9.370	8.022	6.983	6.551	6.166	5.510	4.975	4.531	4.159	3.994	3.841	3.569	3.332	2.857	2.500	2.222	2.000
30	25.808	22.396	17.292	13.765	11.258	9.427	8.055	7.003	6.566	6.177	5.517	4.979	4.534	4.160	3.995	3.842	3.569	3.332	2.857	2.500	2.222	2.000
40	32.835	27.355	19.793	15.046	11.925	9.779	8.244	7.105	6.642	6.234	5.548	4.997	4.544	4.166	3.999	3.846	3.571	3.333	2.857	2.500	2.222	2.000
50	39.196	31.424	21.482	15.762	12.234	9.915	8.304	7.133	6.661	6.246	5.554	4.999	4.545	4.167	4.000	3.846	3.571	3.333	2.857	2.500	2.222	2.000

Table C

PRESENT VALUE OF SUM-OF-YEARS' DIGIT DEPRECIATION

Years of Useful Life	2%	4%	6%	8%	10%	12%	14%	15%	16%	18%	20%	22%	24%	26%	28%	30%	35%	40%	45%	50%
3	0.968	0.937	0.908	0.881	0.855	0.831	0.808	0.796	0.786	0.764	0.745	0.726	0.707	0.690	0.674	0.658	0.621	0.588	0.558	0.531
4	0.961	0.925	0.891	0.860	0.830	0.802	0.776	0.763	0.751	0.728	0.706	0.685	0.665	0.646	0.628	0.611	0.572	0.538	0.507	0.479
5	0.955	0.914	0.875	0.839	0.806	0.775	0.746	0.732	0.719	0.694	0.670	0.647	0.626	0.606	0.588	0.570	0.530	0.494	0.463	0.435
6	0.949	0.902	0.859	0.820	0.783	0.749	0.718	0.703	0.689	0.662	0.637	0.613	0.591	0.570	0.551	0.533	0.492	0.456	0.425	0.398
7	0.943	0.891	0.844	0.801	0.761	0.725	0.692	0.676	0.661	0.633	0.606	0.582	0.559	0.538	0.518	0.500	0.458	0.423	0.392	0.366
8	0.937	0.880	0.829	0.782	0.740	0.702	0.667	0.650	0.635	0.605	0.578	0.553	0.530	0.508	0.488	0.470	0.429	0.394	0.364	0.338
9	0.931	0.869	0.814	0.765	0.720	0.680	0.643	0.626	0.610	0.580	0.552	0.527	0.503	0.482	0.462	0.443	0.402	0.368	0.338	0.313
10	0.925	0.859	0.800	0.748	0.701	0.659	0.621	0.604	0.587	0.556	0.528	0.502	0.479	0.457	0.437	0.419	0.378	0.345	0.316	0.292
11	0.919	0.848	0.786	0.731	0.682	0.639	0.600	0.582	0.565	0.534	0.506	0.480	0.456	0.434	0.415	0.397	0.357	0.324	0.297	0.273
12	0.913	0.838	0.773	0.715	0.665	0.620	0.580	0.562	0.545	0.513	0.485	0.459	0.435	0.414	0.394	0.376	0.338	0.306	0.279	0.257
13	0.907	0.828	0.760	0.700	0.648	0.602	0.562	0.543	0.526	0.494	0.465	0.439	0.416	0.395	0.376	0.358	0.320	0.289	0.264	0.242
14	0.902	0.818	0.747	0.685	0.632	0.585	0.544	0.525	0.508	0.476	0.447	0.421	0.398	0.377	0.358	0.341	0.304	0.274	0.250	0.229
15	0.896	0.809	0.734	0.671	0.616	0.569	0.527	0.508	0.491	0.459	0.430	0.405	0.382	0.361	0.343	0.326	0.290	0.261	0.237	0.217
16	0.890	0.799	0.722	0.657	0.601	0.553	0.511	0.492	0.475	0.443	0.414	0.389	0.367	0.346	0.328	0.312	0.277	0.248	0.225	0.206
17	0.885	0.790	0.710	0.644	0.587	0.538	0.496	0.477	0.460	0.428	0.400	0.375	0.352	0.332	0.315	0.298	0.264	0.237	0.215	0.196
18	0.880	0.781	0.699	0.631	0.573	0.524	0.482	0.463	0.445	0.413	0.386	0.361	0.339	0.320	0.302	0.286	0.253	0.227	0.205	0.187
19	0.874	0.772	0.688	0.618	0.560	0.510	0.468	0.449	0.432	0.400	0.372	0.348	0.327	0.308	0.291	0.275	0.243	0.217	0.196	0.179
20	0.869	0.763	0.677	0.606	0.547	0.497	0.455	0.436	0.419	0.387	0.360	0.336	0.315	0.296	0.280	0.265	0.233	0.208	0.188	0.171
21	0.863	0.754	0.666	0.594	0.535	0.485	0.442	0.424	0.406	0.376	0.349	0.325	0.304	0.286	0.270	0.255	0.224	0.200	0.181	0.164
22	0.858	0.746	0.656	0.583	0.523	0.473	0.431	0.412	0.395	0.364	0.338	0.315	0.294	0.276	0.260	0.246	0.216	0.193	0.174	0.158
23	0.853	0.738	0.646	0.572	0.511	0.461	0.419	0.401	0.384	0.354	0.327	0.305	0.285	0.267	0.252	0.238	0.208	0.186	0.167	0.152
24	0.848	0.729	0.636	0.561	0.500	0.450	0.409	0.390	0.373	0.344	0.318	0.295	0.276	0.258	0.243	0.230	0.201	0.179	0.161	0.147
25	0.842	0.721	0.626	0.551	0.490	0.440	0.398	0.380	0.364	0.334	0.308	0.286	0.267	0.250	0.236	0.222	0.195	0.173	0.156	0.142
30	0.818	0.683	0.582	0.504	0.442	0.393	0.353	0.336	0.320	0.292	0.269	0.249	0.232	0.216	0.203	0.191	0.167	0.148	0.133	0.120
35	0.794	0.648	0.542	0.463	0.402	0.355	0.317	0.300	0.286	0.260	0.238	0.220	0.204	0.190	0.178	0.168	0.146	0.129	0.116	0.105
40	0.771	0.616	0.507	0.428	0.368	0.323	0.286	0.271	0.257	0.233	0.213	0.196	0.182	0.170	0.159	0.149	0.129	0.114	0.102	0.093
45	0.749	0.586	0.476	0.397	0.339	0.296	0.261	0.247	0.234	0.212	0.193	0.178	0.164	0.153	0.143	0.134	0.116	0.103	0.092	0.083
50	0.728	0.559	0.448	0.370	0.314	0.272	0.240	0.227	0.214	0.194	0.176	0.162	0.150	0.139	0.130	0.122	0.106	0.093	0.083	

Source: From tables computed by Jerome Bracken and Charles J. Christenson. Copyright © 1961 by the President and Fellows of Harvard College. Used by permission. See page 443 for explanation of use of this table.

Index

INDEX

*This book has been set in 10 and 9 point
Janson, leaded 2 points. Part numbers are in
42 point Helvetica Medium roman and part
titles are in 24 point Helvetica Regular. Chapter numbers are in 14 and 24 point Helvetica
Regular and chapter titles are in 18 point
Helvetica Medium. The size of the type page
is 27 by 45½ picas.*